T0184689

Communications
in Computer and Information Science   **669**

Commenced Publication in 2007
Founding and Former Series Editors:
Alfredo Cuzzocrea, Dominik Ślęzak, and Xiaokang Yang

More information about this series at http://www.springer.com/series/7899

Yuming Li · Guoxiong Xiang
Hongfei Lin · Mingwen Wang (Eds.)

Social Media Processing

5th National Conference, SMP 2016
Nanchang, China, October 29–30, 2016
Proceedings

 Springer

Editors
Yuming Li
Beijing Language and Culture University
Beijing
China

Hongfei Lin
Dalian University of Technology
Dalian
China

Guoxiong Xiang
Jiangxi Normal University
Nanchang
China

Mingwen Wang
Jiangxi Normal University
Nanchang
China

ISSN 1865-0929   ISSN 1865-0937   (electronic)
Communications in Computer and Information Science
ISBN 978-981-10-2992-9   ISBN 978-981-10-2993-6   (eBook)
DOI 10.1007/978-981-10-2993-6

Library of Congress Control Number: 2016955499

Printed on acid-free paper

This Springer imprint is published by Springer Nature
The registered company is Springer Nature Singapore Pte Ltd.
The registered company address is: 152 Beach Road, #22-06/08 Gateway East, Singapore 189721, Singapore

Preface

We are living in an increasingly networked world. People, information, and other entities are connected via the World Wide Web, e-mail networks, instant messaging networks, mobile communication networks, online social networks, Internet of Things, etc. These generate massive amounts of social data, which present great opportunities for understanding the science of user behavioral patterns and the structure of networks formed by people's interactions. The 5th National Conference on Social Media Processing (SMP) was held in Nanchang, China, in 2016 for the purpose of promoting original research in mining social media and applications, bringing together experts from related fields such as natural language processing, data mining, information retrieval, and social science, and providing a leading forum in which to exchange research ideas and results in emergent social media processing problems.

The conference received 109 submissions, and all papers were peer reviewed by at least three members of the Program Committee (PC) composed of international experts in natural language processing, data mining, information retrieval, and social science. The PC together with the PC co-chairs worked very hard to select papers through a rigorous review process and via extensive discussion. The competition was very strong; only 24 English papers were accepted as conference papers. The conference also featured invited talks from outstanding researchers in social media processing and related areas (the list may be incomplete): Xiaofan Wang (Shanghai Jiaotong University), Xuanjing Huang (Fudan University), Shaoping Ma (Tsinghua University), and Xiaoru Yuan (Peking University).

Without the support of several funding agencies and industrial partners, the successful organization of SMP 2016 would not have been possible. We would also like to express our gratitude to the Steering Committee of the special group of Social Media Processing of the Chinese Information Processing Society for all their advice and the Organizing Committee for their dedicated efforts. Last but not least, we sincerely thank all the authors, presenters, and attendees who jointly contributed to the success of SMP 2016.

September 2016

Yuming Li
Guoxiong Xiang
Hongfei Lin
Mingwen Wang

Organization

Steering Committee Chair

Sheng Li   Harbin Institute of Technology, China

Steering Committee Co-chair

Yuming Li   Beijing Language and Culture University, China

Steering Committee

Shuo Bai	Shanghai Stock Exchange, China
Heyan Huang	Beijing Institute of Technology, China
Xiaoming Li	Peking University, China
Shaoping Ma	Tsinghua University, China
Xiaofeng Meng	Renmin University of China
Jian-Yun Nie	University of Montreal, Canada
Shuicai Shi	TRS
Maosong Sun	Tsinghua University, China
Feiyue Wang	Institute of Automation, CAS, China
Ming Zhou	Microsoft Research Asia

General Chairs

Yuming Li	Beijing Language and Culture University, China
Guoxiong Xiang	Jiangxi Normal University, China

Program Committee Chairs

Hongfei Lin	Dalian University of Technology, China
Mingwen Wang	Jiangxi Normal University, China

Program Committee Area Chairs

Sentiment Computation

Bing Qin	Harbin Institute of Technology, China
Kang Liu	Institute of Automation, CAS, China

Computational Social Sciences

Shizheng Feng	Renmin University of China, China
Huawei Shen	Institute of Computing Technology, CAS, China

Computational Communication

Guojia Song   Peking University, China
Hao Shen   Communication University of China, China

Natural Language Processing

Ruifeng Xu   Harbin Institute of Technology (Shenzhen), China
Qi Zhang   Fudan University, China

Network Science

Yizhou Sun   University of California, Los Angeles, USA
Linyuan Lv   Hangzhou Normal University, China

Machine Learning and Prediction

Jun Zhu   Tsinghua University, China
Jian Tang   Microsoft Research Asia

Program Committee

Wenguang Chen   Tsinghua University, China
Yidong Chen   Xiamen University, China
Zhumin Chen   Shandong University, China
Chong Feng   Beijing Institute of Technology, China
Shi Feng   Northeastern University, China
Shizheng Feng   Renmin University of China, China
Guohong Fu   Heilongjiang University, China
Yue Gao   Tsinghua University, China
Jibing Gong   Institute of Computing Technology, CAS, China
Hanqi Guo   Argonne National Laboratory, USA
Yuhang Guo   Beijing Institute of Technology, China
Yi Han   Institute of Information Engineering, CAS, China
Tingting He   Central China Normal University, China
Yu Hong   Soochow University, China
Zhong Ji   Tianjin University, China
Liang Jie   Peking University, China
Wei Jiang   Beijing University of Technology, China
Shengyi Jiang   Guangdong University of Foreign Studies, China
Ting Jin   Hainan University, China
Aiping Li   National University of Defense Technology, China
Binyang Li   University of International Relations, China
Bing Li   University of International Business and Economics, China
Chenliang Li   Wuhan University, China
Juanzi Li   Tsinghua University, China
Lishuang Li   Dalian University of Technology, China
Ru Li   Shanxi University, China

Shoushan Li	Soochow University, China
Xiangwen Liao	Fuzhou University, China
Chen Lin	Xiamen University, China
Yuan Lin	Dalian University of Technology, China
Dexi Liu	Jiangxi University of Finance and Economics, China
Kang Liu	Institute of Automation, CAS, China
Lizhen Liu	Capital Normal University, China
Ming Liu	Harbin Institute of Technology, China
Pengyuan Liu	Beijing Language and Culture University, China
Shenghua Liu	Institute of Computing Technology, CAS, China
Yang Liu	Shandong University, China
Yiqun Liu	Tsinghua University, China
Zhiyuan Liu	Tsinghua University, China
Jun Ma	Shandong University, China
Wenji Mao	Institute of Automation, CAS, China
Tong Mo	Peking University, China
Risa Na	Dalian University of Technology, China
Haoliang Qi	Heilongjiang Institute of Technology, China
Tieyun Qian	Wuhan University, China
Bing Qin	Harbin Institute of Technology, China
Tong Ruan	East China University of Science and Technology, China
Ying Sha	Institute of Information Engineering, CAS, China
Huawei Shen	Institute of Computing Technology, CAS, China
Yang Shen	Tsinghua University, China
Chuan Shi	Beijing University of Posts and Telecommunications, China
Hanxiao Shi	Zhejiang Gongshang University, China
Shumin Shi	Beijing Institute of Technology, China
Guojie Song	Peking University, China
Wei Song	Capital Normal University, China
Guanglu Sun	Harbin University of Science and Technology, China
Xiao Sun	Hefei University of Technology, China
Hongye Tan	Shanxi University, China
Turgun	Xinjiang University, China
Huaiyu Wan	Beijing Jiaotong University, China
Bailing Wang	Harbin Institute of Technology, China
Bo Wang	Harbin Institute of Technology, China
Daling Wang	Northeastern University, China
Mingwen Wang	Jiangxi Normal University, China
Shuaiqiang Wang	University of Jyvaskyla, Finland
Suge Wang	Shanxi University, China
Ting Wang	National University of Defense Technology, China
Ying Wang	Jilin University, China
Dayong Wu	Institute of Computing Technology, CAS, China
Jinhua Xiong	China.com
Ruifeng Xu	Harbin Institute of Technology, China

Zhiming Xu	Harbin Institute of Technology, China
Xiaoke Xu	Dalian Nationalities University, China
Erhong Yang	Beijing Language and Culture University, China
Zhihao Yang	Dalian University of Technology, China
Tianfang Yao	Shanghai Jiaotong University, China
Lan Yin	Guizhou Normal University, China
Zhengtao Yu	Kunming University of Science and Technology, China
Xiaoru Yuan	Peking University, China
Jian Zhan	Lanzhou University, China
Weidong Zhan	Peking University, China
Guoqing Zhang	Institute of Computing Technology, CAS, China
Hu Zhang	Shanxi University, China
Huaping Zhang	Beijing Institute of Technology, China
Lun Zhang	University of Chinese Academy of Sciences, China
Ming Zhang	Peking University, China
Qi Zhang	Fudan University, China
Yu Zhang	Harbin Institute of Technology, China
Yuejie Zhang	Fudan University, China
Zhichang Zhang	Northwest Normal University, China
Ziqiong Zhang	Beijing Normal University, China
Chengzhi Zhang	Institute of Scientific and Technical Information of China
Dongyan Zhao	Peking University, China
Jun Zhao	Institute of Automation, CAS, China
Shiqi Zhao	Baidu
Shu Zhao	University of California, Berkeley, USA
Xin Zhao	Renmin University of China
Yanyan Zhao	Harbin Institute of Technology, China
Chen Zheng	Anhui University, China
Xiaolong Zheng	Chinese Academy of Sciences, China
Dong Zhou	Hunan University of Science and Technology, China
Huiwei Zhou	Dalian University of Technology, China
Jiali Zuo	Jiangxi Normal University, China
Bin Wang	Institute of Information Engineering, CAS, China

Organizing Committee Chair

Mingwen Wang	Jiangxi Normal University, China

Publication Chairs

Zhiyuan Liu	Tsinghua University, China
Jiali Zuo	Jiangxi Normal University, China

Publicity Chairs

Binyang Li   University of International Relations, China
Fan Xu   Jiangxi Normal University, China

Evaluation Chairs

Shengyi Jiang   Guangdong University of Foreign Studies, China
Huaiyu Wan   Beijing Jiaotong University, China

Workshop Chairs

Huawei Shen   Institute of Computing Technology, CAS, China
Jianyi Wan   Jiangxi Normal University, China

Contents

Learning Cost-Effective Social Embedding
for Cascade Prediction

Wei Liu, Huawei Shen$^{(\boxtimes)}$, Wentao Ouyang, Ge Fu, Li Zha, and Xueqi Cheng

CAS Key Laboratory of Network Data Science and Technology,
Institute of Computing Technology, Chinese Academy of Sciences,
Beijing 100190, China
shenhuawei@ict.ac.cn

Abstract. Given a message, *cascade prediction* aims to predict the individuals who will potentially retweet it. Most existing methods either exploit demographical, structural, and temporal features for prediction, or explicitly rely on particular information diffusion models. Recently, researchers attempt to design fully data-driven methods for cascade prediction (i.e., without requiring human-defined features or information diffusion models), directly leveraging historical cascades to learn interpersonal proximity and then making prediction based on the learned proximity. One widely-used method to represent interpersonal proximity is social embedding, i.e., each individual is embedded into a low-dimensional latent metric space. One challenging problem is to design cost-effective method to learn social embedding from cascades. In this paper, we propose a position-aware asymmetric embedding method to effectively learn social embedding for cascade prediction. Different from existing methods where individuals are embedded into a single latent space, our method embeds each individual into two latent spaces: a latent *influence* space and a latent *susceptibility* space. Furthermore, our method employs the occurrence position of individuals in cascades to improve the learning efficiency of social embedding. We validate the proposed method on a dataset extracted from Sina Weibo. Experimental results demonstrate that the proposed model outperforms state-of-the-art social embedding methods at both learning efficiency and prediction accuracy.

1 Introduction

Online social media, such as Facebook, Twitter, Sina Weibo and WeChat, greatly facilitate information sharing, spreading, and filtering. In online social media, users could post original messages or forward messages that they see from other users. Information propagates along social relationships between users, explicitly or implicitly, forming a series of information cascades. Modeling and predicting cascade dynamics not only have important implications to understanding information propagation, but also have applications in an array of areas, including viral marketing, advertising, and social media analytics. A large amount of existing research devote to the study of information propagation, such as popularity prediction [1–6], influence maximization [7–9], network inference [10–14].

© Springer Nature Singapore Pte Ltd. 2016
Y. Li et al. (Eds.): SMP 2016, CCIS 669, pp. 1–13, 2016.
DOI: 10.1007/978-981-10-2993-6_1

In recent years, cascade prediction emerges as a new research topic. Given a message posted by a certain user, *cascade prediction* aims to predict the individuals who will potentially retweet it [15].

Existing methods for cascade prediction fall into two main paradigms. The first kind of methods exploit demographical, structural, and temporal features for cascade prediction [16–18]. However, these features are not always available in practice. For example, when a WeChat user reshares a message, we are not informed where he/she access the message. Consequently, the applicability of these methods is limited to scenarios where these features are explicit or could be easily inferred. The other kind of methods focuses on leveraging historical cascades for cascade prediction. These methods generally assume that cascades are generated following a particular information diffusion model, like independent cascade model and linear threshold model [19]. By fitting historical cascades, the learned models are used for cascade prediction. Despite their initial success, their performance heavily depends on the underlying information diffusion model and this limits their flexibility of capturing the complex and variational nature of cascade dynamics. Recently, Bourigault et al. proposed to conduct cascade prediction through learning interpersonal proximity from historical cascades [15], embedding each individual into a latent Euclidean space where interpersonal proximity is captured by Euclidean distance. This method is a fully data-driven method, requiring human-defined features or information diffusion models. Yet, it is not cost-effective because all cascades are equally treated and the signals embodied by individual's occurrence position in cascades are not leveraged. In sum, we lack a cost-effective fully data-driven method for cascade prediction.

In this paper, we propose a position-aware asymmetric embedding (PAE for short) method to effectively learn social embedding for cascade prediction. Our method distinguishes itself from existing embedding methods at two key aspects. First, different from existing methods where individuals are embedded into a single latent space, our method embeds each individual into two latent spaces: a latent *influence* space and a latent *susceptibility* space. In this way, our method possesses the flexibility to capture the asymmetric interpersonal influence that is intuitively expected and empirically observed in information diffusion [14,20]. Second, our method takes the occurrence position of individuals in cascades to guide the learning of their embedding. The basic idea is similar to top-k learning to rank in information retrieval [21,22]. Paying more attention to individuals occurring in the top positions of cascades, our method is cost-effective at learning the interpersonal proximity for cascade prediction.

We validate the proposed method on a dataset extracted from Sina Weibo. Experimental results demonstrate that the proposed model outperforms state-of-the-art social embedding methods at both learning efficiency and prediction accuracy.

2   Problem Formulation

The cascade prediction problem addressed in this paper is described as follows: given a message and the source user who originally posts it, cascade prediction aims to predict the individuals who will potentially retweet the message.

A cascade is a sequence of users infected by some information. For example, a cascade could be the list of users who forwarded a message on Sina Weibo. A cascade describes to whom and when an item spreads among users. We use Φ to denote the set of information cascades. For a message m involving n users, its cascade Φ^m is denoted by a user list $\Phi^m = (a_0^m, \ldots, a_n^m)$. The corresponding infected timestamps are denoted as $T^m = (t^m(a_0^m), \ldots, t^m(a_n^m))$, where users are ranked in the ascending order of the time they forward the message m. Here, we use a_0^m to denote the source user of the cascade m and treat the timestamp of a_0^m as 0. All timestamp in T^m is relative to a_0^m. The entire records of information cascades Φ is composed of a set of N users $\mathcal{U} = (a_1, \ldots, a_N)$. We divide Φ into two subsets of distinct cascades, where $\Phi_r \subseteq \Phi$ is the set of training cascades and $\Phi_e \subseteq \Phi$ is the set of testing cascades.

3 Model

3.1 Overview

The central idea in our approach to the cascade prediction problem is to map the observed information diffusion process into a heat diffusion process in a continuous Euclidean space, such that the locations in the latent space well explain the contamination timestamps observed in the training cascades. Specifically, we project each individual as two locations in a latent Euclidean space $Z = R^n$ with n dimensions. The two locations represent a user's influence coordinate and susceptibility coordinate respectively. We learn these coordinates as solving a ranking problem, where we introduce the concept of critical penalty margin. It preserves not only the observed contamination orders but also the distances between pair-wise users in the training cascades. In the latent Euclidean space, users who are infected earlier are closer to the source user than users who are infected later. We illustrate our approach in Fig. 1.

3.2 User Influence and Susceptibility

Influence between users in social networks is usually asymmetric. That is, the influence from user a to user b is usually not identical to the influence from user b to user a. For example, assume there are two users in Sina Weibo, where user a is a movie star and user b is a fan of user a (i.e., user b follows user a); it is more likely that user b will "like" the information published by user a while user a is likely to pay little attention to the information published by user b. In other words, in social networks, some users have high influence while some users have high susceptibility.

To model these aspects, we propose to project each user into two locations in a latent Euclidean space. In particular, the two locations represent a user's influence and susceptibility, depending on whether the user is the source or an infected user in a cascade. Mathematically, we use $y_{a_i} = (y_{a_i}^I, y_{a_i}^S)$ to denote user a's influence coordinate and susceptibility coordinate in the projected Euclidean space.

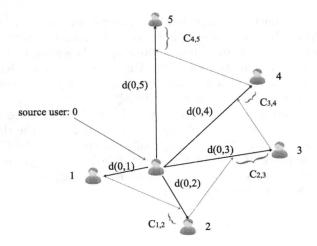

Fig. 1. Embedding social users in latent Euclidean space.

3.3 User Embedding

Consider a geometric manifold $\mathcal{X}$. We follow [15] and define a heat diffusion kernel $E(t, x_1, x_2)$ such that $E : R^+ \times \mathcal{X} \times \mathcal{X} \to R$ computes the heat at location x_2 at time t knowing that the heat source is x_1. It models the heat diffusion when an initial unit heat is positioned at location x_1 at time $t = 0$. In a Euclidean space of n dimensions, the diffusion kernel can be written as:

$$E(t, x_1, x_2) = (4\pi t)^{-\frac{n}{2}} e^{-\frac{\|x_1 - x_2\|^2}{4t}}. \tag{1}$$

We then use this kernel to model the information contamination process and rewrite it as $E_Y(t, a_0, a_i)$, which returns a value corresponding to the contamination score of node a_i at time t knowing that the source of the contamination is a_0. In particular, we write

$$E_Y(t, a_0, a_i) = (4\pi t)^{-\frac{n}{2}} e^{-\frac{\|v_{a_0}^I - v_{a_i}^S\|^2}{4t}}. \tag{2}$$

Note that, in the above equation, the coordinate of the source user a_0 is her influence coordinate (i.e., with the superscript I) while the coordinate of the contaminated user a_i is her susceptibility coordinate (i.e., with the superscript S). This is important in differentiating the role (i.e., the sender or the receiver) of a user in a cascade. If we model only one coordinate for each user as done in [15], the asymmetric interpersonal influence between users in social networks cannot be well addressed.

The diffusion kernel models the contamination propensity of a node at time t given a particular information source. The training cascades Φ_r only provide the infected time of different users in a cascade. Similar to [15], we use the following two constraints derived from the training cascades to restrict the kernel:

$$(1) \quad \forall (a_i, a_j) \in \Phi^m \times \Phi^m, i < j \Rightarrow$$
$$\|y_{a_0^m}^I - y_{a_i}^S\|^2 < \|y_{a_0^m}^I - y_{a_j}^S\|^2$$
$$(2) \quad \forall a_i \in \Phi^m, a_j \notin \Phi^m \Rightarrow$$
$$\|y_{a_0^m}^I - y_{a_i}^S\|^2 < \|y_{a_0^m}^I - y_{a_j}^S\|^2. \tag{3}$$

Note that, we differentiate a user's influence coordinate from her susceptibility coordinate in the above constraints, while [15] does not. The first constraint means that given two contaminated users $a_i \in \Phi^m$ and $a_j \in \Phi^m$ with $i < j$ (where i and j represent the infected orders), the diffusion kernel E_Y should be constrained such that $\forall t$, $E_Y(t, a_0^m, a_i) > E_Y(t, a_0^m, a_j)$. According to (2), this implies $\|y_{a_0^m}^I - y_{a_i}^S\|^2 < \|y_{a_0^m}^I - y_{a_j}^S\|^2$. The second constraint means that given one contaminated user $a_i \in \Phi^m$ and an uncontaminated user $a_j \notin \Phi^m$, the diffusion kernel E_Y should be constrained such that $\forall t$, $E_Y(t, a_0^m, a_i) > E_Y(t, a_0^m, a_j)$. This implies $\|y_{a_0^m}^I - y_{a_i}^S\|^2 < \|y_{a_0^m}^I - y_{a_j}^S\|^2$.

The problem of modeling information cascades then corresponds to finding the optimal coordinates Y of the users in a latent space based on the training cascades Φ_r. We define the corresponding empirical risk of the model as

$$\mathcal{L}(Y) = \sum_{m \in \Phi_r} \Delta(E_Y(., a_0^m, .), m), \tag{4}$$

where $\Delta(E_Y(., a_0^m, .), m)$ is a loss function that measures how much the prediction $E_Y(., a_0^m, .)$ given by the diffusion kernel differs from the observed cascade m. In particular, we define a ranking loss function as

$$\Delta(E_Y(., a_0^m, .), m)$$
$$= \sum_{\substack{a_i \in \Phi^m, \\ a_j \in \Phi^m, \\ i < j}} \max\left(0, C_{i,j} - (\|y_{a_0^m}^I - y_{a_j}^S\|^2 - \|y_{a_0^m}^I - y_{a_i}^S\|^2)\right)$$
$$+ \sum_{\substack{a_i \in \Phi^m, \\ a_j \notin \Phi^m}} \max\left(0, C_{i,j} - (\|y_{a_0^m}^I - y_{a_j}^S\|^2 - \|y_{a_0^m}^I - y_{a_i}^S\|^2)\right), \tag{5}$$

where we call $C_{i,j}$ the *critical penalty margin* and we detail it in the next section. Finally, the problem of learning the optimal coordinates Y^* becomes

$$Y^* = \arg \min_Y \mathcal{L}(Y), \tag{6}$$

which is to minimize the total empirical loss between the predictions and the observed cascades.

3.4   Critical Penalty Margin

The constraints in (5) only encode the relative contamination order of two users. However, they fails to reflect the occurrence positions of users in cascades and how far they are in the cascades. For example, the following two cases result in the same constraint: (1) the source user and the 2nd contaminated user, (2) the source user and the 100th contaminated user. However, the two users in the latter case should be located further in the latent space. To account for this aspect, we design a *position-aware* critical penalty margin $C_{i,j}$ in the loss function.

Before detailing $C_{i,j}$, we first model the *ideal* distance in the latent Euclidean space between user a_0^m and user a_i as $d(0, i) = \log_\mu(1 + i)$ using the information diffusion tree for user a_i, where μ is the average out degree of the information diffusion tree (we set $\mu = 2$ in this paper). We illustrate such distances in Fig. 2. This is inspired by the study in [5], which models an information cascade spreading over the network using an information diffusion tree.

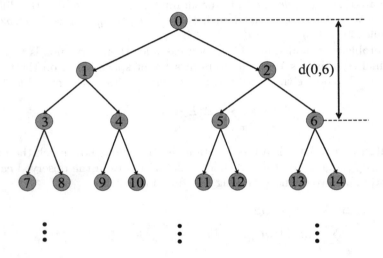

Fig. 2. Information diffusion tree with average out degree 2. User 0 is the source of the cascade and user 1~14 represent the forwarding user in the ascending order of the forwarding time.

We then define the critical penalty margin $C_{i,j}$ as

$$C_{i,j} = \log_\mu(1 + j) - \log_\mu(1 + i) = \log_\mu(1 + \frac{j - i}{1 + i}). \tag{7}$$

If a user a_j is not in the cascade Φ^m, we define $j = \frac{n_m + N}{2}$ where n_m is the number of users involving in the forwarding of message m. The form of $C_{i,j}$ offers the following two benefits. (1) Given i, the critical penalty margin $C_{i,j}$ increases as the value $j - i$ increases. That is to say, the larger the contamination order j is to i (i.e., the latter that a_j is infected), the larger the critical penalty margin $C_{i,j}$ is. In this way, we preserve the distance in addition to the contamination order between two users in the latent space. For example, $C_{1,5} > C_{1,2}$. (2) Given $j - i$, the critical penalty margin $C_{i,j}$ increases as the value i decreases. That is to say,

Algorithm 1. Parameter estimation via gradient descent

Input: set of training cascades Φ_r, dimensions n of latent Euclidean space, maximum epoch M and learning rate η at each iteration
Output: $\forall a_i \in \mathcal{U}$, user coordinates $y_{a_i}^I$ and $y_{a_i}^S$ in latent Euclidean space

Initialize $y_{a_i}^I$ and $y_{a_i}^S$ with random values for each user a_i, and Initialize iteration $k = 0$,
repeat
  for $k = 1$ to M **do**
    $Y^{k+1} \leftarrow Y^k$
    $\forall m \in \Phi_l$, sample $a_i \in \Phi^m$, sample $a_j \in \Phi^m$ with
    $t^m(a_j) > t^m(a_i)$ or $a_j \notin \Phi^m$
    $\hat{d}(0, i) = \|y_{a_0^m}^I - y_{a_i}^S\|^2$
    $\hat{d}(0, j) = \|y_{a_0^m}^I - y_{a_j}^S\|^2$
    $\hat{C}_{i,j} = \hat{d}(0, j) - \hat{d}(0, i)$
    if $\hat{C}_{i,j} < C_{i,j}$ **then**
      compute gradient
    else
      $k = k + 1$
    end if
    aggregate gradient and update parameters
    $y_{a_0^m}^{I(k+1)} = y_{a_0^m}^{I(k)} - \eta \sum_1^{|\Phi_e|} \partial \mathcal{L} / \partial y_{a_0^m}^I$
    $y_{a_i}^{S(k+1)} = y_{a_i}^{S(k)} - \eta \sum_1^{|\Phi_e|} \partial \mathcal{L} / \partial y_{a_i}^I$
    $y_{a_j}^{S(k+1)} = y_{a_j}^{S(k)} - \eta \sum_1^{|\Phi_e|} \partial \mathcal{L} / \partial y_{a_j}^S$
  end for
  $Y \leftarrow Y^k$
until maximum epoch M is reached or gradients vanish

$C_{i,j}$ heavily penalizes errors with regard to the top-ranked users in a cascade and increases the confidence margin for insufficient distance difference between top-ranked users. In this way, we can more accurately predict the cascade for the first few users. In contrast, [15] simply set $C_{i,j} = 1$. As a result, it cannot encode the distance information in the cascades. No matter a user is the 100th contaminated or the 2nd contaminated, they contribute similarly to the loss function.

4 Learning and Prediction

In this section, we describe the method for parameter estimation and cascade prediction. We also analyze the model complexity.

4.1 Parameter Estimation

The optimal values for parameter $\{y_{a_0^m}^I, y_{a_i}^S, y_{a_j}^S\}$ in Eq. (5) can be obtained via minimizing the loss function in Eq. (6) with respect to $y_{a_0^m}^I$, $y_{a_i}^S$ and $y_{a_j}^S$. In this paper, we use the standard gradient descent method, as described in Algorithm 1, where the gradients with respect to $y_{a_0^m}^I$, $y_{a_i}^S$, and $y_{a_j}^S$ are given by

$$\frac{\partial \mathcal{L}}{\partial y_{a_0^m}^I} = 2\left(y_{a_j}^S - y_{a_i}^S\right)$$

$$\frac{\partial \mathcal{L}}{\partial y_{a_i}^S} = 2\left(y_{a_i}^S - y_{a_0^m}^I\right)$$

$$\frac{\partial \mathcal{L}}{\partial y_{a_j}^S} = 2\left(y_{a_0^m}^I - y_{a_j}^S\right). \tag{8}$$

4.2   Cascade Prediction

With the obtained optimal parameters, i.e., Y^*, we can use the learned model to perform cascade prediction on the test cascades Φ_e. For each cascade $m \in \Phi_e$, we compute the Euclidean distance between the influence coordinate $y_{a_0^m}^S$ of user a_0^m and the susceptibility coordinate of every other user in $\mathcal{U}$. Our prediction result is then the user list in the ascending order of the calculated distance values.

4.3   Complexity Analysis

The learning complexity is $\mathcal{O}(2M \times n)$, where M is the number of epochs and n is the dimension of the latent space. The prediction complexity for each cascade is then $\mathcal{O}(2N \times n)$, where N is the total number of users. As the complexity is linear, we can perform cascade prediction in large scale social networks.

5   Experiments

5.1   Dataset

We evaluate the proposed model on a real dataset extracted from Sina Weibo, the largest Chinese microblogging website. The dataset consists of the cascades of tweets pertaining to the documentary entitled "Under the Dome" released by Chai Jing in Sina Weibo. It involves about 2 millions users and spans from February 28, 2015 to March 6, 2015. We construct three datasets, denoted as A_i ($1 \leq i \leq 3$), considering only the top-k (e.g., $k = 4000, 8000, 18000$) active users. For each dataset, 70 % cascades are used for training and the remaining 30 % for testing. Dataset statistics are shown in Table 1.

5.2   Baseline Methods

We compare the proposed position-aware asymmetric embedding (PAE for short) method with three baseline methods, described as follows:

- **Frequency (Freq)**: This heuristic method ranks candidate users according to the frequency that each user involves in cascades in training dataset. It assumes that the user with high activity is more probable to be infected.

Table 1. Dataset statistics.

Dataset	#Users	#Training cascades	#Test cascades
A_1	4,000	1,963	552
A_2	8,000	2,810	809
A_3	18,000	4,045	1,303

– **Matrix factorization (MF)** [23]: We construct an interaction matrix X, with X_{ij} reflecting the frequency that user a_j has been infected by a_i in training dataset. Matrix factorization technique is then used to factorize X, obtaining an influence vector and a susceptibility vector for each user. For cascade prediction, we use the inner product between the influence vector of source user and the susceptibility vector of candidate user as the criteria.
– **Cascade diffusion kernel (CDK)** [15]: This symmetric social embedding model projects each user into a latent Euclidean using a diffusion kernel. Indeed, this model could be viewed as a special case of our model, i.e., symmetric and without considering users' occurrence position in cascades. This model also serves as the state-of-the-art method of cascade prediction.

We choose the three baseline methods with two key considerations: (1) the three methods form a series of methods with new information being added sequentially. The *Freq* method only considers users' activity. The MF method considers the interaction between source user and target user. The CDK method considers users' order occurring in cascades. Finally, our PAE method incorporates the occurrence position of users in cascades. Comparing these methods, we offer readers a clear picture about the role of each factors for cascade prediction. (2) As shown in Ref. [15], the CDK method outperforms the methods that assumes certain underlying diffusion model (e.g., NETRATE [24]), offering us a state-of-the-art method. Moreover, these methods require explicit or implicit network structure, which is not available in our dataset.

For the three latent factor methods (i.e., MF, CDK and PAE), we use the same dimension for fair comparison. In addition, the performance or the three methods depends on the maximum number of iterations and the learning rate. For fair comparison, we use the best parameter configuration for each method with fine-tuning.

Table 2. MAP of the compared models at cascade prediction.

Methods	A_1	A_2	A_3
Freq	0.020	0.014	0.011
MF	0.180	0.135	0.084
CDK	0.212	0.169	0.114
PAE	**0.235**	**0.200**	**0.154**

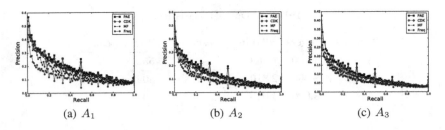

Fig. 3. Precision-Recall curves for different models on different datasets.

5.3   Evaluation Measures

As done in [15], we use Mean Average Precision (MAP) and Precision-Recall curves to evaluate the performance of all the methods for cascade prediction. For each test cascade $m \in \Phi_e$, we compute the *Euclidean distance* between influence coordinate $y_{a_0^m}^S$ of user a_0^m and susceptibility coordinate of every other candidate user and sort them in the ascending order of distance. The user with high rank is more probable to forward the message of source user of cascade. The description of MAP is as follows:

– **Mean Average Precision** measures the prediction performance in the testing cascades. The larger values of MAP indicate better prediction. Let $\gamma_{m,i}$ to be the rank of user a_i for cascade m. Let $A_{m,i}$ be the precision at rank i for cascade m. In other words, the value of $A_{m,i}$ denotes the percentage of infected users among the top i users in prediction users list. The MAP is denoted as:

$$MAP = \frac{1}{|\Phi_e|} \sum_{m \in \Phi_e} \frac{\sum_{a_i \in \Phi^m} A_{m,\gamma_{m,i}}}{|\Phi^m|} \qquad (9)$$

We also visualize model performance by using Precision-Recall curves and it is shown in Fig. 3.

5.4   Experimental Results

We first compare the four methods in terms of their accuracy for cascade prediction. As shown in Table 2, the Freq method performs the worst as expected and the MF method significantly increases the prediction accuracy, confirming that interpersonal influence is a key factor at cascade prediction. The CDK method further improves the prediction accuracy, indicating that users' temporal order in cascades is helpful for learning a better embedding of users. Finally, our PAE method consistently outperforms all the baseline methods in all the three datasets. This is caused that the PAE method separately models users' influence and susceptibility and leverages the occurrence positions of users in

Table 3. Prediction accuracy of PAE with different number of dimensions.

n	10	30	50	70	90	110
MAP	0.095	0.151	0.152	**0.154**	0.154	0.153

cascades for embedding. Moreover, with the increase of data sparsity, i.e., more inactive users are included varying from A1, A2 to A3, the prediction accuracy decreases. However, compared with the CDK method, the superiority of our method increases, with the increasing percent being 10.8 %, 18.3 %, 35.1 % on the three datasets respectively. To offer more details, we show the prediction performance of each method using Precision-Recall curves (Fig. 3).

5.5   Parameters Analysis

We now analyze whether and to what extent the proposed model is affected by parameter configuration, including the dimensionality of latent Euclidean space n, maximum iteration times M and learning rate η at each iteration which is constant in experiment. Limited by space, we only show the results on dataset A_3. Indeed, the results are similar on all the three datasets.

Dimensionality of Latent Space. As shown in Table 3, the prediction accuracy increases when varying the dimension n from 10 to 70. Next, increasing the value of n affect the prediction accuracy slightly. In this paper, if no explicit statement, we use $n = 70$.

Number of Iterations. As shown in Fig. 4, the prediction accuracy increases with the number of iterations in the beginning and then flats. One prominent observation is that our PAE method achieves a good prediction accuracy with only a small number of iterations while the CDK model requires much more iterations. This indicates that our model is cost-effective than the CDK model. One possible explanations is that our model replaces the constant critical penalty

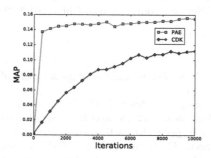

Fig. 4. MAP performance varying with increase of iterations.

Table 4. Prediction accuracy of PAE with different learning rate.

η	0.0004	0.002	0.01	0.05	0.25
MAP	0.140	0.151	**0.154**	0.131	0.078

margin with a varied margin determined according to the occurrence position of users in cascades. This help our model achieve better prediction accuracy with little iterations.

The Learning Rate. The learning rate η represents the step size of gradient descent in the learning process. As shown in Table 4, the prediction accuracy becomes better with learning rate η increasing from 0.004 to 0.01. Then, increasing the value of η results in worse performance because a larger value of learning rate may lead to the lack of convergence. We choose $\eta = 0.01$ in this paper.

6 Conclusions

In this paper, we investigated the problem of cascade prediction using a fully data-driven method, directly leveraging historical cascades to learn interpersonal proximity and then making prediction based on the learned proximity. We proposed a position-aware asymmetric embedding method to effectively learn social embedding for cascade prediction. Different from existing methods where individuals are embedded into a single latent space, our method embeds each individual into two latent spaces: a latent influence space and a latent susceptibility space. Furthermore, our method employs the occurrence position of individuals in cascades to improve the learning efficiency of social embedding. We validate the proposed method on a dataset extracted from Sina Weibo. Experimental results demonstrate that the proposed model outperforms state-of-the-art social embedding methods at both learning efficiency and prediction accuracy.

Acknowledgments. This research is supported by the National Hi-Tech R&D Program of China (863 program) under grant number 2014AA01A302 and 2014AA015103, the National Key Research and Development Program of China (2016YFB0201404), and the National Natural Science Foundation of China (61202215, 61232010).

References

1. Szabo, G., Huberman, B.A.: Predicting the popularity of online content. Commun. ACM **53**(8), 80–88 (2010)
2. Bao, P., Shen, H.W., Jin, X., Cheng, X.Q.: Modeling and predicting popularity dynamics of microblogs using self-excited hawkes processes. In: Proceedings of WWW 2015 Companion, pp. 9–10 (2015)
3. Shen, H., Wang, D., Song, C., Barabási, A.L.: Modeling and predicting popularity dynamics via reinforced poisson process. In: Proceedings of AAAI 2014, pp. 291–297 (2014)

4. Gao, S., Ma, J., Chen, Z.: Modeling and predicting retweeting dynamics on microblogging platforms. In: Proceedings of WSDM 2015, pp. 107–116 (2015)
5. Zhao, Q., Erdogdu, M.A., He, H.Y., Rajaraman, A., Leskovec, J.: Seismic: a self-exciting point process model for predicting tweet popularity. In: Proceedings of KDD 2015, pp. 1513–1522 (2015)
6. Gao, J., Shen, H., Liu, S., Cheng, X.: Modeling and predicting retweeting dynamics via a mixture process. In: Proceedings WWW 2016 Companion, pp. 33–34 (2016)
7. Kempe, D., Kleinberg, J., Tardos, É.: Maximizing the spread of influence through a social network. In: Proceedings of KDD 2003, pp. 137–146 (2003)
8. Chen, W., Wang, Y., Yang, S.: Efficient influence maximization in social networks. In: Proceedings KDD 2009, pp. 199–208 (2009)
9. Cheng, S., Shen, H., Huang, J., Zhang, G., Cheng, X.: StaticGreedy: solving the scalability-accuracy dilemma in influence maximization. In: Proceedings of CIKM 2013, pp. 509–518 (2013)
10. Gomez Rodriguez, M., Leskovec, J., Krause, A.: Inferring networks of diffusion and influence. In: Proceedings of KDD 2010, pp. 1019–1028 (2010)
11. Myers, S., Leskovec, J.: On the convexity of latent social network inference. In: Proceedings of NIPS 2010, pp. 1741–1749 (2010)
12. Rodriguez, M.G., Balduzzi, D., Schölkopf, B.: Uncovering the temporal dynamics of diffusion networks (2011). arXiv:1105.0697
13. Wang, L., Ermon, S., Hopcroft, J.E.: Feature-enhanced probabilistic models for diffusion network inference. In: Flach, P.A., De Bie, T., Cristianini, N. (eds.) ECML PKDD 2012, Part II. LNCS, vol. 7524, pp. 499–514. Springer, Heidelberg (2012)
14. Wang, Y., Shen, H., Liu, S., Cheng, X.: Learning user-specific latent influence and susceptibility from information cascades. In: Proceedings of AAAI 2015, pp. 477–483 (2015)
15. Bourigault, S., Lagnier, C., Lamprier, S., Denoyer, L., Gallinari, P.: Learning social network embeddings for predicting information diffusion. In: Proceedings of WSDM 2014, pp. 393–402 (2014)
16. Guille, A., Hacid, H.: A predictive model for the temporal dynamics of information diffusion in online social networks. In: Proceedings of WWW 2012, pp. 1145–1152 (2012)
17. Bao, P., Shen, H.W., Huang, J., Cheng, X.Q.: Popularity prediction in microblogging network: a case study on Sina Weibo. In: Proceedings of WWW 2013 Companion, pp. 177–178 (2013)
18. Lagnier, C., Denoyer, L., Gaussier, E., Gallinari, P.: Predicting information diffusion in social networks using content and users profiles. In: Proceedings of NIPS 2013, pp. 74–85 (2013)
19. Goldenberg, J., Libai, B., Muller, E.: Talk of the network: a complex systems look at the underlying process of word-of-mouth. Market. Lett. 12(3), 211–223 (2001)
20. Aral, S., Walker, D.: Identifying influential and susceptible members of social networks. Science 337(6092), 337–341 (2012)
21. Niu, S., Guo, J., Lan, Y., Cheng, X.: Top-k learning to rank: labeling, ranking and evaluation. In :Proceedings SIGIR 2012, pp. 751–760 (2012)
22. Cao, Y., Xu, J., Liu, T.Y., Li, H., Huang, Y., Hon, H.W.: Adapting ranking SVM to document retrieval. In: Proceedings of SIGIR 2006, pp. 186–193 (2006)
23. Koren, Y., Bell, R., Volinsky, C.: Matrix factorization techniques for recommender systems. IEEE Comput. 8, 42–49 (2009)
24. Du, N., Song, L., Smola, A., Yuan, M.: Learning Networks of Heterogeneous Influence. In: Proceedings of NIPS 2012, pp. 2780–2788 (2012)

Missing and Spurious Interactions in Heterogeneous Military Networks

Changjun Fan$^{(\boxtimes)}$, Zhong Liu, Baoxin Xiu, and Lianfei Yu

Science and Technology on Information Systems Engineering Laboratory,
National University of Defense Technology, Changsha, Hunan 410073, China
fanchangjun09@163.com

Abstract. As we all know, decision-makers need the high quality battlefield information to design the best operation plans, however, real intelligence data are often incomplete and noisy, where missing links prediction methods and spurious links identification algorithms can be applied. Military organizations could be modeled as heterogeneous complex networks, where nodes represent different types of functional units and edges denote different types of communication links. In this paper, we proposed a combined link prediction index considering both the nodes' types effects and their structural similarities, and demonstrated that it is remarkably superior to all the 25 existing similarity-based methods both in predicting missing links and identifying spurious links in a real military network data; we also investigated the algorithms' robustness under noisy environment, and showed our method maintained the best performance under the condition of small noise. In the end, as the FINC-E model, here used to describe the heterogeneous military organizations, is also suitable to many other social organizations, such as criminal networks, business organizations, etc., thus our method has its prospects in these areas for many tasks, like detecting the underground relationships between terrorists, predicting the potential business markets for decision-makers, and so on.

Keywords: Complex military organization · Link prediction · FINC-E model · Social organization

1 Introduction

The state-of-art complex military organization named "System of System, SOS" has been playing an increasingly significant role in nowadays' warfare, disaster response, nation building, peace operations and counter-terrorism [10] with the rapid development of information technology and military science. Modeling complex military organization is a challenging task, and there are some inspiring works [1–3] in this field, and the most successful one is the FINC model proposed by Dekker [4–7], and Guoli Yang extended it as the FINC-E model [20].

Electronic supplementary material The online version of this chapter (doi:10.1007/978-981-10-2993-6_2) contains supplementary material, which is available to authorized users.

© Springer Nature Singapore Pte Ltd. 2016
Y. Li et al. (Eds.): SMP 2016, CCIS 669, pp. 14–28, 2016.
DOI: 10.1007/978-981-10-2993-6_2

FINC(Force, Intelligence, Networking and C2) methodology classified the nodes into three types: C2 node(C2), like command post, control center, etc., Intelligence node(I), like radar, AWACS, etc., and Force node(F), like missile position; and links provide communications between nodes, indicated by lines or arrows, depending on whether information flow is bidirectional or unidirectional. In FINC-E model, there are five types of links, Intelligence link($I \rightarrow C2$, unidirectional), $C2$ link($C2 - C2$, bidirectional), Fire link($I- > F$, unidirectional), Decision link($C2-F$, bidirectional) and Communication link(I-I, bidirectional). Each node has many attributes, like attack cost, InEdge, OutEdge, etc., each link also has attributes, such as information transfer delay, information load, information accuracy, attack cost, InNode, OutNode, ect. More details see in [20]. In this paper, FINC-E model is utilized to model the heterogeneous military organization.

As for the problem of link prediction, it attempts to estimate the likelihood of the existence of links between nodes based on the attributes of nodes as well as the structure of networks [8,13,14]. Due to its formal simplicity, theoretical value and practical significance, link prediction has attracted increasing attentions from various researches and engineers, such as physicists, mathematicians, computer scientists, statisticians, biologists, etc. As for complex military organization, link prediction may be more significant, since the war determines a country of vital significance, and quality of intelligence is critical to military decisions, as a formal representation of military intelligence, network topology for complex military organization has to be true enough to guarantee the reliability of the subsequent analysis, such as critical operational units analysis, community analysis, network evolving analysis, etc. However, due to the complex battle field situations and the expensive costs of military intelligence collection, it is nearly impossible to obtain an absolute accurate military network, there must be some missing information or spurious noise, in other words, missing links and spurious links in network topology. If we can predict them or identify them in advance with link prediction methods, it would be both meaningful to optimize the military organization structure for our side and attack the other side's critical operational components, which are sure to enhance the accuracy of military decisions and accelerate the process of victory.

Current link prediction methods are mainly designed basing on the definition of node similarity, which assumes that the greater the similarity values between nodes are, the higher the likelihood of the existence of links between them [15]. Another branch is based on the network structure only, which is named structural similarity, and can be further divided into three types: local information based similarity, such as CN index; path-based similarity, such as Katz index; random walk-based similarity, such as ACT index. There are 25 main similarity indexes now, details about them see in SI. And they are utilized to compare the prediction accuracy with the method proposed in this paper. However, all the existing methods may not work well in complex military network, for these methods are only designed for homogeneous networks, but linking behaviors are different between different types of nodes, for example, if there are command nodes and intelligence nodes densely connected in a control-centered military organization, intelligence nodes are more likely to build links with commands nodes than forces nodes. As a result, an index combining this impact and traditional topological similarity is proposed in this paper to improve the link prediction accuracy in complex military organization network.

The major contributions of this study are summarized as follows:

1. For the first time, we quantify the nodes' types effect on their linking behaviors, and empirically proved that it could remarkably improve the prediction accuracy of all the current methods;
2. We design a new link prediction index for heterogeneous military network and it is superior to all the other methods both in missing links prediction and spurious links identification tasks;
3. We investigate the algorithms' robustness under noisy environment, and demonstrate that our method maintains the best performance under the condition of small noise, and we also observe that spurious links are more destructive than missing links in military networks, which is just opposite to that in recommendation systems.

The remainder of this paper is organized as: Sect. 2 describes the methodology in detail, Sect. 3 conducts experiments on a real military network data and compared the performance of our method with all the other methods, Sect. 4 concludes the paper and pointed the further directions.

2   Methodology

Complex military organization can be described as $G(V, E, A, L, W)$ in FINC-E model, where V denotes operation units, E indicates communication links between nodes, A is a set of node types, L represents link types, mainly refers to five types. W is a set of weights, including node weights, like attack costs, and link weight, such as information loads. Just as mentioned in Introduction section, due to the complex battlefield situations and expensive costs of intelligence collection, there are often filled with noisy or incomplete information in the observations, which are reflected as spurious links or missing links respectively in the military network.

To purify the network topology, we used link prediction methods to predicting the missing links and identifying the spurious links based on the known network topology and nodes types information.

For the missing link prediction, the task is to estimate the existence tendency of all the non-observed links, and find the most possible non-observed ones. To test the algorithms' accuracy, the observed links, E, is randomly divided into two parts: the training set, E^T is treated as known information, while the probe set, E^P is used for testing. Obviously, $E^T \bigcup E^P = E$, $E^T \bigcap E^P = \emptyset$.

For spurious link identification, the task is to evaluate the reliability of all the observed links, and identify the most spurious links. To test the algorithm's accuracy, we randomly add some nonexistent links which constitutes the probe set E^P, and the given network (true network) together with the probe set constitute the training set E^T. Clearly, $E^T - E^P = E$, $E^T \bigcap E^P = E^P$.

Traditional methods for predicting missing links and identifying spurious links can be roughly divided into two classes: the probabilistic models and the similarity based algorithms: the former usually requires much information about node attributes, in addition to the observed network topology; the latter assigns a similarity score to every pair of nodes and ranks all links according to their scores. Since it is always very hard to collect enough nodes attributes, similarity based algorithms are thus the practical option, how to define the similarity between nodes is the key point for similarity algorithms, here we proposed the LR (Link Reliability) index, combining both the nodes' types information and their structural similarities.

2.1   Design of LR(Link Reliability) Index

Consider a complex military organization network $G(V, E, A, L, W)$, it is a heterogeneous directed weighted network, and it's difficult to directly conduct link prediction tasks, here we simplified it just a heterogeneous undirected unweighted network based on the following considerations: (1) link directions are totally determined by the two nodes linked, if two nodes' types are known, links between them are determined; (2) weights are often hard to obtain, and they have no obvious effects on linking behaviors between nodes. As a result, in this paper, link prediction is actually conducted in the network $\hat{G}(V, E, A)$, and our index, named Link Reliability (LR) is designed for it.

As we analyzed before, whether two nodes in the military network have links or not depends on two parts, one is the two linked nodes' types, denoted as T, the other is these two nodes' topological similarity, denoted as S. Let R stands for the link reliability, then we may have the following:

$$R = f(T, S) \tag{1}$$

f is the combined function of these two parts' effects.

Next, we deduce the forms of effect of nodes' types T, effect of node structural similarity S and the combined function f.

Effect of Nodes' Types. There are three types of nodes in the military network, and linking behaviors between different types of nodes are different. Here, the stochastic block model is utilized to give the mathematical formula of it. The stochastic block model is a general network model [11], it divides the nodes in the network into several groups, and the existence tendency between nodes is determined by the groups they belong to, nodes in the same group have the same linking behaviors. The model is most suitable for the situations where nodes' types significantly affect their linking behaviors, which is just the case this paper is to address.

A stochastic block model is composed of two parts: one is all the possible group division strategies, denoted as Ω; the other is the linking probability matrix between different groups, denoted as Q. Given a specific block division P and the corresponding linking probability matrix Q, a stochastic block model $M = (P, Q)$

is then determined. The observed network A^O could be regarded as one from an unknown stochastic block model, let Ψ be a certain network property, then it is easy to obtain the following based on Bayes theorem:

$$p(\psi|A^O) = \int_\Theta p(\psi|M)p(M|A^o)dM \tag{2}$$

where Θ stands for all possible stochastic block models, and since $p(M|A^O)p(A^O) = p(A^O|M)p(M)$, formula (2) could be rewritten as:

$$p(\psi|A^o) = \frac{\int_\Theta p(\psi|M)p(A^o|M)p(M)dM}{\int_\Theta p(A^o|M')p(M')dM'} \tag{3}$$

Let Ψ be $A_{xy} = 1$, then $p(\Psi|A^O) = p(A_{xy} = 1|A^O)$ represents the linking reliability of node pair v_x, v_y based on the observed network A^O. Now we can obtain the form of T by proving the following theorem 1. Detailed proof sees the SI.

Theorem 1. *Given a complex military organization network $G(V, E, A)$, let σ_x denotes the type of node v_x, σ_y denotes the type of node v_y, and r_{σ_x,σ_y} is the number of all possible links between these two types of nodes. $l^O_{\sigma_x,\sigma_y}$ represents the observed links between these two types nodes. Then the linking reliability for node pairs $\{v_x, v_y\}$ could be calculated as:*

$$p(A_{xy} = 1|A^O) = \frac{l^O_{\sigma_x,\sigma_y} + 1}{r_{\sigma_x,\sigma_y} + 2} \tag{4}$$

Therefore, formula of T is represented as $T(v_x, v_y) = p(A_{xy} = 1|A^O) = \frac{l^O_{\sigma_x,\sigma_y} + 1}{r_{\sigma_x,\sigma_y} + 2}$.

Effect of Nodes' Structural Similarity. Military network is a sparse network, where there are abundant nodes while with a few links, this may be the result of the hidden hierarchical structure in military organization. In [14], some random walk based indices, such as RWR, SRW, have been empirically demonstrated to be superior to the other methods on spase networks, like the Power network and the Router network. As a result, we utilize the RWR indice, which obtained the best performance among all random walk based methods [14], to measure the effect of nodes' structural similarity in the military network.

Consider a random walker starting from node v_x, who will iteratively move to a random neighbor with probability c and return to v_x with probability $1 - c$. Denote $\vec{q}_x$ as the steady state of this random walker from node v_x, we have:

$$\vec{q}_x = cP^T\vec{q}_x + (1 - c)\vec{e}_x \tag{5}$$

where P is the transition matrix with $P_{xy} = 1/k_x$ if v_x and v_y are connected, and $P_{xy} = 0$ otherwise, $\vec{e}_x$ is the vector with xth element equals 1, and the left elements are all 0s. It can be obviously obtained as follows:

$$\vec{q}_x = (1 - c)(1 - cP^T)^{-1}\vec{e}_x \tag{6}$$

The RWR index is thus defined as

$$s_{xy}^{RWR} = q_{xy} + q_{yx} \qquad (7)$$

where q_{xy} is the yth element of the vector $\vec{q_x}$. A fast algorithm to calculate this index was proposed by Tong et al. [19], and the application of this index to recommender systems can be found in Ref. [17].

Thus the formula of S is $S(v_x, v_y) = s_{xy}^{RWR} = q_{xy} + q_{yx}$.

Form the Combined Function f. Here we just utilize the simplest weighted average form to combine the two parts, which means the Link Reliability value could be calculated as:

$$R = f(T, S, \lambda) = \lambda T + (1 - \lambda)S = \lambda T(v_x, v_y) + (1 - \lambda)S(v_x, v_y) \qquad (8)$$

And $R(v_x, v_y) = \lambda T(v_x, v_y) + (1 - \lambda)S(v_x, v_y)$, form of $T(v_x, v_y)$ and $S(v_x, v_y)$ see formula (4) and (7). Weight parameter λ is proportional to each part's prediction accuracy in specific cases. For instance, for a specific network A, if the first part's accuracy is T_A^{AUC}, the second part's accuracy is S_A^{AUC}, then we obtain:

$$\frac{\lambda}{1 - \lambda} \approx \frac{1 - f(T, S, 0)}{1 - f(T, S, 1)} = \frac{1 - S_A^{AUC}}{1 - T_A^{AUC}} \qquad (9)$$

Thus $\lambda \approx \frac{1 - S_A^{AUC}}{2 - (T_A^{AUC} + S_A^{AUC})}$.

2.2   Evaluation Metrics

Two evaluation metrics adopted here are AUC(Area Under the receiver operating characteristic Curve)[9] and R[21]: AUC is used to measure the algorithms' accuracy in predicting missing links and identifying spurious links, and R is utilized to measure the ability for algorithms to maintain the prediction accuracies under noisy environments.

AUC. The AUC is a way to quantify the accuracy of prediction algorithms. Denote U as all the possible links in the network, E^T is the training set, E^P is the probe set. At each time, we randomly pick a missing link(i.e., a link in E^P) and a nonexistent link(i.e., a link in U-E^T) to compare their scores, if among n independent comparisons, there are n' times the missing link having a higher score and n'' times they have the same score, the AUC value for the missing links prediction task could be calculated as:

$$AUC = \frac{n' + 0.5n''}{n} \qquad (10)$$

The above metric can also be used to quantify the performance on identifying spurious links.

If all the scores are randomly generated from an independent and identical distribution, the AUC values should be about 0.5. Therefore, the degree to which the AUC value exceeds 0.5 indicates how better the algorithm performs than pure chance.

R. The R metric is recently proposed by Zhang et al. [21] to quantify to what extent the link prediction algorithms can resist the noise in the observed network.

$$R = \frac{1}{|L|} \sum_{q=0}^{|L|} \frac{AUC(q)}{AUC(0)} \qquad (11)$$

where $L = ratio * |E^T|$, and $ratio$ is a quantity to measure the fraction of randomly added or deleted links. When $ratio$ is positive, $|ratio| * E^T$ links are randomly added to the training set, when $ratio$ is negative, $|ratio| * E^T$ links are randomly deleted from the training set. In order to keep the network connected, we cannot remove too many links, as a result, we keep $-0.3 \leq ratio \leq 1$, $AUC(q)$ is the AUC value of a link prediction method when q links are added($ratio > 0$) to or deleted($ratio < 0$) from the training set, when $ratio = 0$, $R = 1$.

3   Experiment Design and Result Analysis

In this paper, we provide a real military network, which is from an area's military organization (specific name is anonymized here due to the requirement of secret protections, but detailed network information is described in SI), it contains 89 entities, including 12 command nodes, 26 force nodes, and 51 intelligence nodes, and there are 150 observable links, including 30 Intelligence links, 16 Fire links, 26 Decision links, 51 Communication links and 17 $C2$ links. The topology of the network is drawn as Fig. 1.

3.1   Missing Links Prediction

Divide the network into two parts, the training set E^T contains 90 % of the links, and the remaining 10 % of links constitute the probe set E^P. It is obvious that $E^T + E^P = E$, and $E^T \bigcap E^P = \emptyset$. Compared our proposed method LR with all the other similarity-based indexes on the performance of AUC values. The prediction accuracies measured by AUC are shown in Fig. 2. Each data point is obtained by averaging over 1000 implementations with independently random divisions of the training set and the probe set. It is obvious from the comparisons that our method performs the best among all state-of-the-art algorithms (about 1.26 % higher than the current best method), and its variance value is medium among all, indicating it is also a comparatively stable index.

3.2   Spurious Links Identification

Next we consider the identification of spurious links, where spurious links are those links being observed but not really existent, which may be resulted from

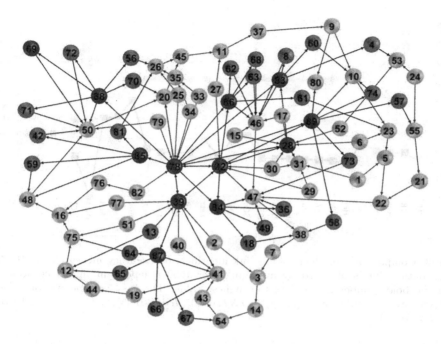

Fig. 1. Topology of the Network. Blue nodes represents the C2 units, like command posts, control center, etc., red nodes denotes the Force units, such as the missile position, and green nodes indicates the Intelligence units, like various optical stations, radar stations. (Color figure online)

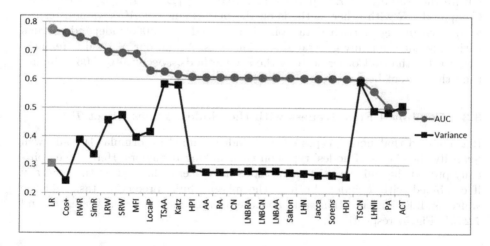

Fig. 2. Comparisons for the missing link prediction accuracy measured by AUC. Each data point is obtained by averaging over 1000 independent implementations, and the bold number emphasizes the highest value. The best parameters for some indexes are: $LR(0.3)$, $Katz(0.01)$, $LHNII(0.9)$, $RWR(0.95)$, $LRW(5)$, $SRW(5)$, $SimRank(0.8)$.

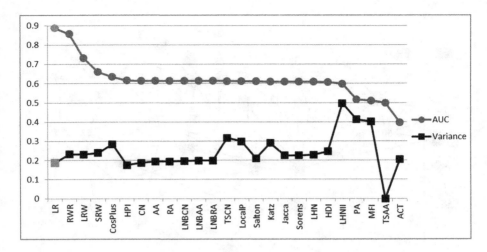

Fig. 3. Comparisons for the spurious link identification accuracy measured by AUC. Each data point is obtained by averaging over 1000 independent implementations, and the bold number emphasizes the highest value. The best parameters for some indexes are: $LR(0.1)$, $Katz(0.01)$, $LHNII(0.9)$, $RWR(0.95)$, $LRW(5)$, $SRW(5)$, $SimRank(0.8)$.

experimental errors or data noise. To test the validity of the algorithms, we randomly add 10% $(0.1|E|)$ nonexistent links to the network data which constitute the probe set E^P, and the original network together with spurious links constitute the training set E^T. It is obvious that $E^T \bigcap E^P = E^P$, $E^T - E^P = E$. Compared LR with other methods on the performance of AUC values, results are shown in Fig. 3. Each data point is averaged over 1000 independent runs with different randomly generated spurious sets. Again, our method is remarkably better than all other state-of-the-art methods, specifically, 3.05% higher than the current best method.

3.3 Combined Effectiveness with the Nodes' Types Effect T

It is claimed that nodes' types effect T index defined in formula (4) could well quantify the effects of nodes' types on their linking behaviors. Here, we empirically proved that all the existent methods have been enhanced on the accuracy if combined with T index, both in the missing links prediction task and the spurious links identification task, and the average rises are 8.39% (Fig. 4) and 7.24% (Fig. 5) respectively.

3.4 Algorithm Robustness

The training set is assumed to be entirely clean in the above tasks, however, in real cases, the reliability of the observed network data could not always be

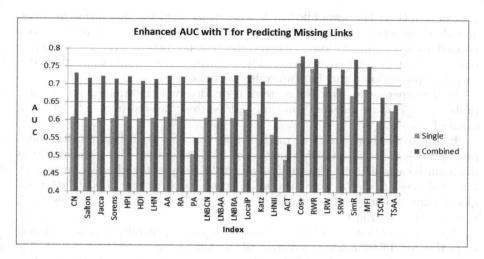

Fig. 4. Enhanced AUC with T for Predicting Missing Links. *Ratio* of the training set is 0.9, and each data point is averaged over 1000 independent implementations. The blue bars are prediction accuracies obtained by the current methods, the red bars are prediction accuracies obtained by current methods combined with T index. The best parameters for some indexes are: $LR(0.3)$, $Katz(0.01)$, $LHNII(0.9)$, $RWR(0.95)$, $LRW(5)$, $SRW(5)$, $SimRank(0.8)$. (Color figure online)

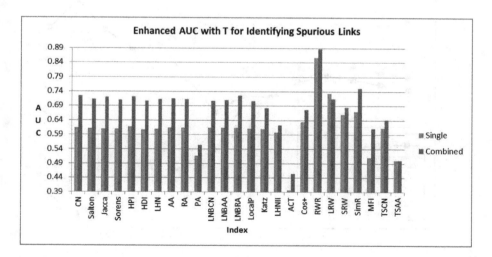

Fig. 5. Enhanced AUC with T for Identifying Spurious Links. *Ratio* of the training set is 0.9, and each point is averaged over 1000 independent implementations. The blue bars are accuracies obtained by the current methods, the red bars are accuracies obtained by current methods combined with T index. The best parameters for some indexes are: $LR(0.1)$, $Katz(0.01)$, $LHNII(0.9)$, $RWR(0.95)$, $LRW(5)$, $SRW(5)$, $SimRank(0.8)$. (Color figure online)

guaranteed, there is always filled with noisy or incomplete information in them, and that's exactly why the link prediction is so important. As a result, when applied to solve application problems, the link prediction methods will most likely work under noisy environment. This section, we investigate to which extent each link prediction algorithm can resist the noise.

In the experiment, after the network is divided into the training set E^T and probe set E^P, some links are randomly added to or deleted from E^T, let *ratio* ranges from -0.3 to 1.

In Fig. 6 we show effects of random noise on link prediction results. More precisely, we investigate the dependence of AUC on $|ratio|$. Since it is hardly to distinguish each of them if putting on all the 26 indexes together, we just select 4 typical ones (*LNBRA* from local information based indexes, *LocalPath* from global information based indexes, *Cos+* from random walk based indexes), and compare them in Fig. 6.

It is observed that (1): AUC decreases with $|ratio|$ generally for most indexes, and AUC of different link prediction algorithms decays with $|ratio|$ with different speed. For example, LR has the highest AUC when $ratio = 0$, when $ratio = 100\%$, it reaches the lowest point among all. This indicates the performance of different link prediction methods in the military network may change dramatically when noise exists, and R value is such an index to quantify the

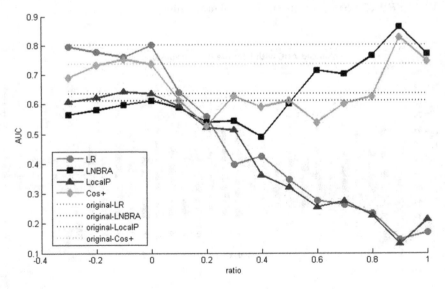

Fig. 6. The dependence of link prediction algorithms' accuracy(AUC) on *ratio* in the military network. The listed link prediction algorithm are LR, $LNBRA$, $LocalP$, $Cos+$. Dashed lines represent the AUC of these prediction algorithms in the clean network (i.e., the network without any noisy or missing links). *ratio* < 0 represents the missing link case and *ratio* > 0 stands for the noisy link case. Each data point is averaged over 100 independent implementations.

different decay speed of AUC, which will be discussed later; (2) randomly removing links are less destructive than randomly adding link given the same $|ratio|$ value. Taking the $Cos+$ index as an example, adding 30% noisy links will decrease AUC from 0.7363 to 0.6260, the drop is 0.1103, while removing the same amount of random links will make the AUC be around 0.6906, the drop is 0.0457. This is on the contrary to results in ref. [21], and the possible explanation may be that for the complex military organization, mistaken information(noisy links) may be more misleading(destructive) than missing information(missing links); (3) LR performs the best as the ratio ranges from -0.3 to 0.2, which means our method is the most robust and efficient one under the condition of small noise.

Next, we utilize R index defined in formula (11) to measure the algorithm robustness when links are randomly added or removed from the training set, and R depends on $ratio$ apparently. In Fig. 7, we investigate the effects of $ratio$ on R. And also we just show LR, $LNBRA$, $LocalPath$ and $Cos+$ for a clear illustration.

It can be observed from Fig. 7 that: (1) the differences between algorithms' R values increase with $ratio$ when $ratio$ is positive, indicating the different decaying speed of different algorithms' robustness; (2) randomly adding spurious links is more destructive to the algorithms' robustness, take LR as an example, given the same $|ratio|$ value, R is 1.056 when $ratio = -0.3$, while 0.8231 when $ratio = 0.3$;

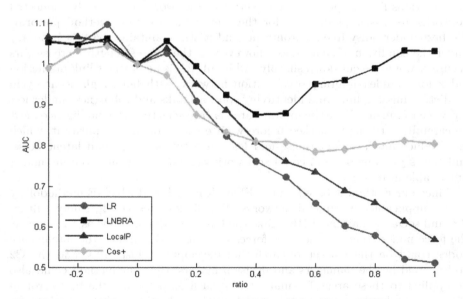

Fig. 7. The dependence of R on $ratio$. The listed link prediction algorithm are LR, $LNBRA$, $LocalP$, $Cos+$. $ratio < 0$ represents the missing link case and $ratio > 0$ stands for the noisy link case. Each data point is averaged over 100 independent implementations.

(3) LR maintains a comparative higher robustness under small noise environment $(-0, 1 \leq ratio \leq 0.1)$.

4   Conclusion and Discussion

This paper tries to address the problem of link prediction in complex military organization network, which is essential for commanders to obtain the qualified intelligence and make the right decisions. Three main contributions are made. Firstly, we measured the nodes' types' effects on their linking behaviors based on the stochastic block model and proved its efficiency empirically. Secondly, we proposed a new link prediction index for complex military organization network, considering both the nodes' types' effect and nodes' structural similarities, and proved it is remarkably superior to all the existent similarity-based indexes, both in predicting missing links and identifying spurious links. Finally, we investigated link prediction algorithms' robustness in the military network under noisy environment, and found that: (1) spurious links are more destructive than missing links for prediction accuracy in military network, which is on the contrary to the results in [21], indicating that mistaken information may be more misleading in military areas; (2) for some indexes, such as $Cos+$ and Local Naive Bayes based indexes, their prediction accuracies may even be improved with a certain spurious links existing, and the hidden reason may account for that the random spurious links improve the connectivity of network, and densely connected networks are easier predictable for these methods; (3) Our method performs the best under noisy-free environment, and it still maintains the best accuracy under the condition of small noise, however, as the noise strength increases, its accuracy would be cut down sharply. All in all, LR is an efficient link prediction index for complex military organization network, with both high accuracy in predicting missing links and identifying spurious links and robustness under low noisy environment. Since the military area is very sensitive, the intelligence must be carefully artificially checked before we use the algorithm to purify it, which may reduce much obvious noise and leave a network with small latent noise, and that's just our method could still work well on, as a result, the method is practicable in reality.

Since our method is based on the FINC-E model, and FINC-E methodology is also applicable to criminal networks [12], disaster rescue [4], safety culture [18] and social management [16]. Take the business organizations as an instance, the force nodes could be the sales forces and business markets; the intelligence nodes could be the market research and development institutes; and the C2 nodes could be the managers and decision-makers, thus our method could also be applied to these areas for many tasks, such as detecting the underground relationships between terrorists, predicting the potential business markets for decision-makers, and so on.

In the future, we should validate the method in more real military network data, and test its applications in the other social organization areas mentioned above. Besides, since the structure of the military organization is changeable overtime, link prediction analysis should be considered in the dynamic environment, as a result, we should further study the link prediction in time-dependent military networks.

Acknowledgements. The authors are grateful to the anonymous referees for their insightful suggestions and comments. This research was supported by the National Basic Research Program of China under Grant No. 71471176, No. 71471174 and No. 61303266. All authors acknowledge the National University of Defense Technology.

References

1. Alberts, D.S., Garstka, J.J., Hayes, R.E., Signori, D.A.: Understanding information age warfare. Technical report, DTIC Document (2001)
2. Alberts, D.S.: The Agility Advantage: A Survival Guide for Complex Enterprises and Endeavors. DoD Command and Control Research Program, Washington, D.C (2011)
3. Cares, J.: Distributed Networked Operations The Foundations of Network Centric Warfare. iUniverse, Bloomington (2006)
4. Dekker, A.: Applying social network analysis concepts to military C4ISR architectures. Connections **24**(3), 93–103 (2002)
5. Dekker, A.H.: C4ISR architectures, social network analysis and the FINC methodology: an experiment in military organisational structure. Technical report, DTIC Document (2002)
6. Dekker, A.H.: Network topology and military performance (2005)
7. Dekker, A.H., et al.: C4ISR, the FINC methodology, and operations in urban terrain. J. Battlef. Technol. **8**(1), 25 (2005)
8. Getoor, L., Diehl, C.P.: Link mining: a survey. ACM SIGKDD Explor. Newslett. **7**(2), 3–12 (2005)
9. Hanley, J.A., McNeil, B.J.: The meaning and use of the area under a receiver operating characteristic (ROC) curve. Radiology **143**(1), 29–36 (1982)
10. Hayes, R.E.: Measuring command and control (c2) effectiveness. In: MORS Workshop-joint Framework for Measuring C2 Effectiveness. Citeseer, Laurel, MD (2012)
11. Holland, P.W., Laskey, K.B., Leinhardt, S.: Stochastic blockmodels: first steps. Soc. Netw. **5**(2), 109–137 (1983)
12. Hutchins, C.E., Benham-Hutchins, M.: Hiding in plain sight: criminal network analysis. Comput. Math. Organ. Theory **16**(1), 89–111 (2010)
13. Lin-yuan, L.: Link prediction on complex networks. J. Univ. Electron. Sci. Technol. China **39**(5), 651–661 (2010)
14. Lü, L., Zhou, T.: Link prediction in complex networks: a survey. Physica A **390**(6), 1150–1170 (2011)
15. Lü, L., Zhou, T.: Link Prediction. Higher Education Press, Beijing (2012)
16. Meyer, M., Zaggl, M.A., Carley, K.M.: Measuring CMOTs intellectual structure and its development. Comput. Math. Organ. Theory **17**(1), 1–34 (2011)
17. Shang, M.S., Lü, L., Zeng, W., Zhang, Y.C., Zhou, T.: Relevance is more significant than correlation: information filtering on sparse data. EPL (Europhys. Lett.) **88**(6), 68008 (2010)

18. Sharpanskykh, A., Stroeve, S.H.: An agent-based approach for structured modeling, analysis and improvement of safety culture. Comput. Math. Organ. Theory **17**(1), 77–117 (2011)
19. Tong, H., Faloutsos, C., Pan, J.Y.: Fast random walk with restart and its applications (2006)
20. Yang, G., Zhang, W., Xiu, B., Liu, Z., Huang, J.: Key potential-oriented criticality analysis for complex military organization based on finc-e model. Comput. Math. Organ. Theory **20**(3), 278–301 (2014)
21. Zhang, P., Wang, X., Wang, F., Zeng, A., Xiao, J.: Measuring the robustness of link prediction algorithms under noisy environment. Sci. Rep. **6** (2016)

Predicting Best Answerers for New Questions: An Approach Leveraging Convolution Neural Networks in Community Question Answering

Jian Wang[✉], Jiqing Sun, Hongfei Lin, Hualei Dong, and Shaowu Zhang

Dalian University of Technology, No. 2 LingGong Road, GanJingZi District, Dalian, China
wangjian@dlut.edu.cn

Abstract. Community Question Answering (CQA) websites are becoming increasingly important sources of information where users can share knowledge on various topics. These websites provide many opportunities for users to seek for help and provide answers, but they also bring new challenges. One of the challenges is that most new questions posted everyday cannot be routed to appropriate users who can answer them. It means that experts are not provided with questions matching their expertise, and therefore new questions cannot be answered in time. Our main goal is to find which user has more potential to be the best answerer for a newly posted question. In this paper, we propose an approach which based on convolutional neural networks (CNN) to predict the best answerer for a new posted question on CQA websites. We have applied our model on the dataset downloaded from StackOverflow, one of the biggest CQA sites. The results show that our approach performs better than Segmented Topic Model.

Keywords: Community question answering · Convolutional neural networks · Expert recommendation · Best answerer · Segmented topic model

1 Introduction

Community Question Answering (CQA) websites receive millions of questions and provide high quality answers to users' questions by cooperating with experts in the community. General sites like Yahoo! Answers, Baidu Knows, Quora and domain-specific CQA websites like Mathematics and StackOverflow have attracted millions of users. In some CQA websites, voting, badges and reputation are provided to measure the quality of answers and answerers.

In CQA websites, a user who submits her or his questions need to wait for other users to answer, which may take several days and the answers sometimes tend to be incorrect, useless or offensive, otherwise the user can use the history profiles of CQA websites which need to deal with word-matching between posted questions and archived questions. In the second method, those questions may have no relevant answers and in this case the user has to seek for other supports.

© Springer Nature Singapore Pte Ltd. 2016
Y. Li et al. (Eds.): SMP 2016, CCIS 669, pp. 29–41, 2016.
DOI: 10.1007/978-981-10-2993-6_3

In CQA sites one of the main problem is the low participation. Only a small part of users are responsible for answering a majority of questions. There are two reasons for low participation, one is a majority of users are not willing to answer questions and the other is users are willing to answer questions, but they cannot find the new questions of interest to them.

Therefore, it is necessary to route questions to experts who have high probability to be best answerers. The research can reduce user's waiting time and make valuable contributions to receive high quality answers. The expert-finding task is primarily addressed by modeling the expertise of a user based on his or her answering history.

Generally there are two methods for finding expert. The first one searches relevant answers for a posted question, and users are ranked by their contributions to those answers. The second method is building a profile for each expert based on his or her previous answers and then uses these profiles to find experts. Our research follows in the second category. Many methods in the second category are classical retrieval models that consider lexical similarity and retrieval good result if sufficient word overlap exists. However, there is little word overlap between new questions and user profiles, therefore these approaches cannot achieve good results.

Traditional sentence classification algorithm extracts a rich set of hand-designed features form sentence, for example, a support vector machine (SVM), often with a linear kernel. In this paper we build a user profile by combining the questions answered by the user for which he or she has been selected as the best answerer in those questions. We regard the task of predicting best answerer as a task of classification. Based on the profiles, we adopt a classification method to predict users' ability to answer the newly posted question and then we ranked users through the probabilities of being the best answerers. We apply our method on StackOverflow which has a corpus of questions and answers. The result shows that our approach outperforms STM based method.

The contributions of our paper are:

- We build a profile for every user and filter some users to be classified.
- We leverage CNN to predict best answerers for new questions on the CQA sites. We utilize CNN to classify the new questions and then we can obtain the probabilities of every user to be the best answer.
- We compare our approach with STM based approach on more than 99000 questions extracted from StackOverflow, one of the biggest CQA sites.

The structure of this paper is as follows. In Sect. 2, we describe the previous related work. In Sect. 3, we formulated the problem. Next we introduce expert retrieval models and our approach in Sect. 4. In Sect. 5 we show and analyze the experiment result. In Sect. 6, we summarize this paper.

2 Related Work

In this section, we review some researches of community question answering sites, expert recommendation and convolutional neural network.

2.1   Community Question Answering

In recent years, CQA sites have built a very big questions and answers repository, such as Yahoo! Answers [1], Baidu Knows [2] and so on. Recommending the answerers for the new questions in CQA sites is a hot topic and its main goal is to decrease users' waiting time.

There are many researches about CQA sites. In [3] Cavusoglu et al. develop a theory of gamification and study the impact of hierarchical badges system. And the result shows that the value of badges and effectiveness of gamification in stimulating voluntary participation. Bhat et al. analyze the significance of tags chosen by the question asker to predict response time of questions [4].

2.2   Expert Recommendation

There are fewer works aiming to solve problem of finding the best answerer for a new question and decreasing users' waiting time, compared with other problems. The task of expert recommendation is to predict the best answerer based on the users' profile for a newly posted question.

Reference [5] uses generative probabilistic model to recommend expert. Reference [6] proposed profile-based models for expert recommending on general documents. In [7] the use of topic models for information retrieval tasks are described. They found topic distribution for words, categories and users in CQA websites. Liu et al. leveraged information retrieval techniques to find experts on CQA site [8]. They computed textual similarity between users' previously answered questions and new questions and then ranked the users according to the similarity. Qu et al. analyzed Yahoo! Answers data and suggested that CQA sites should recommend questions to users who are interested in them [9]. Reference [10] proposed STM model based on LDA to predict the best answerer, and we compare our approach with it. Chang and Pal presented a question routing scheme which takes into account the answering, commenting and voting propensities of the users [11]. They focus on routing a question to a group of users who would be willing to collaborate and provide useful answers to that question. Dong et al. proposed an approach based on distributed representations of words to predict the best answerer for a new questions [12]. Different with above researches, we build profile for every user and utilize CNN to classify every users' profile. Through CNN we can obtain the probability of every user to be the best answerer for the newly posted questions.

2.3   Distributed Representations of Words

In natural language processing (NLP) the most intuitive and most common words vector representations method is one-hot representation which represents every term as a very long vector. The dimension of vector is 1 which stands for the current word, others are 0. For example:

"mother" is represented as [0, 0, 0, 1, 0, 0, 0, ...];
"father" is represented as [0, 0, 0, 0, 0, 0, 1, ...];

This representation of words is very simple, but the relation between any two terms is independent. We cannot see the similarity among terms.

Word2vec is an efficient tool that Google provides to represent terms by means of real value vector. Google adopt Continuous Bag-Of-Words (CBOW) model and Skip-gram model to implement Word2vec [13].

2.4 Convolutional Neural Networks

Deep learning models have achieved remarkable results in computer vision and speech recognition in recent years. Convolutional neural networks (CNN) utilize layers with convolving filters that are applied to local features. CNN models have subsequently been shown to be effective for NLP and have achieved excellent results in semantic parsing, search query retrieval, sentence modeling, and other traditional NLP tasks. The input of CNN is words vector of each word in sentence, and output is the probabilities of the sentence. Yoon Kim report on a series of experiments with CNN trained on top of pre-trained word vectors for sentence-level classification tasks [14]. Collobert et al. propose a unified neural network architecture and learning algorithm that can be applied to various natural language processing tasks and they use sentence approach network to classify sentence [15].

3 Problem Statement

Given a new question q, we will return a ranked list of users of u_1, u_2, ..., u_n who are the best users suited to answer question q.

Every newly posted question includes question title, question body, question tags, question posted time and asker reputation. Question tags are the tags assigned by the user who posted the question. Question title is a short description of the question. Question body is the detailed description of the question. Every answer includes answer content, answer time, best answerer and answer score.

While a user is selected as the best answerer of some questions, we then put those questions to the profile of the corresponding answerer. In this work, we consider active users who have many accepted answers on StackOverflow as the potential answerers for new questions, based on the fact that only few of users on StackOverflow are responsible for a large of number of questions [16, 17]. This means only the profiles of the active users are used as training dataset.

4 Modeling Expert Search

In the CQA websites, when the users want to answer a question, he or she will choose a category that they are interested in and then pick a question from that category. Therefore users' interest can be inferred from the answering history. In this section we try several approaches to rank the users. These methods can be divided into three categories: word-based method, topic-based method and classification-based method. In the first category, we build model through TF-IDF and Language Model. In the second category, we build model through LDA, STM. In the third category, we build model through CNN.

4.1 TF-IDF

TF-IDF is a classical method to compute importance and relevance of a word in a document. Words only appear in a small part documents have a high score than other words. TF-IDF is defined as follows:

$$tfidf = f_{w,d} \times log\left(\frac{|Q|}{f_{w,Q}}\right)$$

Where Q is a document collection, d ϵ Q is a document in collection Q, w ϵ d is a word in document d. $f_{w,d}$ is the number of word w appears in document d. $f_{w,Q}$ is the number of documents in which word w appears. $|Q|$ is the size of corpus.

For the expert retrieval task, given a test question q, we represent test question and each user profile as vector of *tfidf* weights and then calculate the Cosine Similarity between each user profile and each question.

4.2 Language Model

Language model is similar with traditional TF-IDF model that rare terms which occur in only a group of documents in the corpus have a great influence. Some researches show that language model is more effective than TF-IDF.

A question q is represented as q = $\{w_1, w_2, \dots, w_n\}$, where w_i is the i − th word in question q and is a non-stop word. Therefore the probability of generating word w from the user profile can be computed by taking the product of each word's probability in the user profile.

$$P(q|u) = \prod_w P\left(w|\theta_u\right)^{n(w|q)}$$

Where θ_u denotes user profile for user u. $P\left(w|\theta_u\right)$ is the probability of generating word w from user profile θ_u and $n(w|q)$ is the number of word w occurring in the question q. If a word doesn't appear in a given user profile, $P\left(w|\theta_u\right)$ will be 0. So we use a smoothing method. By doing so, we can avoid zero probability for unseen words. The Dirichlet smoothing method:

$$P_{LM}\left(w|\theta_u\right) = \alpha P\left(w|\theta_u\right) + (1 - \alpha)P(w)$$

Where $P(w)$ denotes the background language model built on the entire collection Q and $\alpha \epsilon [0,1]$ is a coefficient to control the influence of the background model and is defined as:

$$\alpha = \frac{\sum_{w \in \theta_u} tf(w, \theta_u)}{\sum_{w \in \theta_u} tf(w, \theta_u) + \mu}$$

Where $tf(w, \theta_u)$ denotes the number of word w in user profile θ_u and parameter u is set to 1000. The background model $P(w)$ can be computed through a maximum likelihood estimation:

$$P(w) = \frac{n(w, Q)}{|Q|}$$

Where $n(w, Q)$ denotes the frequency of words w being in the collection Q and $|Q|$ is the total number of words in the collection.

4.3 Sentence Semantic Representation Model

Sentence Semantic Representation Model (SSRM) leveraged by Dong et al. [12] represents sentence with semantic information. SSRM extracts topic words based on users' tags from users profile and then add up extracted words' vector to be a document vector and compute the similarity between the query and the user profile. Finally they rank the users based on the similarity. They train words distributed representation through skip-gram model.

4.4 Segment Topic Model

Segment Topic Model (STM) introduced by Du et al. [18] is a topic model that discovers the hierarchical structure of topics by using the two-parameter Poisson Dirichlet process, a four-level probabilistic model. STM contains two levels of topic proportions, instead of grouping all the questions of a user under a single topic distribution, it allows each question to have a different and separate distribution over the topics.

Riahi et al. leverage STM to compute the probability of user u being the best answerer and they compare their result with TF-IDF, Language Model and LDA [10].

4.5 Our Approach

We use a variant of CNN architecture for expert recommendation. The model architecture is shown in Fig. 1 and the details are as follows.

Convolutional Neural Networks are biologically-inspired variants of MLPs. CNNs relieve the vanishing gradient problem happened in MLPs by the introduction of sparse connectivity, shared weights, pooling.

In the model, input is the text which correspond to users' profile. Assume a user profile is an ordered list of m words. Each word has an associated vocabulary index j incorporated into the embedding matrix which we use to retrieve the word's vector representation. Let $x_i \in R_k$ be the k-dimensional word vector corresponding to the $i - th$ word in the sentence. A sentence of length n is represented as

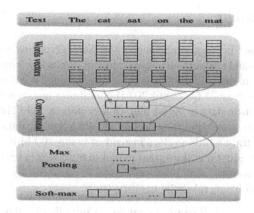

Fig. 1. Model architecture for an example sentence.

$$x_{i:n} = x_1 \oplus x_2 \oplus \dots \oplus x_n$$

Where $\oplus$ is the concatenation operator. In general, and $x_{i:i+j}$ refer to the concatenation of words $x_i, x_{i+1}, \cdots, x_{i+j}$.

A convolution operation involves a filter $w \in R^{hk}$, which is applied to a window of h words to produce a new feature. For example, a feature f_i is generated from window of words $x_{i:i+h-1}$ by

$$f_i = f\left(w \cdot x_{i:i+h-1} + b\right)$$

Here $b \in R$ is a bias term and f is a non-linear function such as the sigmoid function. This filter is applied to each possible window of words in the sentence to produce a feature map

$$C = \left[c_1, c_2, \dots, c_{n-h+1}\right], \, C \in R^{n-h+1}$$

Then we apply a max-pooling operation over the feature map, that is to say take the maximum value $c = \max\{C\}$ as the feature corresponding to this filter. Max pooling is used to capture the most important feature (one with highest value) for each feature map. This pooling scheme naturally deals with variable sentence lengths.

We have described the process by which one feature is extracted from one filter. The model uses multiple filters (with varying window sizes) to obtain multiple features. These features form the penultimate layer and are passed to a fully connected softmax layer whose output is the probability distribution over labels. The output unit corresponds to each candidate answerer respectively. So the number of categories is the number of candidate answerers.

Then we use back-propagation algorithm to further tune the CNN parameters. The gradient of the cross-entropy loss function is computed and back-propagated to the previous layer to update the parameters.

5   Experiment Study

The experiment dataset is based on a snapshot of StackOverflow website. There are a majority of questions and answers on a wide range of topics in computer programming. StackOverflow website provide dataset url[1] for researching. We download all the data from the website which is 25.6G (until 2014) containing questions and answers. The detailed user information data is 790M and all tags data is 3M. There are many other data such as comments, user reputation and so on. We adopt the dataset from the Stack-Overflow website to train words vectors instead of using 100 billion words vectors of Google News and we adopt the Skip-gram model to train words vectors which perform better for infrequent words.

We experiment with several variants of the CNN:

- CNN-rand: In this model all words are randomly initialized and then modified during training.
- CNN-static: In this model words are pre-trained vectors from word2vec. All words are kept static and only the other parameters of the model are learned.
- CNN-non-static: In this model words are pre-trained vectors from word2vec. But the pre-trained vectors are fine-tuned for each task.

When we train the model, input is the question from the users' profile which are represented as distributed representations, output is the probabilities of all the users being the best answerer. If the best answerer for the question q is user u, this is, question q is come from this user's profile, then output corresponding to the user u is 1 and others are 0. When we test a question, we can obtain the probabilities of all the users being the best answerer. We select the user who has a higher probability than others as the best answerer.

We compare our approach with SSRM [12] and STM [10].

5.1   StackOverflow

This section provides readers with the necessary background information to understand the main characteristics of StackOverflow.

StackOverflow contains a variety of tags to distinguish question categories. The asker of a question would assign keywords or tags for it to specify the category of the question. By the March 2014, there are approximately thirty thousand different tags in StackOverflow. Thus StackOverflow participants can get an answer relatively quickly and the answerer can find questions that interests them in a short time based on tags.

StackOverflow has approximately two million users and four million questions. It has been a huge repository. C#, Java, PHP, JavaScript, Android and JQuery are among the hottest topics. Most of the questions are related with programming, algorithms and software tools.

---

[1] https://archive.org/details/stackexchange.

5.2 Dataset

In our experiments, we select a representative subset as the dataset. Tags are good symbols that distinguish different topics. We compute the frequency of top 30 tags with more than 2 answers and Fig. 2 is the frequency line chart while Fig. 3 is the pair-wise frequency line chart. To create a subset that has a similar tag distribution with the original data, we select tags that mostly belong to three categories: (i) tags that are highly frequent and mostly co-occur with other tags, (ii) tags that sometimes co-occur with other tags, (iii) tags that are highly frequent but never co-occur with other tags. These tags are shown in Table 1.

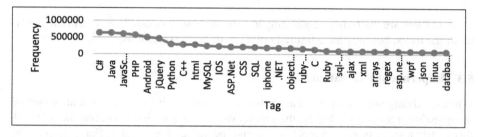

Fig. 2. Distribution of the most frequent tags in StackOverflow

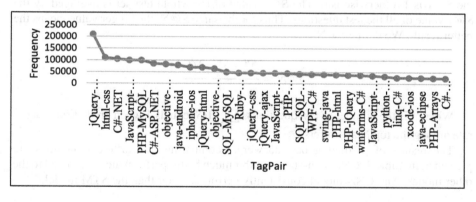

Fig. 3. Distribution of the most co-occurring frequent tags in StackOverflow.

Table 1. 18 Selected tags for the training set

Frequently co-occur	Partially co-occur	Rarely co-occur
C#	Python	Django
SQL	SQL-server	CSS
Linux	Delphi	Ruby
Windows	.NET	Ruby-on-rails
Java	JavaScript	Wpf
C		Iphone
		Android

The data of 18 tags in 2010 are selected as train data and ten thousand questions in 2011 are selected as test questions. The train data are shown in Table 2 and numbers in parentheses are related to candidate answerers. From the table we can see that 56055 users have given at least one best answer, while only 4390 users wrote at least 20 best answers. These 4390 users are very important to questions answering community. They constitute 8 % of all the users, but they have worked out 65 % of all the questions.

Table 2. Data statistics

Questions	Askers	Best answerers
479531(311857)	264053	56055(4390)

And there are 2046 users dedicating at least 40 best answers. They constitute 3.5 % of all the users, but they have figured out 52 % of all the questions.

5.3 Experiment Evaluation

When candidate users are ranked according to our model, if the "real" best answerer of the question it among the top N, the prediction for the question is successful. We call this metric a success-at-N (S@N) metric and the value of S@N is 1. For example, for each question in the test set, if its best answerer is the top one among the predicted users, the S@1 is 1, otherwise is 0. The S@1 value of the whole test set is averaged by the S@1 value of all the test questions. Thus for the same S@N, the bigger value means the better result. We define S@N as:

$$S@N = \frac{\sum_{i=1}^{t} \sum_{j=1}^{N} 1(S)}{t}$$

Where t is the number of test questions, $\sum_{j=1}^{N} 1(S)$ equals 1 when prediction is accurate among the top N answerers.

The results of predicting best answerers comparing five different methods are presented in Table 3. CNN-non-static exhibit much better performance compared to the other modes. And CNN model consistently performs better than the STM model.

Table 3. Results of the best answerers prediction S@N

Method	S@1	S@2	S@3	S@4	S@5
TF-IDF	0.0320	0.0442	0.0560	0.0636	0.0714
Language Model	0.0310	0.0372	0.0442	0.0478	0.0524
LDA	0.0578	0.0765	0.0810	0.0836	0.0856
SRRM	0.0606	0.0801	0.0967	0.1107	0.1206
STM	0.1034	0.1051	0.1192	0.1200	0.1267
CNN-non-static	**0.2734**	**0.2830**	**0.2884**	**0.2928**	**0.2966**

In the experiment, we regard the number of candidate answerers as a hyper-parameter. We use the number of candidate answerers as the output categories, in the CNN model, less categories means much less parameters that need to be trained and this will save a lot training time and gain better generalization. There are 2046 users have dedicated at least 40 best answers, these 2046 are mainly part for the community, thus we select these 2046 users as output categories from 56055 users. But the 10000 test questions belong to 56055 users. The result of three CNN models are shown in Fig. 4. Due to every sentences have different lengths, we cut out the same length from every sentence to try several models. The result shows that in some degree longer sentence has higher S@1 value. However to a certain degree S@1 would not go up. The reason comes down to three points: (i) long sentence contains more useful information, therefore it is benefit to CNN to classify, (ii) mostly sentence length is no more than one hundred, (iii) within a certain sentence length models have learned useful information.

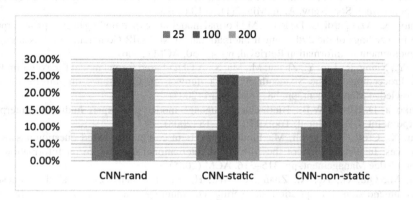

Fig. 4. Results of the best answerer prediction. Y axis shows S@1 values and X axis show three models where different colors stand for different sentence length.

In the Fig. 4, the sentence length are 25, 100 and 200 separately. From the figures we can see that S@N value of CNN-rand model and CNN-non-static model are similar and both S@N value are higher than CNN-static. For CNN-rand model and CNN-non-static model, the fine-tune operation allows them to learn more meaningful representations.

6   Conclusion

Routing a new question to the right group of experts is an important problem in CQA sites. In this paper, we build profiles for every users based on their answering history. Recently neural networks is fashion, thus we leverage word2vec to obtain words distributed representations and leverage CNN to predict best answerers. The result is much better than TF-IDF, Language Model, LDA and STM.

Acknowledgments. We thank the National Key Technology R&D Program (2015BAF20B02), the Natural Science Foundation of China (61272373, 61572098, 61300088), the Liaoning Province Natural Science Foundation of China (2014020003) for the funding support.

References

1. Adamic, L.A., Zhang, J., Bakshy, E., Ackerman, M.S.: Knowledge sharing and Yahoo answers: everyone knows something. In: Proceedings of the 17th International Conference on World Wide Web, pp. 665–674. ACM (2008)
2. Yang, J., Wei, X.: Seeking and offering expertise across categories: a sustainable mechanism works for Baidu knows. In: ICWSM (2009)
3. Cavusoglu, H., Li, Z., Huang, K.W.: Can gamification motivate voluntary contributions? The case of stackoverflow Q&A community. In: Proceedings of the 18th ACM Conference Companion on Computer Supported Cooperative Work & Social Computing, pp. 171–174. ACM (2015)
4. Bhat, V., Gokhale, A., Jadhav, R., Pudipeddi, J., Akoglu, L.: Effects of tag usage on question response time. Soc. Netw. Anal. Min. 5(1), 1–13 (2015)
5. Balog, K., Azzopardi, L., De Rijke, M.: Formal models for expert finding in enterprise corpora. In: Proceedings of the 29th Annual International ACM SIGIR Conference on Research and Development in Information Retrieval, pp. 43–50. ACM (2006)
6. Fu, Y., Xiang, R., Liu, Y., Zhang, M., Ma, S.: A CDD-based formal model for expert finding. In: Proceedings of the Sixteenth ACM Conference on Conference on Information and Knowledge Management, pp. 881–884. ACM (2007)
7. Petkova, D., Croft, W.B.: Hierarchical language models for expert finding in enterprise corpora. Int. J. Artif. Intell. Tools 17(01), 5–18 (2008)
8. Liu, X., Croft, W.B., Koll, M.: Finding experts in community-based question-answering services. In: Proceedings of the 14th ACM International Conference on Information and Knowledge Management, pp. 315–316. ACM (2005)
9. Qu, M., Qiu, G., He, X., Zhang, C., Wu, H., Bu, J., Chen, C.: Probabilistic question recommendation for question answering communities. In: Proceedings of the 18th International Conference on World Wide Web, pp. 1229–1230. ACM (2009)
10. Riahi, F., Zolaktaf, Z., Shafiei, M., Milios, E.: Finding expert users in community question answering. In: Proceedings of the 21st International Conference on World Wide Web, pp. 791–798. ACM (2012)
11. Chang, S., Pal, A.: Routing questions for collaborative answering in community question answering. In: Proceedings of the 2013 IEEE/ACM International Conference on Advances in Social Networks Analysis and Mining, pp. 494–501. ACM (2013)
12. Dong, H., Wang, J., Lin, H., Xu, B., Yang, Z.: Predicting best answerers for new questions: an approach leveraging distributed representations of words in community question answering. In: 2015 Ninth International Conference on Frontier of Computer Science and Technology, pp. 13–18. IEEE (2015)
13. Mikolov, T., Dean, J.: Distributed representations of words and phrases and their compositionality. In: Advances in Neural Information Processing Systems, pp. 3111–3119 (2013)
14. Kim, Y.: Convolutional neural networks for sentence classification. arXiv preprint arXiv: 1408.5882 (2014)
15. Collobert, R., Weston, J., Bottou, L., Karlen, M., Kavukcuoglu, K., Kuksa, P.: Natural language processing (almost) from scratch. J. Mach. Learn. Res. 12(1), 2493–2537 (2011)
16. Wang, S., Lo, D., Jiang, L.: An empirical study on developer interactions in stackoverflow. In: Proceedings of the 28th Annual ACM Symposium on Applied Computing, pp. 1019–1024. ACM (2013)

17. Xia, X., Lo, D., Wang, X., Zhou, B.: Tag recommendation in software information sites. In: Proceedings of the 10th Working Conference on Mining Software Repositories, pp. 287–296. IEEE Press (2013)
18. Du, L., Buntine, W., Jin, H.: A segmented topic model based on the two-parameter Poisson-Dirichlet process. Mach. Learn. **81**(1), 5–19 (2010)

Encoding Dependency Representation with Convolutional Neural Network for Target-Polarity Word Collocation Extraction

Yanyan Zhao[1]([⊠]), Shengqiu Li[2], Bing Qin[2], and Ting Liu[2]

[1] Department of Media Technology and Art,
Harbin Institute of Technology, Harbin, China
`yyzhao@ir.hit.edu.cn`
[2] Department of Computer Science and Technology,
Harbin Institute of Technology, Harbin, China

Abstract. Target-polarity word (T-P) collocation extraction is a basic sentiment analysis task, which aims to extract the targets and their modifying polarity words by analyzing the relationships between them. Recent studies rely primarily on syntactic rule matching. However, the syntactic rules are limited and hard matching is always used during the matching procedure that can result in the low recall value. To tackle this problem, we introduce a dependency representation to explore the most useful semantic features behind the syntactic rules and adopt a framework based on a convolutional neural network (CNN) to extract the T-P collocations. The experimental results on four types of product reviews show that our approach can better capture some latent semantic features that the common feature based methods cannot handle, and further significantly outperform other state-of-the-art methods.

Keywords: Target-polarity word (T-P) collocation extraction · Sentiment analysis · Dependency representation · Convolutional neural network (CNN) · Syntactic rules

1 Introduction

Sentiment analysis deals with the computational treatment of opinion, sentiment and subjectivity in text [15], and has received considerable attention in recent years [10]. Target-Polarity word (T-P) collocation extraction, which aims to extract the collocation of a target and its corresponding polarity word in a sentiment sentence, is a basic task in sentiment analysis. For example, in a sentiment sentence "这款相机拥有新颖的外形" (*The camera has a novel appearance*), "外形" (*appearance*) is the target, and "新颖" (*novel*) is the polarity word that modifies "外形" (*appearance*). According, 〈外形, 新颖〉 (〈*appearance, novel*〉) is the T-P collocation. Generally, T-P collocation is a basic and complete sentiment unit, thus is very useful for many sentiment analysis applications.

© Springer Nature Singapore Pte Ltd. 2016
Y. Li et al. (Eds.): SMP 2016, CCIS 669, pp. 42–53, 2016.
DOI: 10.1007/978-981-10-2993-6_4

Features derived from syntactic parse trees are particularly useful for T-P collocation extraction [1,5]. For example, the syntactic rule "Adj $\overset{\text{ATT}}{\curvearrowleft}$ Noun", where the ATT denotes an attributive syntactic relation, can be used as an important evidence to extract the T-P collocation ⟨外形, 新颖⟩ (⟨*appearance, novel*⟩) in the above sentiment sentence [2,16,19,21].

However, the syntactic rules are limited and thus can result in low recalls. Furthermore, other kind of syntactic feature, such as the syntactic path between the target and the polarity word, is always considered as a whole in the learning or matching procedure. Therefore, the syntactic rule based methods always lack generalization and are prone to lead to data sparsity problems. For example, we can use the syntactic rule "n ← SBV ← v → CMP → a" to extract the T-P collocation ⟨服务, 不错⟩ (⟨*service, good*⟩) in Fig. 1(a). However, the features defined this way may not necessarily capture all useful syntactic information provided by the parse trees for T-P collocation extraction. For example, the T-P collocation ⟨质量, 不错⟩ (⟨*quality, good*⟩) cannot be obtained in Fig. 1(b). The reason is that no rules can be matched during processing, although the syntactic path between "质量" (*quality*) and "不错" (*good*) in Fig. 1(b) is "n ← SBV ← v → VOB → a", which is similar to the syntactic rule "n ← SBV ← v → CMP → a".

That is to say, since previous work treat the syntactic structure as a whole without considering any structured information, it fails to handle similar but not the same syntactic structures. More over, the flat representation of the syntactic rule is difficult to describe the structured syntactic information explicitly. All of these prevent this method from generalizing unseen data well.

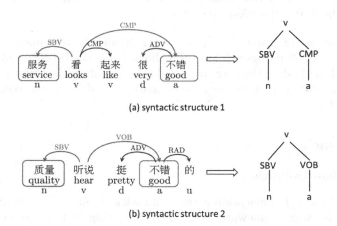

Fig. 1. Example syntactic structures for the T-P collocations. For each syntactic structure, the target is shown with a red box and the polarity word is shown with a green box. The syntactic structure is described by the path between target and polarity word in red color. (Color figure online)

To solve this problem, we propose to use the dependency representation to explore the most useful semantic features behind the syntactic rules. Recently, deep learning techniques have been widely used in exploring semantic representations behind complex structures. This provides us an opportunity to model the dependency representation in a neural network framework. In detail, we combine the word embedding (of the target and polarity word and assisted words on the path) and the syntactic embedding (of the dependencies on the path connecting the target and polarity word) as the dependency representation for a candidate T-P collocation. Then, a convolutional neural network (CNN) is applied over the dependency representation, because CNN is suitable for capturing the most useful features in a flat structure. Recent improvements of CNN have been proven to be efficient for capturing syntactic and semantics between words within a sentence for NLP tasks [4, 11]. CNNs typically use a max-pooling layer, which applies a max operation over the dependency representation to capture the most useful information.

The experimental results on four types of product reviews show that the dependency representation is able to effectively explore the latent semantic features behind the syntactic rules, and furthermore the CNN framework can incorporate the dependency representation very well. It can obtain significant improvements over other syntactic feature based method, including those with heavy hand-engineered features.

In summary, this paper makes the following contributions:

- We propose a dependency representation to describe the T-P collocation and explore the latent general features behind the syntactic rules.
- We present a CNN based framework of using dependency representation to improve the T-P collocation extraction.

This paper is organized as follows: Sect. 2 details the dependency representation and the CNN framework for T-P collocation extraction; Sect. 3 evaluates the proposed method on the corpora from four types of product domains; Sect. 4 provides the related work on sentiment analysis; and lastly we conclude this paper in Sect. 5.

2   Approach

2.1   Problem Definition

We formalize the T-P collocation extraction task as a binary classification problem. In the learning framework, a training or testing instance is formed as a candidate T-P collocation. Specifically, we define that all the nouns are the candidate targets, and all the adjectives are the candidate polarity words. Thus, a sentiment sentence containing n candidate targets and m candidate polarity words can produce $n*m$ candidate T-P collocations. Obviously, this can produce lots of negative instances, so we need some strategies to balance the positive and negative instances. Inspired by the idea from Qiu et al.'s work [16], we filter these instances in which both the targets and the polarity words are not appear in the standard T-P collocations.

Based on the above, for each candidate T-P collocation in a given sentiment sentence, we want to predict if the current collocation is a correct one. That is whether the polarity word in the candidate collocation is really modifying the target.

2.2 Motivation

Syntactic features are very important and widely used in the sentiment analysis tasks. For example, the shortest syntactic paths (such as the structure in Fig. 1) between the targets and polarity words can provide strong evidence for T-P collocation extraction. However, these syntactic features are commonly used in two ways. One is using the syntactic path in the hard matching procedure, we call it path rule based method. The other one is using the syntactic path as a kind of flat feature and then incorporating it into a classifier, we call it feature based method. We can observe that both methods considered the syntactic path as a whole feature, thus they cannot exploit the different perspectives of the syntactic paths.

To better exploit the latent features behind the syntactic paths, we propose to use the lexical and syntactic embedding to respectively capture the lexical and structure information, and then combine them to form a more precise structure to represent the semantics of a candidate T-P collocation. This combined structure is called "dependency representation", as illustrated in Fig. 2. In detail, for a candidate T-P collocation tp, we assume that the "dependency representation" can be interpreted by two parts. One is the lexical embedding, including not only the target and polarity word in tp, but also the words on the syntactic path connecting them; the other one is the dependency embedding, referring to the dependencies on the shortest path. We assume that for each word w in tp, its word embedding is shown as $x_w \in \mathbb{R}^d$, and for each dependency s in tp, its syntactic embedding is shown as $x_s \in \mathbb{R}^d$. Then, for a tp, its dependency representation can be formed as the concatenation of all the words ($x_w \in \mathbb{R}^d$) and the dependencies ($x_s \in \mathbb{R}^d$) on the shortest path.

To explore the different perspectives of the dependency representations, we use a CNN to capture these features. CNN has recently attracted much attention in many natural language processing tasks, such as information extraction [11,14,18], machine translation [13] and text classification [9]. Specially, CNN has a sliding window which can automatically capture different perspectives of a candidate T-P collocation, and has a widely-used max-over-time pooling operation which can retain the most important features.

Therefore, based on the semantic information of the T-P collocations, we propose a very simple dependency representation based CNN framework for T-P collocation extraction. In our framework, we not only consider the lexical information from the target and polarity word, but also consider the words and dependency information on the path between the target and polarity word.

2.3   Framework

Figure 2 illustrates the proposed CNN framework with a concrete example. Suppose that the candidate T-P collocation tp has three words (w_1 and w_3 are the target and polarity word, w_2 is the assisted word on the shortest path) and two dependencies (s_1 and s_2). First, we associate each word w and dependency s with a vector representation $x_w, x_s \in \mathbb{R}^d$. Next, a CNN is designed to model the syntactic features based on the dependency representation of a candidate T-P collocation.

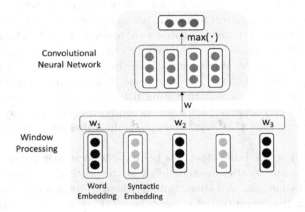

Fig. 2. Convolutional Neural Network for T-P collocation extraction.

As mentioned above, before entering the CNN, each token x_i is transformed into a real-valued vector by looking up the following embedding tables to capture different characteristics of the token:

Word Embedding Table is used to obtain the latent lexical information of the words in the tp. Please note that it can be initialized by some pre-trained word embedding.

Syntactic Embedding Table is used to capture the hidden syntactic properties of the dependencies on the shortest path. In practice, we initialize this table randomly.

For the word token w_i, the vectors are obtained from the Word Embedding Table; and for the syntactic token s_i, we get the vectors from the Syntactic Embedding Table. To better exploit both the lexical and the structural information, we can combine these two types of features. An easy way is to concatenate the two representation together, and then put them into the CNN framework. Then we use a simple but effective way to concatenate them into a single vector x that is called dependency representation, to represent each T-P collocation candidate tp. As a result, tp is shown as $x = [x_{w_1}, x_{s_1}, x_{w_2}, x_{s_2}, \cdots, x_{s_i}, x_{w_j}]$ of size $d \times (i + j)$. Formally,

$$x = x_{w_1} \oplus x_{s_1} \oplus \cdots \oplus x_{w_j}$$

where $\oplus$ is the concatenation operator.

As a sliding window is applied on the representation, we limit the context to a fixed window size k. Inspired by the work from Liu et al. [11], when k = 3, the sliding windows of a candidate tp can be shown as $[s_s w_1 s_1], [s_1 w_2 s_2], ..., [s_{n-1} w_n s_e]$ where s_s and s_e are used to denote the beginning and end of a shortest dependency path connecting the target and polarity word. We define each part in the window processing as $\hat{x}$. Then, for a given dependency representation based concatenated sequence $\hat{x}$, the convolution operation applies a filter w with a bias term b described in the following equation.

$$c = f(w \cdot \hat{x} + b)$$

where f is a non-linear activation function such as rectified linear unit (ReLu) or sigmoid function.

In summary, the dependency representation x is then passed through a convolution layer, a max pooling layer and a sigmoid at the end to perform the candidate T-P collocation classification.

3   Experiments

3.1   Experimental Setup

We conducted the experiments on a Chinese corpus of four product domains, which came from the Task3 of the Chinese Opinion Analysis Evaluation (COAE) [20].[1] Table 1 describes the corpus, where 4,394 sentiment sentences containing 4,800 T-P collocations are manually found and annotated from 478 reviews.

Table 1. Corpus statistics for the Chinese corpus of four product domains.

Domain	# reviews	# sentences	# collocations
Camera	138	1,249	1,335
Car	161	1,172	1,312
Notebook	56	623	674
Phone	123	1,350	1,479
All	478	4,394	4,800

To evaluate the T-P collocation extraction task, we applied the traditional P, R and F-$score$ for the final evaluations. Specially, a fuzzy matching evaluation is adopted for the T-P collocation extraction. That is to say, given an extracted T-P collocation $\langle t, p \rangle$, whose standard result is $\langle t_s, p_s \rangle$, if t is the substring of t_s, and meanwhile p is the substring of p_s, we consider the extracted $\langle t, p \rangle$ is a correct T-P collocation.

---

[1] http://www.ir-china.org.cn/coae2008.html.

3.2   Comparative Systems

To show the impact of the dependency representation and CNN framework, we design two comparative systems as follows.

- **CNN + Path words**: This CNN based system just adopts the word embeddings of the word information on the path, and does not use any syntactic features.
- **CNN + Dependency representation**: This system uses the dependency representation that combines the word embedding and syntactic embedding as the input of CNN, and is also the method proposed in this paper.

Here, both **CNN + Path words** and **CNN + Dependency representation** are based on the 50-d word embeddings trained on a large corpus of Sina Weibo.

Besides, to demonstrate that our proposed method is effective, we compare with two syntactic feature based methods. One is **Path Rule Based** method, which uses nine syntactic path rules. The other one is **Feature Based** method, which uses the syntactic path as a feature.

Path Rule Based. For our baseline system, we used the state-of-the-art method to extract T-P collocations introduced by Qiu et al.'s work [16], who proposed a double propagation method. This idea is based on the observation that there is a natural syntactic relationship between polarity words and targets owing to the fact that polarity words are used to modify targets. Furthermore, they also found that polarity words and targets themselves have relations in some sentiment sentences.

Based on this idea, in the double propagation method, we first used an initial seed polarity word lexicon and the syntactic relations to extract the targets, which can fall into a new target lexicon. Then we used the target lexicon and the same syntactic relations to extract the polarity words and to subsequently expand the polarity word lexicon. This is an iterative procedure, because this method can iteratively produce the new polarity words and targets back and forth using the syntactic relations. We used nine syntactic structure rules proposed by Zhao et al. [21] and the sentences are parsed using a Chinese natural language processing toolkit, Language Technology Platform (LTP) [3].

Feature Based. Similar to the preprocessing in Sect. 2.1, we define that all the nouns are the candidate targets, and all the adjectives are the candidate polarity words. And then lots of candidate T-P collocations are obtained. Based on the training instances, a binary classifier is generated using SVM model.

We adopt several basic features for the target and polarity word in a T-P collocation, such as the basic word feature (w), POS tag feature (t) and their combination context features (01–04) (Table 2). Besides, we also consider the flat syntactic features (05). In this paper, the syntactic path $\mathsf{SynF}(w_{target}, w_{polarity})$ between the target and polarity word is treated as this kind of feature. The detailed descriptions are listed in Table 1.

Table 2. Basic features for T-P collocation extraction

Basic features
01: $w_{i+k}, -1 \leq k \leq 1$
02: $w_{i+k-1} \circ w_{i+k}, 0 \leq k \leq 1$
03: $t_{i+k}, -1 \leq k \leq 1$
04: $t_{i+k-1} \circ t_{i+k}, 0 \leq k \leq 1$
Syntactic features
05: SynF($w_{target}, w_{polarity}$)

For learning, we use the binary SVMLight [7][2]. Because the training and testing instances are unbalanced (the negative instances are 3~4 times more than the positive instances), we tune the cost factor when training with SVM.

3.3 Results for T-P Collocation Extraction

Table 3 shows the experimental results of our proposed method and other comparative systems mentioned in Sect. 3.2.

The system **CNN + Path words** used a CNN with only the word embeddings on the syntactic path. We then add dependency representation to the model, that is the **CNN + Dependency representation** system. Comparing these two systems, we can observe that the **CNN + Dependency representation** system performs significantly ($p < 0.01$) better. This can indicate that the dependency representation is effective, and can greatly improve the performance. Besides, this can also indicate that the syntactic features are useful for T-P collocation extraction, since the system **CNN + Path words** did not use any syntactic features.

Comparing our system **CNN + Dependency representation** system to the other two baselines **Path Rule Based** and **Feature Based**, we can observe that although all of them used the syntactic features, the system **CNN + Dependency representation** achieves the best result. This can indicate that the dependency representation is a better way to describe the syntactic relationship between the target and polarity word, and can exploit the latent semantic

Table 3. Results on T-P collocation extraction using different methods.

Method	P(%)	R(%)	F(%)
CNN + path words	53.8	52.9	53.4
CNN + dependency representation	65.4	72.9	**68.9**
Path rule based	73.7	57.5	64.6
Feature based	49.4	78	60.6

---

[2] http://www.cs.cornell.edu/People/tj/svm_light/.

features behind the syntactic relationship. Moreover, this can also demonstrate that the CNN framework of incorporating the dependency representations is effective for T-P collocation extraction.

4   Related Work

T-P collocation extraction is a basic task in sentiment analysis. In order to solve this task, most methods focused on identifying relationships between targets and polarity words. In early studies, researchers recognized the target first, and then chose its polarity word within a window of size k [6]. However, considering that this kind of method is too heuristic, the performance proved to be very limited. To tackle this problem, many researchers found syntactic patterns that can better describe the relationships between targets and polarity words. For example, Bloom et al. [2] constructed a linkage specification lexicon containing 31 patterns, while Qiu et al. [16] proposed a double propagation method that introduced eight heuristic syntactic patterns to extract the collocations. Xu et al. [19] used the syntactic patterns to extract the collocation candidates in their two-stage framework. Zhao et al. [21] presented a framework that adopted a CRF based sentiment sentence compression model, as a preprocessing step, to improve the T-P collocation extraction task.

Based on the above, we can conclude that syntactic features are very important for T-P collocation extraction. The previous work always focused on the exact matching of syntactic features, such as syntactic paths. In the rule based method, this can result in the low recall values. In the feature based method, this kind of feature are not general and prone to lead to the data sparsity problems. Our proposed dependency representation can explore the latent features, and the CNN model can better capture these features, in order to solve the above problems.

Further more, T-P collocation extraction aims to exploit the relationship between two words, thus can be considered as one kind of relation extraction. Lots of researchers applied CNN based method for relation extraction. Vu et al. [18] presented a new context representation for CNN for relation classification and then combined it with a bi-directional recurrent neural network. Santos et al. [17] tackled the relation classification task using a convolutional neural network that performed classification by ranking (CR-CNN). Liu et al. [11] used a CNN to incorporate the ADP (augmented dependency path) structure for the relation classification task. Besides, CNN is also very popular in the sentiment classification task, Kim [8] reported on a series of experiments with convolutional neural networks (CNN) trained on top of pre-trained word vectors for sentence-level sentiment classification. Ma et al. [12] proposed a dependency-based convolution approach, making use of tree-based n-grams rather than surface ones, to classify the sentiment of a sentence. Inspired by their work, we proposed a new structure *dependency representation* that is incorporated into a CNN framework for the T-P collocation extraction task.

5 Conclusion

In this paper, we propose to extract the T-P collocations by modeling the syntactic features into a neural network framework. We design a new structure called dependency representation, combing the lexical and syntactic information, to describe each T-P collocation. The experimental results on four kinds of product domains show that the dependency representation can explore the latent syntactic features that other feature based methods cannot handle. And furthermore, our CNN framework is able to give statistical significant improvement over other syntactic path based method, indicating our proposed syntactic representation is effective.

In this paper, we only use the syntactic features and omit other useful features, such as the n-gram or POS features. In the future work, we will combine other useful features into the CNN framework. Besides, we observe that the path between the target and polarity word is directed, and Long-Short Term Memory (LSTM) network can better capture this feature due to its special design. Therefore, we will try to use this network to incorporate our proposed dependency representation.

References

1. Abbasi, A., Chen, H., Salem, A.: Sentiment analysis in multiple languages: feature selection for opinion classification in web forums. ACM Trans. Inf. Syst. **26**(3), 121–1234 (2008). http://doi.acm.org/10.1145/1361684.1361685
2. Bloom, K., Garg, N., Argamon, S.: Extracting appraisal expressions. In: HLT-NAACL 2007, pp. 308–315 (2007)
3. Che, W., Li, Z., Liu, T.: LTP: a Chinese language technology platform. In: Coling 2010: Demonstrations, pp. 13–16. Coling 2010 Organizing Committee, Beijing, China, August 2010. http://www.aclweb.org/anthology/C10-3004
4. Chen, Y., Xu, L., Liu, K., Zeng, D., Zhao, J.: Event extraction via dynamic multipooling convolutional neural networks. In: Proceedings of the 53rd Annual Meeting of the Association for Computational Linguistics and the 7th International Joint Conference on Natural Language Processing (Volume 1: Long Papers), pp. 167–176. Association for Computational Linguistics, Beijing, China, July 2015. http://www.aclweb.org/anthology/P15-1017
5. Duric, A., Song, F.: Feature selection for sentiment analysis based on content and syntax models. Decis. Support Syst. **53**(4), 704–711 (2012). http://dx.doi.org/10.1016/j.dss.2012.05.023
6. Hu, M., Liu, B.: Mining and summarizing customer reviews. In: Proceedings of KDD-2004, pp. 168–177 (2004)
7. Joachims, T.: Learning to Classify Text Using Support Vector Machines - Methods, Theory, and Algorithms. Kluwer/Springer, Norwell (2002)
8. Kim, Y.: Convolutional neural networks for sentence classification. In: Proceedings of the 2014 Conference on Empirical Methods in Natural Language Processing (EMNLP), pp. 1746–1751. Association for Computational Linguistics, Doha, October 2014. http://www.aclweb.org/anthology/D14-1181

9. Lee, J.Y., Dernoncourt, F.: Sequential short-text classification with recurrent and convolutional neural networks. In: Proceedings of the 2016 Conference of the North American Chapter of the Association for Computational Linguistics: Human Language Technologies, pp. 515–520. Association for Computational Linguistics, San Diego, June 2016. http://www.aclweb.org/anthology/N16-1062

10. Liu, B.: Sentiment Analysis and Opinion Mining. Synthesis Lectures on Human Language Technologies. Morgan & Claypool Publishers, San Rafael (2012)

11. Liu, Y., Wei, F., Li, S., Ji, H., Zhou, M., Wang, H.: A dependency-based neural network for relation classification. In: Proceedings of the 53rd Annual Meeting of the Association for Computational Linguistics and the 7th International Joint Conference on Natural Language Processing (Vol. 2: Short Papers), pp. 285–290. Association for Computational Linguistics, Beijing, China, July 2015. http://www.aclweb.org/anthology/P15-2047

12. Ma, M., Huang, L., Zhou, B., Xiang, B.: Dependency-based convolutional neural networks for sentence embedding. In: Proceedings of the 53rd Annual Meeting of the Association for Computational Linguistics and the 7th International Joint Conference on Natural Language Processing (Vol. 2: Short Papers), pp. 174–179. Association for Computational Linguistics, Beijing, July 2015. http://www.aclweb.org/anthology/P15-2029

13. Meng, F., Lu, Z., Wang, M., Li, H., Jiang, W., Liu, Q.: Encoding source language with convolutional neural network for machine translation. In: Proceedings of the 53rd Annual Meeting of the Association for Computational Linguistics and the 7th International Joint Conference on Natural Language Processing (Vol. 1: Long Papers), pp. 20–30. Association for Computational Linguistics, Beijing, July 2015. http://www.aclweb.org/anthology/P15-1003

14. Nguyen, T.H., Grishman, R.: Event detection and domain adaptation with convolutional neural networks. In: Proceedings of the 53rd Annual Meeting of the Association for Computational Linguistics and the 7th International Joint Conference on Natural Language Processing (Vol. 2: Short Papers), pp. 365–371. Association for Computational Linguistics, Beijing, July 2015. http://www.aclweb.org/anthology/P15-2060

15. Pang, B., Lee, L.: Opinion mining and sentiment analysis. Found. Trends Inf. Retr. 2(1–2), 1–135 (2008). http://dx.doi.org/10.1561/1500000011

16. Qiu, G., Liu, B., Bu, J., Chen, C.: Opinion word expansion and target extraction through double propagation. Comput. Linguist. 37(1), 9–27 (2011). http://dblp.uni-trier.de/db/journals/coling/coling37.htmlQiuLBC11

17. dos Santos, C., Xiang, B., Zhou, B.: Classifying relations by ranking with convolutional neural networks. In: Proceedings of the 53rd Annual Meeting of the Association for Computational Linguistics and the 7th International Joint Conference on Natural Language Processing (Vol. 1: Long Papers), pp. 626–634. Association for Computational Linguistics, Beijing, July 2015. http://www.aclweb.org/anthology/P15-1061

18. Vu, N.T., Adel, H., Gupta, P., Schütze, H.: Combining recurrent and convolutional neural networks for relation classification. In: Proceedings of the 2016 Conference of the North American Chapter of the Association for Computational Linguistics: Human Language Technologies, pp. 534–539. Association for Computational Linguistics, San Diego, June 2016. http://www.aclweb.org/anthology/N16-1065

19. Xu, L., Liu, K., Lai, S., Chen, Y., Zhao, J.: Mining opinion words and opinion targets in a two-stage framework. In: Proceedings of the 51st Annual Meeting of the Association for Computational Linguistics (Vol. 1: Long Papers), pp. 1764–1773. Association for Computational Linguistics, Sofia, August 2013. http://www.aclweb.org/anthology/P13-1173
20. Zhao, J., Xu, H., Huang, X., Tan, S., Liu, K., Zhang, Q.: Overview of Chinese pinion analysis evaluation 2008. In: The First Chinese Opinion Analysis Evaluation (COAE) 2008 (2008)
21. Zhao, Y., Che, W., Guo, H., Qin, B., Su, Z., Liu, T.: Sentence compression for target-polarity word collocation extraction. In: Proceedings of COLING 2014, the 25th International Conference on Computational Linguistics: Technical Papers, pp. 1360–1369. Dublin City University and Association for Computational Linguistics, Dublin, August 2014. http://www.aclweb.org/anthology/C14-1129

Efficient Community Detection Based on Label Propagation with Belonging Coefficient and Edge Probability

Xinmeng Zhang[1,2(✉)], Yuefeng Li[3], Shengyi Jiang[1,2], Bailin Xie[1,2], Xia Li[2],
Qiansheng Zhang[2], and Meixiu Lu[1]

[1] Cisco School of Informatics, Guangdong University of Foreign Studies,
Guangzhou 510006, Guangdong, China
xmzhanggw@163.com
[2] Social Science Key Laboratory of Language Engineering and Computing
of Guangdong Province, Guangdong University of Foreign Studies,
Guangzhou 510006, Guangdong, China
[3] School of Electrical Engineering and Computer Science,
Queensland University of Technology, Brisbane, QLD 4001, Australia

Abstract. Label propagation algorithm (LPA) has proven to be an efficient means for finding communities in large complex networks, and many improved methods were proposed, but the performance, stability and time complexity of them still need to be improved. In this paper, we investigate the modularity-specialized label propagation algorithm (LPAm), and find that the time complexity of LPAm greatly increased. We prune the LPAm algorithm by only considering neighbors for updating a node's label, which degenerates to a Label propagation algorithm with edge probability and retains the same computational efficiency with LPA. Further, we integrate maximum belonging coefficient into LPA and present an advanced label propagation algorithm by combining maximum belonging coefficient and edge probability (LPAbp), which improves the quality of communities and preserves the merit of high speed of LPA. We also discuss the formation of monster community and time complexity of LPA, LPAm, and our algorithm by experiments on real world networks in form of quantitative analysis. Our proposed algorithms were evaluated on fourteen networks of various types and sizes. Experiments show that the LPAbp algorithm sustains the same time complexity with LPA, hinders the formation of monster community, and exhibits significant improvements in the modularity and Normalized mutual information values of community detection.

Keywords: Complex network · Community detection · Label propagation · Belonging coefficient

1 Introduction

A wide variety of complex systems take the form of networks, sets of nodes joined together in pairs by edges. For example, social networks can be represented

© Springer Nature Singapore Pte Ltd. 2016
Y. Li et al. (Eds.): SMP 2016, CCIS 669, pp. 54–72, 2016.
DOI: 10.1007/978-981-10-2993-6_5

by people as nodes and their relations by edges. The property of community structure appears to be very common to many networks. A community in a network is a subnetwork whose nodes are more densely connected to another than to the nodes outside the subnetwork [1].

Community detection has attracted much interest, and a vast number of methods have been proposed to find reasonably good quality communities in recent years. The most famous algorithm named GN [1] is a divisive algorithm, dividing network by removing edges with highest betweenness scores iteratively, which has very high time complexity $O(nm^2)$. Modularity is the most popular criteria to measure the quality of community detection, and the modularity optimization can be gained by different ways. NM method optimizes modularity by repeatedly merging smaller subnetworks [2]. Blondel proposed a heuristic method based on modularity optimization, which can find communities in large scale sparse networks efficiently [3]. But detecting the highest modularity value in community division is proven to be NP-hard [4], modularity optimization methods are based on approximate optimization. A wide variety of techniques are used to optimize modularity, including spatial clustering [5], dynamic algorithms [6], statistical methods [7], overlapping methods [8–10], semantic network-based algorithms [11], combining content and links algorithms [12], and many more.

Recent years, with the widespread use of Social Media applications, community detection becomes a valuable tool for analyzing large scale social networks [12–17]. But it is a big challenge for the analysis of such networks, because these networks usually are characterized by huge scales, incomplete information, and a highly dynamic nature [12,13]. To handle such large networks, several strategies have been employed to discovery communities in huge networks, including Sampling strategy [18], Multi-level methods [19], Local community detection algorithms [20]. Iterative strategy is a very promising means of scaling community detection, Raghavan et al. proposed a near linear time method to detect community based on label propagation (LPA) [21], which can identify community at very high speed, and its time complexity is $O(m)$. Then LPA is one of the most popular algorithms to detect large networks. However, the original LPA has some drawbacks, such as the occurrence of monster community, weak robustness, and high randomness. Therefore, some improved methods were proposed to solve these problems. Lin improved LPA by using community kernel (CK-LPA). Each node was assigned a corresponding weight according to node importance in the whole network and update node labels in sequence based on weight [22]. Although its time complexity is reported as $O(n + m)$, it takes a lot of time to sort nodes. Leung improved the LPA by using label hop attenuation and node preference to improve the quality of detected communities [23]. Subelj presented two unique label propagation strategies of community formation, namely, defensive preservation and offensive expansion of communities for different types of networks [24]. Barber extended LPA by adding a constraint term to avoid the formation of a monster community, and introduced a modularity-specialized LPA (LPAm) [25], which still has nearly liner time complexity. Liu proposed LPAm+ by combining LPAm and multistep greedy agglomerative algorithm that merge multiple pairs of communities to escape local maxima [26], but the time complexity increases greatly. The LPA algorithm is also used to uncover overlapping community, COPRA algorithm [27] allows nodes to have v labels and belonging coefficient, where v is a parameters. Each node updates its belonging coefficients by averaging the belonging coefficients over all neighbors. Other popular extended LPA algorithms for finding overlapping community including SLPA algorithm [28], BMLPA algorithm [29], and balanced label propagation [30,31]. Recently, to detect communities in massive networks, some parallel version of LPA algorithms are presented, such as parallel SLPA [32], synchronous version of LPA (LPA-S) [33], semi-synchronous version of LPA [34].

We have observed that, during the label propagation process in LPA, the label that a node belongs to is uncertain because of updating label with the most frequent label among neighbors, which can be regarded as a probability. But, the probability is ignored during the label propagation by using Kronecker delta term, which is based on an assumption that neighbors' label is certain. This probability can be expressed by belonging coefficient [27,29], which represents the strength of community that a node belong to. Furthermore, we observed that the time consumption of modularity-specialized LPA (LPAm) increases greatly by contrasting to the original LPA. For updating a node's label, the LPAm needs to check all nodes that have the same label with its neighbors. The number of nodes needs to be checked for updating a node's label is far more than the mean number of neighbors, which leads the time complexity to increase greatly, especially in dense networks.

Based on above observations, first, we modify the updating rule of LPA by adding the maximum belonging coefficient of neighbors, which represents the strength of community that a neighbor belongs to. Then we prune LPAm by only checking neighbors when updating label for a node, which only based on edge probability and can keep the same time complexity with LPA. Finally, two strategies are combined into an advanced label propagation algorithm, denoted LPAbp (Label Propagation Algorithm by combining Belonging coefficient and edge Probability), which gains higher quality community detection and keep the exactly equal time complexity with the original LPA algorithm. We validate the algorithms on fourteen networks. The experiments show that our proposed algorithm is same time complexity with LPA, but gains higher quality of communities.

The structure of the remainder of this paper is as follows. In Sect. 2, we briefly summarize the original operational presentation of LAP, LPAm, and the belonging coefficient according to the COPRA algorithm, which are the bases of next section. In Sect. 3, we discuss the application of maximum belonging coefficient in LPA for finding disjoint communities, and prune LPAm by only considering neighbors for updating a node's label, which indeed is an algorithm based on edge probability and reduces the time complexity greatly. Finally, A new updating label strategy (LPAbp) is presented based on maximum belonging coefficient and the pruning LPAm (edge probability), which the quality of communities greatly. Performance of LPA, LPAm, and our proposed label propagation variant are compared in Sect. 4 on fourteen networks. Finally, we conclude with a summary in last section.

2   The Label Propagation Algorithm

In this section, we give a formal presentation and a briefly surveys of LPA, LPAm, and the belonging coefficient according to the COPRA algorithm, which are the bases of the following discussion.

2.1   LPA

Given the undirected network $G(V, E)$, where V is the set of nodes and E is the set of edges. $N(v)$ denote the set of node v's neighbors. The label propagation algorithm (LPA) [21] is one of the fastest algorithms, which identifies network communities by the following procedure.

1. Initialize each node with a unique label, indicating the community it belongs to.
2. Arrange all nodes in the network in a random order.
3. Then, repeatedly, Each node updates its label with which shared by most of its neighbors. If more than one label have the same frequency among neighbors, one of them is chosen randomly.
4. If every node has a label that is the most frequent label of its neighbors, then stop the label propagation.

Formally, the label updating rule for node v can be described as:

$$l_v^{'} = argmax \sum_{u \in N(v)} \delta(l_u, l) \tag{1}$$

where l_u is the label for node u, $l_v^{'}$ is the new label for node v, $N(v)$ is a set of nodes neighboring v in the network, is the Kronecker delta. If more than one labels satisfies Eq. (1), one of them will be chosen at random.

The most striking feature of LPA is its efficient computation which is near linear time complexity $O(m)$. Initialization takes time $O(n)$, each iteration takes time $O(m)$. It is harder to predict the number of iterations, but it's claimed that more than 95 % of the nodes are labeled correctly by iteration 5 in most networks. Nevertheless, the randomness of update order and the randomness of selecting multiple most frequent labels lead to the instability of LPA algorithm. It's sensitive to the order of nodes to be updated in each step. Sometimes LPA may produce a monster community that occupies most of the nodes, even end up with a trivial solution all nodes are divided into the same community [25, 26].

2.2   LPAm

Barber proposed a modularity-specialized LPA algorithm (LPAm) by adding a constraint term to penalize undesirable solutions which can bring a monotone increase in modularity and prevent the trivial global solution.

Given a network with n nodes and m edges represented by an adjacency matrix A, if there is a connection between nodes u and v, the element A_{uv} is equal to 1, and 0 otherwise.

To consider updating the label for node v, the label updating rule of LPAm [25, 26] is:

$$l'_v = argmax \sum_{u=1}^{n} (A_{uv} - \frac{d_v d_u}{2m}) \delta(l_u, l) \qquad (2)$$

where d_v is the degree of node v, $d_u d_v/2m$ is the edge probability in the null model that an edge exists between nodes u and v. The Eq. (2) appears to require that each possible label be checked for each node, giving $O(n^2)$. But, it is only necessary to consider the labels of the neighbors for each vertex no other label can make a positive contribution to the modularity [25]. However, looking at Eq. (2), it needs to find all the communities that the node v's neighbors belong to, then traverses all the nodes in these communities. Therefore, although it was claimed with near time complexity $O(m)$, it has an obvious far higher time complexity than the original LPA. In some extreme cases, if these communities of node v's neighbors belong to include all communities in the network, every node will be traversed. Testing on fourteen real world networks, we find that the LPAm needs to check about ten times the number of nodes that of LPA for updating a node's label (see the experiment results in Sect. 4).

2.3 Belonging Coefficient

Belonging coefficient represents the strength of community that a node belongs to, which is used to find overlapping community [27, 29]. In the COPRA algorithm, each node v with a set of pairs (c, b), where c is a community identifier and b is a belonging coefficient, indicating the strength that node v belongs to community c, such that all belonging coefficients for v sum to 1. Wu et al. [29] proposed the label c_{max} with maximum belonging coefficient b_{max}, and normalized belonging coefficients of the retained label by dividing by b_{max}.

In original LPA, during the label spreading, a node is assigned to a label with the most frequent label among neighbors, but the frequency may vary from a very small decimal to 1. The most frequency of label among neighbors is the maximum belonging coefficient b_{max} indeed, which can be regarded as probability of node belonging to the label in some sense. But the probability of neighbors belonging to a label is ignored when updating a node's label, the LPA just uses the label c_{max} regardless of the strength of neighbors belong to their label b_{max}.

3 Label Propagation with Belonging Coefficient and Edge Probability

In this section, first, we prone the LPAm algorithm to reduce the time complexity of LPAm to the level of LPA; then apply the maximum belonging coefficient to

LPA; finally, we propose a new label updating rule based on belonging coefficient and edge probability (LPAbp) by combining maximum belonging coefficient and pruning LPAm, and describe the process of the algorithm.

3.1 Label Propagation Based on Edge Probability by Pruning LPAm

To reduce the unpredictable traversal and keep the same time complexity with original LPA, we only retain the penalty term on neighbors by ignoring other nodes with the same label. Therefore, we can rewrite the label updating rule as,

$$l'_v = argmax \sum_{u \in N(v)} (1 - \frac{d_v d_u}{2m}) \delta(l_u, l) \tag{3}$$

where $N(v)$ is neighbors of node v. Equation (3) only requires neighbors to be checked and thus exactly has the same time complexity $O(m)$ with original LPA for each iteration. We find that Eq. (3) degenerates to an label propagation algorithm based on edge probability, where the higher edge probability of pairs of linked nodes in null mode, the lower probability they share the same label. We regard Eq. (3) as a pruning LPAm, which keeps the same time complexity with original LPA algorithm by pruning off the extra traversal of LPAm. We find that Eq. (3) meets the 'latent space' models of sociology and statistics, in which nodes in a network are located somewhere in a Euclidean space and are more likely to be connected if they are spatially close than if they are far apart [35, 36]. A specific functional form is typically assumed for the connection probability and the model is fitted to data using Monte Carlo methods. The variation of edge probability was included in objective functions for community detection [35, 37]. It is clear that an edge is more likely to occur between two nodes with high edge probability; while an edge occurs between two nodes with lower edge probability may be somehow related. In some sense that a pair of linked edges with high edge probability have the low probability of sharing same label, while a pair of linked edges with lower edge probability is more likely to be the same community. In an extreme case, a one-degree node must share the same label with its neighbor; but a node linked to every node may share same label with any node. For example, in social network, such as twitter, a user may likely to fellow a popular user, which doesn't mean they belong to the same community. But if a user fellows an unpopular user, they usually are more similar.

3.2 LPA with Max Belonging Coefficient

Inspired by the COPRA algorithm, we find the belonging coefficient can be used to modify the label updating rule in the LPA algorithm. The LPA algorithm ignores the strength of neighbors' membership of community. In fact, different strength of neighbors' membership of community should have the different contribution to identify the target node's label. If all of node u's neighbors belong to the same community c, the probability of node u belongs to the community is very large. On the other side, if each of its neighbors belongs to different community, it will be labeled with one of neighbors' labels randomly, the strength of node v belongs to the community is rather weak.

According to the BMLPA algorithm, we can find the label c_{max} with maximum belonging coefficient b_{max}. Because of detecting disjoint communities, we only need to calculate and record the maximum belonging coefficient of a node, which can keep the same time complexity with original LPA. Assuming a function $b_{max}(u)$ that maps a node u and label c_{max} to its belonging coefficient,

$$b_{max}(u) = \frac{n_{cmax}}{|N(u)|} \qquad (4)$$

where $b_{max}(u)$ is the maximum belonging coefficient of node u with label c_{max}, n_{cmax} is the number of node u's neighbors that share label c_{max}, $|N(u)|$ is the number of node u's neighbors. Shown as Fig. 1, the central node has five neighbors, each node with the maximum belonging coefficient b_{max}. Nodes 1 and 2 with the label a, nodes 3, 4, and 5 with the label b, according to the original LPA algorithm, the most frequent label is label b, the central node should be labeled b. But the probability of the nodes 3, 4, and 5 belong to community b is so small, and the nodes 1 and 2 have the strong strength belonging coefficient to community a. Intuitively, the central node is more likely to belong to community a.

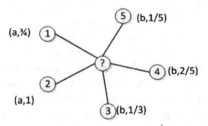

Fig. 1. Effects of belonging coefficient for updating node labels

Based on above analysis, we add the normalized maximum belonging coefficient b_{max} of node v's neighbor to LPA. Thus, the label propagation updating rule in Eq. (1) is rewritten into

$$l'_v = argmax \sum_{u \in N(v)} b'_{max}(l_u)\delta(l_u, l) \qquad (5)$$

where r is a tunable parameter to control the influence of credibility, and $r \in (0, 1)$. The updating rule will be the original LPA when $r = 0$. The b_{max} of a node can be calculated when updating its label in last iteration, which means no extra time consumption increasing. The initial value of b_{max} of a node is assigned with the degree of the node [29], because b_{max} is meaningless for the first iteration.

3.3 LPA Based on Belonging Coefficient and Edge Probability

According to the above analysis, Eq. (5) is a label propagation weighted by neighbors' maximum belonging coefficient, which actually represents a probability of neighbors belong to their communities, while Eq. (3) represents an edge probability of two nodes in null model, where the connection are made randomly between nodes. Then we can produce a new label propagation algorithm based on probability by combining Eqs. (3) and (5). Incorporating Eqs. (3) and (5), we obtain

$$l_v' = argmax \sum_{u \in N(v)} (1 - \frac{d_v d_u}{2m}) b_{max}'(l_u) \delta(l_u, l) \qquad (6)$$

We denote the advanced LPA based on belonging coefficient and edge probability as LPAbp. It is just based on two kinds of probabilities, which both can be calculated in the process of label propagation without extra time consumption. The pseudocode of LPAbp is presented in Algorithm 1.

Algorithm 1. The label propagation algorithm based on probability(LPAbp)

Input: undirected graph $G(V, E)$
Output: communities C (i.e. node labels)
1. Calculate the degree of each node
2. Initialize each node with a unique label and its maximum belonging coefficient with its degree
3. Arrange the nodes in the network in a random order
4. For each node chosen from that specific order, updates its label to the label carried the largest sum by Eq. (6) among its neighbors and updates its bmax by Eq. (4) and ties are broken uniformly randomly
5. If every node has a label that the largest sum by Eq. (6) of their neighbors have, then stop the algorithm. Else, go to (4)

The procedure of LPAbp is very similar to the original LPA. The main difference of two algorithms is the label updating rule in step 4, which can be calculated without extra time consumption. The calculation of nodes' degree in step 1 costs $O(m)$ time, and the edge probability can be calculated according to the degree. According to the original LPA algorithm, the value of n_{cmax} in Eq. (4) will be calculated during the label spreading, which means that the computation of $b_{max}(u)$ don't need any more extra time. Therefore, the time complexity of LPAbp is exactly same with the original LPA for each iteration. In Sect. 4, we will discuss the convergence of LPA and its variants by experiments on 14 networks, which prove that they have the same convergence speed.

In LPA, it's very common that more than one labels are the most frequent ones among neighbors, the new label is chosen at a random from them, which reduce the robustness of algorithm. While our modified label updating rule in step 4 can reduce the randomness of label selecting.

Because the modify label updating rule includes the edge probability of in null model that an edge exists two nodes, a node will tend to adopt the label of a node with lower probability with it, which can hinder the occurrence of monster community. Shown as in Fig. 2, in LPAbp algorithm, for node 4, it will not adopt the label of node 3, because the edge probability between node 3 and node 4 is

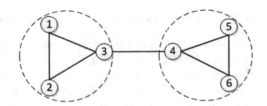

Fig. 2. A schematic representation of a network with two communities (circled by dot line), where nodes 1, 2, and 3 are in same community, the other three nodes belong to another community.

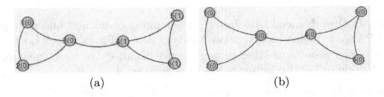

| (a) | (b) |

Fig. 3. This network will be divided two communities (shown as (a), the first figure on the node is the id of node, and the figure in parentheses is the id of community that a node belongs to) by LPAbp algorithm. But a monster community may be produced by LPA algorithm (shown as (b)).

the highest among nodes 3, 4, 5 and 6. Then this network will be divided to two communities, where nodes 1, 2, and 3 will belong to the same community, and the other nodes belong to another community. But, in LPA, if node 4 is updated before nodes 5 or 6, node 4 will select a label randomly from the label of node 3, 5, or 6. If the label of node 3 is selected, another node (5 or 6) may select the label of node 4, and then all nodes will share the same label finally, a monster community occurs. Figure 3 shows the two results of community detection by LPA.

4   Experiments

In this section, we apply LPA, LPAm, and our proposed algorithms to real world networks, and compare the modularity, Normalized mutual information (NMI), time complexity, and the solution of monster community by these algorithms.

4.1   Datasets

We test our modified algorithms, original LPA and LPAm algorithms on 14 real-world networks that are widely used by other researchers for evaluating community detection algorithms. These datasets include different communication, collaboration, social, internet, biological and other networks. Due to simplicity, we treat all the networks as unweighted and undirected. Table 1 lists the features of these networks.

Table 1. The properties of networks used to test label propagation algorithm variants. The sizes of network are described by the number of nodes n and number of edges m. The davg is the average of all nodes' degree; L is the average of path length. The cc is the average clustering coefficient which is the mean value of individual coefficients. The r is the assortativity coefficient which is the Pearson correlation coefficient of degree between pairs of linked nodes.

Datasets	n	m	d_{avg}	L	cc	r
Football	115	613	10.7	2.5	0.403	0.936
NetScience	1536	4112	5.4	4.0	0.619	0.493
Power	4941	6594	2.7	19.0	0.107	0.226
Dolphins	62	159	5.1	3.4	0.303	0.306
PPI	2617	11855	9.1	5.1	0.387	0.469
Hep-th	8361	15751	3.8	7.0	0.636	0.340
Email	1133	6553	11.6	2.0	0.526	0.131
Jazz	198	2906	29.4	1.9	0.665	0.072
Facebook	4039	88234	43.7	3.7	0.617	0.067
Polbooks	105	441	8.4	3.1	0.488	−0.002
Lesmis	77	254	6.6	2.6	0.736	−0.082
Usair	1532	4233	5.5	2.5	0.374	−0.140
Polblogs	1490	16715	22.4	3.2	0.36	−0.187
Karate	34	78	4.6	2.7	0.588	−0.211

Positive values of r indicate a correlation between nodes of similar degree, while negative values indicate relationships between nodes of different degree. In general, r lies between −1 and 1.

4.2 Modularity

The effectiveness of our algorithm is usually measured by modularity [38], which is proposed by Newman to evaluate the effectiveness of community detection algorithm. Modularity measures the fraction of intra-community edges minus its expected value in a null model, which is based on the assumption that a community structure isn't found in random networks. The modularity Q can be described as:

$$Q = \sum_{S=1}^{m} \left[\frac{l_s}{|E|} - \left(\frac{d_s}{2|E|} \right)^2 \right] \tag{7}$$

where l_s is the number of edges between nodes belonging to the s-th community, d_s is the sum of the degrees of these nodes in the s-th community. High values of $Q \in [0,1]$ represents a evident community structure, the values usually are between 0.3 and 0.7 in most real networks. Looking at the parameter r in LPAbp, the application of r indeed tunes the influence of belonging coefficient of neighbors. If $r = 0$, the LPAbp becomes a LPA algorithm based on edge probability.

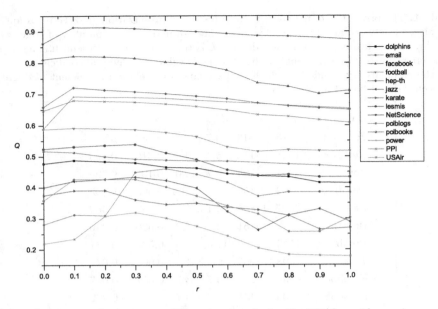

Fig. 4. Average performance on different networks by the LPAbp with varying parameter r over 100 runs

Figure 4 depicts the average performance curves on fourteen real world networks over 100 runs with varying r for LPAbp. The results suggest that the highest modularity value is gained on most networks when r is about 0.1, while the peak modularity is achieved on email, jazz, USAir, and lesmis when r is around 0.4, and we find that these networks have the similar features: shorter mean path length and smaller assortativity coefficient. We examine the LPA, LPAm, and our proposed algorithm one hundred times using these fourteen networks. Table 2 shows the mean modularity by these algorithms. We can see that the LPAbp performs the best among these algorithms, the mean modularity value by LPAbp increases 11.7 % than LPA, and 5.2 % than LPAm, and the LPAbp algorithm also achieves the highest modularity value on ten networks. The LPAbp also runs far more efficient than LPAm (discussion in Sect. 4.4). We find that the original LPA algorithm outperforms the other algorithms on the networks with larger path length, such as power and hep-th. The LPAm algorithm performs the best only on the networks with very short average path length, such as email and jazz.

4.3 NMI

Normalized mutual information (NMI) [39] is another commonly adopted measure to assess the quality of community detection by comparing real communities to the found communities. It is based on a confusion matrix N, where the rows correspond to the real communities, and the columns correspond to the found

Table 2. Mean modularity Q found on 14 networks. Values were calculated from one hundred runs for each network for each of the standard LPA, LPAm, and LPAbp.

Network	LPA	LPAm	LPAbp
Dolphins	0.406	0.484	0.488
Email	0.239	0.490	0.461
Facebook	0.817	0.812	0.817
Football	0.549	0.580	0.594
Hep-th	0.766	0.641	0.721
Jazz	0.215	0.342	0.336
Karate	0.337	0.353	0.393
Lesmis	0.465	0.519	0.535
NetScience	0.913	0.860	0.913
Polblogs	0.345	0.421	0.426
Polbooks	0.480	0.493	0.513
Power	0.802	0.526	0.692
PPI	0.651	0.647	0.679
USAir	0.065	0.317	0.318
Average	0.504	0.535	0.563

communities. The element N_{ij} of N is the number of nodes in the real community i that appear in the found community j. The NMI is defined in Ref. [39] as:

$$I(A,B) = \frac{-2\sum_{i=1}^{CA}\sum_{j=1}^{CB} N_{ij}log(N_{ij}N/N_{i.}N_{.j})}{\sum_{i=1}^{CA} N_{i.}log(N_{i.}/N) + \sum_{j=1}^{CB} N_{.j}log(N_{.j}/N)} \tag{8}$$

where CA is the number of real communities, and CB is the number of found communities. The sum over row i of matrix N_{ij} is denoted N_i, and the sum over column j is denoted $N_{.j}$.

If the communities detected are identical to the real communities, then $I(A,B) = 1$, and $I(A,B) = 0$ for the found communities are totally independent of the real communities. For example, $I(A,B) = 0$ when the entire network is divided to be one community.

Five of the networks in Table 1, namely dolphins, football, karate, polblogs, and polbooks, have been labeled real communities. We measure the NMI score between the real communities and the found communities. We run these algorithms 100 times and choose the average NMI score as the final results. Table 3 compares the results to ground truth (i.e., the true communities). By comparison, the average NMI score by our algorithm is the highest, and our algorithm gains the highest NMI score on three networks. The mean NMI value by LPAbp increases 5.3 % than LPA, and 13.1 % than LPAm.

Table 3. Comparison of NMI for LPA, LPAm, and our algorithm on different networks with known communities.

Network	LPAm	LPA	LPAbp
Dolphins	0.433	0.584	0.525
Football	0.902	0.756	0.866
Karate	0.539	0.572	0.591
Polblogs	0.518	0.598	0.685
Polbooks	0.426	0.519	0.523
Average	0.564	0.606	0.638

4.4   Convergence and Time Complexity

It takes $O(km)$ time complexity in LPA and LPAbp, where m is the number of edges, and k is the times of iteration. The LPAm costs higher time complexity than $O(m)$ for each iteration because more nodes than neighbors need to be checked for updating a node's label. But, the run efficiency of algorithm depends primarily on the times of iteration. As shown in Table 4, the LPAbp reduce the times of iterations slightly, but the average iterations of these algorithms are quite similar, which implies each algorithm can satisfy the stop criteria within about the same number of iterations.

Table 4. Comparison of iterations k for LPA, LPAm, and our algorithm on different networks.

Network	LPA	LPAm	LPAbp
Dolphins	4.2	4.5	4.9
Email	11.3	9.6	7.9
Facebook	8.9	8.8	8.1
Football	3.5	3.4	4.0
Hep-th	11.4	10.6	8.7
Jazz	3.1	5.4	4.4
Karate	3.8	4.1	4.2
Lesmis	4.1	3.8	3.9
NetScience	4.9	5.5	4.6
Polblogs	4.0	7.9	4.7
Polbooks	4.8	5.7	5.5
Power	12.9	7.0	6.2
PPI	9.4	7.0	7.2
USAir	5.0	6.3	6.0
Average	6.5	6.4	5.7

According to the times of iteration, shown as Table 4, all these algorithms have the same convergence speed. The number of edges m can be expressed as nd, where n is the number of nodes in network, and d is the average degree of nodes. The final modified label propagation rule LPAbp, as expressed in Eq. (6), is similar to LPA, only neighbors need to be checked for updating a node's label, then the time complexity of LPA and LPAbp are $O(kd)$. According to the updating rule of LPAm in Eq. (2), for node v, it needs to check all nodes sharing same label with its neighbors. Then the time complexity of LPAm can be represented as $O(knd')$, where d' is the mean number of nodes need to be checked for updating a node's label. The d' is usually more than the mean number of its neighbors d, and it's very varied and unpredictable in each iteration, the worst case is that all nodes in network need to be checked. We first survey the number of nodes for updating a node's label by experiments on real world networks, and calculate the mean value d'. The results are shown as Table 5. The d' for LPAm is almost ten times of d, which means the LPAm needs to check far more nodes than LPA for each iteration.

Table 5. Comparisons of the average number of nodes to be checked for updating a node's label by LPAm and LPA, where the d is the mean degree of nodes, d' is the mean number of nodes to be checked for updating a node by LPAm.

Network	d	d'
Dolphins	5.1	16.8
Email	11.6	125.6
Facebook	43.7	407.4
Football	10.7	31.0
Hep-th	3.8	18.2
Jazz	29.4	153.6
Karate	4.6	13.9
Lesmis	6.6	17.6
NetScience	5.4	7.4
Polblogs	22.4	616.8
Polbooks	8.4	30.4
Power	2.7	6.4
PPI	9.1	57.0
USAir	5.5	74.7
Average	12.1	112.6

The number of node to be considered for updating a node's label shown in Table 4 and the iterations shown in Table 3 illustrate the running time consumption of LPAm, LPA, and LPAbp on different networks. Looking at the time complexity $O(knd')$ for LPAm, and $O(knd)$ for LPA and LPAbp, the n is the

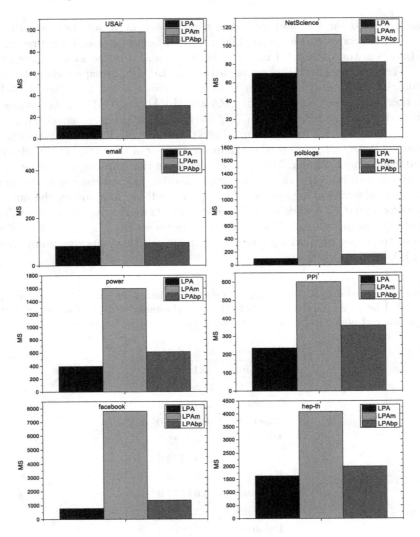

Fig. 5. Comparison of running time for LPA, LPAm, and our proposed algorithm in the networks whose size is more than 1000 (on a PC with Intel Core 2 Duo CPU @2.30 GHz).

same for each algorithm, and k is very similar according to the result shown in Table 3. Therefore, these algorithms except LPAm are the same time complexity. Considering the results shown in Tables 3 and 4, we can see that the time complexity of LPAm is about ten times of LPA and LPAbp.

We run these algorithms 100 times and choose the average running time as the final results. Figure 5 portrays the running time of LPA, LPAm, and our proposed algorithm in networks whose size is larger than 1000, where MS is millisecond in y-axis. Our proposed algorithm have the very approximate running time with original LPA, but the running time of LPAm increases greatly, especially in the networks with higher mean degree, such as polblogs, facebook.

4.5 Solution of Monster Community

The LPA is easy to produce a monster community. During the labels spreading, a small community nearing a large community is prone to be swallowed by the large community, which leads to the formation of a monster community. We count the frequency of occurrence of monster community by running one hundred times over these networks. Monster community only appears in the process of LPA over the following networks, dolphins, jazz, and karate, and the times of occurrence of monster communities over above networks are 1, 26, and 6. Monster community doesn't appear during the process of other algorithms or on other networks. The results show that LPAm, and LPAbp all successfully solve the problem of monster community.

4.6 Conclusions

In this paper, we propose an improved label propagation algorithm LPAbp by combining maximum belonging coefficient and edge probability. The major work conducted in this study is described as follows.

(1) Through the analysis of COPRA algorithm, we discuss the role of belonging coefficient of nodes during the label propagation, and applied the maximum belonging coefficient to the original LPA for finding disjoint communities. The maximum belonging coefficient was used as the weight of neighbor by combining Kronecker delta for updating nodes' label, which provides a possible method for improving label propagation algorithm by combing other methods.

(2) We prune LPAm algorithm by only considering the neighbors for updating a node's label, which degenerates to a label propagation algorithm weighted neighbors by using edge probability, and reduce the time complexity to the level of LPA. We first compare the run efficiency of LPAm and LPA by experiments on real-world networks, and find that the LPAm costs about ten times of time complexity than LPA.

(3) Finally, we proposed an improved LPA algorithm based on belonging coefficient and edge probability by combining the pruning LPAm and maximum belonging coefficient, namely LPAbp, which is the same time complexity with the original LPA but gains higher modularity value than LPAm and LPA.

Our proposed algorithm improves the modularity value greatly than LPA and LPAm, at the same time, it has the same time complexity with LPA, which is far less time complexity than LPAm. Besides, our idea is very ease to be applied to other algorithms, because the probability of link can be regarded as weight of edges which is easy to be added to other algorithms. But our algorithm is still unstable. Although the quality of communities detection is successful than LPA and LPAm on most of networks, but it is worse than LPA on hep-th and power networks and is worse than LPAm on email networks. The reason of failure of our proposed algorithm on these networks is very difficult to be found, it may be has a relationship with the topology of networks. Therefore, our research objective in the future will discover the relationship between the feature of topology of networks and different algorithms.

Acknowledgments. This research is supported by Grant DP140103157 from the Australian Research Council (ARC Discovery Project), the National Natural Science Foundation of China (No. 61402119), the Humanities and Social Sciences Research Youth Foundation of Ministry of Education of China (No. 13YJCZH258), The Training Program for Outstanding Young Teachers in University of Guangdong Province (No. GWTPSY201403), The United Youth Fund Project of Guangdong University of Foreign Studies (No. 12s10).

References

1. Girvan, M., Newman, M.E.J.: Community structure in social and biological networks. Proc. Natl. Acad. Sci. U.S.A. **99**(12), 7821–7826 (2002). USA
2. Newman, M.E.J.: Fast algorithm for detecting community structure in networks. Phys. Rev. E: Stat. Nonlin. Soft Matter Phys. **69**, 066133 (2004)
3. Blondel, V.D., Guillaume, J.L.R., Lambiotte, L.E.: Fast unfolding of communities in large networks. J. Stat. Mech.: Theory Exp. P10008 (2008)
4. Fortunato, S., Castellano, C.: Community structure in graphs. In: Meyers, R.A. (ed.) Computational Complexity, pp. 490–512. Springer, Heidelberg (2012)
5. Yang, B., Liu, J., Feng, J.: On the spectral characterization and scalable mining of network communities. IEEE Trans. Knowl. Data Eng. **24**(2), 326–337 (2012)
6. Morarescu, I.C., Girard, A.: Opinion dynamics with decaying confidence: application to community detection in graphs. IEEE Trans. Autom. Control **56**(8), 1862–1873 (2011). Institute of Electrical and Electronics Engineers
7. Newman, M.E., Leicht, E.A.: Mixture models and exploratory analysis in networks. Proc. Natl. Acad. Sci. U.S.A. **104**(23), 9564–9569 (2007)
8. Wu, Z., Cao, J., Zhu, G., Yin, W., Cuzzocrea, A., Shi, J.: Detecting overlapping communities in poly-relational networks. World Wide Web **18**, 1–18 (2015)
9. Wei, F., Qian, W., Wang, C., Zhou, A.: Detecting overlapping community structures in networks. World Wide Web **12**, 235–261 (2009)
10. Palla, G., Derenyi, I., Farkas, I., Vicsek, T.: Uncovering the overlapping community structure of complex networks in nature and society. Nature **435**, 814–818 (2005)
11. Xia, Z., Bu, Z.: Community detection based on a semantic network. Knowl.-Based Syst. **26**, 30–39 (2012)
12. Ruan, Y., Fuhry, D., Parthasarathy, S.: Efficient community detection in large networks using content and links. In: 22nd International Conference on World Wide Web, pp. 1089–1098. ACM, New York (2013)
13. Lin, W., Kong, X., Yu, P.S., Wu, Q., Jia, Y., Li, C.: Community detection in incomplete information networks. In: 21st International Conference on World Wide Web, pp. 341–350. ACM, New York (2012)

14. Papadopoulos, S., Kompatsiaris, Y., Vakali, A., Spyridonos, P.: Community detection in social media. Data Min. Knowl. Discovery **24**, 515–554 (2012)
15. Peng, D., Lei, X., Huang, T.: DICH: a framework for discovering implicit communities hidden in tweets. World Wide Web **18**, 1–24 (2014)
16. Modani, N., Nagar, S., Shannigrahi, S., Gupta, R., Dey, K., Goyal, S., Nanavati, A.A.: Like-minded communities: bringing the familiarity and similarity together. World Wide Web **17**, 899–919 (2014)
17. Lin, Y.R., Sun, J., Castro, P., Konuru, R., Sundaram, H., Kelliher, A.: MetaFac: community discovery via relational hypergraph factorization. In: 15th ACM SIGKDD International Conference on Knowledge Discovery and Data Mining, pp. 527–536. ACM, New York (2009)
18. Maiya, A.S., Berger-Wolf, T.Y.: Sampling community structure. In: 19th International Conference on World Wide Web, pp. 701–710. ACM, New York (2010)
19. Djidjev, Hristo N.: A scalable multilevel algorithm for graph clustering and community structure detection. In: Aiello, William, Broder, Andrei, Janssen, Jeannette, Milios, Evangelos E. (eds.) WAW 2006. LNCS, vol. 4936, pp. 117–128. Springer, Heidelberg (2008)
20. Ngonmang, B., Tchuente, M., Viennet, E.: Local community identification in social networks. Parallel Process. Lett. **22**, 1240004 (2012)
21. Raghavan, U.N., Albert, R., Kumara, S.: Near linear time algorithm to detect community structures in large-scale networks. Phys. Rev. E: Stat. Nonlin. Soft Matter Phys. **76**, 036106 (2007)
22. Lin, Z., Zheng, X., Xin, N., Chen, D.: CK-LPA: efficient community detection algorithm based on label propagation with community kernel. Phys. A: Stat. Mech. Appl. **416**, 386–399 (2014)
23. Leung, I.X., Hui, P., Lio, P., Crowcroft, J.: Towards real-time community detection in large networks. Phys. Rev. E: Stat. Nonl. Soft Matter Phys. **79**, 066107 (2009)
24. Šubelj, L., Bajec, M.: Unfolding network communities by combining defensive and offensive label propagation. arXiv preprint arXiv:1103.2596 (2011)
25. Barber, M.J., Clark, J.W.: Detecting network communities by propagating labels under constraints. Phys. Rev. E: Stat. Nonl. Soft Matter Phys. **80**, 026129 (2009)
26. Liu, X., Murata, T.: Advanced modularity-specialized label propagation algorithm for detecting communities in networks. Phys. A: Stat. Mech. Appl. **389**, 1493–1500 (2010)
27. Gregory, S.: Finding overlapping communities in networks by label propagation. New J. Phys. **12**, 103018 (2010)
28. Xie, J., Szymanski, B.K.: Towards linear time overlapping community detection in social networks. In: Tan, P.-N., Chawla, S., Ho, C.K., Bailey, J. (eds.) PAKDD 2012. LNCS, vol. 7302, pp. 25–36. Springer, Heidelberg (2012)
29. Wu, Z.H., Lin, Y.F., Gregory, S., Wan, H.Y., Tian, S.F.: Balanced multi-label propagation for overlapping community detection in social networks. J. Comput. Sci. Technol. **27**, 468–479 (2012)
30. Ugander, J., Backstrom, L.: Balanced label propagation for partitioning massive graphs. In: 6th ACM International Conference on Web Search And Data Mining, pp. 507–516. ACM, New York (2013)
31. Šubelja, L., Bajec, M.: Robust network community detection using balanced propagation. Eur. Phys. J. B **81**, 353–362 (2011)
32. Kuzmin, K., Shah, S.Y., Szymanski, B.K.: Parallel overlapping community detection with SLPA. In: 2013 International Conference on Social Computing (Social-Com), pp. 204–212. IEEE Press (2013)

33. Li, S., Lou, H., Jiang, W., Tang, J.: Detecting community structure via synchronous label propagation. Neurocomputing **151**, 1063–1075 (2015)
34. Cordasco, G., Gargano, L.: Community detection via semi-synchronous label propagation algorithms. In: 2010 IEEE International Workshop on Business Applications of Social Network Analysis (BASNA), pp. 1–8. IEEE (2010)
35. Newman, M.E., Peixoto, T.P.: Generalized communities in networks. Phys. Rev. Lett. **115**, 088701 (2015)
36. Hoff, P.D., Raftery, A.E., Handcock, M.S.: Latent space approaches to social network analysis. J. Am. Stat. Assoc. **97**, 1090–1098 (2002)
37. Karrer, B., Newman, M.E.: Stochastic blockmodels and community structure in networks. Phys. Rev. E: Stat. Nonl. Soft Matter Phys. **83**, 016107 (2011)
38. Newman, M.E., Girvan, M.: Finding and evaluating community structure in networks. Phys. Rev. E: Stat. Nonl. Soft Matter Phys. **69**, 026113 (2004)
39. Danon, L., Diaz-Guilera, A., Duch, J., Arenas, A.: Comparing community structure identification. J. Stat. Mech.: Theory Exp. P09008 (2005)

A Novel Approach for Relation Extraction with Few Labeled Data

Xiaobin Wang, Yu Hong[✉], Jianmin Yao, Qiaoming Zhu, and Guodong Zhou

Natural Language Processing Lab, School of Computer Science and Technology,
Soochow University, Suzhou 215006, China
czwangxiaobin@gmail.com, tianxianer@gmail.com, jmyao@szkj.gov.cn,
{qmzhu,gdzhou}@suda.edu.cn

Abstract. Lack of large scale training data is a challenge for conventional supervised relation extraction approach. Although distant supervision has been proposed to address this issue, it suffers from massive noise and the trained model cannot be applied to unseen relations. We present a novel approach for relation extraction which uses the relation definition as a guide and only needs a hundred of high-quality mention examples for training model. In detail, we classify the candidate mention of a specific relation by judging whether the mention is in conformity with the relation's definition through measuring the semantic relevance between the definition and the mention. Our approach is insensitive to class-imbalance problem. And the trained model can be directly applied to classify mentions of newly defined relation without labeling new training data. Experimental results demonstrate that our approach achieves competitive performance and can be incorporated with existing approaches to boost performance.

1 Introduction

Relation extraction (RE for short) is the task of automatically labeling the predefined relation hold between two entities within a sentence (aka. relation mention). Table 1 shows examples of relation mentions labeled by human (entities are underlined). In RE community, two paradigms have been widely investigated, the fully supervised approaches and the distant supervision based approaches.

The conventional supervised approaches have been the most effective approaches so far. They regard the RE task as a classification task, whose models are learned from quantity of handcraft labeled data. However, training data annotation is time-consuming, which limits the application of these approaches in practice. Also, because the relations are labeled on a particular corpus, the resulting classifiers is prone to biasing toward that text domain.

To reduce annotation cost, distant supervision (DS for short), is first proposed by [10] which aligns the Freebase relation tuples to unstructured text to generate train data, and train models in the way analogous to supervised approaches. The DS paradigm is based on the following assumption: Any sentence containing two entities involved in a relation fact from knowledge base

© Springer Nature Singapore Pte Ltd. 2016
Y. Li et al. (Eds.): SMP 2016, CCIS 669, pp. 73–84, 2016.
DOI: 10.1007/978-981-10-2993-6_6

Table 1. Examples of relation mentions

Mention	Relation
Giuffria were signed to MCA Records in 1984	employee_of
He lived in Berkeley, California, from 1955 to 1966	city_of_residence
Google co-founders Page and Brin ...	founded_by
Alitalia Express was based in Rome	city_of_headquarters

(e.g., *FreeBase*) is a positive instance of the corresponding relation. For example, given a fact *(city_of_headquarters, GO, Marsa)*, for sentences like "*GO is based in Marsa, Malta.*" are considered to be positive instances of relation *city_of_headquarters*. DS based approaches suffer from false positive [6,12] and false negative [9,14] problems in training data. Besides, the generation of training data is computation consuming.

We propose a novel approach which is named definition guided relation classification. We address RE by classifying whether the relation mention is satisfied with the relation's definition, which is a sentence that precisely states the meaning of the relation, e.g., "The nationality and/or ethnicity of the assigned person." is the definition of the relation named *per:origin*. To be specific, features reveals semantic relevance are used to determine if the mention is consistent to the definition from the perspective of semantics (including word sense, verb class, frame, etc.). Our approach is inspired by the intuition that the definition is the semantic constraint of the relation mention. For example, a mention of the *city_of_birth* relation should containing senses[1] like "*city*", and "*born*" which are stated in the corresponding relation definition.

Compared with the existing approaches, our approach have three advantages:

1. Insensitive to class-imbalance: lack of training data of one relation can be supplemented by instances of other relation.
2. Low annotation cost: The amount of training data required is very few (100+ sentences in our experiment) and easy to acquire.
3. Low migration cost: The trained model can be applied to new relations without requirement of labeling new training data.

We evaluated our approach on a large manually annotated dataset, it yields a competitive performance and shows potentialities of complementation with existing approaches.

2   Related Work

RE is one of the most popular topics in information extraction area. Many approaches have been developed, such as pattern matching, unsupervised

---

[1] For simplicity, we use concrete words as examples. But in fact, a sense is a more granular semantic unit and is a single meaning of a word that may be ambiguous.

relation discovery and supervised classification. Supervised approaches like feature-based [7, 20, 21] and tree kernel-based [4, 18, 22] are the most commonly used methods and yield relatively high performance. [7] is one of the typical feature-based methods, which employed Maximum Entropy model and combined diverse lexical, syntactic and semantic features. [20] further systematically explored diverse features through a linear kernel and Support Vector Machine model.

To avoid feature engineering, tree kernel-based methods have been proposed, including subsequence kernel on parse tree [18], shortest path kernel on dependency tree [4], convolution kernel on parse tree [19] and tree kernel with context sensitive parse tree [22].

However, supervised approaches may suffer from a lack of labeled data for training. To address this problem, [10] adopted Freebase to perform distant supervision. As described in Sect. 1, original supervision assumption has some limitation. [12] relaxed the assumption to the "at-least-one" and employed multi-instance learning techniques to tackle false positive instances. [6, 16] further improved it to support multi-Instance Multi-Label (MIML) learning. [9, 14, 17] have considered the false negative problem, [9] modified the [16]'s model to learning only from positive and unlabeled data. [17] presented a generative model that directly models DS process and predicted wrong labels. [14] used a knowledge inference method to detect potential false negative instance. Furthermore, [2, 11] infused manual labeled data into the training process of DS model to optimize performance.

3 Approach

3.1 Training and Testing

We address RE as a classification task by classifying whether a mention is satisfied with the specific relation definition. To train the model, we create tuples consisted of both mention and definition as training data. Tuples containing mention along with the definition of its golden relation are labeled as positive instance, or labeled negative otherwise. However, we obtain much more negative instances than positive ones[2]. Too many negative training instances leads to high bias of the classifier, we address this issue by under-sampling negative instances. The sampling ratio was tuned on our development dataset and set to 0.02. The classifier we used is a binary maximum entropy model within the MALLET package developed by [8].

Figure 1 depicts the classification process. Given a mention to be classified, we first combine it with all possible relations' definitions to form several tuples. Then we classify each tuple and output a label indicating whether the mention is in conformity with the definition accompanied with a confidence value. The relation corresponds to the positive label of the maximum confidence is assigned to the mention. If all the labels are negative, the mention is labeled "no_relation".

---

[2] Suppose we have 100 mentions and 50 relations, we can create 100 positive instances and 49 * 100 negative instances.

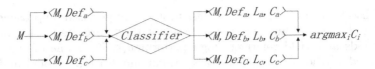

Fig. 1. Process of classification. M denotes a mention, Def_x denotes the definition of relation x, L denotes the predicted label, C denotes the confidence.

Possible relations are selected by appling type constraints. For example, given "*Oabma[PERSON] was born in American[LOCATION]*" (Mentions are preprocessed by NER tagger. The uppercase word in square brackets denotes the type of the entity before it.), we can remove the *per:parents* relation from candidate relation set since the target entity of it must not be a *LOCATION*.

Our approach differs from conventional relation classification approaches in two ways.

On the one hand, the classification instance is different. A mention is an instance traditionally. But we combine a mention and a relation definition to form a instance. Thus we can employ features describing relativeness, such as "*Is there any common words between the mention and the definition*" rather than features describing absolute fact like "*Word A appears in mention.*". Our features are relation independent, in other words, they are not prepared for any specific relation but are effective for all relations including unseen relations.

On the other hand, the classification label is different. Conventionally, a positive label indicates that a mention is a positive instance of specific relation. By contrast, in our model, a positive label means that a mention is in conformity with a specific relation definition. Same classification label can be interpreted to different means depending on the relation definition combined with the mention. If the definition is about relation A, a positive label can be interpreted to that the mention is a positive instance of A. In other words, our classification label is relation independent.

Put them together, relation independent features and labels reap the following benefits: insensitive to class-imbalance issue, lower annotation cost and easily to migrate.

In training stage, since all positive instances are considered as satisfying the definition, we do not distinguish which relation that each of them corresponds to. So lack of instances of one relation does not matter given that the total number of instances is adequate, namely, our model is insensitive to class-imbalance. Further more, annotation cost can be reduced. Suppose we need 100 instances to train a robust classifier and we have 5 relations, we should annotate about 500 instances for training the model sufficiently in conventional approaches (each relation needs sufficient instances). However, only 100 instances are required in our approach due to we do not distinguish relation label.

In testing stage, the cost of model migration is extremely low. Suppose we intend to classify newly defined relation, our approach requires no more than relation definition and few example mentions yet the traditional approaches requires quantity of annotated instances to train new models.

3.2 Features

Classic features employed in relation classification are lexical, syntactic and dependency features. These features are relation related, in other words, they are selected to discriminate pre-defined relations. As mentioned previously, we utilize different kinds of features. In a nutshell, features in our model reveal the relevance between a mention and a relation definition in perspective of semantic, e.g., there are common word senses involved in both mention and definition. We separate the features into three groups and explain their function in the following. Table 2 lists all the features. The means of symbols referred are listed below:

- M: The relation mention to be classified.
- D: The definition of a relation.
- E: Positive example mention (handcraft).
- Words-X: The word set of X(M/D/E), words are in lemma form.
- Verbs-X: The verb classes of the verbs in X(M/D/E).
- Senses-X: The sense set of X(M/D/E).
- KSenses-D: The senses of the key words in D, key words is manually labeled.
- Frame-X: The frame set of X(M/D/E).
- KFrames-D: The frames of the key words in D.

Semantic Relevance: feature 1–6 describe the semantic similarity by indicating if the mention and definition have some overlap in view of word, sense, frame and verb class. Since we consider the abstract semantic apart from simple word surface form, we can measure the similarity between the mention and definition in more abstract level. For example, the word "*spawn*" and "*calve*" don't match in surface, but they belong to the same frame: "*Giving_birth*", so they are semantically similar.

Only concerning semantic overlap may not be enough, as semantics or concepts expressed in definition usually lie on more general level but on specific level in mention. For instance, "*spouse*" in definition and "*wife*" in specific mention. Hence we introduce feature 7–9 to describe the semantic inheritance.

Key Semantic Relevance: A definition may describes many semantics, for instance, given the definition of relation "*date_of_birth*", "*The date on which the assigned person was born.*" Word "*assigned*", "*born*" both describe some semantics, yet the semantic of "*born*" is more important than "assigned". In other words, mention who contains "*born*" has higher possibility to be positive than that only contains "*assigned*". Therefore, feature 11–13 are helpful to address the issue. We take the most indicative words as key words, so that the semantic of these words are key semantic.

Consistency to Examples: Due to the complexity of semantics, measuring similarity and inheritance may be insufficient to judge whether a mention is satisfied to a definition. Suppose we want to judge if "*Amy married Bob.*" is satisfied to the definition of relation "*Spouse*", such as "*The spouse(s) of the*

Table 2. Features and description

ID	Feature name	Description
1	W-OVERLAP	Words-M overlaps Words-D
2	S-OVERLAP	Senses-M overlaps Senses-D
3	S-SIMILAR	Exists at least one sense in Senses-M that is similar to a sense in Senses-D
4	V-OVERLAP	Verbs-M overlaps Verbs-D
5	F-OVERLAP	Frames-M overlaps Frames-D
6	F-RELATED	Exists a frame A in Frames-M and a frame B in Frames-D that A and B are subframes of the same frame
7	S-INHERIT	Exists at least one sense in Senses-M that inherits from a sense in Senses-D
8	WIBI-INHERIT	Exists at least one sense in Senses-M that belong to the category inherited from a category of sense in Senses-D according to the Wikipedia Bitaxonomy [5]
9	WIKI-INHERIT	Exists at least one sense in Senses-M that belong to the category inherited from a category of sense in Senses-D according to the WikiData taxonomy
10	SUBFRAME	Exists a frame in Frames-M that is the subframe of a frame in Frames-D
11	K-RELATED	Senses-M overlaps KSenses-D
12	KF-OVERLAP	Frames-M overlaps KFrames-D
13	K-INHERIT	Exists one sense in Senses-M that inherits from a sense in KSenses-D
14–23		Similar to 1–9, but replace D with E

assigned person.", semantic similarity and inheritance are less helpful, since the sense of *"marry"* is not similar to or inherited from the sense of *"spouse"* but rather the cause of *"Spouse"*. However, if we consider the semantic similarity between the mention and relation mention examples, for instance *"M: Amy married Bob"* and *"E: At Cindy and Dannels Wedding"*, we can determine that this is a mention of *"Spouse"* possibly. (*marry* and *wedding* belong to the same frame.) Hence, we introduce feature 14–23 to describe such relation between mention and examples.

3.3   Semantic Analysis

We conduct semantic analysis (except for frame) using the tool named Babelfy, which jointly performs disambiguation and entity linking based on the BabelNet semantic network [1]. Given an input text, it extracts all the linkable fragments from this text and selects the best candidate meaning for each fragment according to the semantic network, namely BabelNet, using a graph-based method.

BabelNet is both a multilingual encyclopedic dictionary, with lexicographic and encyclopedic coverage of terms, and a semantic network which connects concepts and named entities in a very large network of semantic relations [13]. Each vertex represents a given meaning and contains information obtain from several resources such as WordNet, WikiPedia and VerbNet. Each edge denotes a semantic relation, like HYPERNYM, WIKIDATA_HYPERNYM, SIMILAR TO etc.

We use SEMAFOR[3] to analyze the frame semantic, each word is assigned a frame name (if it exists). Besides, the relations between frames are extracted from the frameNet [3] database.

4   Experiment

4.1   Corpus and Evaluation

Relations concerned in this paper is defined in the TAC-KBP Slot Filling task, which is a shared task proposed by Text Analysis Conference aims at extracting specific attributes (called slots) of given query entity[4]. Most successful Slot Filling systems [2,15] utilized RE techniques to extract slot values from sentences containing query entity and candidate slot value (identified by NER component).

We obtained relation definitions from the Slot Description file[5] provided by the task organizing committee and annotated the key word of each definition manually. Totally 41 definitions (25 of relation regard to person entity and 16 relation regard to organization entity) were obtained and at least one key word per definition was annotated.

Likewise, mention examples can be obtained from the Slot Description file. Each example consists of query entity, slot value and mention sentence. We totally collected 128 mention examples of 41 relations.

We used the corpus released by [2][6] as our evaluation corpus. [2] utilized the Amazon Mechanical Turk to crowdsource annotations. Instead of using all the sentences, we only selected the sentences whose annotation confidence is 1.0. Finally, we obtained 9275 sentences in total. We randomly reserved 1000 sentences as development dataset and kept the other as evaluation dataset.

We made a little change to the KBP Slot Filling relation hierarchy. First, we merged the relations whose fillers are different level of Geo-Political Entities of the same fact to one relation. For example, we replaced *"per:city_of_birth"*, *"per:stateorprovince_of_birth"*, *"per:country_of_birth"* with *"per:place_of_birth"*. Second, we merged the symmetrical relations to one. For example, we replaced *"per:parents"*, *"per:children"* by *"per:parents_or_children"*. Since these relations are too fine-grained, semantic divergence among them are not significant.

---

[3] http://www.cs.cmu.edu/~ark/SEMAFOR/.

[4] http://surdeanu.info/kbp2014/KBP2014_TaskDefinition_EnglishSlotFilling_1.1.pdf.

[5] http://surdeanu.info/kbp2014/TAC_KBP_2014_Slot_Descriptions_V1.1.pdf.

[6] http://nlp.stanford.edu/software/mimlre.shtml.

Table 3. Effectiveness of features.

Model	P	R	F
DefOnly	45.01	48.95	46.90
Def+Key	46.02	50.08	47.96
Def+Key+Exp	44.94	55.76	49.76

*DefOnly uses feature 1–10,
Def+Key uses feature 1–13,
Def+Key+Exp uses all features

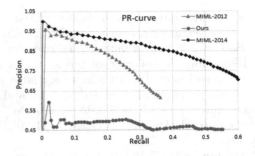

Fig. 2. PRcurve of systems

4.2   Comparison Systems

We compared our approach against two popular approaches proposed by [16] and [2]. They both address the RE task without labeled data. The former (denoted by MIML-2012) is the first MIML-RE (multi-instance multi label relation extraction) model based on distant supervision training paradigm. The latter (denoted by MIML-2014) is the improvement of MIML-2012 which is enhanced with active learning. [2, 16] released their experimental code and pre-trained model, hence, it's convenient to apply their models to produce results on our evaluation dataset.

4.3   Results

Features Analysis. As described in Sect. 3.2, only features that reveal the relations of semantics are used in the classifier. To analysis and compare the effectiveness of features, we trained two special models using part of features listed in Table 2 instead of all the features. We list the performance of each model in Table 3.

Comparing to model DefOnly, model Def+Key shows a little improvement. We believe this improvement gain from adding features describing the relevance to key semantic benefits from emphasizing the key semantic, which weaken the influence of noise in definition. In addition to the semantics in definition, semantics in selected examples reflect the customs of expressing relation, therefore, introducing features describing the similarity between mention and examples increase the recall, this can be concluded from the comparison of model Def+Key+Exp and Def+Key.

System Performance. Similar to previous works, we report precision/recall curves of the models investigated in Fig. 2 and summarize them in Table 4, which lists the performance peaks (highest F1 score). Figure 2 indicates that, MIML-2012 and MIML-2014 have higher precision than our model. But our model obtains a higher best recall rate than MIML-2012, therefore, as showed in Table 4, our model achieves a better performance peak than MIML-2012. We believe that the higher recall benefits from the semantic features we used.

Table 4. Performance of models

Model	P	R	F
MIML-2012	60.78	38.14	46.87
MIML-2014	69.11	60.07	64.28
Ours	44.94	55.76	49.76

Table 5. Performance on some slots

SlotName	P	R	F
per:employee/member_of	62.15	51.75	56.48
org:date_founded	55.68	20.50	29.97
per:date_of_birth	47.09	59.51	52.57

Comparing to lexical and syntactic features, semantic features have better generalization ability. Due to active learning, MIML-2014 yields a significant improvement on MIML-2012. However, it should be noted that our evaluation dataset was used as training set in [2]. In other words, the performance of MIML-2014 may be higher than practical application.

Table 6. Slot wise performance

Slot Name	MIML-2014			Ours			MIML-2012		
	P	R	F	P	R	F	P	R	F
org:alternate_names	0.70	0.79	0.74	0.18	0.18	0.18	0.78	0.20	0.32
org:date_dissolved	0.50	0.30	0.38	0.03	0.61	0.06	0.75	0.30	0.43
org:date_founded	0.63	0.88	0.74	0.69	0.19	0.30	0.74	0.83	0.78
org:founded_by	0.79	0.28	0.41	0.40	0.19	0.26	0.93	0.11	0.19
org:membership	0.78	0.35	0.48	0.31	0.52	0.39	0.85	0.12	0.21
org:number_of_employees_members	0.01	1.00	0.03	0.00	0.00	0.00	0.00	0.00	0.00
org:parents_or_subsidiaries	0.50	0.55	0.52	0.22	0.26	0.24	0.42	0.38	0.40
org:place_of_headquarters	0.81	0.57	0.67	**0.85**	**0.74**	**0.79**	0.83	0.56	0.67
org:political_religious_affiliation	1.00	0.08	0.14	0.03	0.15	0.05	0.00	0.00	0.00
org:shareholders	0.00	0.00	0.00	0.01	1.00	0.02	0.00	0.00	0.00
org:top_members_employees	0.47	0.93	0.62	0.38	0.51	0.43	0.00	0.00	0.00
per:age	0.59	1.00	0.74	0.03	0.08	0.04	0.94	0.71	0.81
per:alternate_names	0.68	0.60	0.64	0.10	0.39	0.15	0.95	0.44	0.60
per:cause_of_death	0.00	0.00	0.00	0.00	0.00	0.00	0.05	1.00	0.10
per:children_or_parents	0.91	0.48	0.63	0.16	0.25	0.20	0.94	0.28	0.43
per:date_of_birth	0.92	0.44	0.59	**0.57**	**0.59**	**0.58**	0.96	0.41	0.58
per:date_of_death	0.71	0.48	0.58	0.38	0.58	0.46	0.90	0.40	0.56
per:employee_or_member_of	0.69	0.53	0.60	**0.62**	**0.46**	**0.53**	0.42	0.09	0.15
per:origin	0.85	0.84	0.85	0.09	0.02	0.03	0.85	0.62	0.72
per:other_family	0.00	0.00	0.00	0.04	0.20	0.07	0.00	0.00	0.00
per:place_of_birth	0.72	0.35	0.47	**0.60**	**0.72**	**0.65**	0.32	0.48	0.38
per:place_of_death	0.78	0.19	0.30	**0.23**	**0.71**	**0.35**	0.47	0.29	0.36
per:place_of_residence	0.46	0.59	0.52	**0.40**	**0.56**	**0.47**	0.42	0.05	0.09
per:religion	0.00	0.00	0.00	0.00	0.00	0.00	0.00	0.00	0.00
per:schools_attended	0.50	0.42	0.45	0.10	0.83	0.18	0.50	0.33	0.40
per:siblings	0.00	0.00	0.00	0.05	0.64	0.10	0.00	0.00	0.00
per:spouse	0.87	0.69	0.77	**0.66**	**0.73**	**0.69**	0.83	0.58	0.68
per:title	0.90	0.90	0.90	0.66	0.73	0.69	0.93	0.59	0.72

We also report the slot wise performance of each model in Table 6. As showed in Table 6, our model achieves competitive results on some slots (shown in bold font), like *org:place_of_headquarters*, *per:place_of_birth*. This result implies the possibility of model combination for purpose of better overall performance. However, the results of our model tends to achieve a higher recall but lower precision, which suggests that features we used is not effective enough, exploring more effective features will be a future work. The variance of slot wise performance is significant, results on several slots are disappointing, we will analysis the cause of error in detail in next section.

Model Migration. Apart from lower annotation cost, our approach is superior to other approaches in model migration. For verification, we excluded some relations in training stage, concretely, we removed the relation definition and mention examples of these relations when training the model. Then, we applied the trained model to classify mentions of these relations. Performance of these relations are listed in Table 5.

Comparing to the performance in Table 6, values in Table 5 are approximate. We think the subtle difference between Table 6 and Table 5 is caused by the change of training dataset (Since we dropped out some relations). It proves the ability of our approach to classify newly defined relation.

5 Error Analysis

Some errors are worth to be analyzed. So we can understand the weakness of our approach and find some research points for future work.

5.1 Absence of Semantic

Since our approach bases on semantic analysis of sentence, the presence of indicating sense is very important, like *"birth"* for relation *"per:date_of_birth"*. However, this condition cannot always be met, semantic is sometimes omitted. For instance, *"Thomas Jefferson (April 13, 1743–July 4, 1826) was the principal author of the United States Declaration of Independence (1776)."* is a mention of relation *"per:date_of_birth"* and *"per:date_of_death"*, but we find no indicating senses like *"birth"*, *"death"* in this sentence. Our approach fails in these cases.

5.2 Complexity of Semantic

Same semantic can be expressed in many forms, the existing semantic analysis tools hardly catch these variance sometimes. For instance, *"The Prince Alfred was a member of the British Royal Family as the fourteenth child and ninth son of King George III and his queen consort Charlotte of Mecklenburg-Strelitz."* The word *"King"* and *"queen"* indicate the *"Spouse"* semantic, but this can not be identified easily. Inference ability is needed to address this challenge.

5.3 Mention Overlap

Mentions like *"The Prince Alfred was a member of the British Royal Family as the fourteenth child and ninth son of King George III and his queen consort Charlotte of Mecklenburg-Strelitz."* contains two or more relations (in this example, *Alfred* is a child of *King George III*, and *Charlotte* is the spouse of *King George III*), so it is satisfied to more than one relation definitions (suppose we can identify all semantic). If the types of the targets of each relation is different, applying type constraints can be helpful, otherwise, the classification result will be uncertain.

6 Conclusion

We present a novel relation extraction approach which conducts classification by measuring the relevance between the testing mention and specific relation definition. It requires only a few training data and can be migrated to new relation with extremely low cost. Our approach achieves a competitive performance on the evaluation dataset and may be combined with existing approaches for the purpose of yielding better performance.

Acknowledgments. This research is supported by the National Natural Science Foundation of China, No. 61672368, No. 61373097, No. 61672367, No. 61272259, No. 61272260, the Research Foundation of the Ministry of Education and China Mobile, MCM20150602 and the Science and Technology Plan of Jiangsu, SBK2015022101. The authors would like to thank the anonymous reviewers for their insightful comments and suggestions. Yu Hong, Professor Associate in Soochow University, is the corresponding author of the paper, whose email address is tianxianer@gmail.com.

References

1. Andrea, M., Alessandro, R., Roberto, N.: Entity linking meets word sense disambiguation: a unified approach. Trans. Assoc. Comput. Linguist. (TACL) **2**, 231–244 (2014)
2. Angeli, G., Tibshirani, J., Wu, J., Manning, C.D.: Combining distant and partial supervision for relation extraction. In: EMNLP-14, pp. 1556–1567. Association for Computational Linguistics (2014)
3. Baker, C.F., Fillmore, C.J., Lowe, J.B.: The berkeley framenet project. In: ACL-98, pp. 86–90. Association for Computational Linguistics (1998)
4. Bunescu, R.C., Mooney, R.J.: A shortest path dependency kernel for relation extraction. In: HLT-EMNLP-05, pp. 724–731. Association for Computational Linguistics (2005)
5. Flati, T., Vannella, D., Pasini, T., Navigli, R.: Two is bigger (and better) than one: the wikipedia bitaxonomy project. In: ACL-14. Association for Computational Linguistics (2014)
6. Hoffmann, R., Zhang, C., Ling, X., Zettlemoyer, L., Weld, D.S.: Knowledge-based weak supervision for information extraction of overlapping relations. In: ACL-HLT-11, pp. 541–550. Association for Computational Linguistics (2011)

7. Kambhatla, N.: Combining lexical, syntactic, and semantic features with maximum entropy models for extracting relations. In: ACL-04, pp. 22. Association for Computational Linguistics (2004)
8. McCallum, A.K.: Mallet: a machine learning for language toolkit (2002)
9. Min, B., Grishman, R., Wan, L., Wang, C., Gondek, D.: Distant supervision for relation extraction with an incomplete knowledge base. In: HLT-NAACL-13, pp. 777–782. Association for Computational Linguistics (2013)
10. Mintz, M., Bills, S., Snow, R., Jurafsky, D.: Distant supervision for relation extraction without labeled data. In: ACL-09, pp. 1003–1011. Association for Computational Linguistics (2009)
11. Pershina, M., Min, B., Xu, W., Grishman, R.: Infusion of labeled data into distant supervision for relation extraction. In: ACL-14, pp. 732–738. Association for Computational Linguistics (2014)
12. Riedel, S., Yao, L., McCallum, A.: Modeling relations and their mentions without labeled text. In: Balcázar, J.L., Bonchi, F., Gionis, A., Sebag, M. (eds.) ECML PKDD 2010, Part III. LNCS, vol. 6323, pp. 148–163. Springer, Heidelberg (2010)
13. Roberto, N., Simone, P.P.: BabelNet: the automatic construction, evaluation and application of a wide-coverage multilingual semantic network. Artif. Intell. **193**, 217–250 (2012)
14. Roller, R., Agirre, E., Soroa, A., Stevenson, M.: Improving distant supervision using inference learning. arXiv preprint arXiv:1509.03739 (2015)
15. Roth, B., Klakow, D.: Combining generative and discriminative model scores for distant supervision. In: EMNLP-13, pp. 24–29. Association for Computational Linguistics (2013)
16. Surdeanu, M., Tibshirani, J., Nallapati, R., Manning, C.D.: Multi-instance multi-label learning for relation extraction. In: EMNLP-CoNLL-12, pp. 455–465. Association for Computational Linguistics (2012)
17. Takamatsu, S., Sato, I., Nakagawa, H.: Reducing wrong labels in distant supervision for relation extraction. In: ACL-12, pp. 721–729. Association for Computational Linguistics (2012)
18. Zelenko, D., Aone, C., Richardella, A.: Kernel methods for relation extraction. J. Mach. Learn. Res. **3**, 1083–1106 (2003)
19. Zhang, M., Zhang, J., Su, J., Zhou, G.: A composite kernel to extract relations between entities with both flat and structured features. In: COLING-ACL-06, pp. 825–832. Association for Computational Linguistics (2006)
20. Zhou, G., Su, J., Zhang, J., Zhang, M.: Exploring various knowledge in relation extraction. In: ACL-05, pp. 427–434. Association for Computational Linguistics (2005)
21. Zhou, G., Su, J., Zhang, M.: Modeling commonality among related classes in relation extraction. In: COLING-ACL-06, pp. 121–128. Association for Computational Linguistics (2006)
22. Zhou, G., Zhang, M., Ji, D.H., Zhu, Q.: Tree kernel-based relation extraction with context-sensitive structured parse tree information. In: EMNLP-CoNLL-07, pp. 728–736. Association for Computational Linguistics (2007)

Segmenting and Characterizing Adopters of E-Books and Paper Books Based on Amazon Book Reviews

Lu Guan[1], Yafei Zhang[1,2], and Jonathan Zhu[1(✉)]

[1] Web Mining Lab, Department of Media and Communication,
City University of Hong Kong, Kowloon, Hong Kong SAR, China
lguan3-c@my.cityu.edu.hk, j.zhu@cityu.edu.hk
[2] Key Laboratory of System Control and Information Processing, Ministry of
Education of China, Department of Automation, Shanghai Jiao Tong University,
Shanghai 200240, China
yflyzhang@sjtu.edu.cn

Abstract. Online product reviews through which consumers express their opinions and experiences with products are extremely valuable for both potential buyers to make informed purchase decisions and retailers to improve their products/services and adjust existing marketing strategies. One of the key challenges for mining product reviews is how to obtain a "ground truth" to guide the segmentation of reviewers properly. We propose a behavior-to-opinion approach, in which users are first categorized based on some unambiguous behavioral patterns (if available) and their online reviews are then classified to reveal unique and detailed characteristics of each user category. In this paper, we identify four categories of book consumers (i.e., kindle-only, print-only, print-to-kindle, and kindle-to-print) based on the long-term patterns of their review behavior. Their review posts are then clustered through *word2vec* and K-means, and four categories of adopters are matched with their concerned word topics. Finally, we find that print-only adopters show significantly different patterns on content-oriented topics as compared to other three groups. Kindle-to-print adopters pay more attention on portability whereas print-to-kindle adopters stress more on money and user experience. Taken together, our work indicates a diversity of characteristics among four categories of book reviewers.

Keywords: Text analytics · Behavioral patterns · E-books · Product reviews

1 Introduction

Online product reviews through which consumers express their opinions and experiences with products are extremely valuable for both potential buyers to make informed purchase decisions and retailers to improve their products/services and adjust existing marketing strategies. One of the key challenges

© Springer Nature Singapore Pte Ltd. 2016
Y. Li et al. (Eds.): SMP 2016, CCIS 669, pp. 85–97, 2016.
DOI: 10.1007/978-981-10-2993-6_7

for mining product reviews is how to obtain a "ground truth" to guide the segmentation of reviewers properly. As a practical solution to the lack of ground truth knowledge for segmentation, we propose a "behavior-to-opinion" approach as outlined in Fig. 1.

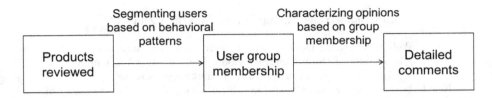

Fig. 1. The behavior-to-opinion approach

The approach involves two stages: (i) users are first divided into a set of groups based on certain behavioral patterns, and (ii) the group memberships are then used to identify opinion characteristics uniquely associated with each group. While the first stage is a usual supervised classification, the first stage is less straightforward conceptually and operationally. Ideally, there is ground-truth knowledge about the relevant group membership that is available in the data or from an external source. However, this is usually not the case. The group membership will have to be learned from the data. We believe that "near ground-truth" knowledge of group membership can be discovered from *unambiguous* and *repeated* behaviors inside product reviews. Amazon review data meet the requirements. First, each review post is dedicated to one and only one product (e.g., print books or kindle books), which ensures the unambiguity of the relevant behavior. Secondly, many reviewers publish multiple posts on the same product, which ensures the stability of the measured membership. Unambiguity and stability jointly provide the necessary face validity for the results of the first stage, which serves the basis for the quality of the second stage.

In the current study, over 7 million users posted reviews exclusively on print books, exclusively on kindle books, exclusively on print and then on kindle, or exclusively on kindle and then on print. We exclude all other users who commented only once on a product or several times in an alternate sequence, which reduces the sample size considerably but safeguards the unambiguity and minimal stability of the derived group membership.

Rogers [1] firstly proposed adopter segmentation in his book *Diffusion of innovations* in 1962 and categorized adopters into innovators, early adopters, early majority, late majority, and laggards. The criterion of this adopter categorization is based on the assumption of normal distribution of innovativeness and the five categories are divided by mean time of adoption plusorminus its one or two times standard deviations. Mahajan and others [2] then developed this adopter categorization using other established diffusion models to fit more products that may not follow normal distributions. Then Zhu and He [3] proposed a dynamic adopter categories including continuous adopters, discontinued adopters, potential adopters, and continuous non-adopters and found distinctive characteristics for the four categories. Based on Zhu and He's categories, we revised the construct to fit our e-books and paper books adopter categories, including kindle-only (continuous e-book adopters), print-only (continuous e-book non-adopters), kindle-to-print (discontinued e-book adopters) and print-to-kindle (transitive e-book adopters). After segmenting the four categories of adopters, we established word vectors using *word2vec*, a deep learning approach for words embedding, and got 2000-dimensional vector representations of more than 30,000 words. Then, we employed K-means model to cluster words with similar meaning into the same cluster or topic. Finally, we conducted multinomial logistic regression analysis and detected features that discriminate the four categories.

2   Methods

2.1   Word Clustering Based on Deep Learning

Understanding the meaning of words or sentences is one of the core issues in natural language processing study. Traditional topic model methods, such as LSA (Latent Semantic Analysis) or LDA (Latent Dirichlet Allocation), are usually count-vector-based, and they care more about co-occurrence patterns of words but not their context. For example, for sentences like "*Tom loves Jessica*" and "*Jessica loves Tom*", traditional methods cannot figure out who loves who but treat these two sentences as the same instead. What's more, these traditional methods rely heavily on dimensionality reduction techniques, which may require more resources to handle on larger data. However, context-predicting models or neural language models stress more on contexts of words and thus can figure out semantic or syntactic relations deeper. Among these context-predicting models, *word2vec* is an efficient embedding method which can provide state-of-the-art results on a lot of natural language tasks [4]. Just as highlighted in Baroni's paper [5], "don't count, predict!", context-predicting methods generally outperform than count models. Furthermore, comparing *word2vec* with other neural-network-inspired word embedding models, e.g. *GloVe* [6], *shape word2vec* is more robust and scales nicely. In other words, although *word2vec* might not be the best approach for every task, it does not significantly underperform in a lot of scenarios [4].

The *word2vec* model and application by Mikolov and his colleagues [7] have attracted a great amount of attention since their release. *Word2vec* works in a way that is similar to deep learning approaches, but is computationally more efficient. It attempts to discover semantic relationships among words through word embeddings, a framework for vector representations of words. The vector representations of words learned by *word2vec* models have been shown to be efficient for learning high-quality vector representations of words from large amounts of unstructured text data, and proven to be useful in various NLP tasks.

Continuous bag-of-words model (CBOW) and Skip-gram model are two main techniques used in *word2vec* to build a neural network that maps words to real-number vectors, with the expectation that words with more similar meanings will be mapped to more similar vectors.

CBOW: Assuming word inputs to the model could be w_{i-2}, w_{i-1}, w_{i+1}, w_{i+2}, and the output will be w_i, where the subscripts from $i-2$ to $i+2$ indicate the index of words in order. Hence we can consider the task as *"predicting the word given its context"*.

Skip-gram: While in this scenario, words input to the model is w_i, and the output could be w_{i-2}, w_{i-1}, w_{i+1}, w_{i+2}. So the task here is *"predicting the context given a word"*. In addition, the window size of context is not limited to its immediate context, and training instances can be created by skipping a constant number of words corresponding to their contexts.

More generally, given word w and its contexts c, we can consider conditional probabilities $p(c|w)$ based on a set of Ω which denotes all word and context pairs derived from the text. Then the objective of the Skip-gram model is to set the parameters θ of $p(c|w; \theta)$ so as to maximize the probability:

$$\arg\max_{\theta} \prod_{(w,c)\in\Omega} p(c|w; \theta) \tag{1}$$

Following a neural-network approach and softmax function, we can obtain:

$$\arg\max_{\theta} \sum_{(w,c)\in\Omega} \log p(c|w; \theta) = \sum_{(w,c)\in\Omega} (\log e^{v_c \cdot v_w} - \log \sum_{c'} e^{v_{c'} \cdot v_w}) \tag{2}$$

where v_c and v_w are vector representations for c and w respectively. Therefore, finding the best parameters θ, which aim to maximize objective function (2), will result in good embedding of words.

However, it's computationally expensive to compute objective (2), therefore *word2vec* model also employs some other tricks, such as hierarchical softmax as well as negative sampling, to make the computation more tractable and efficient in real scenarios. Here we will not address about these methods any more due to space limitations (see Ref. [7] for more detail).

2.2 Logistic Regression

There are plenty of methods to investigate which words are crucial to determine the type of review texts. Among which logistic regression is a widely used method which measures the relationship between the categorical dependent variable and one or more independent variables by estimating probabilities using a cumulative logistic function. The specific model employed by logistic regression, which distinguishes it from standard linear regression, is depicted as follows:

$$\ln \frac{p_i}{1 - p_i} = \beta \cdot X_i = \beta_0 + \beta_1 \cdot x_{1,i} + \beta_2 \cdot x_{2,i} + \ldots + \beta_n \cdot x_{n,i} \tag{3}$$

where n represents the number of features derived from the i-th object X_i, $p_i \in [0, 1]$ means the probability of X_i, while $x_{n,i}$ indicates the n-th feature and β_n represents coefficient corresponding to $x_{n,i}$.

Here in our case, we can depict some typical properties of words as features, such as word topics or word vectors, and then employ logistic regression to find which features are crucial to characterize reviews or reviewers. Generally speaking, for a binary classification problem, features with positive coefficients and high level statistical significance contribute more to the positive category, while features with high level statistical significance but negative coefficients result in negative category.

3   Experiments and Results

3.1   Dataset

We use the Amazon product review data scrapped by McAuley [8], UCSD, with 142.8 million reviews spanning May 1996 - July 2014. Among 82.68 million Amazon reviews (with duplicate items removed), there are 19,446,034 reviews for paper books and 3,310,343 reviews for kindle e-books, with corresponding products number as 1,944,186 books and 435,370 e-books. As shown in Fig. 2, although the original Kindle was introduced in 2007, there appears e-books for sale and receiving reviews on Amazon.com starting from 1998. At that time, the number of e-book reviews per year remained less than four hundred, until 2007, began to dramatically increase.

Table 1. Descriptive statistics of four categories on number of reviewers, average number of reviews and average rating per reviewer

	Print-only	Kindle-only	Print-to-kindle	Kindle-to-print
Num. of reviewers	6,634,219	649,071	175,416	116,537
All category				
Ave. num. of reviews	5.01	2.87	6.58	5.97
Ave. rating	4.292	4.230	4.245	4.256
Prints				
Ave. num. of reviews	2.01	–	1.71	1.51
Ave. rating	4.348	–	4.357	4.405
Kindle				
Ave. num. of reviews	–	1.21	1.18	1.15
Ave. rating	–	4.243	4.167	4.148

– Indicates not applicable in that case

On average, paper book reviewers have the larger average number of reviews than e-book ones (2.60 and 2.23 respectively). One of the possible reasons is that paper book reviewers have much longer review history – 262.5 days on average, whereas e-book reviewers last 75.7 days averagely.

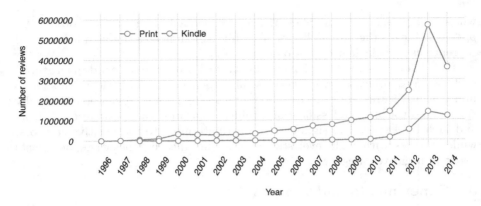

Fig. 2. Number of reviews for paper books and kindle e-books per year

3.2 Adopter Segmentation

As previously discussed, our adopter categories are revised into kindle-only (continuous e-book adopters), print-only (continuous e-book non-adopters), kindle-to-print (discontinued e-book adopters) and print-to-kindle (transitive e-book adopters). To obtain the categories, we firstly extract reviewers who have posted two or more reviews. Then for each reviewer, reviews are placed according to the publish time and each review are labeled as e-book or paper book according to the product it comments on. Reviewers who have only kindle e-book reviews are labeled as kindle-only and so do print-only reviewers. Reviewers who firstly review kindle e-books and then turn to paper books are labeled as kindle-to-print. Similarly, print-to-kindle reviewers refer to those who review paper books and then turn to kindle e-books. The other reviewers who repeatedly changing their review categories are labeled as mix reviewers. Here, we concern more of the difference between the former four kinds of reviewers. Table 1 basic descriptive statistics of four categories.

3.3 Words Clustering Based on Deep Learning Approaches

In order to dig up more discriminating characteristics between the four category adopters, we process the review text of each reviewer in the first step. We combine all the reviews of one reviewer into one paragraph and drop punctuations. Then strings are tokenized into words without stop words and words are further stemmed into their root forms.

Then we conduct *word2vec*, a word embedding model which employs deep learning approaches, to cluster words. *Word2vec* does not need labels in order to create meaningful representations, which is just to our tastes. In this scenario, we apply *word2vec* model to cluster words of reviews about books and kindle. With the aid of *word2vec*, a given word is represented by a vector with a reasonable dimension (tens to hundreds, according to the specification assigned to it).

In our case, we employ the raw text of more than 2 million reviews and train them to get vectors of 36,207 distinctive words with a dimension of 2,000 features. For example, given a word '*media*', it can be represented by a 2,000 dimensional vectors, say $v('media') = [v_1, v_2, \ldots, v_{2000}]$. Thus makes it very convenient to calculate similarity or distance measures for pairs of words.

After obtaining vectors for each word, we then employ K-means clustering method, which has been widely used, to allocate words into different groups, implying that similar words are more likely to be assigned to one group. In this way, words can be grouped into n (=724) different clusters. Examples of clustered words are shown in Appendix.[1]. For example, word '*Instagram*' and word '*Facebook*' are automatically group into the same cluster, which includes only the social applications.

3.4   Characterizing Four Categories of Adopters

To detect the characteristics of four category adopters, we have carried out multi-nominal logistic regression (MLR) using selected features from word clustering as independent variables and the membership of the four category labels as dependent variables. To construct features of each reviewer for MLR analysis, we randomly sample a set of 400,000 reviewers' review texts (100,000 for each category) and calculate each reviewer' cluster occurrence numbers according to his or her review text. Procedures to achieve this for one reviewer are described as follows: for a cluster with n words and each word's term frequency $tf_i, i = 1, 2, \ldots, n$, corresponding to this person's review corpus, the occurrence number of this cluster can be obtained through accumulation, $\sum_{i=1}^{n} tf_i$, and in the same way we can get all cluster numbers of this person. Repeating the steps for all 400,000 reviewers, and therefore all features required are obtained.

Although there are six-pair comparisons among the four adopters, MLR only conduct three pairs with one category as a baseline group. The results of the MLR analysis are shown in Table 2. Here category print-only is used as the baseline category and the MLR model compares print-to-kindle, kindle-to-print, and kindle-only adopters against print-only adopters respectively. The coefficients show the possibility of one individual belonging to one category against the baseline category (print-only adopters) and a negative coefficient for a comparison category represents the probability for one belonging to this comparison category is lower than that for the baseline category. To obtain the statistical significance of the six pairs, we conducted MLR model three times each with print-only, print-to-kindle and kindle-to-print as reference group separately. Full table is shown in Appendix.

The results of Table 2 can be interpreted as follows. Taking cluster 607 as an example, words mentioned about devices have a significant and strong impact in all six comparisons. Kindle-only adopters mention these words most, followed by kindle-to-print adopters, print-to-kindle, and print-only. Similarly, words on UI and interface are significant in all six comparisons and noted most frequently

---

[1] http://weblab.com.cityu.edu.hk/blog/wp-content/uploads/2016/09/Appendix.pdf.

Table 2. Multinomial logistic regression coefficients predicting four categories of adopters

Cluster id	Semantic topic of cluster	Print-to-kindle vs print-only	Kindle-to-print vs print-only	Kindle-only vs print-only
cluster607	devices	0.9369***	1.0544***	1.075***
cluster371	ui/interface	0.2724***	0.2533***	0.3428***
cluster272	light	0.0752***	0.1004***	0.0738***
cluster699	user experience	0.042***	0.037***	−0.1728***
cluster291	money	0.0289***	−0.0259***	−0.1018***
cluster167	misspelling	0.0004	−0.0306***	−0.1799***
cluster183	portable	−0.0548***	−0.0099	−0.115***
cluster564	format	−0.0809***	−0.124***	−0.2464***
cluster494	cookbook	−0.0273***	−0.0836***	−0.1529***
cluster275	law	−0.0278***	−0.0372***	−0.1917***
cluster289	school	−0.0962***	−0.1655***	−0.3383***
cluster216	clothing	−0.0846***	−0.1424***	−0.2412***
cluster197	language	−0.0524***	−0.1137***	−0.1588***
cluster48	comic books	−0.1091***	−0.1658***	−0.343***
cluster89	academic	−0.0756***	−0.1812***	−0.3197***
cluster62	programming	−0.0576***	−0.1943***	−0.2678***
cluster45	erotica	0.1559***	0.1439***	0.1496***
cluster19	social app	0.3529***	0.3385***	0.4064***
cluster104	personal health	0.01*	−0.0005	0.0441***

***, **, and * denote significance at 1, 5, and 10%, respectively.

by kindle-only, followed by print-to-kindle, kindle-to-print and then print-only. Light is also significant, though somewhat weaker, in five of the six comparisons (except in kindle-to-print and print-to-kindle), and the coefficients shows that kindle-to-print and print-to-kindle adopters care more about light than the other two categories. Words of user experience, such as effortless, flawless, etc., are also significant in the prediction direction, with print-to-kindle adopters ranking first in attention. Topic of money significantly distinguishes the four categories, with print-to-kindle adopters as the most concerned group. Words about misspelling have a significant impact in five of the six comparisons (except in print-to-kindle vs print-only), showing that print-to-kindle and print-only adopters mention more about spelling mistakes than the other two categories. Cluster of format is significant in predicted directions of the four categories, with print-only adopters as the most concerned group. Topic of portability shows significance in five of the six comparisons (except in kindle-to-print vs print-only). Kindle-to-print and print-only adopters care more about books' portability topic than print-to-kindle and kindle-only adopters.

We also take some book content topics into considerations, such as cooking, law, school, academic research, language, programming, etc. Whereas for most of the content clusters, print-only adopters concern more than the other three categories. Exceptions are clusters of social apps, erotica and personal health. Cluster of erotica is significant in three comparisons with print-only categories, which represents a lower possibility for print-only adopters to mention sex topic than the other three categories. The significant impacts of words about social apps are in five of the six comparisons (except kindle-only vs print-to-kindle), with large differences between print-only and the other three categories. Significance of cluster about personal health is in five comparisons (except in kindle-to-print vs print-only), showing that kindle-only and print-to-kindle adopters focus more on this topic than the other two categories.

Table 3. Concerned topics for four categories of adopters

Adopters	Function-oriented topics	Content-oriented topics
print-to-kindle	money, light, misspelling, user experience	erotica, social apps, personal health
kindle-to-print	light, portable	
kindle-to-print	devices, ui/interface	
print-only	portable, format, misspelling	cook, academic research, school, law, language, programming

We finally characterize four categories of adopters with function-oriented topics (topics related to interface, portability, etc., not the content of the books) and content-oriented topics. Table 3 matches the topics with the most concerned adopter categories. For topics of misspelling, user experience and portable, the most two related categories of each topic do not show significance in comparison, so the topics appear both in the two categories' lists.

4 Discussion

Comparing print-to-kindle and kindle-to-print adopters' concerned topics, we find that kindle-to-print adopters care more about price and spelling mistakes whereas kindle-to-print adopters pay more attention on portability. Parts of our results can be explained by the *Diffusion of Innovation Theory*. As Rogers [1] proposed that adopters evaluate an innovation on its relative advantage and relative advantage refers to perceived efficiency compared to the current ones. Here in our study, money, light, ui/interface represent the relative advantages of e-books compared to paper books and print-to-kindle adopters (transitive adopters) and kindle-only adopters (the continuous adopters) both show more concerns on these relative advantages. Whereas user experience including words such as effortless, flawless, etc., somehow, represent an individual's personal characteristics and self-efficacy. As Daugherty and others [9] demonstrated that users' adoption and usage of Web technologies, rely on their '*confidence in capability to handle the content online'*, defined as self-efficacy. So here in our study, kindle-to-print and print-to-kindle adopters (e-book adopters) concerns more about user experience than print-only (e-book non-adopters).

Back to the problem of the coexistence of e-book and paper book, in our study, we find that the overall book market is still paper-book-dominated, as when reviewers mention contents in most types of books, including cook, law, school, academic research, language, programming, etc., they are still most probably talking about the print ones. Same situation is also found in reviewer's rating preference, as shown in Table 1, people give much higher average rating on paper books rather than kindle e-books. So does it mean that after more than 20 years' rapid spread, e-book is still in a weak position in book market? The Book Reading 2016 report released by Pew Research Center in September 1, 2016 also supports our conclusion, where they found that 65 % of Americans had read a printed book in the last year, whereas only 28 % of them had read an e-book. Although the proportion of e-book is slowly increasing, the overall pattern tends to be stable. Perhaps that is what really happens in the coexistence of e-book and paper book in book market.

5   Related Work

Our work is related to the following:

Amazon book reviews. Traditionally, book reviews refer to reviews of new books, basically about the content of the books, which can help search for books best meeting personal needs [10]. With the emergence of the Internet, online book reviews are no longer limited to recently published books, but they are still recognized to have an intensive impact on consumers' purchase intension. In these circumstances, online book review data are mainly conducted and analyzed to attract consumers' interest and improve online bookstores' revenue. Chevalier and others [11] investigated the effect of online book review on sales volume at Amazon.com and Barnesandnoble.com and they found that improvements in book reviews can lead to increases in relative sales and negative comments have stronger impact than the positive ones. Also, online book reviews are also analyzed to other purposes, for example, consumers' reputations. David and others [12] scrapped review data from Amazon.com and investigated online consumers' review reputations especially on book review data. They found that hundreds of reviews on Amazon.com might be copies from one another and they finally proposed a framework to discuss the multi-tier online reputation economy. However, to the best of our knowledge, there are few studies conducting online book review data to investigate the adoption of e-book and paper book.

Studies on e-books and paper books. Previous studies investigated the relationship of digital book resources and paper books mainly from aspects of library book usage, academic research and education. Levine-Clark [13] conducted an online survey in University of Denver and found that humanists favor paper books to digital resources at a higher rate than others and humanists care more about content, rather than e-book functions. Bierman and others [14] investigated e-book usage in pure and applied science with their online survey data and they stated an idea that e-books have a growing future in academia, whereas they found no significant difference between usage in pure and applied science. Stephens and others [15] compared the e-book and print collection usage on the Safari Books Online platform, which mainly includes programming and information technology books and found that the digital version received notably higher use than the paper books. Nicholas and others [16] conducted a survey on scholarly e-book usage and found that engineering scholars viewed digital books and resources more often than other subjects' scholars. Slater [17] managed to reason why e-books had not become the cornerstone of the academic library by reviewing previous studies before 2010. Some studies also explore the question why people prefer e-book or not. Knutson and others [18] reported students using e-textbooks for study and proponents in their interview mentioned that e-textbooks can save students' money, lighten backpacks and are convenient to update. Slater [17] mentioned in his study that although e-books can be easier to access initially, paper book can provide easier continual access than the digital versions. He also stated that a poorly designed and confusing interface may be a barrier for e-book users to get used to it.

Most of these studies investigated the difference of digital book resources and paper books from aspects of library book usage, academic research and education. Data used above were basically collected by survey, interviews or from library book collection usage statistics at that time. However, it remains some limitations when using library book collection database or surveying scholars and students to explore these questions. For example, most of the books collected in college libraries are divided by subjects, related to academic study, whereas some other types of common book, such as recipes, erotic books, etc., are rarely included. What's more, most of the digital resources scholars and students view in library collection are technical manuals, thesis and online journals, whereas the real sense of "e-books" are not in concerned and often told to buy them on online bookstores such as Amazon.com. In these circumstances, we believe that conclusions obtained from library and research aspects cannot represent the coexistence of e-books and paper books comprehensively. Further studies are still needed to explore this question under the overall dynamic book market.

Detecting user attributes based on text analysis. Previous studies show that text analysis can help detect users' attributes and profiles. Malouf [19] investigated 77,854 posts on political discussion sites to and classified posters with political orientation labels as left, right and others. They firstly identified texts of posters and then labeled them with the most frequent label in their texts. After combining other approaches as co-citation analysis, they finally get 68.48 % accuracy compared with posters' own descriptions. Pennacchiotti and others [20] inferred twitter user attributes from users' network structure and semantic contents. They employed sentiment analysis and topic models to detect Starbucks fans, user ethnicity, etc., and confirmed that text content can provide high value in user classification. As far as we can see that previous studies generally classify reviewers into several categories based on their text analysis, whereas in our study we propose a new strategy to segment reviewers based on theory first and then characterize reviewer categories based on text analysis.

6   Conclusion and Future Work

In this paper, we conducted a data-driven analysis of the review patterns across four kinds of reviewers with the goal of characterizing reviewers and finding their potential tastes. We found that print-only adopters show significant different patterns with other three categories of e-book adopters in content-oriented topics, in the meantime, e-book adopters show similar concerns but a bit diversified attention to function-oriented topics as depicted in Table 3. When compared with other three types of reviewers, print-only adopters tend to mention words related to programming, language, law, etc., which may indicate that paper books are evolving to the forms as hand-books, tool books and textbooks and also suggest that print-only adopters have the potential demands for skill oriented types of books more than other themes. Therefore, we can recommend more books related to these topics to these reviewers afterwards.

In the case of transitive and discontinuous adopters (print-to-kindle and kindle-to-print), we found that these two categories of adopters both pay more attention to user experience than the other two adopters, which intuitively indicates that user experience may play an important role when people are changing their purchase decision, from books to kindle or from kindle to books. In addition, adopters in group of print-to-kindle care more about price and spelling mistakes whereas kindle-to-print adopters pay more attention on portability. This indicates that price may be one of the key factors that make book adopters divert attention from books to kindle. Therefore, it provides a potential strategy for book retailers to retain consumers as well as for e-book merchants to attract new buyers.

There are also many other interesting avenues to follow in our future work. For instance, do these segmentation and characterizing approaches work the same on other innovation and old technology groups' review, such as MP3 and CD, Amazon Instant video and DVD? Do people's review patterns remain consistently across different products categories? Specifically, for adopters here in kindle-to-print category, do they also pay more attention to price when purchasing other products such as electronics, clothing or movies? These questions remain to be answered by our future works. In addition, in our present work, we emphasis on part of speech of words whereas the sentiment they convey are not considered enough. For example, we know kindle-to-print adopters concern about portable topic, but do they in favor of e-books or paper books in the case of portability is still not so clear and this needs more comprehensive researches both semantically and sentimentally.

References

1. Rogers, E.M.: Diffusion of Innovations. S&S, New York (2003)
2. Mahajan, V., Muller, E., Srivastava, R.K.: Determination of adopter categories by using innovation diffusion models. J. Mark. Res. **27**, 37–50 (1990)
3. Zhu, J.J., He, Z.: Perceived characteristics, perceived needs, and perceived popularity adoption and use of the Internet in China. Commun. Res. **29**, 466–495 (2002)
4. Levy, O., Goldberg, Y., Dagan, I.: Improving distributional similarity with lessons learned from word embeddings. In: TACL, vol. 3, pp. 211–225 (2015)
5. Baroni, M., Dinu, G., Kruszewski, G.: Don't count, predict! A systematic comparison of context-counting vs. context-predicting semantic vectors. In: ACL (2014)
6. Pennington, J., Socher, R., Manning, C.D.: Glove: global vectors for word representation. In: Proceedings of EMNLP, vol. 14, pp. 1532–4315 (2014)
7. Mikolov, T., Dean, J.: Distributed representations of words and phrases and their compositionality. In: Proceedings of NIPS (2013)
8. McAuley, J., Targett, C., Shi, Q., van den Hengel, A.: Image-based recommendations on styles and substitutes. In: Proceedings of SIGIR, pp. 43–52 (2015)
9. Daugherty, T., Eastin, M., Gangadharbatla, H.: E-CRM: understanding Internet confidence and implications for customer relationship management. In: Advances in Electronic Marketing, pp. 67–82 (2005)
10. Lin, T.M., Luarn, P., Huang, Y.K.: Effect of Internet book reviews on purchase intention: a focus group study. J. Acad. Librarianship **31**(5), 461–468 (2005)
11. Chevalier, J.A., Mayzlin, D.: The effect of word of mouth on sales: online book reviews. J. Mark. Res. **43**(3), 345–354 (2006)
12. David, S., Pinch, T.J.: Six degrees of reputation: the use and abuse of online review and recommendation systems. Available at SSRN 857505 (2005)
13. Levine-Clark, M.: Electronic books and the humanities: a survey at the University of Denver. Collect. Build. **26**(1), 7–14 (2007)
14. Bierman, J., Ortega, L., Rupp-Serrano, K.: E-book usage in pure and applied sciences. Sci. Technol. Libr. **29**(1–2), 69–91 (2010)
15. Stephens, J., Melgoza, P., Wan, G.: Safari books online: currency, usage and book release policies of an e-book database. Collect. Build. **27**(1), 14–17 (2008)
16. Nicholas, D., Rowlands, I., Clark, D., Huntington, P., Jamali, H.R., Olle, C.: UK scholarly e-book usage: a landmark survey. ASLIB Proc. **60**(4), 311–334 (2008). Emerald Group Publishing Limited
17. Slater, R.: Why aren't e-books gaining more ground in academic libraries? E-book use and perceptions: a review of published literature and research. J. Web Librarianship **4**(4), 305–331 (2010)
18. Knutson, R., Fowler, G.A.: Book smarts? E-texts receive mixed reviews from students. Wall Street J. **20** (2009). http://www.wsj.com/articles/SB10001424052970203577304574277041750084938
19. Malouf, R., Mullen, T.: Taking sides: user classification for informal online political discourse. Int. Res. **18**(2), 177–190 (2008)
20. Pennacchiotti, M., Popescu, A.M.: A machine learning approach to Twitter user classification. Proc. ICWSM **11**(1), 281–288 (2011)

Emotion Cause Extraction, A Challenging Task with Corpus Construction

Lin Gui[1], Ruifeng Xu[1,2(✉)], Qin Lu[3], Dongyin Wu[1], and Yu Zhou[1]

[1] School of Computer Science and Technology, Harbin Institute of Technology,
Shenzhen Graduate School, Shenzhen, China
`guilin.nlp@gmail.com, wudongyinhit@gmail.com,`
`zhouyu.nlp@gmail.com`
[2] Guangdong Provincial Engineering Technology Research Center
for Data Science, Guangzhou, China
`xuruifeng@hitsz.edu.cn`
[3] Department of Computing,
The Hong Kong Polytechnic University, Hong Kong, China
`csluqin@comp.polyu.edu.hk`

Abstract. In this paper, we present a new challenging task for emotion analysis called emotion cause extraction. In this task, we do not need to identify the emotion category or emotion component of text. We focus on the emotion cause, a.k.a the reason or stimulant of an emotion. Since there is no open dataset available, the lack of annotated resources has limited the research in this area. Thus, we first built an annotated dataset for this task using SINA city news which follows the scheme of W3C Emotion Markup Language. We then present an emotion cause detection method using event extraction where a one-hot representation method is using to represent events in text. Because traditional event representation method does not consider the emotion category caused by the event, we modified the definition of event with a more reasonable improvement. Even with a limited training set, we can still extract sufficient features for analysis. Evaluations show that our approach achieves 7.68 % higher F-measure than other reported methods. The contributions of our work include both resources and algorithm development.

1 Introduction

With the growth of Internet, people can easily share experiences and emotions through this powerful medium anywhere and anytime. How to analyze individual's emotion becomes a new challenge for NLP (Liu 2015). In recent years, studies in emotion analysis (Plutchik 1980; Ekman 1984; Turner 2000) focus on emotion classification (Xu et al. 2012; Beck et al. 2014) including detection of emotions expressed by writers of text (Gao et al. 2013) as well as prediction of reader emotion (Chang et al. 2015). There are also some information extraction tasks in emotion analysis, such as extracting the feeler of emotion (Das et al. 2010). There are some other studies focused on joint learning with sentiment (Luo et al. 2015; Mohtarami et al. 2013), emotion in tweets or blog (Hasegawa et al. 2013; Qadir and Riloff 2014; Ou et al. 2014; Liu et al. 2013;

© Springer Nature Singapore Pte Ltd. 2016
Y. Li et al. (Eds.): SMP 2016, CCIS 669, pp. 98–109, 2016.
DOI: 10.1007/978-981-10-2993-6_8

Quan and Ren 2009), and emotional lexicon construction (Yang et al. 2014; Staiano and Guerini 2014; Mohammad and Turney 2013). However, these works focus on phenomenon in emotion expressions. Sometimes, we care more about the stimuli, or the cause of an emotion. For instance, manufacturers want to know why people love, or hate a certain product. White House also prefers to know the cause of emotional text "Let us hit the streets" rather than the distribution of different emotions.

(Lee et al. 2010; Chen et al. 2010) is the first work on this topic and there are some followers (Ghazi et al. 2015; Russo et al. 2011). There are two main challenges in these studies of emotion cause extraction. The first is that, up to now, there is no open dataset available for emotion cause extraction. This may explain why there are only few studies on emotion causes. The second is that, due to the complexity in annotation, the size of corpus for emotion cause extraction is usually small. Due to this limit, many machine learning methods are not suited for this problem and the most popular method for this problem is rule based method (Gui et al. 2014; Li and Xu 2014; Gao 2015).

In this paper, we first present an annotated dataset for emotion cause extraction to be released to the public. We then present a new emotion cause extraction method. The basic idea is to extract events in the context of emotional text through dependency parsing. Then, a 7-tuples representation structure is used to represent nearby event. Based on this structure based representation of events, a polynomial kernel is used to determine whether an event is emotion cause relevant. This method can detect all possible combinations of lexical structures to obtain sufficient features for emotion analysis using a limited training set. Compare with existing methods, which either use manual rules or commonsense knowledge to extend information, our approach is completely machine learning based and still achieves state-of-the-art performance. The contributions of this work include both resource development and algorithm development.

The rest of this paper is organized as follows. Section 1 provides a review of related works on emotion analysis. Section 2 presents construction of emotion cause extraction corpus. Section 3 gives the event driven emotion cause extraction method and Sect. 4 is the evaluations and discussions. Section 5 concludes this work and gives the future directions.

2 Construction of Corpus

In this section, we first describe the linguistic phenomenon in emotion expressions. It serves as the inspiration to develop the annotated dataset. We then introduce details of annotation scheme and the construction of the dataset.

2.1 Linguistic Phenomenon of Emotion Causes

Emotion causes play an important role in emotion expressions. An emotion cause reveals the stimulus to an emotion. In written text, the cause of an emotion is usually expressed in the context of emotion keywords. Thus, finding appropriate context of emotion keywords in the annotation is the pre-requisite to identify the cause. Finding the relationship between an emotion cause and an emotion keyword is the key to cause extraction.

Another important kind of feature is the presence of conjunctions and prepositions. These cues words indicate the discourse information between clauses. In order to utilize discourse information, the basic analysis unit should be at clause level rather than at sentence level.

The genre of text is also important. Study shows that in informal text, emotion expressions can have overlapping emotion cause and emotion target (Gui et al. 2014). Thus, some causes are simply annotated as the target in informal text. This is why some studies even incorporate cause extraction with target identification to improve performance. However, our focus is on emotion cause identification. So, we us formal news text to avoid the potential mix up. To summarize, we follow three basic principles in construction: (1) Keep the whole context of emotion keywords; (2) The basic processing unit is at clause level; and (3) Use formal text.

2.2   Collection and Annotation

We first take 3 years (2013–15) Chinese city news from NEWS SINA2 of 20,000 articles as the raw corpus. Based on a list of 10,259 Chinese primary emotion keywords (keywords for short) (Xu et al. 2008), we extract 15,687 instances by keyword matching from raw data. Here, we call the presence of an emotion keyword as an instance in the corpus. For each matched keyword, we extract three preceding clauses and three following clauses as context of an instance. If a sentence has more than 3 clauses in each direction, the context will include the rest of the sentence to make the context complete. For simplicity, we omit cross paragraph context.

Note that the presence of keywords does not necessarily convey emotional information due to different possible reasons such as negative polarity and sense ambiguity. For example, "可乐/funny" is an emotion word of "happiness". It can also be the name of a drink. Also, the presence of emotion keywords does not necessarily guarantee the existence of emotional cause neither.

After removing irrelevant those instances there are still 2,105 instances remain. For each emotional instance, two annotators manually annotate the emotion categories and the cause(es) in the W3C Emotion Markup Language (EML) format. Ex1 shows an example of an annotated emotional sentence in the corpus, presented as simplified Chinese, followed by an English translation. To save space, we removed the xml format, the original annotation example will be given as subsidiary file. The basic analysis unit is a clause. Emotion cause is marked as < cause >, and the emotion keyword is marked as < keywords >. Emotion type, POS, position and the length of annotation are also annotated in Emotionml format.

Ex.1: *朱某今年55岁，1979年参加工作时才19岁，已有36年的手艺。"我当时被分配到丹阳南京理发店工作，这是当时丹阳最大的理发店，我在那儿获得了*

好多证书和荣誉" <cause POS="v" Dis="-1">说起自己的荣誉</cause>，朱某很是<keywords type="happiness">自豪</keywords>.

Mr. Zhu is 55 years old. He started work as a barber when he was 19 in 1979, has 36 years of experience. "I was assigned to work at the Barbershop in Danyang, Nanjing, it is the largest barbershop in Danyang. I won many awards and honors there." <cause POS="v" Dis="-1">*talking about his honors*</cause>, *Mr. Zhu is so* <keywords type="happiness"> *pride*</keywords>.

Ex.1 only contains one cause. However, one keyword may have more than one corresponding emotion causes. Here is an example. Ex.2 has two relevant causes for one keyword. In our dataset, only 59 instances have two or more causes.

Ex.2: *劝说过程中，消防官兵了解到，该女子是由于* <cause POS="v" Dis="-2">*对方拖欠工程款*</cause>, <cause POS="v" Dis="-1">*家中又急需用钱*</cause>, <keywords type=sadness>*无奈*</keywords> *才选择跳楼轻生。*

During persuasion, fireman realized that the woman is because of <cause POS="v" Dis="-2">*the hold back wages by the employer*</cause>, *and* <cause POS="v" Dis="-1">*her family requires money in hurry*</cause>, *she feels* <keywords type=sadness>*helpless*</keywords> *and thus attempted suicide.*

2.3 Details of Dataset and Its Annotations

In our dataset, each instance has only one emotion keyword and at least one emotion cause. We ensure the keyword and the causes in the same instance are relevant. Table 1 lists the number of extracted instances, clauses, and emotion causes.

Table 1. The detail of corpus

	Number
Instances	2,105
Clauses	11,799
Emotion cause	2,167
Doc with 1 cause	2,046
Doc with 2 cause	56
Doc with 3 cause	3

From Table 1, we can see that most instances contain only one emotion cause (97.2 %). Only 2.6 % instances have two emotion causes and 0.2 % have three.

Table 2. Distribution of emotions

Emotion	Number	Percentage
Happiness	544	25.83 %
Sadness	567	26.94 %
Fear	379	18.00 %
Anger	302	14.35 %
Hate	225	10.69 %
Surprise	88	4.18 %

The distribution of emotion types lists in Table 2. The distribution of causes' positions is shown in Table 3, from which we can see that 78 % emotion causes adjoin the emotion keywords at the clause level. Obviously, position is an important feature for emotion cause extraction. This motivates us to use distance based features for emotion cause extraction.

Table 3. Cause position of emotions

Position	Num.	Perc.
Previous 3 clauses	37	1.7 %
Previous 2 clauses	167	8.1 %
Previous 1 clauses	1,180	54.45 %
In same clauses	511	23.6 %
Next 1 clauses	162	7.5 %
Next 2 clauses	48	2.2 %
Next 3 clauses	11	0.5 %
Other	42	1.9 %

Table 4 shows the phrase types of emotion causes. Verbs and verb phrases form 93 % of all cause events. Thus, they are the focus of our learning algorithm.

Table 4. Distribution of POS tag

POS	Num.	Perc.
Noun/Noun phrase	147	6.78 %
Verb/Verb phrase	2020	93.21 %

In the annotation process, two annotators work independently. It is important to distinguish clause level and phrase level in cause annotation. The clause level is to label the clause that contains the emotion cause. The phrase level is to determine the boundary of an emotion cause. In the clause level, if two annotators disagree with each other, a third annotator serves as the arbitrator. In the phrase level, the larger boundary of the two annotations is used if they have the same annotation at the clause level. The kappa value on clause level annotation is 0.9287. It means this annotation is very reliable.

3 Event-Driven Emotion Cause Extraction

Due to the complexity of annotation in emotion cause identification, the size of annotated corpus is usually small. Since we aim to use machine learning method to automatically learn and identify causes, we use an event extraction method to detect all possible event in the text. This allows learning from the representation of the event to extract emotion causes.

The basic idea is to use an event representation to capture features for emotion cause identification. For training data, we extract all valid representation for each event, referred to as the ETs (Event Tuples). If an event is a cause, the corresponding ET is positive. Otherwise, the corresponding ET is negative. Then, we train a polynomial kernel SVMs on the training set to classify candidate ETs in the testing set. Since more than 97 % emotion keywords only have one cause, and more than 95 % causes are near the emotion keywords, candidate ETs are extracted from the context of emotion keywords. We only choose the ET with the highest probability in the classification result as the emotion cause.

3.1 Event Extraction

In recent years, there are some related works about the emotion cause extraction, including (Lee et al. 2010; Chen et al. 2010). In these studies, they proposed rule based or machine learning based methods to extract the event cause of an emotion. However, they do not give any formal definition of event.

In this paper, we need to define events first. Inspire by the definition of event in AI, for example, Radinsky (Radinsky et al. 2012) gave a formal definition of an event as "action, actor, object, instrument, location and time", we give a similar definition of event in our study.

Actually, in emotion cause extraction, the components of an event is simpler. We are only interested in the action, actor and object (follow AI's tradition, denote them as P, O_1, O_2). Since Chinese is a SVO language, the actor is the subject and the action is the verb. The subject and the object may have attributes and a predicate may have adverbial and complement. These components may also be helpful in emotion cause extraction. Here, we formally define an emotion cause event as a 7-tuple:

$$e = (ATT_{O_1}, O_1, Adv, P, Cpl, ATT_{O_2}, O_2) \tag{1}$$

Here, Att_{O1} is the attribute of O_1, and Att_{o2} is the attribute of O_2. The Adv is adverbial and Cpl is complement. Note that in some cases, the syntactic components may be implicit and the corresponding attributes can be filled with NIL values.

Note that the core cue in an event is P, the action. So, in our algorithm, we extract **all verbs** from the text, and use the dependency parsing[1] to extract all the relevant

---

[1] https://github.com/HIT-SCIR/ltp.

syntactic components in the clause under our definition above. Then, we can construct an Event Tuples (ETs).

The emotion cause event has 7 components. Since Chinese is a SVO language, the basic level of components are S(subject), V(verb), and O(object). Then, the seven event components can be categorized and to be filled up in the relevant syntactic slots. (Att_{O1}, O_1) belong to S, (Adv, P, Cpl) belong to V and (Att_{o2}, O_2) belong to O. Then we can get the Event Tuples (ETs) based on the definition of an event.

After the construction, the emotion cause extraction becomes a classification problem. If the ET is extract from an emotion cause, then the ET is positive. Otherwise the ET is negative. We need a binary classification algorithm to identify if the ET is emotion cause or not.

3.2 Emotion Cause Classification

After the construction of ETs, we obtain positive and negative ET samples. Due to insufficient amount of samples, it is necessary to dig deep information in the ETs. We choose polynomial kernel based SVMs because it can search all possible syntactic features under a polynomial function.

Event Representation. Consider the definition of an event in our scheme as a 7-tuple:

$$e = (Att_{O1}, O_1, Adv, P, Cpl, Att_{o2}, O_2)$$

We obtain the one-hot representation of each component as the feature respectively. Assume that the representation of each is R_i, here $i \in e$, then we can capture the features of an ET by a joint operation, called ET feature:

$$F = \{R_{Att_{O1}} \oplus R_{O_1} \oplus \ldots \oplus R_{O_2}\} \tag{2}$$

Here, $\oplus$ is the joint operation. It means that just combine the two representations into a new representation by order.

In this paper, we use three kinds of representation method to extract the feature of an event. The first method is a one-hot representation of each component. We use the one-hot representation to extract the feature of each component as a d-dimension vector. Then, we use a joint operation to connect the 7 d-dimension vectors into a 7*d-dimension vector as the representation of the event.

Actually, there are different kinds of representations, such as the word2vec (Mikolov et al. 2013) representation. So, for comparison, we also use the word2vec to capture the representation as the second representation method. The basic idea is similar with the one-hot representation based method. We use the word2vec to obtain the representation for each component. Then, the formula (2) is used to extract the features of an event.

The representation above use the event extraction result which is proposed in the Sect. 3.1. We still need to show if the event extraction is necessary or not. So we proposed the third method for emotion cause representation which does not need the event information. It is based on the clause where the emotion cause appears. For each clause, assume that it contains n words: $w_1, w_2, \ldots, w_n$. The representation of corresponding words are: $R_1, R_2, \ldots, R_n$, then the representation of the emotion cause is:

$$F = \sum_{i=1}^{n} R_i \tag{3}$$

Here, the R is an one-hot representation for the word.

The training data is already in labeled ET format. To prepare testing data, we extract all ETs from a given instance as candidate ETs. Then, we use the classifier to obtain the probability of emotion cause for each ET to produce a ranked list of candidate ETs. The candidate ET with the highest rank will serve as the cause event for the current instance.

The flow chart is shown below in Fig. 1:

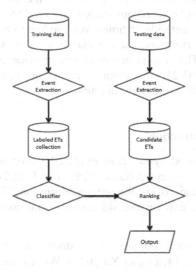

Fig. 1. Flow chart of event-driven emotion cause extraction

Polynomial kernel function. The polynomial kernel is one of the most wildly used kernel function for support vector machines. For any inputs V_1 and V_2, where the V stands for the vector of features, the kernel function is defined as:

$$K_{polynomial}(V_1, V_2) = (\gamma V_1 \cdot V_2 + r)^d \tag{4}$$

Here, V_1 and V_2 are vectors in the feature space. γ, r, and d are parameters. $\cdot$ is the inner product, where:

$$V_1 \cdot V_2 = \sum_{i=1}^{d} v_{1i} \times v_{2i} \tag{5}$$

If $V_1 = \{v_{11}, v_{12}, \ldots, v_{1n}\}$ and $V_2 = \{v_{21}, v_{22}, \ldots, v_{2n}\}$.

This method can search all possible combination in the feature space if the feature is based on one-hot representation. However, the above definition does not consider the syntactical information, so we should combine this method with event extraction. That is the reason why the event extraction is based on dependency parsing is necessary, because it is a syntactical result. In order to prove this point, we compare our method with the clause level one-hot representation, which is non-syntactical, and the word2vec method, where the polynomial kernel may be not useful.

4 Performance Evaluations

4.1 Experimental Setup

In the experiments, we stochastically select 90 % of the dataset as training data and 10 % as testing data. In order to obtain statistically credible results, we evaluate our methods and the reference methods 25 times. We conduct two sets of experiments. The first one evaluates the performance at the clause level to identify the clauses that contain emotion causes. The second one evaluates emotion causes using verb classification. This is because 93.21 % of emotion causes are verb/verb phrase and verbs serve as the action component in event definition.

4.2 Emotion Cause Extraction

We use the measure proposed by Lee (Lee et al., 2010) for emotion cause extraction. This measure is commonly accepted (Gao 2015; Li and Xu 2014). In this measure, if the proposed emotion cause covers the annotated answer, the proposed sequence is considered correct. In the experiment, we compare our method with the following works:

1. **RB** (Rule based method): There are several studies about rule based method (Lee et al. 2010; Gui et al. 2014; Li and Xu 2014). We use the union of the rules, and remove some rules which are not relevant to our dataset.
2. **CB** (Commonsense based method): In order to reproduce this method (Russo et al. 2011), we use the Chinese Emotion Cognition Lexicon (Xu et al. 2013) as the commonsense. The lexicon contains more than 5,000 emotion stimulations and their corresponding reflection words.
3. **ML** (Rule base features for machine learning): Use rules as features, and add other manual features for emotion cause classification (Chen et al. 2010).
4. K_{clause}: Only use the features defined in (3) in the training of classifier for emotion cause extraction.
5. $K_{word2vec}$: Use the word2vec (Mikolov et al. 2013) to learn the continuous representation. Use the representation defined in (2) in the training of classifier
6. K_{ET}: Only use the event extraction based method defined by one-hot representation in the training of classifier for emotion cause extraction.

The performance result is given in Table 5.

Table 5. Performance on corpus

Method	Precision	Recall	F-measure
RB	**0.6747**	0.4287	0.5243
CB	0.2672	**0.7130**	0.3887
RB + CB	0.5435	0.5307	0.5370
RB + CB + ML	0.5921	0.5307	**0.5597**
K_{clause}	0.4793	**0.7058**	0.5695
$K_{word2vec}$	0.4301	0.4233	0.4136
K_{ET}	**0.5924**	0.6139	**0.6029**

From Table 5, we can see that K_{ET} achieves the top performance in F-measure. Compared to other methods, the improvement is significant with p-value less than 0.01 in the t-test.

RB achieves the top precision. However, its F-measure is limited by the low recall. Since CB is opposite to RB, the performance is improved when we use the output of them as features to train a classifier in RB + CB. However, the improvement is quite limited, at 0.0127 in F-measure. The F-measure of our reproduced RB is similar to other references (Gui et al. 2014; Li and Xu 2014) mentioned result. They repeat Lee's (Lee et al. 2014) method and achieve the F-measure with 0.55 more or less.

(Chen et al. 2010) reported that by using handcrafted rules as features to train a classifier with some additional features such as conjunction, action and epistemic verbs, performance can be improved significantly. In our experiment, the result is opposite to this claim. The main reason is the samples in (Chen et al. 2010) are less complex. About 85 % of the emotion causes are in the same clause where the emotion keywords are. Our corpus is quite different. The percentage of causes in the same clause as the emotion keyword itself is only about 23.6 %. (Chen et al. 2010)'s method does not handle long distance relations well. That explains why it does not work well for our dataset. Although (RB + CB + ML) does not perform well, there is still 0.0334 improvement in F-measure compare with RB.

Among our proposed methods, $K_{word2vec}$ achieves 0.4136 in F-measure. Compare to CB and ML, the performance is unsatisfied. However, as a simple feature to represent lexical information, the performance is acceptable. However, compare with the other one-hot representation method, including K_{clause} and K_{ET}, the word2vec is not good. Maybe the joint operation is too simple to handle composition for the complex semantic information. For the non-event-driven method K_{clause}, the performance is 0.5695 in F-measure. It means that the polynomial kernel without consideration the event information can achieves an acceptable performance, because the baseline methods, including RB, CB, ML and the possible combination of these methods, underperforms K_{clause}. However, compare to rule based method, the performance still needs to be enhanced and the event extraction is necessary indeed.

After the combination with ET feature using a event extraction, the performance of K_{ET} achieves a higher level with **0.6029** in F-measure. Compare to RB, the improvement in F-measure is 0.0768. Compare to the combination of existing methods, the improvement is 0.0432. The reason is that our method uses the event information which is at the syntactic level and lexicon level at the same time. This information gives the model generalization ability and achieves a better performance.

5 Conclusion

In this paper, we present our work about the emotion cause. There are two contributions in our paper. We first construct a corpus with annotated emotion cause from news text. We then propose an emotion cause extraction method based on event extraction method. In this method, we use syntactic information to present the emotion cause into an event. Based on this event, a kernel method is designed to extract the emotion cause. Compare with the baseline method, which uses the manually constructed rules and commonsense knowledge to detect the emotion cause, our proposed model can automatically obtain structure features and lexical features to achieve state-of-the-art performance on this dataset. In the future work, we plan to extend this work into English and explore the bilingual method for this problem.

Acknowledgment. This work was supported by the National Natural Science Foundation of China 61370165, 61632011, National 863 Program of China 2015AA015405, Shenzhen Peacock Plan Research Grant KQCX20140521144507925 and Shenzhen Foundational Research Funding JCYJ20150625142543470, Guangdong Provincial Engineering Technology Research Center for Data Science 2016KF09.

References

Chen, Y., Lee, S.Y.M., Li, S., Huang, C.R.: Emotion cause detection with linguistic constructions. In: Proceedings of COLING, pp. 179–187, August 2010

Chang, Y.C., Chen, C.C., Hsieh, Y.L., Hsu, W.L.: Linguistic template extraction for recognizing reader-emotion and emotional resonance writing assistance. In: Proceedings of ACL-IJCNLP, pp. 775–780 (2015)

Das, D., Bandyopadhyay, S.: Finding emotion holder from bengali blog texts—an unsupervised syntactic approach. In: Proceedings of PACLIC, pp. 621–628 (2010)

Ekman, P.: Expression and the Nature of Emotion (1984)

Gao, K., Xu, H., Wang, J.: A rule-based approach to emotion cause detection for chinese micro-blogs. Expert Syst. Appl. **42**(9), 4517–4528 (2015)

Gui, L., Yuan, L., Xu, R., Liu, B., Lu, Q., Zhou, Y.: Emotion cause detection with linguistic construction in chinese weibo text. In: Proceedings of NLPCC (2014)

Ghazi, D., Inkpen, D., Szpakowicz, S.: Detecting emotion stimuli in emotion-bearing sentences. In: Gelbukh, A. (ed.). LNCS, vol. 9042, pp. 152–165 Springer, Heidelberg (2015)

Gao, W., Li, S., Lee, S.Y.M., Zhou, G., Huang, C. R.: Joint learning on sentiment and emotion classification. In: Proceedings of CIKM, pp. 1505–1508. ACM, October 2013

Lee, S.Y.M., Chen, Y., Huang, C.R.: A text-driven rule-based system for emotion cause eetection. In: Proceedings of the NAACL HLT 2010 Workshop on Computational Approaches to Analysis and Generation of Emotion in Text, pp. 45–53, June 2010

Li, W., Xu, H.: Text-based emotion classification using emotion cause extraction. Expert Syst. Appl. **41**(4), 1742–1749 (2014)

Liu, H., Li, S., Zhou, G., Huang, C.R., Li, P.: Joint modeling of news reader's and comment writer's emotions. In: Proceedings of ACL (2), pp. 511–515, August 2013

Li, S., Huang, L., Wang, R., Zhou, G.: Sentence-level emotion classification with label and context dependence. In: Proceedings of ACL, pp. 1045–1053 (2013)

Mikolov, T., Sutskever, I., Chen, K., Corrado, G. S., Dean, J.: Distributed representations of words and phrases and their compositionality. In: Proceedings of NIPS, pp. 3111–3119 (2013)

Plutchik, R.: Emotions: A Psychoevolutionary Synthesis. Harper & Row, New York (1980)

Quan, C., Ren, F.: Construction of a blog emotion corpus for chinese emotional expression analysis. In: Proceedings of EMNLP, pp. 1446–1454, August 2009

Radinsky, K., Davidovich, S., Markovitch, S.: Learning to predict from textual data. J. Artif. Intell. Res. **45**(1), 641–684 (2012)

Russo, I., Caselli, T., Rubino, F., Boldrini, E., Martínez-Barco, P.: Emocause: an Easy-adaptable Approach to Emotion Cause Contexts, pp. 153–160. Investigación (2011)

Turner, J.H.: On the Origins of Human Emotions: A Sociological Inquiry into the Evolution of Human Affect. Stanford University Press, California (2000)

Xu, R., Zou, C., Zheng, Y.: A new emotion dictionary based on the distinguish of emotion expression and emotion cognition. J. Chin. Inf. Process. **27**(6), 82–89 (2013)

Xu, L., Lin, H., Pan, Y., Ren, H., Chen, J.: Constructing the affective lexicon ontology. J. China Soc. Sci. Tech. Inf. **27**(2), 180–185 (2008)

Xu, J., Xu, R., Lu, Q., Wang, X.: Coarse-to-fine Sentence-level emotion classification based on the intra-sentence features and sentential context. In: Proceedings of CIKM, pp. 2455–2458, October 2012

Query Intent Detection Based on Clustering of Phrase Embedding

Jiahui Gu[✉], Chong Feng, Xiong Gao, Yashen Wang, and Heyan Huang

School of Compute Science and Technology, Beijing Institute of Technology, Beijing, China
{gujh,fengchong,gaoxiong,yswang,hhy63}@bit.edu.cn

Abstract. Understanding ambiguous or multi-faceted search queries is essential for information retrieval. The task of identifying the major aspects or senses of queries can be viewed as detection of query intents, where the intents are represented as a number of clusters. So the challenging issue in this task is how to generate intent candidates and group them semantically. This paper explores the competence of lexical statistics and embedding method. First a novel term expansion algorithm is designed to sketch all possible intent candidates. Moreover, an efficient query intent generation model is proposed, which learns latent representations for intent candidates via embedding-based methods. And then vectorized intent candidates are clustered and detected as query intents. Experimental results, based on the NTCIR-12 IMine-2 corpus, show that query intent generation model via phrase embedding significantly outperforms the state-of-art clustering algorithms in query intent detection.

Keywords: Query intents · Term expansion algorithm · Phrase embedding

1 Introduction

An intent of a given query could be viewed as an interpretation of an ambiguous query or an aspect of a broad query. Detection of query intents, namely understanding the search intents of queries, contributes to develop effective web search engines [1].

A query, with diversified aspects, may have multiple intents. The more diversified query intents obtained, the more broad coverage of query aspects are. Research studies have been conducted extensively on the leverage of multiple resources, to better diversify query intents. It is worth noting that the idea of combining multiple resources has been successfully exploited [2, 3], which shows it tends to complete each other, and usually yields to select expansion terms from a good quality. Multi-resources and query expansion strategy [2–5] are leveraged in this paper. Whereas for intents from multi-resources, they may be similar or nearly duplicate. Therefore, researchers study to represent intents by clusters, and focus on measuring the similarities among intents. Specifically, [7] conducts clustering with embedding the subtopics or intents into a unified graph structure. [10] proposes a clustering algorithm to mine the major subtopics of queries, where each subtopic is represented by a number of URLs and keywords. Despite of their usefulness, these works face several unique challenges.

© Springer Nature Singapore Pte Ltd. 2016
Y. Li et al. (Eds.): SMP 2016, CCIS 669, pp. 110–122, 2016.
DOI: 10.1007/978-981-10-2993-6_9

- **Supervised models**. They rely on statistic integrity from external information sources, to weight the explicit query concepts or re-weight the expansion terms.
- **Short text**. The query intents or subtopics, called as phrases, usually contain small number of words, providing limited context information for identifying important query intents, especially for the low-frequency phrases.
- **Phrase mismatch problem**. Short text based clustering methods, such as TF-IDF or inter-domain entropy, focus on the surface information and lose the semantic relations among query intents or subtopics.

To address the first challenge, we present a novel term expansion algorithm, incorporating multi-resources to generate intent candidates. Specifically, the algorithm assigns relative importance weights, based on evidence from lexical statistics (e.g., frequency, string cohesion) of the corpus, to quantify query expansion terms or phrases. As far as we know, we are the first to expand intent candidates with lexical statistics.

In addition, due to the challenges of short text and phrase mismatch, local statistical features don't provide a sufficient information for capturing the semantic meaning. Therefore, for intent candidate clustering, we propose to learn the semantic representations of intent candidates via embedding-based methods. As a case in point, phrase embedding could derive more semantic relatedness between phrases, e.g., "*beautiful youth*" and "*handsome boy*" are similar, while short text clustering couldn't do that.

Thus, synthesizing the methods mentioned above, we propose a query intent detection method, including a term expansion algorithm and a query intent generation model (as Fig. 1). Specifically, the novel algorithm is leveraged to identify a weighted set of query-expansion terms, which could be concatenated with the query to generate intent candidates. Vector representations, learned by phrase embedding, are used as features of the clustering algorithms. Note that, the obtained clusters are viewed as query intents.

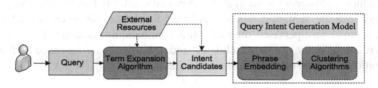

Fig. 1. The process of query intent detection

Experimental results validate the effectiveness of the proposed method, and the main contributions could be summarized as follows: (1) We propose an efficient query intent generation model via semantic representation learning, to cluster intent candidates. (2) We propose a novel term expansion algorithm, by innovatively applying lexical statistics to weight the query-expansion terms. The superiority of the proposed algorithm had been demonstrated by the IMine-2 task in NTCIR-12 [14], in which our best result was ranked No. 2 of all 16 runs in this task[1]. (3) Multiple resources are adopted. Besides,

---

[1] The overview of the NTCIR-12 IMine-2 Task have been released in URL: http://research.nii.ac.jp/ntcir/workshop/OnlineProceedings12/pdf/ntcir/OVERVIEW/01-NTCIR12-OV-IMINE-YamamotoT.pdf.

unsupervised methods are utilized by, in addition to the novel algorithm, as well as the effective model, and could work well for tasks without enough labeled data.

The outline of this paper is as follows. Section 2 summarizes the related work. Sections 3 and 4 formally describes the proposed term expansion algorithm and query intent generation model. Corresponding experimental results are provided in Sect. 5.

2   Related Work

Understanding the ambiguous or multi-faceted queries attracts increasing interests, and extensive approaches have been proposed in [2, 3, 7].

On the perspective of data resources, single resource, such as query logs [8] or Wikipedia [9], achieved relatively good results, but it is difficult to meet the diversity requirement. Therefore, Bouchoucha et al. [3] combined evidence from multiple sources to generate a relevant and diverse list of expansion terms. Bendersky et al. [2] defined a set of external information sources, which they use as a basis for deriving features for either concept weighting or query expansion. However, works [2, 3] were supervised, and depended on statistic integrity from external information resources, to weight the expansion terms. Thus, to avoid these disadvantages, unsupervised method is utilized with the lexical statistics of the corpus to weight query-expansion terms.

Considering the similar query intents or subtopics from multi-resources, clustering algorithms are widely studied. A hierarchical clustering algorithm was used by Tsukuda el al. [15], with the similarity measure of key phrases (n-grams) extracted from snippets. Zhang et al. [7] focused on grouping similar subtopics, by exploiting the dependencies among subtopic candidates based on graph structure. Radlinski et al. [6] clustered similar queries on a click-through bipartite graph to refine the discovered similar queries. These works conducted clustering on short text, and mined similarity features on string surface, which may lose the semantic relation and lead to phrase mismatch. To address the problem, a novel unsupervised method, phrase embedding, is utilized to capture the semantic relations among intent candidates, and perform clustering based on the vector representations, instead of string surface features.

3   Term Expansion Algorithm for Query Intents

This section details the term expansion algorithm, denoted as TEQI. Given a set of raw texts, TEQI first extracts candidate expansion terms, and then a weighting function, based on lexical statistics, is leveraged to obtain a list of query-expansion terms. Following a linear concatenation of the query, intent candidates could be generated.

3.1   Extraction of Candidate Expansion Term

Given the corpus and Chinese queries, we first preprocess them and filter the word segments appeared in both. And put the rest part of the corpus into character set S, namely $S = \{c_1 c_2 c_3 \cdots c_l\}$.. Wherein, l denotes the count of characters in set S. Afterwards, candidate expansion words are extracted by *n-gram* model, in sequence from left to right, and then put into candidate expansion word set (denoted as *CEW*).

3.2 Features of Lexical Statistics

In set *CEW*, there are many noise and meaningless candidate expansion words, e.g., "迅雷下(*xun lei xia*)" and "桌面壁(*zhuo mian bi*)". Thus, the nucleus for selecting effective expansion terms lies in how to measure the properties of word in *CEW*. In our algorithm, the following three features of lexical statistics perform this task.

Frequency (F). A word, with high occurrence frequency in corpus, is intuitively viewed as a potential word. Given word $W_i = c_1 c_2 \ldots c_j$, $1 < j \le n$, the frequency, denoted as F_{w_i}, is calculated using $F_{w_i} = \dfrac{T_{w_i}}{l}$. Where T_{w_i} is the occurrence times of W_i in *CEW*.

String Cohesion (SC). String cohesion emphasizes the correlation of different internal components. The key idea of *SC* is to confirm the word with close internal dependency. Mutual information, with property of reflecting the correlation between two sets of events, becomes a useful criterion to evaluate *SC*. To compute *SC*, we primarily need to enumerate word's cohesive ways, and confirm which two parts the candidate expansion word is composed of. Formally, the *SC* of word W_i is Eq. (1):

$$SC_{W_i} = min\left\{ \log_2 \frac{F_{w_i}}{F_{c_1} * F_{c_2 \ldots c_j}}, \log_2 \frac{F_{w_i}}{F_{c_2 \ldots c_{j-1}} * F_{c_j}} \right\} \tag{1}$$

Wherein, SC_{W_i} denotes the string cohesion of word W_i, and F_c is the frequency of character c. Take "国家公园(*National park*)" for example, *SC* is computed as follows:

$$SC_{国家公园} = min\left\{ \log_2 \frac{F_{国家公园}}{F_{国} * F_{家公园}}, \log_2 \frac{F_{国家公园}}{F_{国家公} * F_{园}} \right\} \tag{2}$$

String Liberalization (SL). String liberalization indicates the neighborhood feature of a string, which is the diversity of adjacent characters. If atring could be a potential word, it will have abundant left and right character sets, and high liberalization. Branch entropy, measuring the degree of uncertainty, is usually leveraged to measure *SL*. For word W_i, define its left character set as $C_l = \{c_1, c_2 \cdots c_i\}$ and right character set as $C_r = \{c_1, c_2 \cdots c_r\}$. Then the left and right branch entropy, respectively marked as *HL* and *HR*, are computed using Eqs. (3) and (4). Also, *SL* takes the smaller one, as Eq. (5). Where $F(c_i w_i)$ and $F(w_i c_j)$ respectively denote the string frequency of $c_i w_i$ and $w_i c_j$.

$$HL_{w_i} = -\sum_{c_i \in C_l} \left[F(c_i w_i) \times \log F(c_i w_i) \right] \tag{3}$$

$$HR_{w_i} = -\sum_{c_j \in C_r} [F(w_i c_j) \times \log F(w_i c_j)] \tag{4}$$

$$SL_{w_i} = min\{HL_{w_i}, HR_{w_i}\} \tag{5}$$

3.3 Ranking and Intent Candidate Generation

Considering the aforementioned features, the weighting function is proposed to detect query-expansion terms with explicit meaning. Accordingly, we score the candidate expansion words in *CEW* using a linear weighted combination of the three features, and rank them based on this score. Formally, the score of a word could be written as:

$$R_w = \alpha_1 F_w + \alpha_2 \widehat{SC}_w + \alpha_3 \widehat{SC}_w \tag{6}$$

Wherein $w \in CEW$, $\sum_{i=1}^{3} \alpha_i = 1$, $\alpha_i \in [0,1]$, α_i are the weights measuring the importance of three features. $\widehat{SL}_w$ and $\widehat{SC}_w$ denote the normalization forms of *SC* and *SL*. This formula captures our intuition that the more a term is ranked on top with high score, the more important it is to the query. Therefore, the top *K* terms from ranked set *CEW* are chosen, and then put into the query-expansion terms set (denoted as *EW*).

Finally, the term expansion algorithm could be briefly summarized in algorithm 1.

Algorithm 1: Term expansion algorithm of query intents (TEQI)

Input: The preprocessed character set *S*, threshold for value *K*, feature weights α_i ($i \in [1,3]$)
Output: A list of query-expansion terms *EW*
Begin:
    Extract *n-grams* (n$\in$[2,10]) from set *S* as set *CEW*
    Initialize *EW* $\leftarrow$ $\emptyset$
    Foreach *n-gram named w in set CEW* do
        Compute F, SC, SL, R_w
        Rank the set *CEW* by R_w
    Extract the top *K* expansion terms in set *CEW* to *EW*
    Return *EW*
End.

Intent Candidate Generation. After obtaining the set *EW*, the intent candidates are generated by the linear concatenation of the query *Q*, and the expansion terms.

4 Query Intent Generation Model via Phrase Embedding

A query intent generation model is outlined in Fig. 2. Taking the intent candidates, from the output of TEQI and resource *related search*, as input, the model is composed of semantic representation learning, and intent candidate clustering. More precisely, the former, based on phrase embedding, learns to map intent candidates into vector representations, which then are used as features of the K-means and Spectral Clustering algorithm to conduct clustering. Specifically, *phrase* is a sequence of Chinese characters, which is larger than a word and smaller than a sentence, such as "**优胜**美地瑜伽会所 (*Yosemite Yoga Club*)" and "夏威夷旅游攻略 (*Tourism strategy of Hawaii*)".

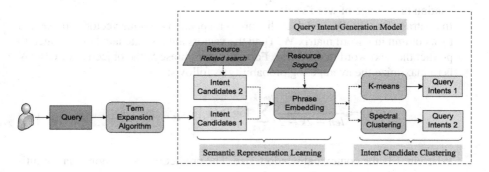

Fig. 2. The detailed description of query intent detection

4.1 Semantic Representation Learning

To learn semantic representations among intent candidates, we propose phrase embedding method based on word vectors. Firstly, we sketch previous methods for learning word vectors, which are the inspiration of our method. Then our phrase embedding based on the CBOW (continuous bag-of-words) and Skip-gram model are introduced.

(1) Learning word vectors

For Skip-gram model, it aims to predict the context words given a target word in a sliding window. The vector of target word is used as features to predict the context words. Given a phrase $S = \{w_1, w_2, \ldots, w_{len}\}$, the objective is to maximize the average log probability:

$$\mathcal{L}(S) = \frac{1}{len} \sum_{t=1}^{len} \sum_{-k \leq c \leq k} \log \Pr(w_{t+c} | w_t) \tag{7}$$

Wherein, *len* is the context size of the target word w_t. k is the contextual window size Skip-Gram formulates the probability $\Pr(w_c | w_i)$ using a softmax function as Eq. (8):

$$\Pr(w_c | w_t) = \frac{e^{\overline{w_c} \cdot \overline{w_t}}}{\sum_{w_i \in V} e^{\overline{w_c} \cdot \overline{w_{len}}}} \tag{8}$$

Wherein, $\bar{w}_t$ and $\bar{w}_c$ are respectively the vector representations of target word w_t and context word w_c, and V represents the word vocabulary.

Each of $y_{w_{t'}}$ is un-normalized log-probability for each output word $w_{t'}$, computed as:

$$y_{w_t} = \mathbf{U}h(w_{t-k}, \ldots, w_{t+k}; \mathbf{W}) + b. \tag{9}$$

Wherein, $\mathbf{U}$ and b are the softmax parameters. And $h(\cdot)$ is constructed by a concatenation or average of word vectors.

In contrast, for CBOW model, each word is mapped to a unique vector, represented by a column in a word matrix $\mathbf{W}$. Then the vectors are concatenated or averaged to predict the next word in a context. Formally, for phrase S, the objective of CBOW is to maximize the average log probability as follows:

$$\mathcal{L}(S) = \frac{1}{len - 2k - 2} \sum_{t=k+1}^{len-k} \log \Pr(w_t | w_{t-k}, \ldots, w_{t+k}) \tag{10}$$

Wherein, k is the contextual window size. The prediction task is done via a multi-class classifier, such as softmax as Eq. (11):

$$\Pr\left(w_t | w_{t-k}, \ldots, w_{t+k}\right) = \frac{e^{y_{w_t}}}{\sum_{w_i \in V} e^{y_{w_i}}} \tag{11}$$

(2) Phrase Embedding based on CBOW(PE-CBOW)

Following the inspiration of algorithms for word embeddings, wherein word vectors are asked to contribute to a prediction task about the next word in the sentence. In the proposed model, the phrase vectors are also asked to contribute to the prediction task of the next word given many contexts. There are three-layers: input layer, project layer and output layer. Wherein, words text window $\{w_1, w_2, \ldots, w_{len}\}$, and phrase ID are the inputs. Every phrase, which acts as a virtual word and is denoted by phrase ID, is mapped to a unique vector $\bar{s}$, represented by a column in matrix $\mathbf{S}$, and every word is also mapped to a unique vector $\bar{w}_i$, represented by a column in matrix $\mathbf{W}$ [12].

Afterward, the phrase vector $\bar{s}$, and word vectors $\{\bar{w}_1, \bar{w}_2, \ldots, \bar{w}_{len}\}$. are averaged to predict the next word in a context. Obviously, compared to the word vector framework, the only change is in Eq. (9), where $h(\cdot)$ is constructed from $\mathbf{W}$ and $\mathbf{S}$. Note that, the contexts are fixed-length (length is len) and sampled from a sliding window over the phrase. The phrase vector is shared across all contexts generated from the same phrase, and the word vector matrix $\mathbf{W}$ is shared across phrase.

(3) Phrase Embedding based on Skip-Gram(PE-SG)

The CBOW-based model above loss information about word order. Furthermore, the skip-gram based model generates word vectors, which ignores the context words in the input, but force the model to predict words randomly sampled from the fix-length contexts of phrase in the output. That is, only phrase vector $\bar{s}$ is used to predict the next word in a text window. The contextual words arno longer used as inputs, whereas they become what the output layer predict. Typically, we sample a text window at each iteration of stochastic gradient descent, then sample a random word from the text window and form a classification task given the sentence vector.

(4) Training Phrase Embedding Models

To make the models efficient for learning, the techniques of hierarchical softmax are used when learning CBOW and Skip-Gram [13]. In the proposed work, the structure of the hierarchical softmax is a binary Huffman tree, which is a good speedup trick because frequent words could be accessed quickly. Moreover, SogouQ[2] resource is adopted to train CBOW and Skip-Gram model. And the vectors are initialized by random with the dimensionality of 100, based on the training method of stochastic gradient descent and backpropagation. Afterwards, the vector representations of intent candidates could be obtained, and then viewed as features of the intent candidate clustering.

4.2 Intent Candidate Clustering

After learning the semantic representations of the intent candidates, K-means and Spectral Clustering (denoted as **SpeC**) are leveraged to group them. Note that the query intents are represented by the generated clusters. The cluster numbers are set between 5 and 10 for the 100 queries, according to objective value, that is the maximal sum of intra cluster similarities. Symbol E is set to represent clustering results in experiments, namely *intent candidates predicted partition*.

5 Experiments

To evaluate the performance of our approach, we conduct the following experiments: (1) we study the impact of term expansion algorithm with extensive experiments, as well as explore its sensitivity to parameter tuning of weights and the number of expansion terms; (2) we compare our methods to several baselines.

5.1 Datasets

Experiments were conducted by incorporating multiple external resources, which could be briefly summarized, as Table 1.

Table 1. Description of datasets used in experiments

Datasets	Descriptions
Queries	The 100 Chinese queries from the NTCIR-12 IMine-2 subtask[a]
C_0	The IMine-2 Chinese web corpus, provided by IMine-2 subtask[b]
C_1	Dataset, collected from search engines[a]
C_2	Dataset from "相关搜索 (Related search)" at the bottom of webpages[a]
SogouQ	Dataset, utilized to train the phrase embedding models in Sect. 4.1

[a]http://www.dl.kuis.kyoto-u.ac.jp/imine2/dataset/

[b]For each query, top 200 pieces of snippets are crawled from the retrieval webpages of the search engines, e.g., Baidu, Google, Bing and Yahoo.

---

[2] http://www.sogou.com/labs/dl/q.html.

Note that, datasets of TEQI comprises C_0 and C_1. Next, to create gold standard for evaluation of the generated intent candidates in Sect. 3.3, eleven annotators manually label the extracted expansion terms in set EW. An expansion term could be viewed as an effective query-expansion term if at least seven annotators agree with it. The annotation leads to 950 expansion terms. And the labeled dataset are partly available online[3]. For example, "*cvs usage*" is an effective query-expansion term, while "*cvs job*" isn't.

In addition, datasets of query intent generation model are composed of C_2, SogouQ and the output of TEQI. For *Intent candidate standard partition(S)*, corresponding to E described in Sect. 4.2, 3,914 intent candidates are collected, and then manually grouped into clusters according to the content words by eleven annotators [7]. An intent candidate could be mapped into a cluster if at least seven annotators agree with it.

5.2   Experimental Setup

There are four parameters in TEQI algorithm: K in the number of expansion terms, and α_1, α_2 and α_3 in ranking function. After some preliminary experiments, the optimal values utilized are $K = 12, \alpha_1 = 0.4, \alpha_2 = 0.3, \alpha_3 = 0.3$.

Evaluation metrics.   Precision (p), recall (r), f-measure (*f-measure*) are utilized, and are computed by Eq. (14) [7]. However, for TEQI, the focus is to extract effective query-expansion terms, and we couldn't assume how many expansion terms the corpus should have. Thus, to evaluate TEQI, p is selected and computed by the function in [11].

$$p(S_j, E_i) = \max \frac{|S_j \cap E_i|}{|E_i|}, r(S_j, E_i) = \max \frac{|S_j \cap E_i|}{|S_j|}, i \in [1, n] \tag{12}$$

$$p_k = \frac{1}{n} \times \sum_{j \in [1,n]} p(S_j, E_i), r_k = \frac{1}{n} \times \sum_{j \in [1,n]} r(S_j, E_i) \tag{13}$$

$$p = \frac{1}{100} \times \sum_{k \in [1,100]} p_k, r = \frac{1}{100} \times \sum_{k \in [1,100]} r_k, f - measure = \frac{2 \times p \times r}{p + r} \tag{14}$$

Wherein character E_i and S_j respectively denote cluster i in *experimental partition* and cluster j in *standard partition* for the same query. $p(E_i, S_j)$ returns the *precision(p)* between E_i and S_j. n is the number of clusters for query k.

Baselines.   We include two categories of comparison methods:

Text-based baselines: **K-means** and **Spectral Clustering** (denoted as **SpeC**) are two state-of-art text clustering approaches, and are chosen as our baselines, using the Python library sklearn with default parameters.

---

3 https://github.com/keaigongzhugu/labeled-dataset.

Embedding-based methods: We construct four variants: **K-means+PE-CBOW, K-means+PE-SG, SpeC+PE-CBOW** and **SpeC+PE-SG**. The main difference between **Text-based baselines** and **Embedding-based methods**, is that the former utilizes statistical information (e.g., TF-IDF) for intent candidates clustering, while the latter conducts cluster, based on phrase embedding method. The variant of **K-means+PE-CBOW** means applying PE-CBOW model to learn vector representations of intent candidates, and then using K-means to conduct cluster. It's similar to another three variants, such as **K-means+Skip-gram, SpeC+CBOW** and **SpeC+Skip-gram**.

5.3   Evaluation of Term Expansion Algorithm

5.3.1   The Performance of TEQI

After training TEQI described in Sect. 3, 1,084 intent expansion terms are obtained. Wherein, 950 are meaningful and 134 are not. Thus, the p value is 0.8764. What's more, Table 2 shows the results of TEQI in the participation of IMine-2 Query Understanding subtask. The evaluation D-nDCG, I-rec and D-#nDCG@l measure the overall relevance and diversity in terms of all the possible intents [14].

Table 2. Results of TEQI in IMine-2 subtask

Teams	I-rec@10	D-nDCG@10	D-#nDCG@10
IRCE	0.4827	0.4290	0.4558
rucir	0.6125	0.6402	0.6264
thuir	0.6287	0.4814	0.5550
TEQI	**0.6240**	**0.5498**	**0.5869**

In terms of precision and evaluation metrics in Table 2, TEQI is desirable in extracting relevant and diverse query-expansion terms. Instead of relying on statistics integrity to weight expansion terms, unsupervised lexical statistics is successfully exploited. And also, a linear weighted combination of the features is utilized to score the query-expansion terms, which has the better computational efficiency. Therefore, the results indicate the superiority of our TEQI algorithm.

In addition, to illustrate the performance of TEQI, we show four examples of results in Table 3. With the limitation of space, the original query is omitted. The first example is a vertical-oriented query, the second is faceted query, and the third is an ambiguous query. We could see that TEQI often gives more specific expansion terms, and distills diverse and compact query intents. This means that the considered multi-resources are complementary in terms of coverage of query intents: the intents by some resources can be recovered by other ones.

Table 3. Examples of intent candidates from TEQI

Queries	刘兰芳评书	速度与激情	星光大道
Query-expansion Terms	有声小说	迅雷下载	朱军
	在线观看	手机游戏	最新一期
	完整版 mp3 下载	剧情介绍 全集	在线观看电视节目

5.3.2 Influence of Parameters to TEQI

An analysis is provided in Table 4, to discuss the combination of the lexical statistic features with varying weights α_i in Eq. (7). **F** is the frequency feature, **SC** is the string cohesion feature and **SL** is the string liberalization feature, mentioned in Sect. 3.2.

Table 4. The precision values with varying weight α_i

Features	α_1	α_2	α_3	p	Features	α_1	α_2	α_3	p
F	1	0	0	0.3040	F+SC+SL	0.8	0.1	0.1	0.4236
SC	0	1	0	0.2461		0.5	0.3	0.2	0.7421
SL	0	0	1	0.2615		0.2	0.5	0.3	0.5826
F+SC	0.5	0.5	0	0.4045		0.1	0.8	0.1	0.4167
F+SL	0.5	0	0.5	0.4051		0.2	0.3	0.5	0.6416
SC+SL	0	0.5	0.5	0.3612		0.1	0.2	0.7	0.4241
F+SC+SL	**0.4**	**0.3**	**0.3**	**0.8764**		0.3	0.3	0.4	0.7954

Single feature, like **F**, is adopted when $\alpha_1 = 1$, $\alpha_2 = 0$ and $\alpha_3 = 0$. It's same to **SC** and **SL**. **F+SC** employs string frequency and string cohesion with $\alpha_1 = 0.5$, $\alpha_2 = 0.5$ and $\alpha_3 = 0$, which is similar to **F+SL** and **SL+SC**. All features are considered for **F+SC +SL**. Due to the space limitation, fourteen groups of α_i settings are exhibited.

Obviously, in all cases, the combination of **F+SC+SL** performs significantly better than the application of single or two features. Besides, the best result is obtained with $\alpha_1 = 0.4, \alpha_2 = 0.3$ and $\alpha_3 = 0.3$, which clearly demonstrates the performance benefits from appropriate weight settings, and the combination of three lexical statistic features.

What's more, in Fig. 3, we plot the impact of parameter K (in terms of precision p) with setting $\alpha_1 = 0.4$, $\alpha_2 = 0.3$ and $\alpha_3 = 0.3$. The figure indicates that our setting $K = 12$ is good for the TEQI algorithm, as a lower value may generate less expansion terms and a higher value may induce more noisy terms.

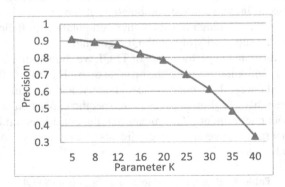

Fig. 3. The precision values with varying parameter K

5.4   Comparison Analysis on Intent Detection

In this subsection, we further employ **Text-based baselines** to compare with our **Embedding-based methods**. In Table 5, we summarizes the detailed comparing results of our methods and baselines. From the table, our method, **SpeC+PE-SG**, significantly outperforms other methods in precision, recall and f-measure. It proves the superiority of the proposed method. More precisely, we have the following observations.

Table 5. The perormance of all clustering methods

Categories	Methods	p	r	f-measure
Text-based	K-means	0.6024	0.6008	0.6016
	Spectral clustering	0.6313	0.6387	0.6350
Embedding-based	K-means+PE-CBOW	0.7516	0.7328	0.7421
	K-means+PE-SG	0.7824	0.7645	0.7733
	SpeC+PE-CBOW	0.8013	0.7907	0.7960
	SpeC+PE-SG	**0.8254**	**0.8162**	**0.8208**

For the comparison of Spectral Clustering and K-means, **SpeC** clearly performs more effective in all cases. The reason is that **SpeC**, applying to non-flat geometry, could identify any shapes of the sample space. However, **K-means** is sensitive to noise and outliers. Accordingly, the properties confirm the superiority of spectral clustering.

The results, in Table 5, verify that **PE-SG** models achieve better effects, indicating that it's better in learning precise semantic relations. Specifically, CBOW model fails to work well, since it is a distributed bag-of-words approach, in which word ordering and semantic interaction between words are not taken into account. However, Skip-gram model considers how each phrase is composed, and succeed to recognize many sophisticated linguistic phenomena. Therefore, the improvement is obvious.

What's more, embedding-based methods receive high performance across all evaluation metrics, as compared to text-based clustering baselines, such as **K-means** and **SpeC**. This is because short text-based clustering suffers from the ignorance of low frequency and string mismatch phrases. Whereas our methods incorporate semantic knowledge into intent candidates, it alleviates the low frequency and string mismatch problem. On the clustering task, our method has an absolute improvement of 19.41 % in terms of precision. Overall, the results in Table 5 showcase the desirable efficiency of semantic clustering than short text clustering.

6   Conclusion and Future Work

In this paper, we propose a novel unsupervised approach for the task of query intent detection, by incorporating the lexical statistics and phrase embedding method. It could jointly optimize the expansion term extraction and semantic clustering, and encourage the former algorithm to enhance the latter. Experimental results, on multi-resources, validate that the proposed approach performs the best, and shows improvement over the compared methods, especially for short texts.

References

1. Liu, Y., Song, R., Zhang, M., Dou, Z., Yamamoto, T., Kato, M.P, Ohshima, H., Zhou, K.: Overview of the NTCIR-11 IMine task. In: NTCIR (2014)
2. Bendersky, M., Metzler, D., Croft, W. B.: Effective query formulation with multiple information sources. In: Proceedings of the Fifth ACM International Conference on Web Search and Data Mining, pp. 443–452. ACM (2012)
3. Bouchoucha, A., Nie, J.Y., Liu, X.: Université de Montréal at the NTCIR-11 IMine task. In: NTCIR(2014)
4. Cui, H., Wen, J.R., Nie, J.Y., Ma, W.Y.: Query expansion by mining user logs. IEEE Trans. Knowl. Data Eng. **15**(4), 829–839 (2003)
5. Bai, J., Song, D., Bruza, P., Nie, J. Y., Cao, G.: Query expansion using term relationships in language models for information retrieval. In: Proceedings of the 14th ACM International Conference on Information and Knowledge Management, pp. 688–695. ACM (2005)
6. Radlinski, F., Szummer, M., Craswell, N.: Inferring query intent from reformulations and clicks. In: Proceedings of the 19th International Conference on World Wide Web, pp. 1171–1172. ACM (2010)
7. Zhang, Z., Sun, L., Han, X.: Learning to mine query subtopics from query log. In: ACL Short papers, vol. 2, p. 341 (2015)
8. Jiang, D., Leung, K.W.T., Ng, W.: Query intent mining with multiple dimensions of web search data. World Wide Web **19**(3), 475–497 (2016)
9. Li, C., Yan, N., Roy, S.B., Lisham, L., Das, G.: Facetedpedia: dynamic generation of query-dependent faceted interfaces for Wikipedia. In: Proceedings of the 19th International Conference on World Wide Web, pp. 651–660, ACM (2010)
10. Hu, Y., Qian, Y., Li, H., Jiang, D., Pei, J., Zheng, Q.: Mining query subtopics from search log data. In: SIGIR (2012)
11. Mei, L., Huang, H., Wei, X., Yuan, P., Mao, X.L.: FCL: a new network words extraction approach based on statistical language knowledge. Chinese National Conference on Social Media Processing. Communications in Computer and Information Science, vol. 568, pp. 119–130. Springer, Singapore (2015)
12. Le, Q.V., Mikolov, T.: Distributed representations of sentences and documents. ICML **14**, 1188–1196 (2014)
13. Mikolov, T., Dean, J.: Distributed representations of words and phrases and their compositionality. Adv. Neural Inf. Process. Syst. (2013)
14. Yamamoto, T., Liu, Y., Zhang, M., Dou, Z., Zhou, K., Markov, I., Kato, M.P, Ohshima, H., Fujita, S.: Overview of the NTCIR-12 IMine-2 task. In: Proceedings of the NTCIR (2016)
15. Tsukuda, K., Dou, Z., Sakai, T.: Microsoft research Asia at the NTCIR-10 Intent Task. In: NTCIR (2013)

Individual Friends Recommendation Based on Random Walk with Restart in Social Networks

Jibing Gong[1,2,3], Xiaoxia Gao[1,2(✉)], Yanqing Song[1,2],
Hong Cheng[4], and Jingjing Xu[1,2]

[1] School of Information Science and Engineering, Yanshan University,
Qinhuangdao City, China
gongjibing@gmail.com, gaoxxysu@gmail.com, songyqysu@gmail.com,
xujjysu@gmail.com
[2] The Key Laboratory for Computer Virtual Technology and System Integration
of Hebei Province, Yanshan University, Qinhuangdao City, China
[3] State Key Lab of Mathematical Engineering and Advanced Computing,
Wuxi, China
[4] Department of Systems Engineering and Engineering Management,
The Chinese University of Hong Kong, Hong Kong, China
hcheng@se.cuhk.edu.hk

Abstract. In social networks, current friend/user recommendation methods are mainly based on similarity measurements among users or the structure of social networks. In this paper, we design a novel friend recommendation method according to a new individual feature *intimacy degree*. Intimacy degree reflects the degree of interaction between two users and further indicates how close two users pay attention to each other. Specifically, we first formally define this problem and perform a theoretical investigation of the problem based on random walk with restart model. And then we design an individual friend recommendation algorithm based on the social structures and behaviors of users. At last, we conduct experiments to verify the method on a real social data set. Experimental results show that the performance of friend recommendation outperforms the existing methods, and the proposed algorithm is effective and efficient in terms of PV Value, UV Value and Conversion Rate.

Keywords: Friend recommendation · Intimacy degree · Random walk model · Social network analysis

1 Introduction

Recommendation is an effective way to reduce the cost for finding information and also a powerful way to attract customers. The flourish of the dynamic social networks provides a new environment for validating the recommendation methods, at the same time brings new challenges, e.g., how to recommend friends according to interaction information?

© Springer Nature Singapore Pte Ltd. 2016
Y. Li et al. (Eds.): SMP 2016, CCIS 669, pp. 123–133, 2016.
DOI: 10.1007/978-981-10-2993-6_10

This paper systematically investigates the friend recommendation problem, and proposes a novel method according to a new individual feature intimacy degree. *Intimacy degree* is defined as the total number of reviewing, forwarding, making comments, clicking a like, replying and making @relationship which two friends give each other in social networks. As we know, interaction relation is a kind of equivalent relation and thus interaction degree can be regarded as one new feature for friend recommendation among users in social networks [1]. According to this above idea (as illustrated in Fig. 1), we propose a novel method based on the social structures and behaviors of users for friend recommendation. Specifically, we first extract friend relationships data and their interacting activities data from social networks. And then we compute the intimacy degree between target users and candidate friends using random walk algorithm (RW) based on a bipartite graph. Finally, we build an individual friends recommendation model in order to provide intelligent recommending service in social networks.

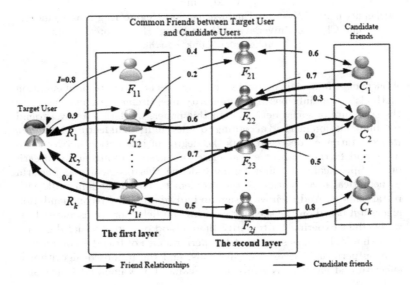

Fig. 1. The architecture of our method

In Fig. 1, I means the set of intimacy degree values, F_{1_i} denotes the ith user in the first layer of friends of Target User, C_k means the kth candidate user being recommended to Target User, F_{2_j} states the jth user in the second layer of friends of Target User, and R_k is the Ranking value of the kth candidate friend.

Individual friend recommendation is an important task in various social-network-based applications such as searching product information and rating, recommending advertisement and services, as well as public sentiment surveillance. But, some challenges still exist:

- Due to the network heterogeneity, it is difficult to find an appropriate method to model social networks in order to make friend recommendation.
- Due to the dynamics of users behaviors and the importance of users interaction, it is challenging to design an effective model to utilize the two properties for friend recommendation.
- It is non-trivial to find a dynamic united model considering the above factors to make individual and effective friend recommendation. In addition, it is very hard to obtain the large volume of real data to validate the proposed recommending methods.

The main contributions of this paper are as follows:

- Aiming at the shortcomings of the existing friend recommendation model of social networks, this paper presents an individual recommendation model based on the social structures and behaviors of users.
- This paper designs a random walk recommendation algorithm, gives algorithm scheme and conducts the implementation of the algorithm.
- We conduct experiments to verify the method on a real social data set. Experimental results show that the performance of friend recommendation outperforms the existing methods, and the proposed algorithm is effective in terms of PV Value, UV Value and Conversion Rate. All data and codes are publicly available.

The rest of our paper is organized as follows. Section 2 describes related work. Section 3 gives the proposed individual friend recommendation algorithm based on random walk (RW). Section 4 describes experimental details and validations of our results, and Sect. 5 offers concluding remarks.

2   Related Work

Most recommendation systems are based on Bipartite Graph, and model connections between two user sets. A bipartite graph (or bigraph) is a graph whose vertices can be divided into two disjoint sets U and V (that is, U and V are each independent sets) such that every edge connects a vertex in U to one in V. Generally, there are edges between two parts and there is not edge among the nodes in the same part. The recommendation system based on bipartite graph hides the characteristics of information between users, and makes the relationship between users abstracted into a mapping recommendation relationship between M users and N users. If user i chooses or has browsed user j, then an edge will exist in the bipartite graph, denoted as $e_{ij} = 1$, otherwise $e_{ij} = 0$ and in this way it will constitute an $M + N$ bipartite graph. The target of such algorithm is to establish a connection between i and the user which has not been selected, recommend Top N users to user i according to the users preferences, use w_{ij} representing user is preferences to user j [2].

Content-based recommendation technology is to analyze the target user information that is selected or browsed by the user [3]. The recommendation process of collaborative filtering system is divided into two steps: the first step is using the existing users history information to calculate the similarity between users [4,5], sorting the neighbor users with similarity degree, and selecting Top N users with a high degree of similarity [6,7]. The second step is computing the score of Top N neighbor users to target user, the user with the higher score will be recommended to target user [8]. Recommendation system based on the structure has also been applied in heterogeneous social networks [9,10]. It can be extended to the individual setting by combining the user behavior logs and user preference information. Additional information such as tags can eventually be integrated into the scope list to improve the accuracy of individual recommendation [11].

3 Individual Friend Recommendation Algorithm Based on RW

Compared to existing friend/user recommendation methods, our individual friend recommendation method is based on the social structures and behaviors of users. Thus, it no longer depends on the users profile information, and instead uses both historical friend and interaction relationships of users. This strategy can help the method effectively avoid the recommendation problems caused by missing users information. Theoretically, our solution should have better recommendation results than existing friend recommendation methods, and better help social network users to find more potential friends.

3.1 Problem Definition

A simple network relationship can be commonly defined as a relational graph, which consists of a set of users (called points), as well as correlation which is called edges between users (such as friend relationship, fans relationship and so on). It can be expressed as $G = <V, E>$ based on graph theory, where V represents the set of all points, E represents the set of all edges on the relational graph. The problem discussed by this paper is: given a point a in V, how to find the most relevant point of a in V. In order to solve this problem, our solution is that we compute and obtain the set of neighbor points which have the largest similarities with a. According to the above way, we calculate all points in set V.

A recommendation relationship can be defined as a bipartite graph relationship formed by users. The bipartite graph network is commonly defined as $G = <U \cup I, E>$, It is shown in Fig. 2.

In Fig. 2, U denotes a set of users, I means another set of users, E states a relationship set between U and I. In our proposed method, U is the set of target users that will receive candidate friends list with ranking values, I is the set of candidate friends that will be recommended to one target user, E means relationships among users, such as friend relationships, fans relationships, comment relationships, @ relationships, and so on.

$$U \qquad E \qquad I$$

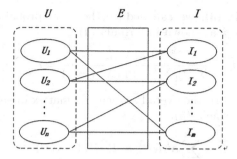

Fig. 2. Bipartite graph of User to User (U2U) degree

3.2   The Method

Random Walk Algorithm.

Aiming at the characters of social networks, this paper is based on the Random Walk algorithm, and introduces an individual friend recommendation method using interaction information to rate the friends of target user. Random Walk (RW) model uses first order Markov Model and thus the status of users probability at the time of $t + 1$ only can be influenced by the time of t on the graph structure, but not by other time. It is expressed by formula (1).

$$\Pr\left(X_{u,t+1} = i \mid X_{u,t}\right) \tag{1}$$

where i represents the set of candidate friends in the system, and m represents the size of the set of candidate friends. So a directed graph G=$< V, E >$ which has m points can be established. Weight $P_{i,j}$ represents the probability moving from point i to point j on the graph. According to the description of formula (1), we get formula (2).

$$P_{i,j} = \Pr\left(X_{u,t+1} = j \mid X_{u,t} = i\right) \tag{2}$$

We can get a $m \times m$ state transition probability matrix P (also, **intimacy transition probability matrix**) according to formula (2). In formula (2), u means the set of all users in the recommending system, n states the size of the user set, $\bar{P}_{i,j}^k$ stands for the column vector of matrix P, $\bar{R}_{u,\_}^*$ denotes the row vector of matrix P, as well as represents the rating value from user u to user m. According to the active information of users on the network, we can establish a $n \times m$ dimensional information matrix between target users and candidate friends. And then, we can obtain the probability transition matrix from target users to candidate friend j at the time of t.

$$\Pr\left(X_{u,t} = j\right) = \alpha \sum_{i=1}^{m} \Pr\left(X_{u,t-1} = i\right) P_{i,j} = \alpha^k \sum_{i=1}^{m} R_{u,i}^* P_{i,j}^k = \alpha^k \bar{R}_{u,\_}^* \bar{P}_{\_,j}^k \tag{3}$$

According to formula (3), we can deduce the total probability formula from target friends to user j, as shown in formula (4).

$$\Pr\left(X_u = j\right) = \frac{\sum_{k=1}^{x} \Pr\left(X_{u,k} = j\right)}{\sum_{k=1}^{x} \sum_{i=1}^{m} \Pr\left(X_{u,k} = i\right)} = c \sum_{k=1}^{x} \alpha^k \bar{R}_{u,-}^* \bar{P}_{-,j}^k \tag{4}$$

According to formula (4), the overall sequencing matrix of each user ratings for all users is given in formula (5).

$$\tilde{R} = \sum_{k=1}^{x} \alpha^k R P^k = R\alpha P \left(1 - \alpha P\right)^{-1} \tag{5}$$

where matrix $\tilde{R}$ reflects the rating that target user to user, we can sequence the ratings that target user to all users according to this matrix, and we can receive the users Top N recommendation by using the result of sequencing.

Random Walk with Restart Algorithm Based on the Bipartite Graph.

Random Walk with Restart(RWR) algorithm calculates similarity between one point and point j according to formula (6).

$$R_t = \left(1 - c\right) \tilde{W} R_{t-1} + c e_j \tag{6}$$

where $c \in (0, 1)$ is restarting probability, $\tilde{W}$ is adjacency matrix, e_j is an initial vector, and R_t is probability distribution vector after t times iteration.

The next key step is how to abstract the friend relation, fans relation, comment relation, retransmission relation and @ relation among users to a target user-user Bipartite Graph, establish grade mechanism among users, then introduce random walk with restart quick algorithm which is based on Bipartite Graph, and individually recommend friends to a target user.

As mentioned above, we can give the process of the **Random Walk with Restart Algorithm** based on the Bipartite Graph, as shown in Table 1.

4   Experimental Results

4.1   Experimental Setup

In this paper, we use Microblog social data from Sina Mobile Client Platform (shortly SMCP) as experimental datasets, and design three solutions to validate our methods on three groups of datasets. Every dataset includes 100,000 users. The detailed information of experimental settings is displayed in Table 2.

New Recommendation strategy: our presented recommendation strategy, New Algorithm: our proposed algorithm, Old Recommendation strategy: the existed recommendation strategy from SMCP, and Old Algorithm: the existed algorithm from SMCP.

In Table 2, the first solution consists of New Recommendation strategy and New Algorithm, the second solution includes New Recommendation strategy and Old Algorithm, and the third solution contains Old Recommendation strategy and Old algorithm.

Table 1. The description of the algorithm based on random walk with restart.

Input:	The normalized matrix $\tilde{W}$ and the start vector r_0
Output:	Stationary distribution probability r
First:	Through $\tilde{W}$ to construct the state transition matrix M
Second:	Segmentation matrix M is $M = M_1 + M_2$, among them M_1 contains all the internal relations, M_2 contains all the cross relations
Third:	Initializer$_{(k)}^{(0)} = \left(r_1^0, r_2^0, ..., r_n^0\right), m = 1$
Fourth:	For $i = 1, 2, ... N$, calculating $\phi_i^{(m-1)} = \dfrac{r_i^{(m-1)}}{\left\|r_i^{(m-1)}\right\|_1}$
Fifth:	Construct the aggregation matrix $A^{(m-1)}$, among them $\left(A^{(m-1)}\right)_{ij} = \phi_i^{(m-1)} M_{ij} e_j$
Sixth:	To solve the characteristic vector $\xi^{(m-1)} = \xi^{(m-1)} A^{(m-1)} + c_{1 \times N}$
Seventh:	For $i = 1, 2, ... N$, get W_i and ξ_i^m

Table 2. The detailed information of the experimental setting

Dataset no	Dataset size	Recommendation strategy	Algorithm
1	100000	New	New
2	100000	New	Old
3	100000	Old	Old

4.2 Evaluation Metrics

- **PV Value (Page View):** It is the number of page views or page exposure. The PV value of one webpage within a day is the total number of visiting this page this day.
- **UV Value (Unique Visitor):** It refers to page independent visiting. A page within a day of the UV value that is the day how many users access the page, a user logs in the page several times a day is only remembered once, that is, UV values of 1.
- **CR (Conversion Rate):** It is defined as the UV value divided by the PV value of the day. The conversion rate is an important indicator of the validation of a recommendation.

4.3 Recommendation Performance Analysis

At the end of the first round launching our experimental scheme, we obtained experimental data from SMCP servers and listed the PV and UV values of these three group experiments in Tables 3, 4, and 5.

In one experimental period, Conversion Rates of the three groups can be obtained and listed in Table 6. According to the result data, we can give the trend graph of Conversion Rate, as shown in Fig. 3.

Table 3. The PV and UV values of the first group experiment.

Time	Login PV	Login UV	Follow PV	Follow UV	Conversion Rate
2012/4/4	423183	31860	992	742	2.33 %
2012/4/5	385415	31050	1131	910	2.93 %
2012/4/6	394291	30708	893	643	2.09 %
2012/4/7	371477	29861	743	411	1.38 %
2012/4/8	373583	30106	528	434	1.44 %
2012/4/9	393173	32448	926	545	1.68 %
2012/4/10	396847	31651	765	608	1.92 %

Table 4. The PV and UV values of the second group experiment.

Time	Login PV	Login UV	Follow PV	Follow UV	Conversion Rate
2012/4/4	403972	30959	902	673	2.17 %
2012/4/5	360750	29859	976	749	2.51 %
2012/4/6	373079	29570	827	588	1.99 %
2012/4/7	342670	28688	568	364	1.27 %
2012/4/8	339181	29095	564	390	1.34 %
2012/4/9	354664	31212	791	477	1.53 %
2012/4/10	355508	30626	798	543	1.77 %

Table 5. The PV and UV values of the third group experiment

Time	Login PV	Login UV	Follow PV	Follow UV	Conversion Rate
2012/4/4	434946	31867	937	646	2.03 %
2012/4/5	389522	30801	932	746	2.42 %
2012/4/6	399585	30564	868	668	2.19 %
2012/4/7	373897	29440	598	408	1.39 %
2012/4/8	368926	29792	507	400	1.34 %
2012/4/9	392042	32107	769	464	1.45 %
2012/4/10	393412	31342	713	511	1.63 %

Table 6. Conversion Rates in one experimental period

Group No	Day 1	Day 2	Day 3	Day 4	Day 5	Day 6	Day 7
Group I	2.33	2.63	2.09	1.68	1.74 %	1.98	2.22
Group II	2.17	2.51	1.99	1.57	1.64 %	1.83	2.07
Group III	2.13	2.32	1.98	1.45	1.65 %	1.75	1.93

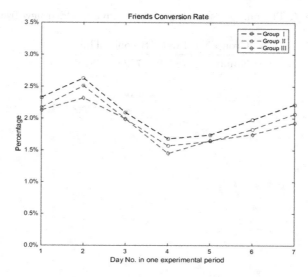

Fig. 3. The trend graph of Conversion Rates

From Fig. 3, the recommended conversion rate of the first group is greater than the second group, and the second group is greater than the third group. The results show that the recommendation effect based on the individual recommendation algorithm is better than the existing recommendation algorithm. At the same time, the experimental results also show that the user acceptance of a recommendation algorithm not only depends on the results of the algorithm itself, but also depends on a good recommendation strategy.

We utilize Sina Microblog Mobile Client Service Platform (SMCP) as the experimental environment. But, due to the limitations of the use of habits and mobile terminal platform, the proportion of users to add friends through the mobile terminal platform is relatively small.

We randomly select three groups of users from the whole micro blog platform data. Although our proposed algorithm is a little better than the existing recommendation one, the advantage is not great. The reason is that the advantages of our algorithm had been scattered to the data of the entire platform when SMCP keeps on running.

4.3.1 Determinating N Value of Top N in Recommendation Results

In this paper, our proposed individual recommendation algorithm adopted recommendation mode of Top N. So, how to determine the value of N became a key problem. In our experiments, we determine the range of N values by analyzing the situation of adding new friends of users from datasets during the experimental period.

Table 7. The number statistics of users having added new friends

Group No	First	Second	Third
Number	78419	77329	78159

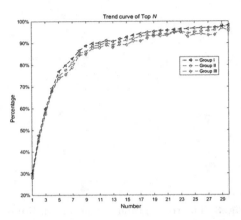

Fig. 4. The trend curve of Top N

We selected users who had added new friends in the experiment period from these three groups of experimental data, and then computed the distribution of each group of the number of the users following behaviors. The number statistics of users that had added new friends or conducted following behaviors are given in Table 7.

From Table 7, the number of adding new friends from three groups in the experimental period had little difference. The reason is that the advantage of our individual recommendation algorithm is weaken by the massive data from entire SMCP. In addition, the distribution trend graph of the number of following new friends in very group of users is given in Fig. 4.

From Fig. 4, the attention/following number of three experimental groups is within 10 in terms of 86 % of users. During the experimental period, it is smaller than 30 in terms of 97 % of users. From the experimental results, it is acceptable that the Top N values were recommended to 0~30. If recommending results were updated more quickly, the value of N can be relatively smaller. Our experimental period is set as 7 days, so it is more reasonable that we took the value N as 30.

5   Conclusions

In this paper, we study a novel problem of individual friend recommendation in social networks, with the objective of finding an effective and dynamic model to utilize the social structures and behaviors of users for friend recommendation. We formally define this problem and perform a theoretical investigation of the problem based on random walk with restart model. We design an individual friend recommendation algorithm and conduct experiments to verify the method on a real social data set. Experimental results on a real social dataset demonstrate the effectiveness and efficiency of the proposed method.

Acknowledgements. The research is supported by the National High Technology Research and Development 863 Program of China under Grant No. 2015AA124102, the Hebei Natural Science Foundation of China under Grant No. F2015203280, the Open Project Program of the State Key Laboratory of Mathematical Engineering and Advanced Computing, and the National Natural Science Foundation of China under Grant No. 61303130. © Springer-Verlag Berlin Heidelberg 2011.

References

1. Zhang, J., Tang, J., Liang, B.Y., Yang, Z., Wang, S.J., Zuo, J.J., Li, J.Z.: Recommendation over a heterogeneous social network. In: Proceedings of the 9th International Conference on Web-Age Information Management (WAIM 2008), pp. 309–316 (2008)
2. Deshpande, M., Karypis, G.: Item-based top-N recommendation algorithms. ACM Trans. Inf. Syst. **22**, 143–177 (2004)
3. Cai, Y., Leung, H., Li, Q., Tang, J., Li, J.Z.: Recommendation based on object typicality. In: Proceedings of the Nineteenth Conference on Information and Knowledge Management (CIKM 2010), pp. 1529–1532 (2010)
4. Xu, B., Bu, J., Chen, C., Cai, D.: An exploration of improving collaborative recommender systems via user-item subgroups. In: Proceedings of the 21st International Conference on World Wide Web, Lyon, France, pp. 21–30 (2012)
5. Cai, Y., Leung, H., Li, Q., Han, H., Tang, J., Li, J.Z.: Typicality-based collaborative filtering recommendation. IEEE Trans. Knowl. Data Eng. (TKDE) **26**(3), 766–779 (2014)
6. Tang, J., Wu, S., Sun, J., Su, H.: Cross-domain collaboration recommendation. In: Proceedings of the Eighteenth ACM SIGKDD International Conference on Knowledge Discovery and Data Mining (KDD 2012), pp. 1285–1293 (2012)
7. Hilmi, Y., Mukkai, S.K.: A random walk methed for alleciating the sparsity problem in collaborative filtering. In: Proceedings of the 4th ACM Conference, pp. 131–138 (2008)
8. Zhang, M., Tang, J., Zhang, X.C., Xue, X.Y.: Addressing cold start in recommender systems: a semi-supervised co-training algorithm. In: Proceedings of the 37th International ACM SIGIR Conference on Research and Development in Information Retrieval (SIGIR 2014), pp. 73–82 (2014)
9. Chiang, M.F., Liou, J.J., Wang, J.L., Peng, W.C., Shan, M.K.: Exploring heterogeneous information networks and random walk with restart for academic search. Knowl. Inf. Syst. **36**, 1–24 (2013)
10. Dong, Y.X., Tang, J., Wu, S., Tian, J.l., Nitesh Chawla, Rao, J.H., Cao, H.H.: Link prediction and recommendation across heterogeneous social networks. In: Proceedings of 2012 IEEE International Conference on Data Mining (ICDM 2012), pp. 181–190 (2012)
11. Liang, H., Xu, Y., Li, Y., Nayak, R., Tao, X.: Connecting users and items with weighted tags for personalized item recommendations. HT 2010, pp. 51–60. ACM (2010)

A Case Study on Active Learning for Event Extraction

Kai Wang, Yingying Qiu, Yu Hong$^{(\boxtimes)}$, Yadong Chen, Jianming Yao,
Qiaoming Zhu, and Guodong Zhou

Natural Language Processing Lab, School of Computer Science and Technology,
Soochow University, Suzhou 215006, China
wangkainlp@gmail.com, yyinqiu@gmail.com, tianxianer@gmail.com,
chinachenyadong@gmail.com, jmyao@szkj.gov.cn, {qmzhu,gdzhou}@suda.edu.cn

Abstract. Supervised event extraction methods suffer from the lack of high-quality event corpora. Active learning is applied to improve the efficiency of manual annotation. In particular, we introduce the uncertainty of argument classification into the active learning for pipeline and joint extraction models. For the pipeline model, we drive active learning to identify and annotate the most informative instances at each extraction stage. It proceeds step-by-step and iteratively until the extraction at each stage reaches the optimal state. While for the joint model, we incorporate active learning with structural perceptron to identify the informative and interdependent event constituents. Experiments on ACE 2005 English corpora show that active learning for pipeline and joint model yield promising improvement.

Keywords: Event extraction · Active learning · Structural perceptron

1 Introduction

Event extraction is an important task in Automatic Content Extraction (ACE). The goal is to precisely extract triggers and closely related arguments (participants) in raw event mentions. The performance of event extraction depends heavily on the quality and quantity of the labelled corpora. However, the existing corpora is small-scaled, such as English ACE 2005[1], which only contains 599 documents. In terms of quality, a trigger expression might represent different event types in different contexts and it may also be annotated as different event types in the same contexts due to different annotators, which may result in uneven quality of trigger annotation. From the instances:

E1: *He **attacked** me.*
E2: *Iraqi **attacked** on U.S. forces.*
E3: *He **left** the company.*
E4: *He **left** the Microsoft.*

---

[1] http://www.nist.gov/speech/tests/ace/2005.

© Springer Nature Singapore Pte Ltd. 2016
Y. Li et al. (Eds.): SMP 2016, CCIS 669, pp. 134–142, 2016.
DOI: 10.1007/978-981-10-2993-6_11

E5: *The outlines for the international stability force were decided at a **conference**.*
E6: *Campbell apologized to British Columbians in a tearful news at a **conference**.*

It's easy to identify the candidate trigger "*attacked*" in above mentioned sentences (E1 and E2) as an Attack event in ACE, while it's relatively difficult to identify "*left*" in sentence E3 as a Transport event and "*left*" in sentence E4 as an End-position event. It's rather difficult to identify the event type of a candidate trigger due to ACE's annotation specifications. For example, the candidate trigger "*conference*" in above mentioned sentences (E5 and E6) represent the same meaning. However, E5 has been annotated as an event with the type of *Meet* while E6 not.

To address the problem, we utilize active learning to improve the quality of corpora and the efficiency of manual annotation. Current active learning method for event extraction [1] only consider the uncertainty of trigger classification, but ignore the uncertainty of argument classification. Thus we introduce the uncertainty of argument classification into active learning for pipeline [2,3] and joint extraction models [4], because the sentences which contain event mentions hold more entities (candidate arguments) than that not. Table 1 shows the statistics.

Table 1. Entitiy distributions of the sentences that contain or not event mentions.

Entity	Contain	Not contain
0–2	755(19.0 %)	7,095(57.2 %)
3–5	1,410(35.6 %)	3,568(28.7 %)
>=6	1,801(45.4 %)	1,746(14.1 %)

The paper is organized as: Sect. 2 briefly introduces pipeline and joint extraction models, Sects. 3 and 4 give the cooperation method with active learning, Sect. 5 shows experimental results, Sect. 6 overviews related work, and finally we conclude the paper in Sect. 7.

2   Pipeline and Joint Extraction Models

The pipeline model consists of two sequential stages: trigger and argument classification. Figure 1 shows an example of pipeline extraction. It firstly classifies the word "*wounded*" as the trigger of an *Injure* event, and secondly employs the event type *Injure* as a new feature for the determination of related arguments, such as those in the example: "*seven people*", "*the terrorists*", and "*Bagdad*" which respectively play the roles of *Victim*, *Agent* and *Place*.

Pipeline model generally suffers from the error propagation. Li et al. [4] attempts to fix the problem by joint model. Instead of the pipeline model predicting the type of a trigger or an argument respectively, the joint model predict

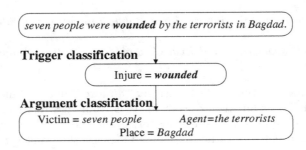

Fig. 1. A two-stage pipeline model

them simultaneously by a structured representation consisting of the sequence of triggers, arguments, and other words. The structured representation of sentence "*Gates founded Microsoft.*" is shown as follows.

$\mathbf{x}=< Gates_{PER}, founded, Microsoft_{ORG} >$
$\mathbf{y}=< \varnothing, Star\_Org(Agent,Org), \varnothing>$

where $\mathbf{x}$ is the input of the sentence and $\mathbf{y}$ is the structured predication of $\mathbf{x}$; The trigger *founded* evokes the *Start_Org* event, and the arguments *Gates* and *Microsoft* act as the roles *Agent* and *Org*; The argument *Gates* or *Microsoft* does not evoke any event type, thus the event type is empty with $\varnothing$.

3   Active Learning for Pipeline Model

The active learning for pipeline model begins instances selection by preferring the most informative instances in trigger classification until they are performing sufficiently well, at which point the instances are selected in argument classification.

We employ an uncertainty metric to measure the prediction reliability for trigger or argument classification. In particular, the prediction probabilities on K types of trigger or argument are denoted as $P = \{p_1, p_2 \ldots p_K\}$. The uncertainty metric U of a trigger or an argument can be simply picked as the maximum probability in P.

$$U = 1 - p_{max} \tag{1}$$

The prediction reliability of a sentence is under the joint action of triggers and arguments in it, which is denoted as follows:

$$Q_{pipeline} = \alpha \cdot U_{trg} + \beta \cdot U_{arg} \tag{2}$$

The contributions of the trigger classification and the argument classification are assigned by the weighting coefficients α and β, respectively. The higher value of $Q_{pipeline}$ indicates the more uncertainty of a sentence. U_{trg} and U_{arg} denote the average uncertainties of all triggers and arguments in a sentence.

$$U_{trg} = \frac{\sum_{word} U_{word}}{n_{word}} \tag{3}$$

$$U_{arg} = \frac{\sum_{trg} \sum_{ner} U_{ner}}{n_{trg} \cdot n_{ner}} \tag{4}$$

Given a sentence, U_{word} denotes the uncertainty of a word as candidate trigger, and n_{word} is the number of words in the sentence; U_{ner} denotes the uncertainty of a given entity as candidate argument; n_{trg} and n_{ner} denote the number of triggers and entities in the sentence, respectively.

Then we propose an algorithm of active learning for our pipeline model in event extraction, as shown in Algorithm 1.

We initialize $\alpha = 1$ and $\beta = 0$ to prefer most uncertain instances in trigger classification at the beginning of instances selection, with an aim to reduce error propagation. Lines 8–11 update the weight α and β according to the relative variation of the average uncertainties of trigger and argument classification in different iterations. Generally, the average uncertainty value would be reduced with increasing iteration number. In addition, the decreasing magnitude of average uncertainties of trigger or argument classification means that the importance of the corresponding subtask would increase more rapidly.

4   Active Learning for Joint Model

Generally, a joint model predicts the triggers and arguments simultaneously in event extraction. It is able to effectively reduce the error propagation in pipeline method. However, to the joint model, the search space becomes much more complex. To solve the problem, we incorporate active learning to select informative instances from unlabelled data for annotation step (see the 3rd line of Algorithm 2). Different from the learning process in pipeline model, i.e., step by step and independently at each stage, the active learning towards joint model predicts the uncertainty of event constitutes simultaneously. It regards a structured representation (a sequence) of triggers, arguments and other common words as an inseparable unit. The query function in active learning for joint model is applied to measure the uncertainty of an unlabelled sentence.

$$Q_{joint} = \frac{score_2}{score_1 - score_2} \tag{5}$$

where $score_i$ denotes the score of the i-th candidate result of a sentence; Algorithm 2 depicts the active learning method for joint model.

5   Experiments

5.1   Experimental Setting

Data sets: We employ the ACE 2005 English corpus as the benchmark data, which involves 33 event subtypes. The corpus contains 599 documents and

---

Algorithm 1. active learning for pipeline model

Require:
    S_l: labelled data set
    S_u: unlabelled data set
    n: batch size
    T: number of iterations
    λ: update rate
Ensure:
    C_{trg}: trigger classifier
    C_{arg} argument classifier
1: **Initialize:** $\alpha = 1, \beta = 0$
2: **Repeat** $t = 1 \cdots T$
3: Learn classifier C_{trg} and C_{arg} from S_l
4: Use classifier C_{trg} and C_{arg} to classify instances in S_u
5: Choose the n most uncertain predicted instances S_s to manual label according to $Q_{pipeline}$
6: Add instances S_s to S_l with their manual labels and remove S_s from S_u
7: Calculate the average uncertainties all the triggers and arguments in $S_u : \overline{U}^t_{trg} = (\sum_{s \in S_u} U^t_{trg}) / |S_u|$ and $\overline{U}^t_{arg} = (\sum_{s \in S_u} U^t_{arg}) / |S_u|$
8: $\Delta^t_{trg} = (\overline{U}^{t-1}_{trg} - \overline{U}^t_{trg}) / \overline{U}^t_{trg}, \Delta^t_{arg} = (\overline{U}^{t-1}_{arg} - \overline{U}^t_{arg}) / \overline{U}^{t-1}_{arg}$
9: $\Delta^t_{trg} = \Delta^t_{trg} / (\sqrt{\Delta^t_{trg}})^2 + \Delta^t_{arg})^2, \Delta^t_{arg} = \Delta^t_{arg} / (\sqrt{\Delta^t_{trg}})^2 + \Delta^t_{arg})^2$
10: $\alpha = \alpha + \lambda \cdot \Delta^t_{trg}, \beta = \beta + \lambda \cdot \Delta^t_{arg}$
11: $\alpha = \alpha / \sqrt{\alpha^2 + \beta^2}, \beta = \beta / \sqrt{\alpha^2 + \beta^2}$
12: **Until** certain number of instances are labelled

16,375 sentences. We randomly select 200 sentences as the seed set for active learning and 2,000 ones as the test set. The remaining 14,175 sentences are used as the unlabelled set. The batch size for active learning is set as 200.

Classification algorithm: We utilize maximum entropy classifier of Mallet Toolkits[2] in pipeline model and structured perceptron in joint model.

Feature: The feature used in the classifiers focus on lexical, syntactic and entity level [4].

Evaluation metric: We evaluate the event extraction models with the learning curves for trigger classification and argument classification (F_1_score).

5.2   Experimental Results

In this section, we evaluate active learning methods for pipeline and joint models in event extraction. For comparison, we implement six systems in Table 2.

    Figures 2 and 3 depict the learning curves of trigger classification and argument classification for each active learning method. The horizontal axes denote

---

[2] http://mallet.cs.umass.edu.

Algorithm 2. active learning for joint model

Require:
   S_l: labelled data set
   S_u: unlabelled data set
   n: batch size
   T: number of iterations
Ensure:
   C_{joint}: joint model of extraction
1: **Repeat** $t = 1 \cdots T$
2: Learn joint model C_{joint} from S_l
3: Use joint model C_{joint} to to tag instances in S_u
4: Choose the n most uncertain predicted instances S_s to manual label according to
   Q_{joint}
5: Add instances S_s to S_l with their manual labels and remove S_s from S_u
6: **Until** certain number of instances are labelled

Table 2. Experimental systems.

Systems	Description
PipeRan	Using random instances selection in active learning for pipeline model.
JointRan	Using random instances selection in active learning for joint model.
Trigger	Using active learning for pipeline model and only consider the uncertainty of trigger classification.
CoTesting	Considering both the uncertainty of trigger classification and that of sentence-based event type classification [1].
PipeUni	Using active learning for pipeline model and setting uniform weight of Eq. (2) with $\alpha = 1$, $\beta = 1$.
PipeDyn	Using active learning for pipeline model with query function Eq. (2).
Joint	Using active learning for joint model with query function Eq. (5).

learning iterations, and the vertical axes denote F_1_score. According to these figures, Trigger significantly outperforms PipeRan and JointRan, verifying the effectiveness of active learning to reduce annotation efforts.

PipeDyn slightly outperforms Trigger, demonstrating the advantages of considering both the uncertainties of trigger classification and argument classification in the query function, because the sentences which contain event mentions hold more arguments than that do not. PipeDyn is superior to PipeUni in trigger classification, on account of preferring most uncertain instances in trigger classification at the beginning annotation to reduce error propagation. While PipeDyn is comparable to PipeUni in argument classification, it is because PipeUni pays

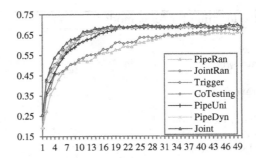

Fig. 2. Learning curves for trigger classification

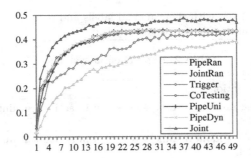

Fig. 3. Learning curves for argument classification

more attention to argument classification than PipeDyn at the beginning of instances selection.

Joint performs better than CoTesting, demonstrating the joint model is more compatible to the active learning methods. The reason is that CoTesting ignores the uncertainty of argument classification, while Joint introduces the uncertainty of argument classification into active learning via structured representation.

6   Related Work

Most studies about ACE event extraction rely on pipeline models which consist of separate local classifiers for trigger classifier and argument classifier [2,3,5–9]. Sequential pipelines with multiple stages usually suffer from error propagation. While for the joint model based method, Li et al. [4] propose a joint framework based on structured perceptron, which extracts triggers and arguments together.

Different training instances differ in containing quantity of information which greatly effect the extraction performance. Hence, we propose active learning to improve the quality of corpora and the efficiency of manual annotation. Active learning has been widely used in a variety of NLP tasks: POS tagging [10], named entity recognition [11], entity-centric relation extraction [12], and event extraction [1].

7   Conclusion

We apply active learning into pipeline model and joint model in event extraction with the goal of reducing human annotation requirements and achieving higher performance only by a smaller number of training instances. Experimental results show the effectiveness of active learning to achieve comparable performance with lower annotation costs, and active learning for joint model achieves the best performance.

Acknowledgments. This research is supported by the National Natural Science Foundation of China, No. 61672368, No. 61373097, No. 61672367, No. 61272259. The authors would like to thank the anonymous reviewers for their insightful comments and suggestions. Yu Hong, Professor Associate in Soochow University, is the corresponding author of the paper, whose email address is `tianxianer@gmail.com`.

References

1. Liao, S., Grishman, R.: Using prediction from sentential scope to build a pseudo co-testing learner for event extraction. In: Proceedings of the 5th International Joint Conference on Natural Language Processing, pp. 714–722 (2011)
2. Ji, H., Grishman, R.: Refining event extraction through cross-document inference. In: Proceedings of the Meeting of the Association for Computational Linguistics, 15–20 June 2008, Columbus, Ohio, USA, ACL 2008, pp. 254–262 (2008)
3. Hong, Y., Zhang, J., Ma, B., Yao, J., Zhou, G., Zhu, Q.: Using cross-entity inference to improve event extraction. In: Meeting of the Association for Computational Linguistics: Human Language Technologies, pp. 1127–1136 (2011)
4. Li, Q., Ji, H., Huang, L.: Joint event extraction via structured prediction with global features. In: ACL (1), pp. 73–82 (2013)
5. Grishman, R., Westbrook, D., Meyers, A.: NYU's English ACE 2005 system description. J. Satisf. **51**(11), 1927–1938 (2005)
6. Ahn, D.: The stages of event extraction. In: Proceedings of the Workshop on Annotating Reasoning About Time Events, pp. 1–8 (2006)
7. Liao, S., Grishman, R.: Using document level cross-event inference to improve event extraction. In: Proceedings of the 48th Annual Meeting of the Association for Computational Linguistics, pp. 789–797. Association for Computational Linguistics (2010)
8. Li, P., Zhou, G., Zhu, Q., Hou, L.: Employing compositional semantics and discourse consistency in Chinese event extraction. In: Joint Conference on Empirical Methods in Natural Language Processing and Computational Natural Language Learning, pp. 1006–1016 (2012)
9. Chen, Y., Xu, L., Liu, K., Zeng, D., Zhao, J.: Event extraction via dynamic multi-pooling convolutional neural networks. In: The Meeting of the Association for Computational Linguistics (2015)
10. Ringger, E., Mcclanahan, P., Haertel, R., Busby, G., Carmen, M., Carroll, J., Seppi, K., Lonsdale, D.: Active learning for part-of-speech tagging: accelerating corpus annotation. In: Linguistic Annotation Workshop, pp. 101–108 (2007)

11. Tomanek, K., Hahn, U.: Semi-supervised active learning for sequence labeling. In: Proceedings of the Meeting of the Association for Computational Linguistics and the International Joint Conference on Natural Language Processing of the AFNLP, 2–7 August 2009, Singapore, ACL 2009, pp. 1039–1047 (2009)
12. Roth, D., Small, K.: Active learning for pipeline models. In: AAAI Conference on Artificial Intelligence, pp. 683–688 (2008)

Word Representation on Small Background Texts

Lishuang Li[✉], Zhenchao Jiang, Yang Liu, and Degen Huang

School of Computer Science and Technology, Dalian University of Technology,
Dalian, Liaoning, China
{lilishuang314,jzc_nlp}@163.com, 1396924332@qq.com,
huangdg@dlut.edu.cn

Abstract. Vector representations of words learned from large scale background texts can be used as useful features in natural language processing and machine learning applications. Word representations in previous works were often trained on large-scale unlabeled texts. However, in some scenarios, large scale background texts are not available. Therefore, in this paper, we propose a novel word representation model based on maximum-margin to train word representation using small set of background texts. Experimental results show many advantages of our method.

Keywords: Natural language processing · Maximum margin · Word representation · Small background texts

1 Introduction

Word vectors can be used as extra features or inputs to learning algorithms in natural language processing (NLP) applications. Previous word representation methods leveraged techniques such as language model [1], skip-gram model, continuous Bag-of-word (CBOW) model [2], matrix factorization [3], Convolutional Neural Networks [4, 5], Dirichlet Multinomial Mixture Model [6], morpheme [7], word ambiguity, word proximity [8], dependency [9], and bilinear energy function [10], and most of them utilized neural networks where logistic function and softmax function were often implemented at the final layer.

Word representations in previous works were often trained on large-scale unlabeled texts. For example, Pennington et al. (2014) used Wikipedia, Gigaword 5 and Common Crawl to learn word representations, each of which contained billions of tokens. There was not always a monotonic increase in performance as the amount of background texts increased.

On the other hand, background texts in some domain are still a comparatively scarce resource, especially in non-English languages, such as electronic medical record, traditional Chinese medicine side effect, English-Oromo machine translation, and certain Kaggle competition including a text field of description of education projects. For these NLP applications, it is difficult to obtain large-scale background texts, thus it is difficult to give full play to the role of previous word representation models. Although Convolutional Neural Networks based model [5] and Dirichlet Multinomial Mixture Model [6] have been proposed for sentiment analysis and

© Springer Nature Singapore Pte Ltd. 2016
Y. Li et al. (Eds.): SMP 2016, CCIS 669, pp. 143–150, 2016.
DOI: 10.1007/978-981-10-2993-6_12

clustering of short texts, they did not aim to provide word embeddings for general NLP applications as skip-gram [2] and GloVe [3] did. Therefore, a word representation method using small background texts is motivated.

The goal of this paper is to learn word representation using small background texts to improve the performance of NLP systems such as relation extraction and sentiment analysis. Inspired by the advantages of Support Vector Machine (SVM) in solving the small data set, we focus on how to effectively train word representations on small background texts and propose a novel word representation model based on maximum-margin theory, which efficiently learns high-quality vector representation of words from small set of unlabeled texts.

Experimental evidence shows that existing word vectors trained on large collections of texts are not good enough in specialized domains, domain-oriented word representations can perform better than general-purposed ones, and can improve the performance of NLP systems.

Experimental results show that word vectors trained by GloVe using Wikipedia 2014 (6B tokens)[1] reach an F-score of 53.3 % on AIMed, whereas those trained by our method using MedLine abstracts (33,491 tokens) reach 61.9 % F-score, which motivates us to propose a novel domain-oriented word representation method, especially on small background texts.

2 Method

We train target words by its surrounding words since context can make explicit the meaning of a word. For each target word i, the corresponding word vector $x^{(i)}$ is trained using back-propagation algorithm, which will be illustrated in detail in the following

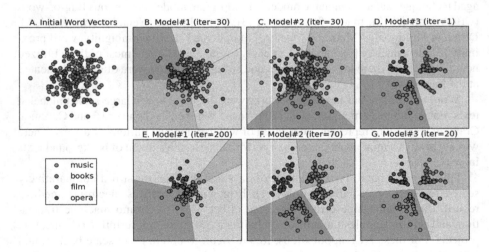

Fig. 1. Word representations trained by the three models.

[1] http://nlp.stanford.edu/projects/glove/.

sections. To give an intuitive comparison and further illustrate our motivation, we collect 200 instances from Freebase[2] falling into 4 domains, music, book, film and opera, initialized as shown in Fig. 1(A).

2.1 Model#1

For a given surrounding word y, the objective of the word representation is to let the prediction $\hat{y}^{(i)}$ equal to $y^{(i)}$,

$$\hat{y}^{(i)} = \arg\max_k \frac{\theta_k^T x^{(i)}}{\sum_j \theta_j^T x^{(i)}} \tag{1}$$

where $x^{(i)}$ is the corresponding word vector of target word i, and θ is the parameter of the model (weight matrix). To achieve this, on each training iteration we perform:

$$\theta_j := \theta_j - \alpha \sum_{i=1}^m x^{(i)} \left(y^{(i)} - \hat{y}^{(i)} \right) \tag{2}$$

and

$$x^{(i)} := x^{(i)} - \alpha \left(y^{(i)} - \hat{y}^{(i)} \right) \theta^T \tag{3}$$

so that the parameters and word vectors can be updated on each training iteration, where α is the learning rate.

As shown in Fig. 1 (B and E), during the training, the word vectors are easy to move toward the origin to minimize the errors. However, once a point x_i is close to the origin, it only needs to move a little step near the origin to correct the classification according to the update rules. Consequently, it will never escape the region around the origin, which is unfavorable to learn of distributed representation.

2.2 Model#2

Due to the limitation of Model#1, we improve the word representation model by incorporating the idea of sigmoid function. Thus the objective of the new model is to minimize cost function as (4):

$$J(\theta) = -\frac{1}{m} \sum_{i=1}^m \sum_{j=1}^k 1\left\{ y^{(i)} = j \right\} \log \frac{e^{\theta_j^T x^{(i)}}}{\sum_{l=1}^k e^{\theta_l^T x^{(i)}}}, \tag{4}$$

where $1\{\cdot\}$ is the indicator function, so that $1\{$a true statement$\} = 1$ and $1\{$a false statement$\} = 0$. On each training iteration we perform:

---

2 https://www.freebase.com/.

$$\theta_j := \theta_j + \alpha \frac{1}{m} \sum_{i=1}^{m} x^{(i)} \left(1\{y^{(i)} = j\} - \frac{e^{\theta_j^T x^{(i)}}}{\sum_{l=1}^{k} e^{\theta_l^T x^{(i)}}} \right) \tag{5}$$

and

$$x^{(i)} := x^{(i)} + \alpha \frac{1}{m} \sum_{i=1}^{m} \sum_{j=1}^{k} 1\{y^{(i)} = j\} \left(\theta_j^T - \frac{\sum_{l=1}^{k} \theta_l^T e^{\theta_l^T x^{(i)}}}{\sum_{l=1}^{k} e^{\theta_l^T x^{(i)}}} \right). \tag{6}$$

As shown in Fig. 1 (C and F), each point keeps moving all the time as long as the prediction is not equal to $y^{(i)}$. Finally the word vectors are well distributed as shown in Fig. 1 F, which is much better than Model#1 does (Fig. 1 E).However, Model#2 takes 70 iterations to converge, which we think is not fast enough.

2.3 Model#3

To overcome the shortage of Model#2 and train word vectors in less iterations, we introduce the idea of maximum-margin. The cost function of Model#3 is:

$$J(\theta) = \max\left(0, 1 + \max_{t \neq y^{(i)}} \theta_t^T x^{(i)} - \theta_{y^{(i)}}^T x^{(i)} \right) \tag{7}$$

On each iteration if:

$$1 + \max_{t \neq y^{(i)}} \theta_t^T x^{(i)} - \theta_{y^{(i)}}^T x^{(i)} > 0, \tag{8}$$

we perform:

$$\theta_t := \theta_t - \alpha x^{(i)} \tag{9}$$

and

$$\theta_{y^{(i)}} := \theta_{y^{(i)}} + \alpha x^{(i)} \tag{10}$$

and

$$x^{(i)} := x^{(i)} - \alpha \left(\theta_t - \theta_{y^{(i)}} \right). \tag{11}$$

As shown in Fig. 1 (D and G), all the points are well separated at the first iteration (D), and remain approximately constant in subsequent iterations (G). Model#3 takes 1 iteration (Fig. 1 D) and obtains almost the same word representation as Model#2 which takes 70 iterations (Fig. 1 G).It can be inferred thatModel#3 give better word vectors for specialized domain tasks, because it uses less iterations to converge, while word vectors are well separated.

2.4   Optional Model#3

The parameters θ and word vector $x^{(i)}$ are trained by stochastic gradient descent. To update the word vector $x^{(i)}$ and parameter θ of Model#3, $\max_{t \neq y^{(i)}} \theta_t^T x^{(i)}$ should be first calculated. Usually the vocabulary size of background texts ranges from thousand to billion, and correspondingly there are at least thousands of rows in θ, which makes the computational cost too much to afford. Therefore, although Model#3 has been much faster than Model#2, an optional version of Model#3 is proposed to modify the model by removing $\max_{t \neq y^{(i)}} \theta_t^T x^{(i)}$ when the computational cost cannot be afforded.

3   Experimental Settings

Since the ultimate goal of word representation is to boost the learning models for NLP systems, we think it is better to evaluate word representation immediately in a certain NLP scenario, rather than just testing whether word vectors can encode word analogies by vector equations or not [2]. Therefore, in this paper, we evaluate the word representation models on a practical biomedical NLP task.

3.1   Evaluation Method

We subject word vectors into Protein-Protein Interaction Extraction (PPIE) task as [11] did. By doing so, we clearly see how word representations influence the extraction performance and further give some recommendations about how to choose word representation models for NLP systems.

All evaluation results are reported using the F-score. For PPIE, we perform pair-wise 10-folds cross-validation (randomly partitioned) on each corpus and report the macro-average F-score.

3.2   Dataset

The dataset consists of two parts: the first one to train word representations is background texts from MedLine, and the second one to evaluate the performance of word representations contains five publicly available PPI corpora: AIMed [12], BioInfer [13], HPRD50 [14], IEPA [15] and LLL [16]. To study the influence of corpus size, we build 19 background text sets, with different number of sentences ranging from 10 thousands to 1 million.

3.3   Group Settings

We compare Model#3 with Skip-gram model, CBOW model, and GloVe model. To study the relationship between word representation and background text size, and compare the performance of the four models in detail, we train word representations over 19 set of background texts, and shows their performance by integrating the word vectors into PPIE system.

4   Results and Discussion

4.1   Model Analysis: Background Text Size

In Table 1, due to space limitation, we only report the F-scores on the two largest corpora: AIMed and BioInfer. We show the performance on the PPIE task for word vectors trained on the 19 set of background texts.

Table 1. Evaluation of four word representation models with background text ranging from 10–1000 thousands sentences. PPIs are extracted using logistic regression. The dimension of all word vectors are 400.

Text Size	AIMed				BioInfer			
	SG	CBOW	GloVe	Model#3	SG	CBOW	GloVe	Model#3
10t	37.0 %	36.5 %	0.0 %	61.3 %	53.6 %	53.4 %	37.0 %	73.6 %
20t	40.9 %	39.1 %	9.8 %	60.3 %	56.0 %	53.8 %	43.1 %	73.7 %
30t	43.8 %	42.3 %	11.2 %	60.7 %	58.7 %	57.6 %	43.7 %	72.0 %
40t	40.7 %	41.0 %	12.7 %	60.5 %	59.6 %	58.0 %	45.2 %	73.0 %
50t	46.8 %	42.8 %	15.8 %	61.4 %	61.2 %	58.6 %	45.6 %	72.1 %
60t	47.0 %	43.6 %	20.1 %	60.9 %	61.0 %	60.2 %	48.9 %	73.5 %
70t	45.7 %	45.0 %	23.3 %	59.7 %	62.5 %	61.4 %	50.5 %	72.8 %
80t	50.2 %	47.6 %	21.9 %	61.0 %	63.6 %	61.9 %	50.8 %	72.9 %
90t	47.2 %	46.6 %	31.8 %	60.1 %	63.8 %	62.7 %	53.0 %	72.3 %
100t	51.8 %	49.0 %	29.6 %	61.0 %	63.6 %	63.0 %	52.3 %	73.2 %
200t	53.9 %	51.8 %	45.4 %	60.5 %	67.9 %	67.9 %	59.1 %	73.2 %
300t	54.6 %	52.9 %	49.1 %	60.0 %	67.8 %	67.4 %	61.9 %	73.8 %
400t	54.6 %	54.2 %	49.8 %	60.7 %	69.0 %	67.6 %	64.1 %	73.1 %
500t	54.1 %	54.6 %	51.6 %	60.1 %	70.3 %	69.4 %	65.5 %	72.9 %
600t	54.9 %	55.8 %	52.9 %	61.3 %	69.7 %	68.5 %	66.2 %	73.2 %
400t	57.2 %	54.9 %	53.5 %	61.0 %	70.3 %	69.7 %	66.1 %	73.4 %
800t	55.1 %	55.3 %	55.1 %	60.9 %	69.7 %	69.0 %	66.3 %	72.2 %
900t	54.5 %	54.0 %	56.4 %	59.8 %	70.0 %	69.2 %	67.3 %	72.7 %
1000t	57.2 %	55.9 %	54.7 %	62.0 %	70.2 %	69.8 %	67.2 %	72.5 %

Interestingly, we observe that, on AIMed and BioInfer, the performance of Model#3 is independent of the size of background texts. Unlike Skip-gram, CBOW and GloVe, the number of training sentences hardly influences the performance of Model#3. For example, on AIMed, word vectors trained on background texts with 10 thousands sentences achieve an F-score of 61.3 %, while those trained on 1000 thousands sentences achieve an F-score of 62.2 % and Table 1 shows the similar performance on BioInfer. It is a good feature of Model#3 to keep steady performance on different size of background texts, and it is a good feature for NLP domains with scarce resources.

Since the maximum-margin theory is used most notably for SVM, which has performed many advantages in solving the small data set [17], it is easy to understand why

Model#3 performs well even using small background texts even with 10 thousands sentences. Therefore, Model#3 is recommended for NLP scenarios with small background texts, especially when less than 200 thousands background sentences are available.

4.2 Model Analysis: Comparison with Other Word Representation Models

As the previous sections have described, the performance of Model#3 is almost dependent of training background text size, whereas Skip-gram, CBOW and GloVe do not. For example, on AIMed, word vectors trained using Skip-gram model on background texts with 10 thousands sentences achieve an F-score of 37.0 %, and the performance gets better as the size of background texts increases, and achieves an F-score of 62.2 % when trained on 1000 thousands sentences.

Generally, the performance of all models has a ceiling, e.g., the F-score of CBOW on AIMed halts between 54.6 % and 55.9 % after 300t. In our experiments, Model#3 obviously performs better than the other models of the same group as shown in Table 1.

5 Conclusion

Domain-oriented word representations can perform better than general-purposed ones in NLP systems. In this paper, we propose a novel word representation model based on maximum-margin theory for NLP scenarios with small background texts, and compare it with Skip-gram, CBOW and GloVe. The experimental results show several advantages of our method.

Firstly, we theoretically illustrate that Model#3 converges much faster than Model#1 and Model#2 while Model#3 can obtain ideal word representations. Secondly, we show that Model#3 performs better than Skip-gram, CBOW and GloVe when trained on less than 1 million of background sentences in our experiments. Thirdly, we find that Model#3 performs more steadily in all groups of experiments mainly due to the theory of maximum-margin. Therefore, Model#3 is recommended for NLP scenarios with small background texts.

In our future works, we plan to incorporate richer information such as dependency to improve Model#3 to learn better word representation on small background texts.

Acknowledgments. The authors gratefully acknowledge the financial support provided by the National Natural Science Foundation of China under No. 61672126, 61173101, 61672127. The Titan X used for this research was donated by the NVIDIA Corporation.

References

1. Bengio, Y., Ducharme, R., Vincent, P., Janvin, C.: A neural probabilistic language model. J. Mach. Learn. Res. **3**, 1137–1155 (2003)
2. Mikolov, T., Chen, K., Corrado, G., Dean, J: Efficient estimation of word representations in vector space. arXiv preprint arXiv:1301.3781 (2013)

3. Pennington, J., Socher, R., Manning, C.D.: Glove: global vectors for word representation. In: Proceedings of the 2014 Conference on Empirical Methods in Natural Language Processing, Doha, Qatar, pp. 1532–1543 (2014)
4. Collobert, R., Weston, J., Bottou, L., Karlen, M., Kavukcuoglu, K., Kuksa, P.: Natural language processing (almost) from scratch. J. Mach. Learn. Res. (JMLR) **12**, 2493–2537 (2011)
5. Dos Santos, C.N., Gatti, M.: Deep convolutional neural networks for sentiment analysis of short texts. In: Proceedings of COLING 2014, Dublin, Ireland, pp. 69–78 (2014)
6. Yin, J., Wang, J.: A dirichlet multinomial mixture model-based approach for short text clustering. In: Proceedings of the 20th ACM SIGKDD International Conference on Knowledge Discovery and Data Mining, New York, USA, pp. 233–242 (2014)
7. Qiu, S., Cui, Q., Bian, J., Gao, B., Liu, T.-Y: Co-learning of word representations and morpheme representations. In: Proceedings of COLING 2014, the 25th International Conference on Computational Linguistics: Technical Papers, Dublin, Ireland, pp. 141–150 (2014)
8. Qiu, L., Cao, Y., Nie, Z., Yu, Y., Rui, Y.: Learning word representation considering proximity and ambiguity. In: Proceedings of the Twenty-Eighth {AAAI} Conference on Artificial Intelligence, Québec, Canada, pp. 1572–1578 (2014)
9. Levy, O., Goldberg, Y.: Dependency-based word embeddings. In: Proceedings of the 52nd Annual Meeting of the Association for Computational Linguistics, Maryland, USA, pp. 302–308 (2014)
10. Mnih, A., Hinton, G.: Three new graphical models for statistical language modelling. In: Proceedings of the 24th International Conference on Machine Learning, Corvallis, USA, pp. 641–648 (2007)
11. Li, L., Jiang, Z., Huang, D.: A general instance representation architecture for protein-protein interaction extraction. In: 2014 {IEEE} International Conference on Bioinformatics and Biomedicine, Belfast, United Kingdom, pp. 497–500 (2014)
12. Bunescu, R., Ge, R., Kate, R.J., Marcotte, E.M., Mooney, R.J., Ramani, A.K., Wong, Y.W.: Comparative experiments on learning information extractors for proteins and their interactions. Artif. Intell. Med. **33**, 139–155 (2005)
13. Pyysalo, S., Ginter, F., Heimonen, J., Björne, J., Boberg, J., Järvinen, J., Salakoski, T.: BioInfer: a corpus for information extraction in the biomedical domain. BMC Bioinform. **8**, 1 (2007)
14. Fundel, K., Küffner, R., Zimmer, R.: RelEx—relation extraction using dependency parse trees. Bioinform. **23**, 365–371 (2007)
15. Ding, J., Berleant, D., Nettleton, D., Wurtele, E.: Mining MEDLINE: abstracts, sentences, or phrases. In: Proceedings of the Pacific Symposium on Biocomputing, Lihue, Hawaii, pp. 326–337 (2002)
16. Nédellec, C.: Learning language in logic-genic interaction extraction challenge. In: Proceedings of the 4th Learning Language in Logic Workshop (LLL 2005), Bonn, Germany (2005)
17. Byun, H.-R., Lee, S.-W.: Applications of support vector machines for pattern recognition: a survey. In: Lee, S.-W., Verri, A. (eds.) SVM 2002. LNCS, vol. 2388, pp. 213–236. Springer, Heidelberg (2002)

Extracting Opinion Expression with Neural Attention

Jiachen Du[1], Lin Gui[1], and Ruifeng Xu[1,2(✉)]

[1] Shenzhen Engineering Laboratory of Performance Robots at Digital Stage,
Harbin Institute of Technology Shenzhen Graduate School, Shenzhen, China
dujiachen199165@gmail.com, guilin.nlp@gmail.com,
xuruifeng.hits@gmail.com
[2] Guangdong Provincial Engineering Technology Research Center
for Data Science, Guangzhou, China

Abstract. Extracting opinion expressions from raw text is a fundamental task in sentiment analysis and it is usually formulated as a sequence labeling problem tackled by conditional random fields (CRFs). However CRF-based models usually need abundant hand-crafted features and require a lot of engineering effort. Recently deep neural networks are proposed to alleviate this problem. In order to extend neural-network-based models with ability to emphasize related parts in text, we propose a novel model which introduces the attention mechanism to Recurrent Neural Networks (RNNs) for opinion expression sequence labeling. We evaluate our model on MPQA 1.2 dataset, and experimental results show that the proposed model outperforms state-of-the-art CRF-based model on this task. Visualization of some examples show that our model can make use of correlation of words in the sentences and emphasize the crucial parts for this task to improve the performance compared with the vanilla RNNs.

Keywords: Opinion expression extraction · Sequence labeling · Recurrent neural network · Neural attention

1 Introduction

Recently, researchers from many subareas of Natural Language Processing and Machine Learning have been working on the sentiment analysis and related tasks [8, 13, 14, 17, 20]. In this work, we focus on one fundamental task in sentiment analysis—the detection of opinion expressions—both direct subjective expressions (DSEs) and expressive subjective expressions (ESEs) as defined in Wiebe et al. [18]. DSEs are explicit mentions of private states or speech events expressing private states; and ESEs are expressions that indicate sentiment, emotion, etc. without explicitly conveying them.

Opinion expressions extraction has often been treated as a sequence labeling task in previous works. This approach usually uses the conventional B-I-O tagging scheme to convert the original opinion expressions to sequences of tagging tokens: B indicates the beginning of an opinion expression, I is for the token within the range of opinion expression, O is the tag used to denote token outside any opinion expression. Since two

© Springer Nature Singapore Pte Ltd. 2016
Y. Li et al. (Eds.): SMP 2016, CCIS 669, pp. 151–161, 2016.
DOI: 10.1007/978-981-10-2993-6_13

The	United	States	wanted	this	very	much
O	O	O	B_DSE	I_DSE	I_DSE	I_DSE

The	committee	as	usual	has	refused
O	O	O	B_ESE	I_ESE	O

Fig. 1. Example Sentences with opinion expression B-I-O labels

types of opinion expressions (DSE, ESE) are used in annotation, there are five tagging labels in this task: B_DSE, I_DSE, B_ESE, I_ESE and O. The example sentences in Fig. 1. show this tagging scheme. For instance, the DSE "wanted this very much" results in one B_DSE tag for "wanted" and three I_DSE tags for "this very much".

Conditional random fields (CRFs) [10] have been quite successful for different sequence labeling problem in sentiment analysis including opinion target extraction [15], opinion holder recognition [11] etc. The state-of-the-art models of opinion expression extraction are also CRF [2] and variant of CRF that relaxes the Markovian assumption [21]. However, the success of CRFs depends heavily on the use of an appropriate features set and carefully manual selection, which requires a lot of engineering effort.

In recent years, there is no doubt that deep learning has ushered in amazing technological advances on natural language processing (NLP) researches. Deep learning models automatically learn the latent features and represent them as distributed vectors, outperforming CRF-based model in several tasks of NLP. For example, Yao et al. applied Recurrent Neural Network (RNN) to name entity recognition task, and showed that RNN obtains state-of-the-art result in this task [22]. Based on the aforementioned architectures, a new direction of neural networks has emerged. It learns to focus "attention" to specific parts of text as the simulation of human's attention while reading. The researches on neural network with attention mechanism show promising results on a sequence-to-sequence (seq2seq) tasks in NLP, including machine translation [1], caption generation [19] and text summarization [16].

Motivated by the recent researches on attention model of neural networks, we explore to apply recurrent neural network with attention to opinion expression extraction which can be treated as an instance of seq2seq learning tasks. In general, we except that the neural attention model would make use of correlation of words in the sentences and emphasize the crucial parts for this task to improve the performance compared with the vanilla RNNs.

The rest of this paper proceeds as follows. In Sect. 2, we present our recurrent neural network with attention model. In Sect. 3, we show the experimental results on MPQA dataset and analyze them. In Sect. 4, we conclude and discuss future work.

2 Methodology

This section describes a novel architecture for opinion expression extraction. The new architecture consists of a bidirectional recurrent neural network with long short-term memory (LSTM) as an word encoder, a decoder that outputs the predicted B-I-O tags of opinion expressions, and a neural attention layer that softly aligns the word sequences and output sequences.

2.1 RNN with Long Short-Term Memory

An RNN [4] is a kind of neural network that processes sequences of arbitrary length by recursively applying a function to its hidden state vector $h_t \in \mathbb{R}^d$ of each element in the input sequences. The hidden state vector at time-step t depends on the input symbol x_t and the hidden state vector at last time-step h_{t-1} is:

$$h_t = \begin{cases} 0 & t = 0 \\ g(h_{t-1}, x_t) & \text{otherwise} \end{cases} \tag{1}$$

A fundamental problem in traditional RNN is that gradients propagated over many steps tend to either vanish or explode. It makes RNN difficult to learn long-dependency correlations in a sequence. Long short-term memory network (LSTM) was proposed by [7] to alleviate this problem. LSTM has three gates: an input gate i_t, a forget gate f_t, an output gate o_t and a memory cell c_t. They are all vectors in $\mathbb{R}^d$. The LSTM transition equations are:

$$\begin{aligned} i_t &= \sigma(W_i x_t + U_i h_{t-1} + V_i c_{t-1}), \\ f_t &= \sigma(W_f x_t + U_f h_{t-1} + V_f c_{t-1}), \\ o_t &= \sigma(W_o x_t + U_o h_{t-1} + V_o c_{t-1}), \\ \tilde{c}_t &= \tanh(W_c x_t + U_c h_{t-1}), \\ c_t &= f_t \odot c_{t-1} + i_t \odot \tilde{c}_t, \\ h_t &= o_t \odot \tanh(c_t) \end{aligned} \tag{2}$$

where x_t is the input at the current time step, σ is the sigmoid function and $\odot$ is the elementwise multiplication operation. In our model, we use the output vector o_t of each time step as the representation of input sequence.

2.2 Bidirectional RNNs

Observe that with above definition, LSTMs only have information about the past, when making a decision on input x_t. This limits LSTMs to make use of previous sequential information which is important for most NLP tasks. To capture long-distance dependencies from the future as well as from the past, Graves and et al. proposed to use bidirectional LSTMs which allow bidirectional links in the network [6]. For the Elman-type RNN in Sect. 2.1, the bidirectional variant of it is:

$$\overrightarrow{h_t} = \overrightarrow{g}(\overrightarrow{h_{t-1}}, x_t)(\overrightarrow{h_0} = 0)$$
$$\overleftarrow{h_t} = \overleftarrow{g}(\overleftarrow{h_{t+1}}, x_t)(\overleftarrow{h_T} = 0) \tag{3}$$
$$h_t = [\overrightarrow{h_t}, \overleftarrow{h_t}]$$

where $\overrightarrow{g}$ and $\overleftarrow{g}$ are forward and backward transitional functions, they use different weight matrices and bias vectors. The concatenated vector $h_t = [\overrightarrow{h_t}, \overleftarrow{h_t}]$ combines vectors of the same time-step from both directions. We can thus interpret h_t as an intermediate representation summarizing the past and the future, which is then used to make decision on the current input. Similarly, unidirectional LSTMs can be extended to bidirectional LSTMs by allowing bidirectional connections in the hidden layers.

2.3 Stacked RNNs

Here, we describe briefly the underlying framework, called *Stacked RNNs* proposed by (El Hihi and Bengio) [3] on which we build a novel architecture that model attention. In the Stacked RNNs framework, there are $k(k > = 2)$ RNNs RNN$_1$, RNN$_2$, ..., RNN$_k$ where the jth RNN receive $(j - 1)$th RNN's output as its input and feed its output into the $(j + 1)$th RNN, meanwhile the first RNN receives the word sequences as its input and the last RNN omits the vector representation of the labels which are used to predict the targets. Suppose the output of jth RNN on time-step t is h_t^j, the stacked RNNs can be formulated as:

$$h_t^j = \begin{cases} x_t & j = 0 \\ g(h_{t-1}^j, h_t^{j-1}) & \text{otherwise} \end{cases} \tag{4}$$

The function g used in (4) can be replaced by any RNN transition function, In this paper, we use bidirectional LSTM described in Sect. 2.2. Figure 2 demonstrates a stacked RNN consisting two LSTMs, the input sequence is the vectors of words in sentences and the output sequence is the B-I-O tags of opinion expressions. In order to make the stacked RNNs to be extended easily, we use stacked bidirectional LSTMs with depth of 2 as our basic model in this paper.

2.4 Stacked RNNs with Neural Attention

Recently, researches on neural network with attention mechanism show promising results on a sequence-to-sequence (seq2seq) tasks in NLP, including machine translation [1], caption generation [19] and text summarization [16]. For opinion expression extraction, we proposes to use neural attention to focus the important parts in the sentences. As we described in Sect. 2.3, we use stacked bidirectional-LSTMs with depth of 2 as our basic model. For the attention model, the input of the second LSTM on each time step t is a weighed sum of the first LSTM's output vectors. The input vector of the second LSTM on time t, i_t^2 is represented by

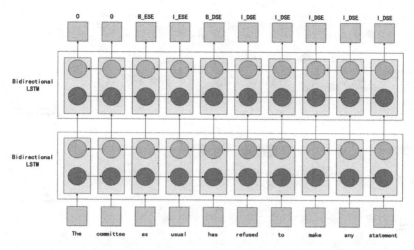

Fig. 2. Demonstration of stacked RNNs for emotion expression extraction, the input of the whole model is the word embeddings and the output is the predicted B-I-O tags. In this paper we use stacked bidirectional LSTMs with depth of 2 as our basic model

$$i_t^2 = \sum_{s=1}^{T} \alpha_{ts} h_s^1 \qquad (5)$$

In Eq. (5), h_s^1 is the output vector of the 1st LSTM on time step s, α_{ts} is the weight value that maps output sequence of the 1st LSTM $[h_1^1, h_2^1, \ldots, h_T^1]$ to input vector of the 2nd LSTM. α_{ts} can also be consider as a value that indicates how much of a difference the sth word will make to the decision of the tth label. The weight α_{ts} is obtained by

$$e_{ts} = \tanh(W^1 h_s^1 + W^2 h_{t-1}^2 + b)$$
$$\alpha_{ts} = \frac{\exp(e_{ts}^T e)}{\sum_{k=1}^{T} \exp(e_{tk}^T e)} \qquad (6)$$

In Eq. (6), W^1 and W^2 are parametric matrices that will be tuned in training phase, b is the bias vector. e in this equation is a vector with the same length with e_{ts}, and is jointly trained with all other parameters. The first line in this equation can be treated as a fully-connected neural network whose input is the output vectors of the emitted vectors of both LSTMs with separated parametric matrix. The second line in Eq. (6) is also a fully-connected neural network but with a softmax activation function that outputs the attention weights. The whole model is illustrated in Fig. 3.

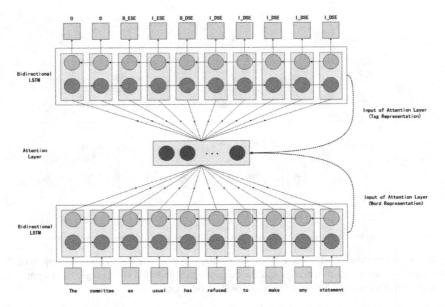

Fig. 3. Stacked RNNs with neural attention. For the sake of simplicity, the attention layer in this figure is represented by a abstract part.

3 Experiments

In this section, we investigate the empirical performance of our proposed model on opinion expression extraction and compare it with state-of-the-art models for this task. We use MPQA 1.2 corpus[1] [18]. It contains 535 news documents of 11,111 sentences annotated with both DSEs and ESEs labels at phrase level. As in previous work, we use 135 documents as a development set and employ 10-fold cross validation on the remaining 400 documents. The summary statistics of MPQA 1.2 is listed in Table 1.

Table 1. Summary statistics of the MPQA 1.2 datasets.

	DSE	ESE
Sentences with opinion (%)	55.89	57.93
Words with opinion (%)	5.82 %	8.44 %
Maximum of Length	15	40
Minimum of Length	1	2
Average of Length	1.86	3.33

---

[1] Available at http://www.cs.pitt.edu/mpqa/.

3.1   Evaluation Metrics

We use precision, recall, and F1-measure to evaluate the performance of the model. Since the boundaries of opinion expressions are hard to define even for human annotators [18], we use *Binary Overlap* and *Proportional Overlap* as two soft measures to evaluate the performance. Breck et al. firstly introduced the *Binary Overlap* measure to opinion expression extraction which counts every overlapping match between a predicted and true expression as correct [2]. And *Proportional Overlap* is a stricter measure that computes the proportion of overlapping spans [9].

3.2   Model Training and Hyper-parameters

The model can be trained in an end-to-end way by back-propagation, where the objective function is cross-entropy of error loss. Training is done through gradient descent with the Adadelta update rule. In all of these experiments, the word embeddings are initialized with the publicly available word2vec vectors that were trained on 100 billion words from Google News [12]. Other parameters are set as follows. The number of hidden units of both LSTM is 32, dropout rate is 0.5 and mini-batch size is 128. These hyper-parameters are chosen via a grid search on the development set.

3.3   Baselines

To illustrate the performance boost of our proposed attention model, we compare our model with some baseline methods. Since we use bidirectional LSTM as component of our model, we implement an RNN with LSTM memory unit as a baseline. We also compare our model with stacked LSTM with depth of 2.

- **Bi-LSTM:** LSTM for sequence labelling. [5]
- **Bi-LSTM(stacked):** stacked model of two bi-directional LSTMs [8].
  We also compare our model with the following state-of-the-art models:
- **CRF:** Features used in CRF are words, part-of-speech tags and membership in a manually constructed opinion lexicon (within a $[-1,+1]$ context window) [2].
- **Semi-CRF:** Since Semi-CRF is a variant of traditional CRF model that relaxes the Markovian assumption and focus on the phrase level features rather than token-level features. Semi-CRF also use parse trees to generate the candidate segments of sentences [21].

3.4   Results and Analysis

Since our model is based on RNNs, we firstly conduct experiments to confirm that our model outperforms vanilla bidirectional LSTM and stacked LSTM. The experimental results are shown in Table 2. We notice that vanilla bidirectional LSTM performs the worst among all the models since it cannot extract high-level features for this task. Two-layer LSTM uses deeper architecture "in space" to give LSTM additional power to tackle complex problems, and it obtains higher F1 scores than the vanilla LSTM. Our model which introduces the attention layer to stacked LSTM gives the best performance among the three models. For F1 scores, our model outperforms stacked LSTM with maximum absolute gains of 2.80 % for DSE, and 3.39 % for ESE. All differences are statistically significant at the 0.05 level. These results can demonstrate that neural attention model can emphasize the crucial parts for specific tasks and improve the performance of RNNs on sequence labeling problems.

Table 2. Experimental evaluation of our proposed model and baseline methods

Task	Model	P		R		F1	
		Bin	Prop	Bin	Prop	Bin	Prop
DSE	Bi-LSTM	64.31	61.21	70.90	65.33	67.44	62.25
	Bi-LSTM(stacked)	64.80	63.22	72.15	65.35	68.27	63.28
	Bi-LSTM(stacked) + Att	**67.82**	**64.32**	**74.89**	**65.89**	**71.17**	**65.10**
ESE	Bi-LSTM	56.34	48.20	70.00	52.18	62.43	50.11
	Bi-LSTM(stacked)	57.10	48.37	70.48	54.20	63.09	51.12
	Bi-LSTM(stacked) + Att	**63.29**	**48.69**	**70.02**	**55.97**	**66.48**	**52.06**

Table 3 shows comparison of our model to the previous best results in the literature. In term of F1 value, our model performs best for both DSE and ESE detection. Semi-CRF with its high recall, performs comparably to our model on F1 measure. Note that our model does not have to access any hand-crafted features other than word embeddings pre-trained by word2vec. In general, CRF models achieve high precision but low recall on both DSE and ESE detection (Note that it obtains best precision for binary and proportional measures, however it performs worst for recall measure). While Semi-CRF exhibit a high recall, low precision performance, since it use a more relaxed Marcovian assumption. Compared with Semi-CRF, our model produces even higher recall and comparable precision. We can observe that our model obtains higher F1 scores than Semi-CRF — 71.17 vs. 71.15 (binary overlap) and 65.10 vs. 64.27 (proportional overlap) for DSEs; 66.48 vs. 66.37 (binary overlap) and 57.57 vs. 50.95 (proportional overlap) for ESEs.

Table 3. Results of our proposed model against CRF-based models.

Task	Model	P		R		F1	
		Bin	Prop	Bin	Prop	Bin	Prop
DSE	CRF	**82.28**	**74.96**	52.99	46.98	64.45	57.74
	Semi-CRF	69.41	61.67	73.08	**67.22**	71.15	64.27
	Our Model	67.82	64.32	**74.89**	65.89	**71.17**	**65.10**
ESE	CRF	68.36	**56.08**	51.84	42.26	58.85	48.10
	Semi-CRF	**69.06**	45.64	64.15	**58.05**	66.37	50.95
	Our Model	63.29	**48.69**	**70.02**	55.97	**66.48**	**52.06**

3.5   Case Study

In order to validate that our model is able to select salient parts in a text sequence, we visualize the attention layers in Fig. 4. For an example sentence from the MPQA dataset in which our model predicted all labels correctly. The example sentence and its corresponding labels are:

Nevertheless	he	wanted	to	clarify	some	of	Powell	's	statement
O	O	B_DSE	B_DSE	B_DSE	O	O	O	O	O

This sentence contains a DSE *"wanted to clarify"* which is a verb phrase. In order to understand the attitudes and feelings which this phrase conveys, we have to consider its corresponding object — *"Powell's statement"*. We except our attention model can recognize this correlation and emphasize it for extracting the correct opinion expressions.

In Fig. 4. deeper colors mean higher attention and pale colors indicate lower attention. First of all, we can observe that for each label, the highest attention value is always associate with its corresponding word in the sentence. This result is consistent to our expectation, since each word has the biggest influence on its corresponding label. We can also find that except *"wanted to clarify"* 's own words, the phrase *"Powell's statement"* has the most highest attention value on the labels of this DSE. This means our model can emphasize words related to the opinion expressions other than the corresponding ones in text. This example shows that introducing attention mechanism gives RNNs additional power to tackle more complicated sequence labeling problems that involve semantic understanding.

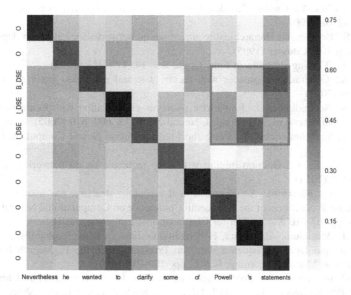

Fig. 4. Visualization of attention signals in sample sentences in the MPQA dataset. (Color figure online)

4 Conclusion

In this paper, we improve the traditional recurrent neural networks (RNNs) by introducing the attention mechanism to tackle the opinion expression extraction task. The new model can emphasize the most important parts in text and evaluate the correlation of each words in sentence with their expression labels (DSE and ESE). Experimental results show that attention layer gives RNNs additional power to process more complicated sequence labeling problems such as opinion expression extraction. Since our model can produce higher recall on both DSE and ESE, it outperforms traditional CRF-based methods on MPQA dataset.

In the future, we would like apply our models to other sequence labeling tasks in sentiment analysis including opinion holder extraction, aspect-based sentiment analysis, etc.

Acknowledgement. This work was supported by the National Natural Science Foundation of China 61370165, 61632011, National 863 Program of China 2015AA015405, Shenzhen Peacock Plan Research Grant KQCX20140521144507925 and Shenzhen Foundational Research Funding JCYJ20150625142543470, Guangdong Provincial Engineering Technology Research Center for Data Science 2016KF09.

References

1. Bahdanau, D., Cho, K., Bengio, Y.: Neural machine translation by jointly learning to align and translate. arXiv preprint arXiv:1409.0473 (2014)
2. Breck, E., Choi, Y., Cardie, C.: Identifying expressions of opinion in context. In: IJCAI, pp. 2683–2688 (2007)
3. El Hihi, S., Bengio, Y.: Hierarchical recurrent neural networks for long-term dependencies. In: NIPS, p 409. Citeseer (1995)
4. Elman, J.L.: Finding structure in time. Cogn. Sci. **14**, 179–211 (1990)
5. Graves, A.: Generating sequences with recurrent neural networks. arXiv preprint arXiv: 1308.0850 (2013)
6. Graves, A., Schmidhuber, J.: Framewise phoneme classification with bidirectional LSTM and other neural network architectures. Neural Netw. **18**, 602–610 (2005)
7. Hochreiter, S., Schmidhuber, J.: Long short-term memory. Neural Comput. **9**, 1735–1780 (1997)
8. Irsoy, O., Cardie, C.: Opinion mining with deep recurrent neural networks. In: EMNLP, pp. 720–728 (2014)
9. Johansson, R., Moschitti, A.: Syntactic and semantic structure for opinion expression detection. In: Proceedings of the Fourteenth Conference on Computational Natural Language Learning, pp. 67–76. Association for Computational Linguistics (2010)
10. Lafferty, J., Mccallum, A., Pereira, F.: Conditional random fields: probabilistic models for segmenting and labeling sequence data. In: Proceedings of the Eighteenth International Conference on Machine Learning, ICML, pp. 282–289 (2001)
11. Lu, B.: Identifying opinion holders and targets with dependency parser in Chinese news texts. In: Proceedings of the NAACL HLT 2010 Student Research Workshop, pp. 46–51. Association for Computational Linguistics (2010)

12. Mikolov, T., Sutskever, I., Chen, K., et al.: Distributed representations of words and phrases and their compositionality. In: Advances in Neural Information Processing Systems, pp. 3111–3119 (2013)
13. Pang, B., Lee, L.: A sentimental education: sentiment analysis using subjectivity summarization based on minimum cuts. In: Proceedings of the 42nd Annual Meeting on Association for Computational Linguistics, p 271. Association for Computational Linguistics (2004)
14. Pang, B., Lee, L., Vaithyanathan, S.: Thumbs up?: sentiment classification using machine learning techniques. In: Proceedings of the ACL-2002 Conference on Empirical Methods in Natural Language Processing, vol. 10, pp. 79–86. Association for Computational Linguistics (2002)
15. Pontiki, M., Galanis, D., Papageorgiou, H., et al.: Semeval-2015 task 12: aspect based sentiment analysis. In: Proceedings of the 9th International Workshop on Semantic Evaluation (SemEval 2015), Denver, Colorado, pp. 486–495. Association for Computational Linguistics (2015)
16. Rush, A.M., Chopra, S., Weston, J.: A neural attention model for abstractive sentence summarization. arXiv preprint arXiv:1509.00685 (2015)
17. Tang, D., Wei, F., Yang, N., et al.: Learning sentiment-specific word embedding for Twitter sentiment classification. In: ACL (1), pp. 1555–1565 (2014)
18. Wiebe, J., Wilson, T., Cardie, C.: Annotating expressions of opinions and emotions in language. Lang. Resour. Eval. **39**, 165–210 (2005)
19. Xu, K., Ba, J., Kiros, R., et al.: Show, attend and tell: neural image caption generation with visual attention. arXiv preprint arXiv:1502.03044 2:5 (2015)
20. Xu, R., Gui, L., Xu, J., et al.: Cross lingual opinion holder extraction based on multi-kernel SVMs and transfer learning. World wide web **18**, 299–316 (2015)
21. Yang, B., Cardie, C.: Extracting opinion expressions with semi-Markov conditional random fields. In: Proceedings of the 2012 Joint Conference on Empirical Methods in Natural Language Processing and Computational Natural Language Learning, pp. 1335–1345. Association for Computational Linguistics (2012)
22. Yao, K., Zweig, G., Hwang, M.-Y., et al: Recurrent neural networks for language understanding. In: INTERSPEECH, pp. 2524–2528 (2013)

Topic Model Based Adaptation Data Selection for Domain-Specific Machine Translation

Liang Yao, Mengyi Liu, Yu Hong[(✉)], Hao Liu, and Jianmin Yao

Provincial Key Laboratory for Computer Information Processing Technology,
Soochow University, Suzhou, China
liangysky@gmail.com, mengyiliu22@gmail.com, tianxianer@gmail.com,
liuhao1992@gmail.com, jyao@suda.edu.cn

Abstract. Current domain-specific machine translation (MT) suffers from the lack of high-quality bilingual corpora. Existing work in this field has shown the advantage of Adaptation data selection (Ada-selection) for enriching the corpora. Encouraged by the empirical finding that topic distribution is conductive to characterizing a distinctive domain, we propose to use topic model to improve Ada-selection. Based on a joint LDA approach, we incorporate topic distribution in measuring the relevance between the target domain and the candidate parallel sentence pairs. On the basis, we select the highly relevant candidates as the high-quality domain-specific bilingual corpora. In practice, we apply our method for the acquisition of domain-specific corpora from the general-domain. Experiments on an end-to-end domain-specific MT task show that our method outperforms the state of the art, yielding at least 1.5 BLEU points at different scales of training data.

Keywords: Statistical machine translation · Specific-domain machine translation · Topic model · Data selection

1 Introduction

Domain-specific bilingual corpora are helpful for building a proper translation model for a specific domain. The so-called domain-specific samples are defined as the parallel sentences or aligned words that strictly adhere to the pragmatic nature of the domain. For example, the word mouse refers to a rat in most cases in the domain of *biological science*, though it means a cursor position indicator (CPI) in the domain of *computer science*. Correspondingly, the translations of the word aligned with in the domains are very different:

 # Biological Science (mouse⇒rat)

鼠 */Chinese; ratte/German; rata/Spanish*

 # Computer Science (mouse⇒CPI)

鼠标 */Chinese; maus/German; ratón/Spanish*

Obviously, the former are proper samples in a translation task specific to the domain of *biology*, while the latter the *computer science*.

Y. Li et al. (Eds.): SMP 2016, CCIS 669, pp. 162–171, 2016.
DOI: 10.1007/978-981-10-2993-6_14

However, there are always few available domain-specific parallel sentences for the uncommon domains. To overcome the problem, we introduce Ada-selection method into data acquisition. Supervised by priori knowledge in small-scale in-domain training data, Ada-selection method automatically selects the domain-relevant parallel sentence pairs from large-scale general-domain corpora. The selected pairs are then merged with the original training data as new in-domain samples. The method, hence, complies with the basic assumption that the domain-relevant samples are specific to the domain in language use, either for source language or target.

Previous work in literature has proved that the expanded training data by Ada-selection can improve the performance of domain-specific MT. [14] redistributed the weight of each training sentence to assign higher weight for domain-relevant data using information retrieval models. [9,24] selected sentence pairs from general-domain corpora by language model perplexity, which are computed with respect to in-domain training data. [1] expanded the language model method and tried to rank the sentence pair by bilingual cross-entropy difference of in-domain and out-domain. [7] further exploited neural language model for Ada-selection in order to eliminate the data sparse problem caused by conventional language model. [12] uses translation models trained on small-scale in-domain corpus and also achieves promising results. Existing methods are mainly based on statistics, such as lexical co-occurrence, but ignore the underlying semantic information behind the bilingualism. Motivated by the advantages of topic models in detecting the embedded semantic concepts in raw texts, we propose to use topic model to improve Ada-selection.

2 Similar Topic Distribution

We argue that high-quality domain-relevant samples are closely related to the main topics in the target domain. Figure 1 shows two domain-relevant samples with bilingual topic distributions, which are inferred by using bilingual topic model.

Source: *Missile <u>shooting area</u> visualization is important to achieve shooting simulation training.* **[Sample 1]**

  Domain: *science and military*

  Translation: 投射区域 (*Means: a place allocated for missile launching*)

Source: *To choice reasonable <u>shooting area</u> is important to improve shooting percentage.* **[Sample 2]**

  Domain: *sports*

  Translation: 射门区域 (*Means: scoring regions in sports competitions*)

Figure 1 indicates that the translation of the same sample (shooting area) varies due to different domains. In the domain of *military*, it means a place allocated for missile launching. While in the domain about sports, it refers to the scoring regions. Thus, given a document about *military*, we prefer to select sample 1 for domain-specific MT system. We achieve this by measuring the domain relevance of a sample based on its topic distribution. Figure 1 indicates

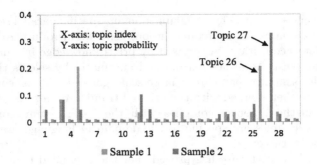

Fig. 1. Topic distributions of the samples 1 & 2.

that sample 1 has a highest probability over topic 26 and sample 2 obtains the highest probability over topic 27. Table 1 shows the top 10 most likely words of topic 26 and 27.

Table 1. Top10 most likely words of topic 26 and 27

Topic 26		Topic 27	
Word	Probability	Word	Probability
信息(info)	0.0252	两(two)	0.0251
系统(system)	0.0151	球(ball)	0.0103
provide	0.0048	三(three)	0.0089
network	0.0040	match	0.0061
数据(data)	0.0038	sports	0.0051
服务(service)	0.0038	参加	0.0050
data	0.0038	Beijing	0.0049
system	0.0037	Olympic	0.0047
network	0.0037	上(up)	0.0043
computer	0.0036	swim	0.0038

From Table 1, we infer that topic 26 is more relevant to the *military* domain because that the words "信息 (*info*)", "系统 (*system*)" and "*network*" are frequently used in the domain of *military*. Similarly, topic 27 is more relevant to the *sports* domain. Thus, we can conclude that the high-quality domain-relevant samples are closely related to the main topics in the target domain.

3   Methodology

The available data for Ada-selection process include small-scale domain-specific corpora C_s and large-scale general-domain corpora C_g. We drive the Ada-selector to go through every pair of parallel sentences in C_g, verify their relevance to the target domain, and select the most relevant pairs as high-quality domain-specific samples.

3.1   Bilingual Relevance

For a sentence pair e_g in C_g, we measure its relevance to the target domain D by bilingual topic probabilities of e_g in C_g:

$$R(D|e_g) = \sum_{i=1}^{K} P(D|t_i) \cdot P(t_i|e_g) \tag{1}$$

where t denotes a topic, while K the number of assigned topics. $P(t|e)$ is bilingual topic probability. It represents the degree in which a parallel sentence pair e associates with t. $P(D|t)$ is the probability which reflects the relevance between t and the target domain D. We calculate $P(t|e)$ by [20]'s joint LDA approach (Sect. 3.2), while $P(D|t)$ by projection approach (Sect. 3.3).

In our experiments, we rank all e_g in C_g, and select top N samples to enlarge C_s. On the basis, we use the expanded C_s to train the MT system.

3.2   Bilingual Topic Probability

[20] proposed a simple but efficient joint LDA approach, in which two sides of a large parallel corpus are concatenated at sentence level. Therefore, the training corpus is a combination of each source sentence and its translation in the same line. The LDA model is estimated from the bilingual traing corpus using [4]. Figure 2 shows the framework of the joint LDA model. In Fig. 2, each sentence pair is represented by a sequence of n words shown as the colored circle. z_i indicates the i-th topic variable and k is the number of topics. α, β, Θ is the hyper-parameter used in LDA model.

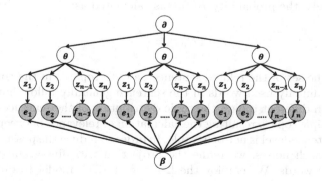

Fig. 2. Framework of the joint LDA model.

3.3   Topic Projection for Topic-Domain Relevance Measurement

Topic projection is a cluster of related samples to the topic t in a dataset (see Fig. 3). It reveals the topic distribution over the dataset. We apply such a projection for the calculation of $P(D|t)$ in equation (1), viz., probability which reflects the relevance between topic t and the target domain D. In particular, we develop a sentence-level projection approach and a word-level approach.

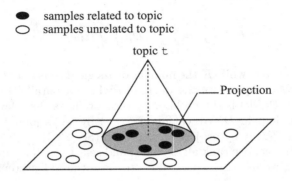

Fig. 3. Projection on target domain

For the case of sentence-level projection, we employ [20]'s joint LDA to obtain the topic probability $P(t|e)$ for a sentence pair e. We assume that e is only related to the topic t if t has the maximum probability $P(t|e)$ in all topics, i.e., $argmax P(t|e)$. In the same way, we detect the related topic for every sentence pair in C_g, building one-to-many t-e mapping table. Based on this table, we can easily collect all sentence pairs related to a given topic. By the table, we obtain the projection of a topic t to the target domain D by the intersection between the related sentence pairs of t and all sentence pairs in C_s, i.e., $J_s = S_q \bigcap C_s$. Correspondingly, the probability $P(D|t)$ is calculated as:

$$P(D|t_i) = \frac{|J_s|}{|S_g|} \qquad (2)$$

where, S_g is the set of the related sentence pairs to topic t_i in the corpora C_g.

As the commonly used words in the sentence generally follow homogeneous distribution on different topics, the topic distribution of the sentence-pair tends to prefer multiple topics, resulting the calculation of relevance between topic and domain in sentence-level is not believable. In order to reduce the possible negative influences of such noises, we refine the projection with fine-grained linguistic units, such as words. We employ the [20]'s joint LDA model to obtain topic-word probability $P(w|t)$ over all topics. On the basis, we modify the projection and $P(D|t)$ as below:

$$P(D|t_i) = \sum_{w \in C_g} \frac{|W_s|}{|W_g + W_s|} \cdot P(w|t_i) \tag{3}$$

where, W_g denotes the number of words existed in the corpora C_g. W_s denotes the number of words existed in the corpora C_s.

4 Experiments

4.1 Experimental Settings

In order to evaluate the proposed Ada-selection method, we conduct a spoken-language-oriented English-to-Chinese MT task. We employ two kinds of corpora for topic model training, CAS and CWMT09. CAS is constructed by Chinese Academy of Science [12], containing 350K parallel sentence pairs. The corpora cover multiple domains, such as Environment, Legislation, Politics, etc. CWMT09 contains 50k parallel sentence pairs in real spoken dialogue. Furthermore, the WEB corpora are used in the Ada-selection process for the expansion of training data of a domain-specific MT system. WEB was mined from the Internet by [13]'s acquisition method which contains 16M sentence pairs. We employ two kinds of in-domain corpora, 863 SLT04 and 863 SLT05. 863 SLT04 contains 870 parallel sentence pairs in real spoken dialogue with 4 Chinese reference translations for each. We use it as the development set. 863 SLT05 contains 856 English sentences along with 4 Chinese references. We used it as the test data.

We employ hierarchical phrase-based models [5] to carry out our experiments. A 4-gram language model is trained on the monolingual data which contains 5M Chinese sentences [12] using SRILM toolkit [21]. We evaluate translation results by the case-insensitive BLEU-4 [18]. We use the GibbsLDA++ [4] for topic modeling[1]. The number of topics n is specified as 30[2].

4.2 Main Results

We have built two baseline systems, respectively named BCWMT and BWEB. BCWMT is trained on the corpora CWMT09. BWEB is trained on the corpora WEB. Table 2 shows the translation performance on the development data 863 SLT04 (Dev) and the test data 863 SLT05 (Tes).

The results illustrate that BWEB outperforms BCWMT. The former is trained over a large-scale bilingual corpora, while the latter a small-scale corpora in the domain of interest. The reason is that the large scale parallel sentences cover more bilingual translation knowledge. By contract, the small-scale in-domain corpora suffers from sparse prior knowledge available for training, which degrades the translation performance. However, it raises the question

---

[1] http://gibbslda.sourceforge.net/.

[2] We determine n by testing {5, 15, 30, 50, 100} in our experiments. We find that n = 30 gets a better performance than other values.

Table 2. Translation performance of the baseline systems.

Sys	#Dev	#Tes
BCWMT	15.01	**21.99**
BWEB	27.72	**34.62**

whether it is necessary to employ Ada-selection to refine the training data. To answer the question, we reproduce two Ada-selection methods and ours (See Table 3), use them to refine the corpora WEB, and retrain the baseline systems with the refined data. In addition, we will verify the validity of our topic model based selection methods by comparing with the state of the art.

Table 3. Adaptation data selection methods

> **NN:** Data selection by perplexity score of the Recurrent Neural LM, with the RNNLM Toolkit. (Duh et al., 2013).
>
> **BTM + BLM:** Selection by combining translation and language models in two directions. (Liu et al., 2014).
>
> **SL:** Selection by bilingual topic models with the Sentence-level projection (subsection 3.3).
>
> **WL:** Selection by bilingual topic models with the Word-level projection (subsection 3.3).

Figure 4 shows the performance achieved on different scale (N) of training data selected by the Ada-selection methods from WEB. It shows that all the Ada-selection methods help the translation system achieve better performance by using 1M training data ($N=1M$). The scale is much smaller than that of WEB (16M). Considering that such training data are selected from WEB by the Ada-selection methods, we conclude that the methods are effective in detecting the samples adherent to the characteristics of the target domain.

It has been also proved that it is necessary to refine training data in a domain-specific translation task. It is because that the translation system doesn't need to take into account large-scale domain-irrelevant knowledge and noisy rules in the learning process any more. In all, Ada-selection improves learning performance but reduces the time-consuming for learning. In addition, our Ada-selection methods (**SL** and **WL**) outperform others. The minimum performance gain for both is about 1.5 BLEU points (see that at $N=1.2M$ in Fig. 4).

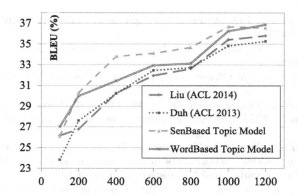

Fig. 4. Results of the MT systems only trained on the selected adaptation data.

It illustrates that the topic-topic relevance can indeed serve as an effective measure in determining the degree with which a bilingual sample adheres to the target domain. It also supports the assumptions: 1) pragmatics is closely related to the domain, and 2) topics can reveal the characteristics of the domain. Therefore, the topic-level domain relevance helps discover the samples in which the pragmatics adheres to the target domain. The samples, correspondingly, can be used as reliable training data in a domain-specific task.

5   Conclusion

We propose a topic model based Ada-selection method. Experiments show that it outperforms the traditional methods. In addition, our methods make full use of the limited in-domain data and can be easily implemented. In the future, we will study on the method of embedding deep semantic information into bilingual domain relevance measurement.

Acknowledgements. This research is supported by the National Natural Science Foundation of China, No. 61672368, No. 61373097, No. 61672367, No. 61272259. The authors would like to thank the anonymous reviewers for their insightful comments and suggestions. Yu Hong, Professor Associate in Soochow University, is the corresponding author of the paper, whose email address is tianxianer@gmail.com.

References

1. Axelrod, A., He, X., Gao, J.: Domain adaptation via pseudo in-domain data selection. In: Proceedings of the Conference on Empirical Methods in Natural Language Processing, pp. 355–362. Association for Computational Linguistics (2011)
2. Bertoldi, N., Federico, M.: Domain adaptation for statistical machine translation with monolingual resources. In: Proceedings of the Fourth Workshop on Statistical Machine Translation, pp. 182–189. Association for Computational Linguistics (2009)

3. Blei, D.M., Lafferty, J.D.: A correlated topic model of science. Ann. Appl. Stat. **1**(1), 17–35 (2007)
4. Blei, D.M., Ng, A.Y., Jordan, M.I.: Latent dirichlet allocation. J. Mach. Learn. Res. **3**, 993–1022 (2003)
5. Chiang, D.: Hierarchical phrase-based translation. Comput. Linguist. **33**(2), 201–228 (2007)
6. Cui, L., Zhang, D., Liu, S., Chen, Q., Li, M., Zhou, M., Yang, M.: Learning topic representation for SMT with neural networks. In: ACL (1), pp. 133–143. Citeseer (2014)
7. Duh, K., Neubig, G., Sudoh, K., Tsukada, H.: Adaptation data selection using neural language models: experiments in machine translation. In: Meeting of the Association for Computational Linguistics, pp. 678–683 (2013)
8. Eidelman, V., Boyd-Graber, J., Resnik, P.: Topic models for dynamic translation model adaptation. In: Proceedings of the 50th Annual Meeting of the Association for Computational Linguistics: Short Papers-Volume 2, pp. 115–119. Association for Computational Linguistics (2012)
9. Foster, G., Goutte, C., Kuhn, R.: Discriminative instance weighting for domain adaptation in statistical machine translation. In: Proceedings of the 2010 Conference on Empirical Methods in Natural Language Processing, pp. 451–459. Association for Computational Linguistics (2010)
10. Gong, Z., Zhang, Y., Zhou, G.: Statistical machine translation based on LDA. In: 2010 4th International on Universal Communication Symposium (IUCS), pp. 286–290. IEEE (2010)
11. Gong, Z., Zhou, G., Li, L.: Improve smt with source-side topic-document distributions. In: MT Summit, pp. 496–501 (2011)
12. Liu, L., Hong, Y., Liu, H., Wang, X., Yao, J.: Effective selection of translation model training data. In: Meeting of the Association for Computational Linguistics, pp. 569–573 (2014)
13. Liu, L., Hong, Y., Lu, J., Lang, J., Ji, H., Yao, J.M.: An iterative link-based method for parallel web page mining. In: Proceedings of the 2014 Conference on Empirical Methods in Natural Language Processing, pp. 1216–1224. Association for Computational Linguistics (2014)
14. Lü, Y., Huang, J., Liu, Q.: Improving statistical machine translation performance by training data selection and optimization. In: EMNLP-CoNLL, vol. 34, pp. 3–350 (2007)
15. Matsoukas, S., Rosti, A.V.I., Zhang, B.: Discriminative corpus weight estimation for machine translation. In: Proceedings of the 2009 Conference on Empirical Methods in Natural Language Processing, pp. 708–717. Association for Computational Linguistics (2009)
16. Moore, R.C., Lewis, W.: Intelligent selection of language model training data. In: Proceedings of the ACL 2010 Conference Short Papers, pp. 220–224. Association for Computational Linguistics (2010)
17. Och, F.J.: Minimum error rate training in statistical machine translation. In: Proceedings of the 41st Annual Meeting on Association for Computational Linguistics-Volume 1, pp. 160–167. Association for Computational Linguistics (2003)
18. Papineni, K., Roukos, S., Ward, T., Zhu, W.J.: BLEU: a method for automatic evaluation of machine translation. In: Meeting on Association for Computational Linguistics, pp. 311–318 (2002)
19. Pecina, P., Toral, A., Way, A., Papavassiliou, V., Prokopidis, P., Giagkou, M.: Towards using web-crawled data for domain adaptation in statistical machine

translation. In: Proceedings of the 15th Conference of European Association for Machine Translation, pp. 297–304 (2011)

20. Rubino, R., De Souza, J., Foster, J., Specia, L.: Topic models for translation quality estimation for gisting purposes. In: Machine Translating (2013)

21. Stolcke, A., et al.: Srilm-an extensible language modeling toolkit. In: INTER-SPEECH, vol. 2002, p. 2002 (2002)

22. Su, J., Wu, H., Wang, H., Chen, Y., Shi, X., Dong, H., Liu, Q.: Translation model adaptation for statistical machine translation with monolingual topic information. In: Meeting of the Association for Computational Linguistics: Long Papers, pp. 459–468 (2012)

23. Tam, Y.C., Lane, I., Schultz, T.: Bilingual LSA-based adaptation for statistical machine translation. Mach. Transl. **21**(4), 187–207 (2008)

24. Yasuda, K., Zhang, R., Yamamoto, H., Sumita, E.: Method of selecting training data to build a compact and efficient translation model. In: IJCNLP, pp. 655–660 (2008)

25. Zhao, B., Xing, E.P.: BiTAM: bilingual topic admixture models for word alignment. In: ACL 2006, International Conference on Computational Linguistics and Meeting of the Association for Computational Linguistics, Proceedings of the Conference, Sydney, Australia, 17–21 July 2006

26. Zhao, B., Xing, E.P.: HM-BiTAM: bilingual topic exploration, word alignment, and translation. In: Advances in Neural Information Processing Systems, pp. 1689–1696 (2007)

Early Detection of Promotion Campaigns in Community Question Answering

Xin Li[(⊠)], Yiqun Liu, Min Zhang, and Shaoping Ma

State Key Laboratory of Intelligent Technology and Systems,
Tsinghua National Laboratory for Information Science and Technology,
Department of Computer Science and Technology,
Tsinghua University, Beijing 100084, China
x-108@163.com, {yiqunliu,z-m,msp}@tsinghua.edu.cn

Abstract. As is the case with many social media websites, the Community Question Answering (CQA) portal has become a target for spammers to disseminate promotion information. Previous works mainly focus on identifying low-quality answers or detecting spam information in question-answer (QA) pairs. However, these works suffer from long delay since they all rely on the information of answers or answerers while questions have been displayed on the websites for some time and attracted certain user traffic. As a matter of fact, spammers on CQA platforms also act as questioners and involve promotion information in their questions. So if they can be detected as early as possible, the questions will not appear on the websites and affect legitimate users. In this paper, we design a framework for early detection of promotion campaigns in CQA based on only question information and questioner profile. First, we propose a novel sampling method for identifying the questions that contain promotion information, which compose the positive dataset. We also sample an unlabeled dataset of unsolved questions during a certain period of time. Then, we compare the characteristics of question information and user profiles between the two datasets, which are also used as features in the learning process. Finally, we apply and compare several PU (Positive and Unlabeled examples) learning algorithms to find positive examples in the unlabeled dataset. In our approach, no answer side information is needed, which means that it can detect spamming activities as soon as the question is posted. Experimental results based on about 0.7 million questions derived from a popular Chinese CQA portal indicate that our approach can detect questions related to promotion campaigns as effectively as but more efficiently than the state-of-the-art QA pair level detection methods.

Keywords: Early detection · Promotion campaign · Community Question Answering · PU learning

This work was supported by Natural Science Foundation (61672311, 61622208, 61532011, 61472206) of China and National Key Basic Research Program (2015CB358700).

Y. Li et al. (Eds.): SMP 2016, CCIS 669, pp. 172–185, 2016.
DOI: 10.1007/978-981-10-2993-6_15

1   Introduction

Community Question Answering (CQA) platforms provide Web users with the convenience of seeking and releasing information. Due to its large number of audience, CQA also suffers from quality issues [15,21]. The dissemination of promotion information is one of the most serious problems faced by CQA portals [1,2,4], where spammers conduct promotion campaigns when posting questions or answers. Additionally, crowd-turfing systems have become popular tools for organizing fraudulent activities among large numbers of people on various websites, such as microblogs, online forums, e-commerce sites and search engines [5,16–18]. These crowd-turfing platforms are also manipulated by spammers to organize promotion campaigns on CQA portals. Users may be misled by spammers' questions or answers to visit certain websites or purchase certain products. Therefore, it is important to detect spammers' promotion information as early as possible so that it would not reach a larger audience.

Although promotion campaigns make the CQA environment less credible and more noisy, few techniques exist to assist the CQA portals with early detection of promotion activities. Most existing works focus on estimating the quality of question-answer pairs [6,7,9,14], which extract various kinds of features from both answer and question and apply a learning model to estimate the quality. However, low-quality questions/answers cannot be regarded as equivalent to those containing promotion information, since paid experts from crowdsourcing systems may carefully design the QA pairs to make them seemingly useful. Another attempt is detecting promotion campaigns in answers or QA pairs [10], which makes use of promotion channels involved in the answers to detect promotion information. However, these works suffer from long delay because they all rely on the information of answers or answerers, which can only be collected after certain answers are provided. In many cases, posters from crowdsourcing systems have shown signs of promotion campaigns in their questions. Based on this observation, we aim to detect promotion information as early as possible. The proposed methodology is based on question information and user profiles only, which can be eliminated before reaching many CQA users.

Figure 1 shows two examples of promotion campaigns in CQA. Figure 1(a) is an unsolved question[1], which can be judged as promotion according to the question title. Figure 1(b) is a solved question[2]. Though we cannot make a judgment based on the question alone, we can determine according to the QA pair. For the second case, if we take into full account the profile of the questioner, who posted a large number of similar questions and selected the answers containing promotion information of certain stores or products as best answers, we can still make a judgment without the information of the answer. The examples indicate that although most exiting works on promotion campaign detection rely on QA pairs, we can make judgment about the promotion without answers. This kind

---

[1] http://wenwen.sogou.com/z/q627682313.htm.
[2] http://wenwen.sogou.com/z/q625841351.htm.

Fig. 1. Two examples of promotion information in CQA. (a) Q: which is the best office furniture store in Chengdu? Sichuan xxx office furniture store, selling office chairs, office desks, reception desks.... (b) Q: which is the most popular wedding photography shop in Chengdu? A: It should be xxx wedding photo studio, which is famous in Chengdu....

of judgment method is faced with more challenges, but the advantage it brings is noticeable because promotion activities can be stopped as soon as they appear.

The examples give us two inspirations. First, question information is useful for promotion campaign detection. Second, the profile of the questioner contributes to the detection of promotion campaigns. Spammers generally behave differently from legitimate users, thus we can identify them based on their profiles and history behavior patterns (as for the case in Fig. 1(b), the username of the questioner contains a large proportion of non-alphanumeric characters, which seems to be an auto-generated one). In this paper, we design a framework for early detection of promotion campaigns in CQA based on only question information and user profile. The main contributions of this paper can be summarized as follows:

- A novel sampling method based on the data collected from a crowd-turfing website is proposed for identifying the questions that contain promotion information, which compose the positive dataset. An unlabeled dataset is also sampled from the unsolved questions during a certain period of time for comparison.
- Characteristics of question information and user profiles are compared between the two datasets and features are derived for PU learning algorithms.
- An evaluation dataset is constructed that contains about 0.7 million questions from a popular Chinese CQA portal and also a large number of annotated fraudulent/legitimate questions, which will be open to the public after the double-blind review process.

Our approach is different from previous works on detecting the spamming activities of questioners cooperating with answerers [1,2]. These works also place attention on the effects of questioners and many of our detected samples belong to this spamming category, but they rely on the information of both questions and answers and cannot achieve the goal of early detection.

The remainder of this paper is organized as follows. After a discussion of the related work in the next section, we introduce the sampling strategy for the datasets in the Sect. 3. Then, we compare the characteristics between the datasets and apply the PU learning algorithms for classification in the Sects. 4 and 5, respectively. The Sect. 6 presents the experimental results and discussion. Finally, the Sect. 7 concludes the paper.

2 Related Work

Most existing approaches for the detection of promotion campaigns rely on the information from answers or answerers to finish the detection task. Li et al. [10] believe that spammers usually adopt promotion channels, such as (shortened) URLs, telephone numbers and social media accounts, to connect to users to achieve promotion goals. So they propose an "answerer-channel" bipartite graph propagation algorithm to diffuse promotion intents and detect answers containing promotion campaigns. They also utilize the spamming scores of users and channels derived from the propagation algorithm as features to train a supervised learning model to decide whether a QA pair is spam. Chen et al. [1,2] address a special case of promotion campaigns where spammers ask questions and select their self-posted answers as best answers. They argue that features used in traditional quality estimation methods, such as textual similarities between questions and answers, are no longer effective. Instead, they combine more context information, such as writing templates and a user's reputation track, to form a new model to detect promotion campaigns. However, these methods will not work until an answer is given to the question. As shown in Fig. 1, enough information can be excavated from the questions and questioners, thus promotion activities can be early detected and eliminated before reaching many CQA users.

3 Dataset

In this section, we introduce the sampling strategy for the datasets, including a positive set and an unlabeled set.

3.1 Positive Set

Crowd-turfing websites provide paid services for organizing promotion campaigns on CQA portals [1,2]. Spammers will create multiple accounts in CQA, use some of them to post questions and others to answer the questions. Generally, these answers will be selected as best answers to attract CQA users [1,2].

Figure 2 shows the user profiles of the questioner and the answerer for the QA pair in Fig. 1(b). We can see that the spammer accounts are mostly used as either concentrated questioners or answerers. The questioner posts multiple questions but few answers, while the answerer posts several answers but no questions. Besides, the acceptance ratio of the answerer account is extremely high since its answers are selected as best answers by its partners.

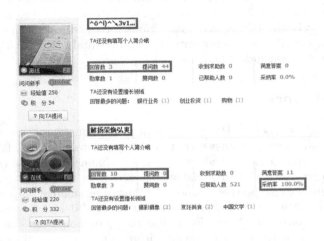

Fig. 2. User profiles of the questioner (above) and the answerer (below) for the QA pair in Fig. 1(b), including answers, questions, votes, acceptance ratio, experience, credit points, etc. The questioner posts 3 answers and 44 questions. The answerer posts 10 answers and 0 questions, whose acceptance ratio is 100 %.

According to our observations, we propose a sampling strategy based on propagation on the "questioner-best answerer" bipartite graph. $G = (V_q \cup V_a, E)$ denotes the bipartite graph, where $q \in V_q$ represents a questioner, $a \in V_a$ represents an answerer, and $e_{qa} \in E$ represents that questioner q selects at least one answer from answerer a as the best answer. For each step of the propagation, all the answerers whose answers are selected as best answers by given questioners are diffused, or vice versa. In the first step, we find 100 tasks of organizing promotion campaigns on CQA portals from a crowd-turfing website[3] and sample 1,043 questions that match these tasks, which are posted by 27 questioners. We conduct the propagation with 5 steps. The numbers of questioners, answerers and questions found in each step are shown in Table 1. It is obvious that the propagation does not converge since with iterations going on, the number of questions increases exponentially. This is reasonable because if a spammer selects one answer from a legitimate user as best answer, or if one of a spammer's answers is selected as best answer by a legitimate user (not quite common but sometimes it happens), noise will be introduced into the positive set and

---

[3] http://www.sandaha.com/.

spread promptly. To evaluate the precision, we randomly sample 100 QA pairs in each step to check whether they contain promotion information. The precision for each step is shown in the last column in Table 1, which indicates that the precision maintains high within the first 3 steps, while as the iteration continues, the precision drops dramatically. To obtain a positive set with high precision, we use the dataset propagated to the third step, including 38,843 questions posted by 1,346 users.

Table 1. Statistics for each step of the propagation

Step	#questioner	#answerer	#question	precision
1	27	–	1,043	100 %
2	27	803	11,393	100 %
3	1,346	803	38,843	100 %
4	1,346	4,584	55,877	82 %
5	6,908	4,584	232,907	54 %

We aim to characterize what kinds of questions will lead to promotion campaigns, so we use the information of both questions and answers when sampling the positive set. However, to achieve the goal of early detection, we will only use the question information and user profiles of questioners in the learning process.

3.2 Unlabeled Set

Considering the fact that spamming activities happen a lot in CQA [4,10], it is difficult to obtain a large set containing only negative examples. On the other hand, if we sample high-quality QA pairs with certain methods (for example, QA pairs posted by expert users), the examples will be biased and cannot be applied to real circumstances. Instead, we sample an unlabeled set for comparison and use PU learning algorithms to detect positive examples from the unlabeled set. With the help of a major CQA portal, we get all the active users (who have posted at least one question during a certain period of time) in the community in May, 2015. We aim to test the effectiveness of our approach on early detection of promotion campaigns without answers, so we only sample all the unsolved questions posted by these users in May. The unlabeled set consists of 660,505 questions posted by 517,027 users. The summary of the two datasets is shown in Table 2.

4 Characteristics

In this section, we compare the characteristics of user profiles and question information between the positive set and the unlabeled set, which are also utilized as features in the learning process.

Table 2. Summary of the datasets

	#questioner	#question
Positive set	1,346	38,843
Unlabeled set	517,027	660,505

4.1   User Profile

In order to achieve their spamming goals, spammers generally behave differently from legitimate users. We compare the cumulative distribution function (CDF) of several properties of questioners between positive set and unlabeled set, as shown in Fig. 3. The properties are important aspects of a user, which can all be collected at the time of submitting queries, which means that they can be adopted in the early detection process. For example, number of votes means the number of times a user's answers are voted by other users, which well represents the quality of the user's answers. While experience and credit points indicate the frequency of a user interacting with the community, which are good metrics to estimate the user's activeness.

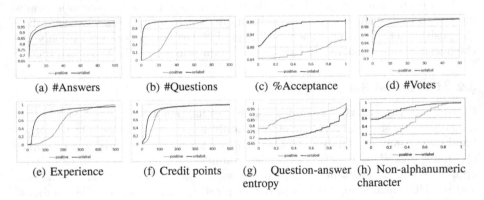

(a) #Answers   (b) #Questions   (c) %Acceptance   (d) #Votes

(e) Experience   (f) Credit points   (g) Question-answer entropy   (h) Non-alphanumeric character

Fig. 3. Comparison of user profiles between positive set and unlabeled set

- (a) Number of answers: positive users typically give fewer answers than unlabeled users. 77.8 % of positive users give no answers, while 68.8 % of unlabeled users give no answers.
- (b) Number of questions: positive users post a lot more questions than unlabeled users. 75.9 % of positive users post more than 20 questions, while only 3.5 % of unlabeled users post over 20 questions.
- (c) Acceptance ratio: positive users typically have higher acceptance ratios than unlabeled users. 8.2 % of positive users have an acceptance ratio of 100 %, while only 0.7 % of unlabeled users have an acceptance ratio of 100 %.

- (d) Number of votes: positive users typically receive fewer votes than unlabeled users, which suggests that although positive users' answers are more likely to be selected as best answers, they are less likely to be preferred by other users.
- (e)–(f) Experience & credit points: From the figures we can see that positive users are generally more active than unlabeled users.
- (g) Question-answer entropy: if a user posts m questions and n answers, the proportion of questions and answers is $p = \frac{m}{m+n}$ and $q = \frac{n}{m+n}$, respectively. Then the question-answer entropy of the user is $-p * \log(p) - q * \log(q)$. The figure shows that positive users typically have a lower question-answer entropy than unlabeled users, which is in consistence with our previous observation that spammer accounts are mostly concentrated questioners or answerers.
- (h) Proportion of non-alphanumeric characters in the username: the usernames of positive users contain a remarkably higher proportion of non-alphanumeric characters than those of unlabeled users. This may be because the usernames of spammer accounts are mostly auto-generated. (Inspired by [20], we add more username related features, such as the number of unique characters in the username, the entropy of the character distribution of the username and so on. Due to space limitation, we do not show the comparison here.)

4.2 Question Information

For question information, we extract textual features and posting time of the question for classification.

Textual Features. Though pretending to be legitimate users, spammers may organize their questions differently and use specific words to achieve their promotion goals. Therefore, we use the bag-of-words features. The whole set of questions in the training set is denoted as Q. After Chinese word segmentation for the question texts in Q, we obtain a vocabulary $V = \{w_1, \ldots, w_n\}$. Then the textual feature vector for a question q is $\{f_1, \ldots, f_n\}$, where $f_i = tf(w_i, q) * idf(w_i, Q)$, $tf(w_i, q)$ is the term frequency of w_i in q and $idf(w_i, Q)$ is the inverse document frequency of w_i in Q.

Posting Time. Intuitively, a spammer's promotion campaign is a job rather than a leisure activity, so there ought to be more promotion posts on weekdays than on weekends. Figure 4 shows that the number of questions in the positive set drops drastically on Sunday, while more questions in the unlabeled set are posted on weekends when legitimate users have more spare time to browse the community. The result verifies our assumption, which is consistent with [3]. Thus, we add 7 binary features $\{f_1, \ldots, f_7\}$, where $f_i = 1$ indicates that the posting time of the question is the i-th day in a week, and $f_i = 0$ otherwise.

Sentiment Score. Generally, a question in CQA should be an interrogative sentence inquiring knowledge on certain topics, the sentiment of which is more

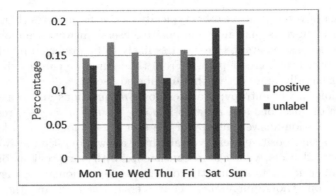

Fig. 4. Comparison of posting time throughout a week

neutral. While the promoting question shown in Fig. 1(a) is not a typical inter-rogative sentence. The questioner is not actually making an enquiry but pro-moting a brand, which makes the sentiment of the question more positive. Therefore, we use the sentiment analysis tool proposed in [8] to analyze the question text, which outputs the probability distribution of three kinds of senti-ments for a sentence, i.e., positive, negative and neutral. We add three features $\{f_{positive}, f_{negative}, f_{neutral}\}$ into the feature set, where f_s denotes the probabil-ity of sentiment s for the question.

A summary of the feature set is shown in Table 3.

Table 3. Summary of the feature set

Category	Feature description
User profile	Number of answers posted by the questioner
	Number of questions posted by the questioner
	Acceptance ratio of the questioner
	Number of votes by other users
	Experience value given by the community
	Credit points given by the community
	Question-answer entropy of the questioner
	Username related features (proportion of non-alphanumeric characters, number of unique characters, entropy of the character distribution...)
Question information	Bag-of-words features of the question text
	Posting time of the question
	Sentiment score of the question text

5   Learning Process

We have obtained a small set of positive examples and a large set of unlabeled examples, and then we analyze the characteristics for both sets and extract multiple features. In this paper, four state-of-the-art PU learning algorithms are implemented and compared to identify positive examples in the unlabeled set, which are described as below:

- **LPU**: *L*earning from *P*ositive and *U*nlabeled Examples [11] is a two-step learning process. In the first step, LPU tries to identify a set of reliable negative examples from the unlabeled set. In the second step, LPU builds a set of classifiers by iteratively applying a classification algorithm and then selects a good classifier from the set.
- **PEBL**: *P*ositive *E*xample *B*ased *L*earning [19] for Web page classification.
- **UBSD**: [12] propose a *U*ser *B*ehavior-based *S*pam-*D*etection algorithm, which is based on the Naïve Bayesian-learning framework.
- **OSVM**: *O*ne-class *SVM* [13] is an extension of standard SVM, which is appropriate for one-class classification in the context of information retrieval.

6   Experimental Results

We have tried different combinations of identification techniques and classification algorithms for LPU. It is observed that Roc-SVM gives the best results, where Rocchio technique and SVM algorithm are applied in the first and the second step, respectively.

6.1   Comparison of PU Learning Algorithms

We aim to test the ability of finding positive examples in the unlabeled set. A PU learning algorithm outputs a score for each example in the unlabeled set as the confidence value of the example being positive. To compare the performance of promotion campaign detection with different PU learning algorithms, we randomly sample 2,000 questions in the unlabeled set and manually label them as spam or nonspam. If the question contains promotion information explicitly or misleading information that will lead to promotion campaigns (as the two examples in Fig. 1), we label it as spam. Otherwise, it is labeled as nonspam. In total, 94 out of the 2,000 questions are labeled as spam. Each time we apply a PU learning algorithm, the questions receive different scores, thus having different rankings. We rank the 2,000 questions in a descending order of the score each time a PU learning algorithm completes and compare the Area Under Curve (AUC) values, as shown in Table 4.

The results show that OSVM performs the worst, which only makes use of the positive examples and misses the useful information in the unlabeled set. While LPU, PEBL and USBD take full advantage of the unlabeled examples and give better performances. Among them, LPU is able to achieve the highest AUC value as it intelligently selects the best classifier in the classification step.

Table 4. AUC values with different PU learning algorithms

Algorithm	AUC value	Improvement
OSVM	0.6398	–
UBSD	0.9197	43.7%
PEBL	0.9360	46.3%
LPU	**0.9416**	**47.2%**

6.2 Feature Analysis

To evaluate the contribution of different types of features, we adopt a leave-one-out strategy. Each time we use the whole feature set except one kind of features to evaluate the performance loss. Since LPU gives the best performance, we adopt it for the classification. We use the same 2,000 labeled examples and rank them after running the LPU algorithm with each feature set. Table 5 compares the AUC values leaving out the top-5 most important features in descending order of performance loss.

Table 5. Comparison of AUC values and performance loss leaving out different kinds of features

Features left out	AUC value	Performance loss
None	0.9416	–
Bag-of-words features	0.8506	9.7%
Posting time of the question	0.8804	6.5%
Username related features	0.9100	3.4%
Question-answer entropy	0.9137	3.0%
Acceptance ratio	0.9191	2.4%

From the results, we can see that question information related features are among the most important features. User profile related features such as username and question-answer entropy can also assist to achieve a higher AUC value. The results indicate that question information is more important on the detection of promotion campaigns than user profiles, because spammers may pretend to be legitimate users through various methods, but their questions have to show signs of promotion information to achieve their promotion goals.

6.3 Timeliness in Detection

To evaluate the effectiveness of our approach on early detection, we choose two state-of-the-art QA pair based promotion campaign detection methods [2, 10] for comparison as described in the related work. The unlabeled set consists of all the unsolved questions posted in May, when no answers are available to those questions. So we apply the baseline methods at the end of each week after May 31st to test how the newly posted answers to the questions help baseline methods detect promotion campaigns. When a new answer is available for a question, we also add the features extracted from both answer side and answerer side (similar with those in Table 3) into the learning process to enhance our detection method. For a question, if one of the QA pairs is detected as involving promotion information, we regard the question as a promoting question. At the end of each week, we randomly sample 100 questions from the results of detected promoting questions by each method for manual labeling and compute the precision. We conduct the experiments for 12 weeks from June to August and calculate the percentage of detected promoting questions each time we apply the baseline methods. We compare the percentage of detected promotion questions and corresponding precision scores of both our approach and the baselines on different dates, shown in Fig. 5.

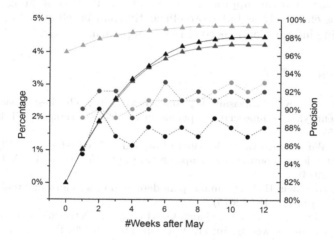

Fig. 5. Comparison of percentage of detected promoting questions (solid) and precision (dashed) between our approach and baseline methods (red: our approach, blue: [10], black: [2]) (Color figure online)

As shown in the figure, the percentage of promoting questions detected by our approach reaches 4 % when no answers are available because we do not rely on answers. With the increasing information of answers, our approach is able to detect more promoting questions and remains stable at about 4.8 % after 8 weeks. The baseline methods are able to detect more promoting questions in the first few weeks but speed down after 5 weeks, because most answers are given shortly after the questions are posted and the questions receive almost no answers after 10 weeks. While our approach is able to achieve the same effects with baseline methods 9 weeks earlier. Additionally, the precision of our approach is around

90 % at the beginning and increases with more answer information, which is comparable with [10]. Overall, since our approach is based on only questions and questioners, we can accurately detect promotion campaigns much earlier than baseline methods. Besides, with more answers available to the questions, our approach is able to detect more promoting questions.

7   Conclusion

Traditional quality estimation methods and promotion campaign detection approaches in CQA rely on both information of questions and answers. In this paper, we design a framework for early detection of promotion campaigns based on only questions and questioners. We first propose a novel sampling method to obtain a positive set and an unlabeled set. Then, we compare the characteristics of user profiles and question information between the two sets. Finally, we use the LPU algorithm to classify positive examples from the unlabeled set. Experimental results show that our approach can detect questions containing promotion campaigns as effectively as but more efficiently than baseline methods because no answer side information is needed in our approach.

References

1. Chen, C., Wu, K., Srinivasan, V., Bharadwaj, R.K.: The best answers? Think twice: identifying commercial campagins in the CQA forums. JCST **30**(4), 810–828 (2015)
2. Chen, C., Wu, K., Srinivasan, V., Bharadwaj, R.K.: The best answers? Think twice: online detection of commercial campaigns in the CQA forums. In: ASONAM, pp. 458–465 (2013)
3. Chen, Y.-R., Chen, H.-H.: Opinion spam detection in web forum: a real case study. In: WWW, pp. 173–183 (2015)
4. Ding, Z., Gong, Y., Zhou, Y., Zhang, Q., Huang, X.: Detecting spammers in community question answering. In: IJCNLP, pp. 118–126 (2013)
5. Fayazi, A., Lee, K., Caverlee, J., Squicciarini, A.: Uncovering crowdsourced manipulation of online reviews. In: SIGIR, pp. 233–242 (2015)
6. Harper, F.M., Raban, D., Rafaeli, S., Konstan, J.A.: Predictors of answer quality in online Q&A sites. In: SIGCHI, pp. 865–874 (2008)
7. Jeon, J., Croft, W.B., Lee, J.H., Park, S.: A framework to predict the quality of answers with non-textual features. In: SIGIR, pp. 228–235 (2006)
8. Jiang, F., Liu, Y., Luan, H., Sun, J., Zhu, X., Zhang, M., Ma, S.: Microblog sentiment analysis with emoticon space model. JCST **30**(5), 1120–1129 (2015)
9. Li, B., Jin, T., Lyu, M.R., King, I., Mak, B.: Analyzing and predicting question quality in community question answering services. In: WWW, pp. 775–782 (2012)
10. Li, X., Liu, Y., Zhang, M., Ma, S., Zhu, X., Sun, J.: Detecting promotion campaigns in community question answering. In: IJCAI, pp. 2348–2354 (2015)
11. Liu, B., Dai, Y., Li, X., Lee, W.S., Yu, P.S.: Building text classifiers using positive and unlabeled examples. In: ICDM, pp. 179–186 (2003)
12. Liu, Y., Chen, F., Kong, W., Yu, H., Zhang, M., Ma, S., Ru, L.: Identifying web spam with the wisdom of the crowds. TWEB **6**(1), 1–30 (2012)

13. Manevitz, L.M., Yousef, M.: One-class SVMs for document classification. J. Mach. Learn. Res. **2**, 139–154 (2002)
14. Shah, C., Pomerantz, J.: Evaluating and predicting answer quality in community QA. In: SIGIR, pp. 411–418 (2010)
15. Suryanto, M.A., Lim, E.P., Sun, A., Chiang, R.H.: Quality-aware collaborative question answering: methods and evaluation. In: WSDM, pp. 142–151 (2009)
16. Tian, T., Zhu, J., Xia, F., Zhuang, X., Zhang, T.: Crowd fraud detection in internet advertising. In: WWW, pp. 1100–1110 (2015)
17. Wang, G., Wilson, C., Zhao, X., Zhu, Y., Mohanlal, M., Zheng, H., Zhao, B.Y.: Serf and turf: crowdturfing for fun and profit. In: WWW, pp. 679–688 (2012)
18. Xu, H., Liu, D., Wang, H., Stavrou, A.: E-commerce reputation manipulation: The emergence of reputation-escalation-as-a-service. In: WWW, pp. 1296–1306 (2015)
19. Yu, H., Han, J., Chang, K.C.-C.: PEBL: positive example based learning for web page classification using SVM. In: SIGKDD, pp. 239–248 (2002)
20. Zafarani, R., Liu, H.: 10 bits of surprise: detecting malicious users with minimum information. In: CIKM, pp. 423–431 (2015)
21. Zhang, K., Wu, W., Wu, H., Li, Z., Zhou, M.: Question retrieval with high quality answers in community question answering. In: CIKM, pp. 371–380 (2014)

Generating User-oriented Text Summarization Based on Social Networks Using Topic Models

Bo Xu, Hongfei Lin[✉], Huihui Hao, Zhihao Yang, Jian Wang, and Shaowu Zhang

School of Computer Science and Technology, Dalian University of Technology,
Dalian, 116024, Liaoning, China
hflin@dlut.edu.cn

Abstract. Text summarization techniques are widely used to generate abstracts of documents automatically, facilitating users to capture the needed information from a large amount of documents. However, it poses a great challenge to satisfy the information needs of users in different roles while keeping the most important information. To solve this problem, we propose a novel framework on text summarization, which incorporates historical information of users to generate a user-oriented personalized summarization. The framework adopts two topic models to model the comments of doctors and patients from health-related social networks about certain diseases, and then identifies topics that the two kinds of users are interested in. Based on the identified topics, we propose three methods for sentence ranking to generate summarizations about the diseases for doctors and patients, respectively. Experimental results show a high similarity between the generated summarization and the real interests of different users, better meeting the information needs while keeping the summarization performance.

Keywords: Text summarization · Topic models · User-oriented summarization

1 Introduction

Text summarization is an important task in the area of text mining, which can provide the main information about the original text with a concise paragraph [1]. With the development of scientific techniques and the Internet, especially the social network, there exist large amounts of data on the web available for users to fulfill their information need, which also poses a great challenge for summarization systems to generate effective abstract paragraphs for different users.

In this paper, we mainly focus on two aspects of the summarization systems: how to extract the key information from documents, and how to extract the information a certain user really cares about. Most existing methods on summarization focus on the former one [2, 3], and the latter one is less studied. Intuitively, users in different roles may want to know different aspects about the same document. For example, doctors may view articles about human immunodeficiency virus (HIV), focusing on their research or treatment, while patients prefer to pay more attention to the prevention and symptom of HIV. Some studies have attempted to summarize the comments of different users to improve the performance. For example, Ma et al. [4] propose a topic-driven

© Springer Nature Singapore Pte Ltd. 2016
Y. Li et al. (Eds.): SMP 2016, CCIS 669, pp. 186–193, 2016.
DOI: 10.1007/978-981-10-2993-6_16

reader comments summarization system to tackle this problem. However, it remains a problem on how to interpret the information needs and interests of users. To model the users' interests, we attempt to utilize the data from social networks because users' posts on the web every day to express their feelings, which reflects the habits and interests of the users.

In this paper, we propose a novel user-oriented summarization framework by incorporating users' interests. Specifically, we acquire the real-time data that users' posts on the web, and then conduct topic modeling on these data with state-of-the-art topic models to model their interests. Finally, we incorporate the topic information into the summarization process to measure the importance of sentences. We examine the performance of our framework based on posts from the health-related forum MedHelp, and model the interests of doctors and patients, respectively. Experimental results show that our framework can effectively summarize the documents, and provide useful summaries for users in different roles to meet diversified information needs.

The rest of this paper is organized as follows: We give detailed descriptions of our user-oriented framework in Sect. 2. In Sect. 3, we introduce the experimental settings, and show the performance of our framework. Finally, we conclude the paper in Sect. 4.

2 Automatic Generation of User-oriented Disease Summarization

2.1 Data Collection

To obtain the related corpus about certain diseases, one intuitive way is to extract related citations in MEDLINE and take the contents of all the abstracts as the candidate sentences. However, the obtained corpus may comprise irrelevant sentences because of the noises in the raw text. To solve the problem, we propose to use SemRep [5] to acquire relevant corpus for our framework. SemRep is a program that can automatically extract semantic predications from biomedical free text. We download all the citations of articles for a certain disease, use SemRep to extract the semantic relations in these documents, filter the irrelevant sentences to the disease, and finally obtain the candidate sentence set for further refinement.

In order to model users' interests, we resort to health-related forum MedHelp, which is a popular online communication platform for doctors and patients in the United States established in 1994. Since there are many comments on MedHelp, it may be an effective resource to model users' interests. It should also be noticed that due to the particularity of biomedical field, there exists a lot of terminologies. By observing the comments, we find that the comments of patients are usually colloquial, while the comments of doctors tend to be more specialized and professional. So before modeling users' preference, we utilizes open-access and collaborative consumer health vocabulary (OAC CHV) to standardize the comments of different users, namely mapping the oral terms in comments to concepts in Metathesaurus of UMLS [6].

2.2   Topic Modeling

The task of this step is mainly about modeling the comments achieved in the previous step to model topics that users are interested in. To achieve it, topic model is used. It originates from Latent Semantic Analysis (LSA) [7] and can find the implicit topics in documents automatically. In this model, the basic idea is that documents are represented as random mixtures over latent topics, where each topic is characterized by a distribution over words. Here we used two useful topic models, pLSA [8] and LDA [9] to model the comments that patients and doctors made on HIV. After modeling the topics on users' comments by both of pLSA and LDA, we can obtain the topics that different users are interested in, and each topic corresponds to a group of related terms, which would be used in the next step.

2.3   Summary Generation

Summary generation is to automatically generate user-oriented summarization based on the topic models. Specifically, we rank the candidate sentences in consideration of user preferences to obtain the final summarization. To measure the relevance degrees of each sentence with respect to users' topics, we propose three methods to calculate the weight of sentences, which is described as follows in more details. After weighting on sentences, we sort these sentences, and top-ranked ones will be chosen as the final summary in our framework.

Sentence Ranking based on Topic Term Frequencies. This method assumes that if one of topic terms occurs once in a sentence, then add 1 point to the sentence, otherwise not. After the calculation, we normalize the score by the length of the sentence as follows.

$$Score(S_j) = \frac{\sum_{t \in topic, t \in S_j} freq(t)}{\sum_{t \in S_j} freq(t)} \tag{1}$$

where S_j is the jth candidate sentence, t is one term in S_j, and *topic* refers to the topic term set.

Sentence Ranking based on Topic Term Weights. The second method assumes that if one of the topic terms occurs once in a sentence, then add the weight of the topic term to the sentence, where the weight is obtained as $P(w|z)$ by topic modeling. Similarly, we normalize the score using the total weights of all the words in the candidate sentence.

$$Score(S_j) = \frac{\sum_{t \in topic, t \in S_j} weight(t)}{\sum_{t \in S_j} weight(t)} \tag{2}$$

Sentence Ranking based on Okapi BM25. In the third method, we introduce a classic information retrieval scoring function, Okapi BM25, to measure the importance of sentences. Specifically, given a topic covering topic terms $z_1, z_2, \ldots, z_n$, the similarity between the sentence and the topic can be computed as follows.

$$Score(S_j) = \sum_{i=1}^{n} IDF(z_i) \times \frac{f(z_i, s_j) \times (k+1)}{f(z_i, s_j) + k \times (1 - b + b \times \frac{|S_j|}{avg|S|})} \tag{3}$$

where $f(z_i, S)$ is the frequency of z_i in sentence S, $|S|$ is its length, $avg|S|$ denotes the average length of sentences in candidate set. k and d are parameters and empirically set to be 1.2 and 0.75, respectively. IDF is the inverse document frequency.

Remove Redundancy. After weighting the candidate sentences, we find that similarities among sentences in a summary may increase the redundancy of the summary. Therefore, in this step, we introduce a state-of-the-art method, called Maximal Marginal Relevance (MMR) [10], to remove the redundancy in the set of candidate sentences. The intuition of the methods is that if the sentence has a high similar degree with the ones already in the summary, then it should be punished.

Specially, let S be the set of sentences in the final summary, C be the set of candidate sentences. The MMR algorithm can be described as follows.

Step 1: Set $S = \Phi$, $C = \{s_i \mid i = 1,2, ..., n\}$. Compute scores for each sentences in C using Eqs. (1), (2) and (3).

Step 2: Rank the candidate sentences based on the scores in a descending order.

Step 3: Take the sentence with the highest score to S, and update the remaining scores using the following equation.

$$Score(S_j) = Score(S_j) - w * sim(S_j, S_i), i \neq j \tag{4}$$

where w is the penalty factor, $sim(S_j, S_i)$ measures the similarity between the sentence S_j and S_i by cosine similarity.

Step 4: Repeat Step 2 and Step 3 until a fix-length summary is obtained.

In our experiment, we empirically set the w to be 2.0 and the length of summary to be 300 words. After removing the redundancy of candidate sentences, we obtain the final sentences to form the outputted summary of our overall framework. Next, we will examine the performance of our framework by extensive experiments.

3 Experiments

3.1 Experimental Settings

Our framework mainly focuses on generating patient-oriented and doctor-oriented summaries about HIV. As described before, we generated 4 groups of summaries: lda_doc, lda_pat, plsa_doc, plsa_pat, in which doc and pat denote doctor and patient, respectively. lda and plsa refer to the two topic modeling approaches we used to generate the summaries. In our experiment, we empirically set the length of final summary as 300 words. For the corpus we used, we collected all the articles about HIV in MEDLINE between the year of 2010 and 2012, and achieved 4,581 sentences related to HIV as the candidate sentences. Meanwhile, we crawled all comments about HIV in the forum "Ask a Doctor" in MedHelp, which contains 25,837 pieces of comments of doctors and 39,553 pieces of comments of patients. For the systems we compared, we choose three state-of-the-art systems as baseline systems, namely MEAD [11], LexRank [12] and SumBasic [13]. Besides, we also compare our framework with one method based on SemRep, which sorts sentences with the BM25 model after relation extraction, filtering and expansion with SemRep. For the evaluation measures, we evaluate extracted summaries mainly using ROUGE [14] measure and semantic similarity with manually generated summaries [15].

3.2 Summary Performance

We evaluate the summary produced by our framework in comparison with the Wikipedia definition and the manual constructed summary using sentence ranking method based on topic term frequencies. For the evaluation by definitions on Wikipedia, we list the ROUGE scores at different levels in Table 1.

Table 1. Performance of all summaries evaluated by the referenced summary on Wikipedia

Methods	ROUGE-1	ROUGE-2	ROUGE-SU4
MEAD [11]	0.3403	0.0526	0.1088
LexRank [12]	0.3613	0.0579	0.1306
SumBasic [13]	0.3194	0.0411	0.1067
SemRep	0.3665	0.0684	0.1465
lda_doc	**0.4241**	0.0579	0.0165
lda_pat	0.3874	0.0474	**0.1544**
plsa_doc	0.3613	0.0421	0.1297
plsa_pat	0.3874	**0.0947**	0.1481

In the table, we compare our user-oriented summaries with the baseline systems to examine the performance. From the table, we find that our framework achieves better performance than the state-of-the-art systems. For the four groups of summarizations by our framework, the performance of LDA based summarizations is slightly better than pLSA based ones both for the doctor and the patient. We also find that performances of summarizations for doctors and patients are incomparable, indicating the information needs of these two kinds of users are different.

Since the Wikipedia-based evaluation cannot distinguish the information needs for users in different roles, we further evaluate our framework by manually created user-oriented summaries to enhance the evaluations. We asked two groups of experts to make summaries for HIV, one is for doctors and the other is for patients. Table 2 shows the ROUGE scores of our summaries. From the tables, we find that the average performance of our method outperforms the baseline systems in terms of all the evaluation measures, which shows that the user-oriented topic modeling is useful for generating summaries. We also find LDA based summarization is more suitable for patient-oriented topic modeling, and pLSA based summarization is more suitable for doctor-oriented topic modeling.

Table 2. Performance of summaries for doctors evaluated by the manual created summary

Users	Methods	ROUGE-1	ROUGE-2	ROUGE-SU4
For doctors	MEAD [11]	0.3071	0.0376	0.0954
	LexRank [12]	0.2490	0.0250	0.0715
	SumBasic [13]	0.2988	0.0500	0.1014
	SemRep	0.3403	0.5000	0.1245
	lda_doc	0.3444	0.0250	0.1170
	plsa_doc	**0.3900**	**0.0625**	**0.1492**
For patients	MEAD [11]	0.2652	0.0366	0.0702
	LexRank [12]	0.1971	0.0293	0.0473
	SumBasic [13]	0.2530	0.0585	0.0813
	SemRep	0.2895	0.0463	0.0948
	lda_pat	**0.3212**	**0.0610**	**0.1051**
	plsa_pat	0.3090	0.0561	0.0967

To examine whether the summaries generated by our framework are coherent with the users' interests, we measure the coherence degree by semantic similarity. To compute semantic similarity between words, we used word2vec [16] tool to represent words as real-valued vectors, and compute their cosine similarity. Here we extracted all the articles related to HIV in MEDLINE from the year 2003 to 2009 to train the word vectors. Table 3 shows our results. In the table, lda_doc, lda_pat, plsa_doc, plsa_pat refers to the topic distribution produced by LDA or pLSA for doctors and patients, respectively. From the table, we can find that semantic similarity by our method is higher than those based on other methods, which indicates that our user-oriented summaries can better meet the information need of users in different roles.

Table 3. Semantic Similarity Between Summaries and Corresponding Topics

Methods	lda_doc	lda_pat	plsa_doc	plsa_pat	Average
MEAD [11]	0.3174	0.4080	0.3472	0.2889	0.3404
LexRank [12]	0.2234	0.2898	0.2581	0.1922	0.2409
SumBasic [13]	0.2221	0.3088	0.2552	0.1896	0.2439
SemRep	0.2560	0.3364	0.3021	0.2193	0.2785
Ours	**0.3693**	**0.4894**	**0.3902**	**0.3804**	**0.4073**

3.3 Comparison of Three Sentence Ranking Methods

We also compare the proposed three sentence ranking methods. Figure 1 shows that experimental results evaluated by ROUGE-1 in terms of Wikipedia definitions and semantic similarities, where Frequencies, Weights and BM25 refers to sentences ranking methods based on topic term frequencies, topic term weights and Okapi BM25 model, respectively. In the left panel, it seems difficult to tell which method is the best one. The reason for the observation can be that ROUGE-1 only takes co-occurrence into account for evaluation, and wouldn't care about what weight of a term is. In the right panel, the method by computing term frequencies achieves the highest semantic similarity, followed by the way of summing up all weights of terms, which show that topic term frequencies based sentence ranking is more effective to measure the importance of sentence to generate the summary.

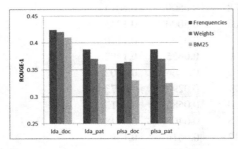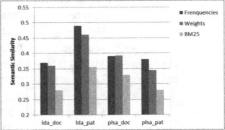

Fig. 1. ROUGE-1 scores (left) and semantic similarity (right) of sentence ranking methods

4   Conclusion

In this paper, we proposed a novel user-oriented text summarization system. We take doctors and patients as experiment subjects, and model their preferences about HIV with pLSA and LDA to find their interests. Then with these topics, generate doctor-oriented and patient-oriented summaries. From experimental results, we find that our summaries have a high semantic similarity with users' topics and therefore meet their information need better. Meanwhile, the generated summaries achieve the best summarization performance compared with the baseline methods. In future work, we will apply our framework for more specific users and other popular diseases to generate more personalized summarization.

Acknowledgements. This work is partially supported by grant from the Natural Science Foundation of China (No. 61277370, 61402075, 61572102), Natural Science Foundation of Liaoning Province, China (No. 201202031, 2014020003), State Education Ministry and The Research Fund for the Doctoral Program of Higher Education (No. 20090041110002), the Fundamental Research Funds for the Central Universities. The 12th five year national science and technology supporting programs of China under Grant No. 2015BAF20B02.

References

1. Luhn, H.P.: The automatic creation of literature abstracts. IBM J. Res. Dev. **2**(2), 159–165 (1958)
2. Louis, A., Joshi, A., Nenkova, A.: Discourse indicators for content selection in summarization. Paper Presented at the Proceedings of the 11th Annual Meeting of the Special Interest Group on Discourse and Dialogue (2010)

3. Zhang, H., Fiszman, M., Shin, D., Wilkowski, B., Rindflesch, T.C.: Clustering cliques for graph-based summarization of the biomedical research literature. BMC Bioinform. **14**(1), 182 (2013)
4. Ma, Z., Sun, A., Yuan, Q., Cong, G.: Topic-driven reader comments summarization. Paper Presented at the Proceedings of the 21st ACM International Conference on Information and Knowledge Management (2012)
5. Rindflesch, T.C., Fiszman, M.: The interaction of domain knowledge and linguistic structure in natural language processing: interpreting hypernymic propositions in biomedical text. J. Biomed. Inf. **36**(6), 462–477 (2003)
6. Zeng, Q.T., Tse, T.: Exploring and developing consumer health vocabularies. J. Am. Med. Inf. Assoc. **13**(1), 24–29 (2006)
7. Deerwester, S.C., Dumais, S.T., Landauer, T.K., Furnas, G.W., Harshman, R.A.: Indexing by latent semantic analysis. JASIS **41**(6), 391–407 (1990)
8. Hofmann, T.: Probabilistic latent semantic indexing. Paper Presented at the Proceedings of the 22nd Annual International ACM SIGIR Conference on Research and Development in Information Retrieval (1999)
9. Blei, D.M., Ng, A.Y., Jordan, M.I.: Latent dirichlet allocation. J. Mach. Learn. Res. **3**, 993–1022 (2003)
10. Carbonell, J., Goldstein, J.: The use of MMR, diversity-based reranking for reordering documents and producing summaries. Paper Presented at the Proceedings of the 21st Annual International ACM SIGIR Conference on Research and Development in Information Retrieval (1998)
11. Radev, D., Allison, T., Blair-Goldensohn, S., Blitzer, J., Celebi, A., Dimitrov, S., Liu, D.: MEAD-a platform for multidocument multilingual text summarization (2004)
12. Erkan, G., Radev, D.R.: LexRank: Graph-based lexical centrality as salience in text summarization. J. Artif. Intell. Res. (JAIR) **22**(1), 457–479 (2004)
13. Vanderwende, L., Suzuki, H., Brockett, C., Nenkova, A.: Beyond SumBasic: Task-focused summarization with sentence simplification and lexical expansion. Inf. Process. Manag. **43**(6), 1606–1618 (2007)
14. Lin, C.-Y.: Rouge: a package for automatic evaluation of summaries. Paper Presented at the Text Summarization Branches Out: Proceedings of the ACL-04 Workshop (2004)
15. Achananuparp, P., Hu, X., Shen, X.: The evaluation of sentence similarity measures. In: Song, I.-Y., Eder, J., Nguyen, T.M. (eds.) DaWaK 2008. LNCS, vol. 5182, pp. 305–316. Springer, Heidelberg (2008)
16. Mikolov, T., Chen, K., Corrado, G., Dean, J.: Efficient Estimation of Word Representations in Vector Space. arXiv preprint arXiv:1301.3781 (2013)

Discovering Region Features
Based on User's Comments

Huangliang Sun, Olaoluwa Esho$^{(\boxtimes)}$, Junling Liu, and Lingyu Pang

School of Information and Control Engineering, Shenyang Jianzhu University,
Shenyang 110168, China
{sunhl,liujl}@sjzu.edu.cn, oksesho@yahoo.com

Abstract. With the development of web 2.0 technology, people can not only have access to information on the internet but can express their opinions, engage in on-line discussion and interact within the network's platform. By analyzing user comment from the same region, we can understand the implied region features and trending topics in that region. Region features can be categorized as an event or topic therefore it can be labeled based on the user's comment.

In this paper, we propose the discovery of similar topics based on semantics and level or extent of attention focusing on the user's comment data. Semantics represents the user's comment while level of attention represents the amount of user's comment on a news topic, therefore, semantics and the level of attention reveals the user's comment behavior. This paper uses the *LDA* and *K-means* clustering algorithm to analyze similar topics in a region and proposes methods to determine region features. By analyzing the region features and the similar region topics, the labeled region topics can be used for advertisement, improve business strategies, and as a reference for regional administration and planning which has a practical significance.

Keywords: Region feature · User comment · Feature measurement · Similar regions

1 Introduction

With the popularity and rapid development of web 2.0, many web applications like Twitter, Sina news, Baidu, Tencent, MicroBlog have been the front runners for acquiring information. With the popularity of these applications, users can no longer obtain information passively but more users can both actively and passively obtaining information by making comments on a news topic, publishing blogs, sharing information (pictures, videos), rating contents (movies, songs) across various networking platforms. The way users publish information through on-line web services reflect the propensity of their opinions. For instance, the views and emotional expressions of a user in real-time social events can be used to analyze on-line public opinions. Regulators can grasp public opinions direction in real time, monitor hot topic which plays an important role in maintaining a

© Springer Nature Singapore Pte Ltd. 2016
Y. Li et al. (Eds.): SMP 2016, CCIS 669, pp. 194–206, 2016.
DOI: 10.1007/978-981-10-2993-6_17

healthy, civilized, and secured network environment. The hotspot of user's views and comments shows the obvious regional feature, for instance, some areas are sensitive to political topics while other areas focus more on economy topics.

Social media networks have the ability to provide users with location-based services through signing in from a GPS compatible cellphone combined with the location information. For example, users of Twitter social network can include the current location when tweeting or posting images; users of Foursquare platform can sign in to search for places, such as hotels, shopping malls and movies theaters. Also, website like Flickr allows users to upload photos and add a text label to the images uploaded which can be tagged with the current location.

This paper uses comment of users from various regions to find regional feature. A large amount of data from users comment was used to find topics and users interest in a region, which was then used to analyze user's focus, life pattern, social activities and regional function.

The rest of this paper is structured as follows. In Sect. 2, we discuss related works, a detailed description of the data is presented in Sect. 3 while Sects. 4 and 5 discusses methods of discovering regional features and how to extract the regional features based on the extent of attention. In Sect. 6 we presents the experimental results. Finally, this work is concluded in Sect. 7.

2 Related Work

There have been various analysis on geographical topic and label of regional function in related studies both locally and abroad [3], regional function and geographical topic are indicated by location labeling (e.g.interest points) or user's behavior in a region and geographic coordinate. [12,15] presented a method for expressing location information by using location labeling in distinguishing the functions in different locations. However this analysis was done without putting into consideration the latitude and longitude information in user's activity areas. Other research [6,11,13] represents location as the coordinates used to describe the user's activity area. Their analysis was without functional feature that includes location and they hypothesized that similar location has the same functional features. Eisentein et al. [11] used the regional bivariate Gaussian distribution to create position coordinates. Sizov [13] introduced GeoFolk Model to manage geographic reference documentation, where each geographic region represents a different function of a topic. Other research work used transportation data with the combination of mobile data to infer travel purpose and extract human activities [5,7], they mined transportation data from multi-data source to infer the purpose of travel. [4] used travel activities based on spatiotemporal points to mine various human activity pattern from mobile data but they did not determine the region features.

Many studies combined location labeling, latitude and longitude information for analysis. Literature [8] mentioned geographical pictures often reflect the popular tourist attractions, and check-in data shows the daily life preferences of the natives. The author analyzed geographically labeled photos and check-in data to find the region of interest in a city. Literature [9] divided a city into several region thereby functional feature can be inferred according to the personal Mobility Patterns (GPS) and Point of Interests (POIs) in each region. The strength of each function in different position can be determined.

Yin et al. [6] used photo data from Flickr to propose a hybrid model based on *PLSA* that includes text and location information, and compared geographical distributions among the preferences with the same topic. Jiang et al. [9] used clustering algorithm to cluster crowd into different types of groups while including time and space factors. They found space-time structure of city diversity by estimating and visualizing cumulative spatial density of the period of people's activity in each group. Ferrari et al. [10] used *LDA* topic model to extract urban pattern through location-based social networks. According to statistical feature of the data, geographic spatial region caused by social media is also used to label regional function. Qi et al. [16] found that the number of the taxi passengers getting on or off can define activity intensity in a region and regional function. Wakamiya et al. [14] observed urban region function by the data tweeted by users in the city through the Twitter social media. In their paper, they divided a day into four average periods and labeled the functions of each region by counting the change in regularity of the number of group publishing micro-blog, number of micro-blog and number of regional group movement in each region over each period of time.

According to user's comment and the analysis of regional feature, this paper proposes discovering similar topic in a region based on semantic and level of attention with its method. This paper uses *LDA* and *k-means* algorithm to analyze similar topics in a region according to user's specific comment, and proposes methods to measure the discrepancy of regional feature according to user's comment sequence.

3   Data Preparation

On-line news sites provide information on different categories of topic. In general, popularly labeled topics are closely related to people's lifestyle or user's preference. These categories of topics are more descriptive and general. Analyzing comments in these popularly labeled topics makes it easier to understand the behavior of user's comments. After analyzing the number of comments in each category of topics from the sina network [1], this paper chose eight popular categories with comments as the experimental data.

The eight categories includes sports, politics, society, science and technology, health, finance, education and environment. This paper adopts the following form of comment sets; $User_{id}$, $Location$, $post_{time}$ and $text$ as shown in Table 1.

Definition 1. *User's comment is expressed as ($User_{id}$, $Location$, $Post_{time}$, $Text$), where $User_{id}$ represents User's ID or nickname; $Post_{time}$ represents the time Users publish comments; $Text$ represents the content of the User's comments. User's comment sets D is made up of many comments $\{d1, d2, d3, \cdots, d_n\}$.*

Table 1. User comments

User-id	Location	Post-time	Text
Nini**	Beijing	2014-04-19	winner takes all, Outstanding!
yy****an	Sichuang Chengdu	2014-04-27	Happy!!!
Pinglun	Shandong Jinan	2014-05-18	An opportunity to qualify for European cup has been wasted!!

3.1   Region Division

The content of the news and the degree of topic attention in a population are related to, or depends on, administrative region. This paper focuses on administrative areas. In User's comments, location includes two information *"province+ city"*. This paper uses *"province"* to separate region. For example, *Location = "Beijing"*, *Region = "Beijing"*, *Location = "Sichuang Chengdu"*, *Region = "Sichuang"*.

Definition 2. *Regional user's comment set* $D_j = \{d_{1,j}, d_{2,j}, d_{3,j}, \cdots, \}$, *where* D_j *is User's comment in Region j and $d_{m,j}$ is the number of comment m in region j.*

Definition 3. *Regional topic comment set* $D_{i,j} = \{d_{i,1}, d_{i,2}, d_{i,3}, \cdots\}$, *where* $D_{i,j}$ *is the comment set in $Topic_{(i)}$ of $Region_{(j)}$, $d_{i,n}$ which represent the number of comment n in set $Topic$ $D_{i,j}$.*

4   Discovering Similar Topic Region Based on Semantic

This paper proposes discovering similar topic region based on semantics from User's comments on a Topic. Semantics reveal User's comment behavior and shows how users tend to discuss a topics. User's comments reflect their views, opinions and emotions about the topic. Generally, people living in different region have different preference or concerns. People living in the same geographical location will tend to have similar environment and living habits. Therefore User's in these regions will have similar views and opinions on a topic. Finding a region with a similar topic provides a reference for planning, development and resource allocation among these regions. This paper identifies the topic distribution in each region through semantics by analyzing the contents of User's comment. Then it captures the region with similar topic feature after performing clustering analysis on the region. The process is shown in Fig. 1.

To discover region of similar topics, this paper uses *LDA* [2] to learn regional topic distribution feature. Each document in the document set is represented by $d = \{w_1, w_2, \cdots, w_n\}$, where w_n is Word number n. A document set is made up of M documents represented by $D = \{d_1, d_2, \cdots, d_M\}$. For Document generation, the steps are described as follows.

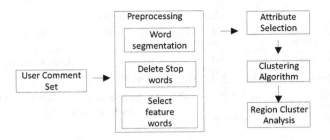

Fig. 1. Region similar topic discovery process.

1. For a document in the document set, determining the length of document N is important, where N is subject to *Poisson Distribution*, $N \sim Poisson(\xi)$, N.
2. For Document d of the document set, the document-topic distribution vector θ is generated according to *Dirichlet Distribution*, Dir (α).
3. For every Topic z, the topic-word distribution vector φ is generated according to Dirichlet Distribution, Dir (β).
4. For each word w in the document set,
    (a) Choosing a *Topic z* from Multinomial distribution Multinomial (θ).
    (b) Choosing a word w_n from polynomial conditional probability distribution Multinomial (φ).
    Repeat the above process for N times to finish generating the document.

The key to building the *LDA* Model is by implying topic-word distribution φ and document-topic distribution θ. In *LDA* Topic Model, Parameter θ and φ represent document-topic probability distribution matrix and topic-word probability distribution matrix. The process of modeling *LDA* is generating θ and φ matrix and learning document-topic matrix D.

This paper preprocesses text data of user's comment contents in advance. After preprocessing, removing the noise data from meta-data makes the original text to comply with the algorithm requirements. Data preprocessing in this paper includes Chinese word segmentation, part of speech tagging, deleting stop word and extracting topic feature word.

This paper adopts *ICTCLAS* (Institute of Computing Technology, Chinese Lexical Analysis System), which provides functions like Chinese word segmentation, part of speech tagging and named entity recognition.

The word segmentation stand-alone speed is $500\,\text{KB/s}$, and accuracy is as high as $98.45\,\%$ which is the best Chinese word segmentation system for this process. For stop word, this paper adopts the method for creating a stop word list. There are many meaningless words for a *Topic* in the document with high frequency, like "of", "the". The contribution of the words called stop word to document's *Topic* is little. Removing stop words from preprocessed result can improve the efficiency of text topic learning. This paper chose stop word table set to delete stop word. The set includes Harbin Institute of Technology stop word list, Sichuang University and intelligence laboratory stop words library and Baidu stop word list.

It is widely believed that semantic content information is expressed by nouns, verbs and adjectives in a text. So after word segmentation and deleting stop words, this paper extracts the words with nouns ($/n$), adjective ($/a$) and verb ($/v$) as topic feature words. It's difficult to express a clear meaning by single word. So this paper reserves the single words or phrase as topic feature words, which are made up of two or more words. After text preprocessing, the $Text$ shown in Table 1 obtains the form: "Winner takes all, Outstanding", "Happy", "An opportunity to enter the European Cup has been wasted".

Definition 4. *Regional feature comments $d_m, j = \{w_1, w_2, w_3, \cdots\}$, where w_n is the topic feature word, $w_n \in v$, v is the list of topic feature word.*

The regions with similar topics have the tendency to have the same topic distribution. The User's comments from all categories are classified as documents and are used as input to the LDA model. This paper makes the probability distribution the topic features distribution vector in a region, and computes regional similarity by computing cosine similarity of topic tendency distribution in each region, then uses K-Means algorithm to perform clustering analysis on the region.

Definition 5. *Regional topic features distribution vector: $d_j =< p_{j,1}, p_{j,2}, p_{j,3}, \cdots >$, where p_j is the probability of Region j for a given Topic l. The cosine similarity between two regional feature distribution vector can be used to find region similarity. The equation of region similarity is as follows:*

$$RegionSim(d_1, d_2) = \frac{d_1 \cdot d_2}{\|d_1\| \times \| d_2 \|}$$

$$= \frac{\sum_{l=1}^{k} P_{t,l} \cdot P_{s,l}}{\sqrt{\sum_{l=1}^{k} P_{t,l}^2} \cdot \sqrt{\sum_{l=1}^{k} P_{s,l}^2}} \tag{1}$$

The process for discovering similar topic region clustering algorithm is as follows:

- Step one: Text preprocessing.
- Step two: For all news topics, enter regional feature contents with topic feature words into LDA topic model. making all contents in each region a document.
- Step three: Entering the number of topics and topic words, Parameter α and β. Then getting the result θ, region - theme probability distribution, and then computing regional similarity.
- Step four: Entering the number of category. Using K-Means to perform clustering analysis on the region based on region similarity.

The recognition of similar topic region through clustering algorithm is shown in Algorithm 1.

Algorithm 1. Similar Region Clustering

```
Input: K(the number of cluster), document-topic distribution matrix
Output: C_k: K clusters in region set
```
1 **while** $\Delta C_k \neq 0$ **do**
2   **for** *each Cluster* C_i **do**
3   Computing the average of all objects to get a new center of
      the cluster;
4   Update Cluster C_k;

5 **return** C_k;

---

5   Extracting Regional Feature Based on Comments Attention

The Information on user's comments not only includes semantic information of comments, but also includes the number of user's who commented on the news topic. The amount of comment in a region on a specific topic can be referred to as *"The user comments level of attention"*. The *level of attention* is used to quantify the user comment data set. The *level of attention* describes the extents of attention on a topic of interest of the user and helps to understand the focus of attention and living habit at that particular region. For example, people of one region pay more attention to the latest phone model and they discuss about it while people from other region are less interested in it. Discovering these region features can be very useful to the local administrative department, business advertising, planning and marketing. This section discusses the method on how to extract region feature. We use the frequency of Users comments from all region comment based on different category of news to represent region model. We propose three methods to measure the region feature. Maximum feature measurement, Minimum feature measurement, and Maximum offset distance.

From the measured region feature we can determine the most important and less important topic category from each region. Preprocessing is not needed, because we only make use of the comments frequency from each region.

Definition 6. *User's comments set* $C = \{c_1, c_2, c_3, \cdots\}$, $c_i = \{d_1, d_2, d_3, \cdots\}$, *expresses the User comments set of* i^{th} *category,* d_m *is the* m^{th} *user comment.*

Definition 7. *Regional comment pattern* $PR = <valueR_{(1)}, valueR_{(2)}, \cdots, valueR_{(n)}>$ *is the comment vector of user interested in different news topic category in a region R. And* $valueR_{(i)}$ *is the number of user's* i^{th} *comment in Region R.*

Figure 2 is regional comment pattern diagram, where every curve represents a region comment model. In this figure, *category* represent i^{th} topic category, *value* is the number of comment on a topic. *regionA*, *regionB*, *regionC* and *regionD* represent the comment sequence of every region's for different topic. Due to varying population in different regions, the number of comments differs.

Therefore a region with more population tends to have more comment. In order to have a balanced data, this paper normalizes on every comment model. In the normalization process, this paper calculate the proportion of every category value of a topic and the sum thus every $valueR_{(i)}$ is a number between [0,1]. The normalization process formula is as follows in Eq. 2 and the result is shown in Fig. 3

$$value_{r,j}(i) = \frac{value_i}{\sum_{i=1}^{n} value_i}, \ i = 1, 2, \cdots, n \tag{2}$$

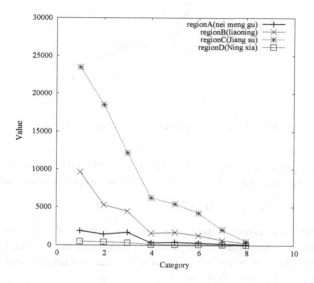

Fig. 2. Region comment pattern

Definition 8. *Comment frequency $value_{rj}(i)$ represent the comment frequency of ith topic category in region rj.*

The regional model based on comment frequency $P_{rj} = <value_{rj}(1), value_{rj}(2), value_{rj}(3), \cdots >$ is the sequence vector of user's comment frequency for different topic category in region $rj.value_{rj}(i)$

This paper uses the regional feature measurement to find the most abnormal dimension in every region's model, that is which category abnormal in every region or have abnormal dimensionality in comment frequency sequence of every region. This paper proposes three methods to measure regional feature which includes the following: Maximum feature measurement, Minimum feature measurement, Maximum offset distance. In maximum feature measurement, the most abnormal dimension of the comment sequence vector is the maximum frequency

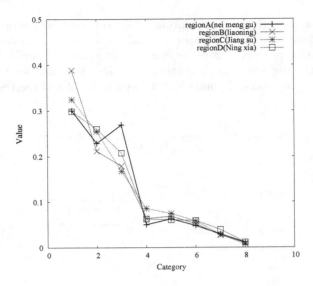

Fig. 3. Normalized region comment pattern

vector, which represent the category with the maximum comment frequency of every region. The maximum feature measurement formula is as follows in Eq. 3

$$max(j) = Max\{value_{rj}\}, \ i = 1, 2, \cdots, n \tag{3}$$

In minimum feature measurement, the most abnormal dimension of comment sequence vector is the minimum frequency vector, that is, it is the category with minimum comment frequency of every region. The minimum feature measurement formula is as follows. Equation 4

$$min(j) = Min\{value_{rj}\}, \ i = 1, 2, \cdots, n \tag{4}$$

Both maximum feature measurement and minimum feature measurement are based on absolute maximum and absolute minimum of comment frequency, but maximum offset distance is based on relative maximum and relative minimum of comment frequency. This can be used to discover the most abnormal dimension of every region. The maximum offset distance is compared to an *average model*, and the *average model* is obtained calculating the average comment frequency sequence value of all region. In order to eliminate the influence of extreme value, this paper removes the average tail, removes top and bottom 10 % extreme value of every vector of all p_{rj}, then calculates the average value. We call the *average model* the *stability model*, the formula to calculate the stability model is as follows in Eq. 5:

$$value_i = \frac{\sum_{j \in S} value_{rj}(i)}{|S|}, \ i = 1, 2, \cdots, n \ and \ j \in S. \tag{5}$$

Definition 9. Stability model $P = <Value_1, Value_2, Value_3, \cdots>$ *is the aver-age model vector of all region,* $Value_i$ *represent comment frequency value of* i^{th} *category topic. After calculating the* stability model, *the maximum range shift of every region is calculated. The maximum offset distance is max difference of one vector of region model vector compared with* stability model. *Maximum offset distance formula of every region is as follows in Eq. 6:*

$$d_{max}(j) = Max\{\frac{value_i - value_{rj}(i)}{value_i}\}$$
$$i = 1, 2, \cdots, n, j = 1, 2, \cdots, k$$

(6)

Because the frequency of comments on different topic category varies, we calculate the value of $|value_i - value_{rj}(i)|$ which is the vector difference between *region model and stability model.* The higher the value of $value_{rj}$ the higher the value of the vector difference $|value_i - value_{rj}(i)|$. Also, the smaller the values of $value_i$ the smaller the value of the vector difference. The regional feature measurement can be used to calculate the most abnormal dimension, only calculating $|value_i - value_{rj}(i)|$ will not discover the abnormal dimensions that is in the region. So this paper uses the ratio of $|value_i - value_{rj}(i)|$ to $Value_i$ to calculate the maximum value from all categories.

6   Experiments

This paper's uses the data set on active user comment from the Sina's News Network, and crawled eight categories of Topics from users comment data between 2013/9 to 2014/6 which consist of over 2,347,245 amount of data. In this experiment, we performed the test on 31 provinces to find region feature and similar regional clusters.

6.1   The Result of Similar Region Cluster Analysis

For the similar regional cluster analysis, the input of *LDA* model are $\alpha = 50/K, \beta = 0.1, K = 8, T = 10$. This paper chose $k = 3, k = 5$ *and* $k = 7$ as the number of clusters to find region cluster (Table 2).

According to the clusters, we discovered geographical distribution, so we can infer that neighboring geographical region have similar topic distribution feature. Because people who live in neighboring region have similar environment and living habit.

6.2   The Result of Region Feature

In the experiment on region feature discovery, we separately compared maximum feature measurement, minimum feature measurement and maximum offset distance measurement. And chose the top-10 of the result as the output.

Table 2. Cluster result for k=7

Cluster	Region
Cluster 1	Guangdong, Heilongjiang, Hubei, Zhejiang
Cluster 2	Fujian, Hebei, Henan
Cluster 3	Beijing, Hainan, Shanxi
Cluster 4	Guizhou, Jiangsu, Liaoning,Tibet, Yunnan, Chongqing
Cluster 5	Anhui, Guangxi, Hunan, Qinghai, Shandong, Shanghai, Sichuang, Xinjiang
Cluster 6	Gansu, Shanxi
Cluster 7	Jilin, Jiangxi, Neimenggu, Ningxia, Tianjin

For maximum feature measurement, we discovered all region belong to sports category except Tibet which is Politics category. Maximum feature represent the category with the most user comment in the region. Sports category have the most user, therefore the number of comment on sports is the most in every region, but we can't conclude that these regions possess sports feature. Table 3 shows the top-10 result of minimum feature. From this table we can see all region belong to the environment category. The result shows the category that has the least user comment in this region.

Table 3. Result of minimum feature measurement

top-10	Region	Category-min
1	Liaoning	Environment
2	Guizhou	Environment
3	Henan	Environment
4	Shanxi	Environment
5	Chongqin	Environment
6	Zhejiang	Environment
7	Tibet	Environment
8	Jilin	Environment
9	Hainan	Environment
10	Ningxia	Environment

Table 4 shows the top-10 result of maximum offset distance measurement. From this table we can see the category of every region feature is different because maximum offset distance calculates the relative maximum frequency of every category. The relative *stability model*, indicates average comment situation. The maximum offset distance shows the relative comment minimum or relative comment maximum in the category of any region, which means that

Table 4. Result of maximum offset distance measurement

top-10	Region	Category-d_{max}
1	Liaoning	Environment
2	Beijing	Environment
3	Guizhou	Environment
4	Chongqin	Environment
5	Jiangxi	Environment
6	Anhui	Education
7	Fujian	Education
8	Qinghai	Environment
9	Tianjin	Environment
10	Shanghai	Science and technology

maximum offset distance is category with farthest distance from the stability model compared with other categories from the region.

From the experimental result Beijing and Tianjing province exhibit maximum offset distance in environment category while in fact, Beijing and Tianjing had severe haze occurrences from 2013/9 to 2014/6. Due to the continual severe air pollution, people from Beijing and Tianjing pay more attention to the environmental problems.

7   Conclusion

The paper proposes the discovery of regional feature through semantics and the level of attention from the user's comment behavior. In the analysis of topic's in similar region, we use the *LDA* and k-means to perform similar regional cluster analysis. In finding regional feature, this paper proposed three measurement methods based on user level of attention. Finally, this paper performed experiments on real data set from a news website and got the regions with the similar topic tendency and compared the three measurement methods.

References

1. Sina network. http://news.sina.com.cn/zt
2. Datatang. http://www.dataatang.com/data/19300
3. Zheng, Y., Yuan, N.J., Xie, X.: Discovering functional groups of an area (2015). http://www.freepatentsonline.com/y2015/0363700.html
4. Yuan, Y., Raubal, M.: Analyzing the distribution of human activity space from mobile phone usage: an individual and urban-oriented study. Int. J. GIS **30**(8), 1594–1621 (2016). doi:10.1080/13658816.2016.1143555

5. Zhong, C., Huang, X., Arisona, S.M., Schmitt, G., Batty, M.: Inferring building functions from a probabilistic model using public transportation data. Comput. Environ. Urban Syst. **48**, 124–137 (2014). http://www.sciencedirect.com/science/article/pii/S0198971514000854

6. Yin, Z., Cao, L., Han, J., Zhai, C., Huang, T.: Geographical topic discovery and comparison. In: Proceedings of the 20th International Conference on World Wide Web (WWW 2011), pp. 247–256. ACM, New York (2011). http://dx.doi.org/10.1145/1963405.1963443

7. Liu, F., Janssens, D., Cui, J., et al.: Building a validation measure for activity-based transportation models based on mobile phone, data. Expert Syst. Appl. **41**, 6174–6189 (2014). http://www.sciencedirect.com/science/article/pii/S0957417414002036

8. Liu, J., Huang, Z., Chen, L., Shen, H.T., Yan, Z.: Discovering areas of interest with geo-tagged images and check-ins. In: Proceedings of the 20th ACM International Conference on Multimedia, MM 2012 (2012). http://doi.acm.org/10.1145/2393347.2393429

9. Jiang, S., Ferreira Jr., J., Gonzalez, M.C.: Discovering urban spatial-temporal structure from human activity patterns. In: Proceedings of the ACM SIGKDD International Workshop on Urban Computing (UrbComp 2012), pp. 95-102. ACM, New York (2012). http://dx.doi.org/10.1145/2346496.2346512

10. Ferrari, L., Rosi, A., Mamei, M., Zambonelli, F.: Extracting urban patterns from location-based social networks. In: Proceedings of the 3rd ACM SIGSPATIAL International Workshop on Location-Based Social Networks (LBSN 20011), pp. 9–16. ACM, New York (2011). http://dx.doi.org/10.1145/2063212.2063226

11. Eisenstein, J., O'Connor, B., Smith, N.A., Xing, E.P.: A latent variable model for geographic lexical variation. In: Proceedings of the 2010 Conference on Empirical Methods in Natural Language Processing (EMNLP 2010), pp. 1277–1287. Association for Computational Linguistics, Stroudsburg (2010)

12. Hao, Q., Cai, R., Wang, C., Xiao, R., Yang, J.-M., Pang, Y., Zhang, L.: Equip tourists with knowledge mined from travelogues. In: Proceedings of the 19th International Conference on World Wide Web (WWW 2010), pp. 401–410. ACM, New York (2010). http://dx.doi.org/10.1145/1772690.1772732

13. Sizov, S.: GeoFolk: latent spatial semantics in web 2.0 social media. In: Proceedings of the Third ACM International Conference on Web Search and Data Mining (WSDM 2010), pp. 281–290. (2010). http://dx.doi.org/10.1145/1718487.1718522

14. Wakamiya, S., Lee, R., Sumiya, K.: Crowd-sourced urban life monitoring: urban area characterization based crowd behavioral patterns from Twitter. In: Proceedings of the 6th International Conference on Ubiquitous Information Management and Communication (ICUIMC 2012), Article 26, pp. 1–9. ACM, New York (2012). http://dx.doi.org/10.1145/2184751.2184784

15. Wang, C., Wang, J., Xie, X., Ma, W.-Y.: Mining geographic knowledge using location aware topic model. In: Proceedings of the 4th ACM Workshop on Geographical Information Retrieval (GIR 2007), pp. 65–70. ACM, New York (2007). http://dx.doi.org/10.1145/1316948.1316967

16. Qi, G., Li, X., Li, S., Pan, G., Wang, Z., Zhang, D.: Measuring social functions of city regions from large-scale taxi behaviors. In: WIP of PERCOM 2011: Work in Progress Workshop (2011). http://hal.archives-ouvertes.fr/hal-01301930

Extraction of Expert Relations Integrated with Expert Topic and Associated Relationship Features

Jiaying Hou, Zhengtao Yu$^{(\boxtimes)}$, Yu Qin, and Xudong Hong

School of Information Engineering and Automation,
Kunming University of Science and Technology, No. 727 South Jingming Rd.,
Chenggong District, Kunming 650500, China
ztyu@hotmail.com

Abstract. In order to utilize the topic features and the associated relationship features of experts to identify expert relations effectively, a novel extraction method of expert relations is proposed with the integration of expert topic and associated relationship features in this article. Firstly, the expert topics are extracted according to the idea that cooperative experts share the same topic distribution by integrating the expert cooperation network with Probabilistic Topic Models based on LDA Model. Secondly, the associated relationship features are extracted with the utilization of the attributes characteristics, such as the links among homepages, the mutual following on the Blogs. Finally, Markov Network is used to construct the extraction model of expert relations by integrating expert topics and associated relationship features. The experimental results have demonstrated that the proposed method that integrated with expert topic and the associated relationship features of experts supports the extraction of expert relations and shows promising performance.

Keywords: Expert topic · Associated relationship features · Expert relations · Markov network

1 Introduction

As an applied fundamental research in the field of information processing, Experts retrieval that is of important application value in such cases as scientific research and enterprise management has been one of the most effective methods to obtain expert information nowadays. Experts do not exist in isolation in this complex social network. Instead, they're connected with each other through complicated relations to constitute an expert relationship network to share knowledge in the same domain. Actually Experts retrieval is supported by this important resource of relationship network, while the expert relations extraction task has become an important link in the construction of expert relationship network. Since the expert relations extraction result will determine directly the construction quality of the expert relationship network, it has become particularly important on how to extract the expert relations in an accurate and efficient way.

At present, it is the entity relationship extraction task which received the most attention among the aspects of relationship extraction, defined in the Automatic content

© Springer Nature Singapore Pte Ltd. 2016
Y. Li et al. (Eds.): SMP 2016, CCIS 669, pp. 207–219, 2016.
DOI: 10.1007/978-981-10-2993-6_18

extraction Evaluation Conference. The methods for solving the task of relations extraction both home and abroad were mainly divided into such groups: the first method based on pattern matching, for example, Yangarber [1] has put forward advanced pattern matching method based on the sample generalization. It solves the disadvantage that traditional method consume manpower and materials and bad portability and customization especially at the scenario level, improve the efficiency of entity relations extraction; The second method based on machine learning, for example, Zhao [2] uses feature vector and the entity pair was expressed as feature vector by using information such as terms, lexical, entity category, get the classification model to realize the entity relations extraction through Supporting Vector Machine training. Zhou [3] adding the phrase information feature into the feature set to improve the performance of extraction based on Zhao. Like Suzuki [4], the example is transformed into the way of the structural sequence, and the weight factor was added into while extracting the same sub sequences of different instances, and get some effect. On the basis of the shortest path tree, Yu [5] added entity related semantic information and put it in the node to form the path tree with reconciled Syntactic and entity semantic information, and get the categorizer with the training of convolution tree kernel function, complete the extraction task very well; The third method based on entities relationship extraction, for example, Han [6] puts forward a extraction method of character entity relationship based on supporting the vector machine, they take the character context and the part of speech as the feature words, use the method of self-expansion to expand the feature words, classify the character relationship in the method of supporting the vector machine. Yao [7] puts forward an extraction method of character social relationship in large scale on the basis on web and introduced the simulated annealing method, iteratively excavate the minimum description model set of character social relationship contained in the webpage, take the advantage of the redundancy of web information, and extract the relationship effectively and accurately. Li [8] puts forward a recognition method of character relationship based on sequential pattern mining; this method was used for the character entity relation extraction and could automatically extract the sequential pattern which expresses the relationship of character in large corpus.

Regarding the task described as above, good achievements have been made in the entity relationship extraction and the character relationship extraction. However as a special community in the character entity, experts are known for their professional knowledge and skills in a specific field. For example, when two experts often become co-authors on their published papers, it's very likely that they might be the experts working in the same research field. Hence from the perspective of topic analysis, it's very possible that they might have the same topic distribution. The analysis on expert resources reveals that there're lots of expert correlation characteristics contained on the expert homepages, their Blog pages and the papers, such as the homepage link, the mutual following on the Blogs, the same organization and the co-authorship etc. In fact, all of these correlations and the similar topic distribution between the experts are able to provide an effective guidance to the extraction of expert relations.

On account of all these as above, this paper makes an attempt to construct a Markov network-based expert relations extraction model to extract the expert relations through the integration of expert topic and associated relationship features.

2 Analysis on the Expert Topic and Associated Relationship Features

2.1 Analysis on the Expert-Related Resources

Expert relations are implied in massive expert resources such as the expert homepages, their blogs and papers etc. In the face of such a vast data pool, it becomes extremely necessary to make a screening and analysis on the above network resources: An expert homepage always contains the following basic attributes of an expert, including his (her) organization, his (her) research field and his (her) academic achievements etc. with the availability of a homepage link to the other experts' homepages. The expert's blog always contains an interest list, where the mutual following between the experts is able to reflect intuitively the expert relationship. Meanwhile the content published by the expert on his (her) blog is able to reflect the expert's domain knowledge. In normal cases, since an expert always collaborates with the other experts to publish an academic paper, then the author list on the paper will also reflect intuitively the expert relationship. Actually the paper in itself is able to reflect the expert's domain knowledge.

The analysis reveals that: the attributes of an expert and the indexical links in homepages, the interest list and the content on an expert's blog, the author list and the content of the paper written by the experts will provide a powerful support to the extraction of expert topic and associated relationship features.

2.2 Analysis on the Expert Topic

Since the article published by an expert is always involved with several collaborators, then it's feasible to establish an expert collaboration network based on the collaboration relationship between the experts. In such a network, all of the collaborators are those experts who would share knowledge in the same field. That's to say, all of these experts will show an extremely similar topic distribution. On account of this, it's applicable to integrate the expert collaboration network constructed based on the collaboration relationship between the experts into a probabilistic topic model LDA to build an expert topic extraction model for the extraction of expert topic. This process can be formally represented with the model as shown in the following formula:

$$M(C,G) = (1 - \pi)[-p(\overline{w}|\overline{z}, \overline{\beta})p(\overline{z}|\overline{\alpha})]$$
$$+ \frac{\pi}{2} \sum_{<v,\overline{v}> \in E} c(v,\overline{v}) \sum_{j=1}^{k} \left(f(Q_j, v) - f(Q_j, \overline{v}) \right)^2 \tag{1}$$

where C represents the set of the experts' papers and G represents the expert collaboration network, while $p(\overline{w}|\overline{z}, \overline{\beta})$ indicates the process of term sampling based on β, which is the parameter of the prior distribution for the determined topic $\overline{z}$ and the term distribution. $p(\overline{z}|\overline{\alpha})$ is the process of topic sampling according to α, the parameter of the prior distribution for topic distribution. $c(v,\overline{v})$ represents the times of cooperation between the expert v and the expert $\overline{v}$ on the edge of $<v,\overline{v}>$ in an expert network.

The parameter π is an equilibrium factor. $f(Q_j, v)$ represents the conditional probability $p(Q_j|v)$ that the expert v is allocated to the topic Q_j under the condition that the expert v is given, while $f(\theta_j, \bar{v})$ represents the conditional probability $p(\theta_j|\bar{v})$ that the expert $\bar{v}$ is allocated to the topic θ_j under the condition that the expert $\bar{v}$ is given. k is the number of the topics and $\sum_{j=1}^{k} (f(Q_j, v) - f(Q_j, \bar{v}))^2$ represents the sum of differences between the expert v and the adjacent expert $\bar{v}$ regarding the topic distribution of k topics. Hence when $M(C, G)$ reaches the minimum, it means that both of the expert - topic probability distribution and the topic - topic term probability distribution will be obtained. In this case, adopt the Gibbs sampling [9] method to solve the expert topic model.

2.3   Analysis on the Associated Relationship Features

The expert relations are quite complex. In this paper, it takes the friendship, the colleagueship and the guidance relationship between the experts into account to make an analysis and automatic extraction. All of these three expert relationships are implied in various expert resources but show different features. The analysis on these three expert relationships reveals the following relationship characteristics.

Generally there won't be a link available on an expert's homepage pointing to the homepages of the other experts, who are just friends of this expert, but they might be mutually followed on their blogs. It's very rare that these experts would collaborate on the same paper since they're generally working in different organizations. However in the case that these experts are colleagues, it would be easy to find an indexical link between their homepages. But it's rare that these experts would follow each other on their blog pages. Since they're working in the same organization, they might collaborate frequently on the papers. Meanwhile the colleagueship between the experts is featured with transmissibility. That's to say, if the expert e_1 is determined as a colleague of the expert e_2, who is also the colleague of the expert e_3, then the expert e_1 can also be considered as a colleague of the expert e_3. In the case that there's a guidance relationship between the experts, it would be easy to find an indexical link between their homepages. Also these experts are always mutually followed on their blog pages. Although they might work in different organizations, they still would collaborate on the same papers. However frequent collaboration on papers can only happen in a certain period, since guidance relationship is of certain timeliness. For example, when Che Wanxiang was studying for a doctor's degree under the guidance of Liu Ting from 2004 to 2008, it happened very often that they collaborated on paper publishing in this period. However this could rarely happen in the other periods. The description of the associated relationship features of expert is shown in Table 1.

Where, use expert evidence document to identify undirected graph model [10] and then to identify experts' homepage automatically. To determine the situation of links among homepages through regular expression matching to obtain the URL link address of the homepage. Then remove the tag from the homepage. Use the Chinese lexical analysis system ICTCLAS of the Chinese academy of Science to segment the terms. Using the method of multi-page Chinese expert metadata extraction based on 3D model

Table 1. Associated relationship features of expert

Type of relations	Associated relationship features			
	Homepage Link	Blog attention	Organization	Collaboration on Papers
Friendship	Not available	Yes	Generally different	Rare
Colleagueship	Available	Rare	Same	Frequent
Guidance relationship	Available	Yes	Might not be the same	Frequent only in a certain period

to extract two kinds of expert metadata information [11], namely, name and organization. Use expert name disambiguation method based on semi supervised graph clustering [12] to solve the problem of the same name as the expert's name, in order to get the accurate expert information. As to the experts' blog information, a web crawler developed by the lab itself has been used to get the experts' blog content and their interest list on the blogs. Regarding the collection of the papers published by the experts, manually collect the papers published by the experts to extract the author list and the publishing time on every paper. The author list will be used to calculate the frequency of the collaboration between the experts, while the publishing time of the paper will be used to analyze the timeliness of the co-authorship.

3 Construction of Expert Relations Extraction Model Integrated with Expert Topic and Associated Relationship Features

3.1 Description of Expert Relations Extraction Model

The Markov Network in the probability graph model [13, 14] is an undirected graph model with strong learning ability and reasoning ability and can express the complicated relations in the network node effectively. From the above analysis, topic features and associated relationship features both have good supporting functions for the extraction of expert relations. We extract relations between experts through constructing the Markov Network to integrate expert topic and associated relationship features. Experts' relations extraction model based on Markov Network diagram shown in Fig. 1:

Where e_1 and e_2 represent separately the experts whose relations are to be extracted, $d_{e1,1}$ and $d_{e2,1}$ represent separately the homepage of the expert e_1 and the expert e_2, $d_{e1,2}$ and $d_{e2,2}$ represent separately the blog page of the expert e_1 and the expert e_2, $d_{e1,3}$ and $d_{e2,3}$ represent separately the collection of the papers published by the expert e_1 and the expert e_2, t_{e1} and t_{e2} represent separately the topic of the expert e_1 and the expert e_2, while $d_{e1,1} - d_{e2,1}$, $d_{e1,2} - d_{e2,2}$ and $d_{e1,3} - d_{e2,3}$ jointly represent the associated relationship features. $t_{e1} - t_{e2}$ represents the expert topic, $d_{e1,1} - d_{e2,1}$ represents that if there's an indexical link available between the expert homepages and if the same organization has been extracted from the expert homepages. $d_{e1,2} - d_{e2,2}$ represents the mutual following of the experts on their blog pages, $d_{e1,3} - d_{e2,3}$

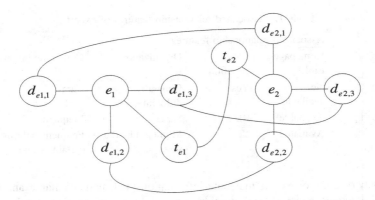

Fig. 1. The extraction model of expert relations based on Markov network

represents the co-authorship between the experts on the papers and $t_{e1} - t_{e2}$ represents the similarity between the expert topics.

3.2   Representation of Expert Relations Extraction Model

3.2.1   Construct Markov Network

Domingos and Richardson [15] in the University of Washington in 2004 put forward Markov Network for the first time, and demonstrates the possibility that the Markov Network as a statistical relational learning unified framework [15]. At present, the international artificial intelligence community generally accepted Markov Network to combine the first order predicate logic and probability graph model perfectly. It provides an effective method for the representation and processing of complexity and uncertainty problem. It is a undirected graph probability model, each vertex representing the random variable or the random vector, and the edges represent the conditional dependence between variables. For any edge, the maximum clique (full connected sub graph) is called factor. In the learning task, Markov Network was usually expressed in a log linear model, namely, each factor is represented as the index weighted sum of the feature function of the variable set. The formula listed as below:

$$P(X_1, X_2, \cdots X_n) = \frac{1}{Z} \exp(\sum_i \omega_i f_i(C_i))$$ (2)

where the characteristic function $f_i(C_i)$ is an arbitrary real-valued function for the variable set C_i and w_i is the weight of the characteristic function $f_i(C_i)$. For calculation purpose, the characteristic function can be defined by the following formula:

$$f_i(C_i) = \begin{cases} 1 & \textit{Conformity between the characteristics and the tags} \\ 0 & \textit{Inconformity between the characteristics and the tags} \end{cases}$$ (3)

If there's an indexical link available between the homepages of the experts whose relations are to be extracted, then there should be undirected edges available for the connection between the directional characteristics of the links in a Markov network, otherwise no edges will be available for the connection. If the experts whose relations are to be extracted work in the same organization, then there should be undirected edges available for the connection between the organization characteristics in a Markov network, otherwise no edges will be available for the connection. If mutual following can be found on the blogs of the experts whose relations are to be extracted, then there should be undirected edges available for the connection between the characteristics of blog attention in a Markov network, otherwise no edges will be available for the connection. In the case that the experts whose relations are to be extracted have been collaborating on paper publishing frequently, there should be undirected edges available for the connection between the co-authorship characteristics in a Markov network; otherwise no edges will be available for the connection. When the topics of the experts whose relations are to be extracted are quite similar, then there should be undirected edges available for the connection between the topic features in a Markov network, otherwise no edges will be available for the connection.

The approach to judge similar topic is: Since the extracted topic always consists of a series of topic terms, then the topic can be represented with a topic term vector. When the cosine of the included angle between the vectors is used to describe the similarity degree of the topics, the topic similarity can be calculated according to the formula shown as below:

$$\text{Sim}(t_i, t_j) = \frac{\vec{t_i} \times \vec{t_j}}{|\vec{t_i}| \times |\vec{t_j}|} \tag{4}$$

where $Sim(t_i, t_j)$ represents the topic similarity between the expert i and the expert j, $\vec{t_i}$ represents the topic vector of the expert i and $\vec{t_j}$ represents the topic vector of the expert j. Through the definition of a threshold, the topics are similar when the vector is greater than the threshold. Otherwise it can be determined that the topics are not similar.

3.2.2 Formalized Representation of the Model

Expert relations extraction can be transformed into an expert relations classification problem to get the solutions. The core is to solve the probability of the relations, which can be respectively classified into friendship, colleagueship or the guidance relationship under the condition that the experts have conformed to certain associated relationship features and topic. When a type of relations shows the maximum probability, it means that this is also the final relations between the experts. According to the joint probability distribution in a Markov network as shown in Formula (2), the joint probability distribution of the expert relations extraction model based on the Markov network can be expressed with Formula (5) as shown below:

$$P(X = x) = \frac{1}{Z}\exp\left[\sum_m \omega_m f_m(C_m)\right] \tag{5}$$

where x represents a type of expert relations, $P(X = x)$ represents the probability that the expert relation X is affiliated to x, Z is a normalization factor and m represents the type of the characteristic. When $m = 5$, it indicates the integration of the expert topic on the basis of Table 1 to achieve a unified representation of the expert relations characteristics, which are shown in Table 2.

Where $f_m(C_m)$ represents the characteristic function of the variable set C_m and w_m is the weight of $f_m(C_m)$. Regarding the following four characteristics including the similar

Table 2. Characteristics of expert relations

Type of relations	Expert topic	Associated relationship features				
	Domain related knowledge	Homepage Link	Blog attention	Organization	Collaboration on papers
Friendship	Might not similar	Not available	Yes	Generally different	Rare
Colleagueship	Similar	Available	Rare	Same	Frequent
Guidance relationship	Similar	Available	Yes	Might not be the same	Frequent only in a certain period

domain knowledge, the availability of homepage link, the same organization and the blog attention, their characteristic function is:

$$f_m(C_m) = \begin{cases} 1 & \text{Conform to the type of characteristic} \\ 0 & \text{Otherwise} \end{cases} \qquad (6)$$

As to the co-authorship characteristic, it can be integrally grouped into frequency and infrequency. In the case of frequent collaboration, there're two situations: frequent collaboration and frequent collaboration only in a certain period. Hence the characteristic function can be:

$$f_m(C_m) = \begin{cases} 1 & \text{Frequent collaboration} \\ 1/2 & \text{Frequent collaboration in a certain period} \\ 0 & \text{Rare collaboration} \end{cases} \qquad (7)$$

3.3   Probability Inference and Parameter Learning for Expert Relations Extraction Model

Under the condition of the known Markov Network, the probability inference process of Markov was to solve the problem of maximum likelihood (MPE problems) [13, 16] interpretation for this model. The inference process of extraction model of expert relations was to solve the maximum probability of classification of expert relations under the condition that the associated relationship features and topic between the experts was known. Probability formula as below:

$$\arg \max P(R_x | G_M) = \arg \max P(X = x)$$

$$= \arg \max \left\{ \frac{1}{Z} \exp \left[\sum_m \omega_m f_m(C_m) \right] \right\} \tag{8}$$

$$\propto \arg \max \left\{ \sum_m \omega_m f_m(C_m) \right\}$$

where, $\arg \max P(R_x | G_M)$ represents that in the case of given relation Markov Network G_M, expert relations belongs to the maximum probabilities of the category R_x. Since the normalization factor Z and the exponential function exp will not affect the maximum probability, and therefore there is more than the equivalent conversion.

For the probability graph model, the inference algorithm is generally effective, such as the Cliquetree Propagation algorithm and the Variable Elimination algorithm as well as approximate inference algorithm of Monte Carlo algorithm. In this paper, the Gibbs sampling algorithm is used to solve the Formula (8).

For the parameters learning method of probabilistic graph, there are two kinds, namely, structure learning and parameter learning [13, 16]. The structure learning should consider the structure of the network and consider the parameters in the net-work. And the parameters learning only consider the network parameters in the existing network structure. As the structure of the network of the extraction model of expert relations based on the Markov Network was confirmed in this paper, so parameter learning method is considered for estimating the parameters of the model. In this paper, the maximum likelihood estimation is used to estimate the weight of the feature. Process as follows:

Firstly, take the logarithm of the joint probability distribution in Formula (6) to obtain the corresponding likelihood function as shown in Formula (9).

$$\log P(X = x) = \sum_m \omega_m f_m(C_m) - \log Z \tag{9}$$

Then calculate the partial derivative of a random weight in Formula (8) with the derivation process shown in Formula (10).

$$\frac{\partial}{\partial \omega_m} \log P(X = x) = \frac{\partial}{\partial \omega_m} \sum_m \omega_m f_m(C_m) - \frac{\partial}{\partial \omega_m} \log Z$$

$$= \sum_m f_m(C_m) - \frac{1}{Z} \frac{\partial}{\partial \omega_m} Z$$

$$= \sum_m f_m(C_m) - \frac{1}{Z} \sum_{x'} \frac{\partial}{\partial \omega_m} \exp \left[\sum_m \omega_m f_m(C_m) \right] \tag{10}$$

$$= \sum_m f_m(C_m) - \sum_{x'} P_{\omega_m}(X = x') \sum_m f_m(C'_m)$$

where $\sum_m f_m(C_m)$ represents the sum of the characteristic values for m features and $\sum_{x'} P_{w_m}(X = x') \sum_m f_m(C'_m)$ represents the sum of probabilities for all possible value assignments. Obtain the present weight through Formulas (9) and (10) and then get all of the unknown weights according to the gradient descent algorithm.

4   Experiments and Analysis

4.1   Experiment Data Preparation

In order to verify the effectiveness of the expert relations extraction integrated with expert topic and associated relationship features, this paper collects randomly totally 200 experts, who are artificially tagged into the following three types of relationships, including friendship, colleagueship and guidance relationship in Natural Language Processing and Information Retrieval. Where the correlation characteristics of 150 tagged experts are used as the training data and the rest are used as the test data.

4.2   Experimental Evaluation

In order to evaluate comprehensively the effectiveness of the extracted model, this paper makes a statistical analysis on different methods in terms of the following two indicators, Precision (P) and Recall(R) in the experiment, based on which F value is used as the final evaluation index to evaluate the effectiveness of the mentioned method, since F value is able to reflect perfectly the effect in recognizing the expert relations. The increase in F value represents a better recognition effect. Meanwhile this paper provides the following formulas to calculate separately the Precision Recall and F-value. T_p is the number of identifying expert relations correctly based on model, F_p is the number of identifying expert relations based on model. F_n is the number of pair of experts whose relations are to be extracted.

$$\mathrm{Pr}\,e = \frac{T_p}{F_p}, \mathrm{Rec} = \frac{T_p}{F_n} \quad F - value = \frac{2 \times P \times R}{P + R} \tag{11}$$

4.3   Experimental Design and Analysis

In order to verify the effectiveness of the method proposed in this paper, which designs two experiments for the verification of the model. In Experiment I, it makes a contrast on the Precision, Recall and F-value in the expert relations extraction task separately through our method, the SVM method [6] and the Sequence Pattern Mining method [8]. In Experiment II, it makes a contrast on the F values of the expert relations extraction models with and without considering the expert topic in the expert relations extraction task.

Experiment I: It makes an extraction of the expert's friendship, colleagueship and guidance relationship separately through the method proposed in this paper, the SVM method and the sequential pattern mining method and then calculates Precision 、 Recall and the F value according to the extraction result. The expert relations extraction results through the above three methods in the contrast experiment are shown in Table 3:

Table 3. Contrast results based on different methods

	SVM	Sequence pattern mining	Our approach
P (%)	72.27 %	75.14 %	77.35 %
R (%)	68.61 %	70.47 %	72.06 %
F (%)	70.39 %	72.73 %	74.61 %

The analysis on the experimental results in Experiment I reveals that Precision, Recall and the F value have been improved to some extent through our method compared with the SVM method and the sequential pattern mining method. Also the integration of the expert topic and associated relationship features contributes to the better recognition of expert relations.

Experiment II: Firstly, utilize the method proposed in this paper to extract the expert relations and then calculate the F value according to the extraction result. After that, construct an expert relations extraction model without the consideration of the expert topic. The F values of both models will be calculated according to Formula (11) with the results obtained in the contrast experiment as shown in Fig. 2.

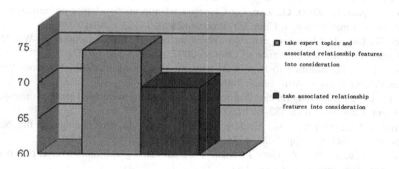

Fig. 2. Influence of different number of features of experts on F-value in the test sets

The analysis on the experimental results in Experiment II reveals that without the consideration of the expert topic, the expert relations extraction model based on the Markov network won't perform as well as the model that has taken the expert topic into account in terms of the F value. Since the expert topic is able to represent the expert's domain knowledge, then the topic would play a good supporting role in the recognition of the expert relations.

5 Conclusions

Combined with their own characteristics of the experts, this paper makes an analysis on the friendship, the colleagueship and the guidance relationship between the experts. Through the integration of the expert topic and the associated relationship features, this paper constructs an expert relations extraction model based on the Markov Network. The experimental result shows that the expert relations extraction model proposed in this paper has performed very well in the recognition of the friendship, the colleagueship and the guidance relationship. Then our further research will focus on the consideration of a method to quantize the strength of the expert relations for the accurate extraction of the expert relations and at the same time for the quantization of the expert relations strength to improve further the expert relations extraction model.

References

1. Yangarber, R., Grishman, R.: NYU: description if the proteus/PET system as used for MUC-7. In: Proceedings of the 7th Message Understanding Coferences, pp. 117–121 (1998)
2. Zhao, S., Grishman, R.: Extracting relations with integrated information using kernel methods. In: Proceeding ACL 2005 Proceedings of the 43rd Annual Meeting on Association for Computational Linguistics, pp. 419–426 (2005)
3. Zhou, G., Su, J., Zhang, J., Zhang, M.: Exploring various knowledge in relation extraction. In: Proceeding ACL 2005 Proceedings of the 43rd Annual Meeting on Association for Computational Linguistics, pp. 427–434 (2005)
4. Suzuki, J., Isozaki, H., Maeda, E.: Convolution kernels with feature selection for natural language processing tasks. In: Proceedings of the 42nd Annual Meeting of the Association for Computational Linguistics, pp. 199–206 (2004)
5. Yu, H., Qian, L., Zhou, G., Zhu, Q.: Chinese semantic relation based on unified syntactic and entity semantic tree. J. Chin. Inf. Process. 24(5), 17–23 (2010)
6. Han, B., Lin, H.: Characters extraction based on support vector machine. In: Wu, H. (ed.) Information Control Conference of Chinese 2007, pp. 335–341 (2007)
7. Yao, C., Di, N.: Solution to large scale extraction of social relations of persons based on web. Pattern Recogn. Artif. Intell. 740–744 (2007)
8. Li, D., Luo, Z.: Persons relationship recognition based on sequential pattern mining. Adv. Comput. Linguist. China 582–587 (2009)
9. Griffths, T.L., Steyvers, M.: Finding scientific topics. In: Proceedings of the National Academy of Sciences, pp. 5228–5235 (2004)
10. Mao, C., Yu, Z., Wu, Z., Guo, J., Xian, Y.: Undirected graph model for expert evidence document recognition. J. Softw. 24(11), 2734–2746 (2014)
11. Pan, X., Shen, T., Yu, Z., Wu, Z., Guo, J.: Multi-page Chinese expert metadata extraction method based on the 3D model. J. Comput. Inf. Syst. 9(6), 2251–2259 (2013)
12. Jiang, J., Yan, X., Yu, Z., Guo, J., Tian, W.: A Chinese expert disambiguation method based on semi-supervised graph clustering. Int. J. Mach. Learn. Cybern. 5(1), 1–8 (2014)
13. Jordan, M.I.: Graphical models. Stat. Sci. 19(1), 140–155 (2004). (Special Issue on Bayesian Statistics)
14. Koller, D., Friedman, N.: Probabilistic Graphical Models: Principles and Techniques. The MIT Press, Cambridge (2009)

15. Domingos, P., Richardson, M.: Markov logic: a unifying framework for statistical relational learning. In: Proceedings of the ICML 2004 Workshop on Statistical Relational Learning and its Connections to Other Fields, Banff, pp. 49–54 (2004)
16. Koller, D., Friedman, N.: Probabilistic Graphical Models: Principles and Techniques. Massachusetts Institute of Technology Press, Cambridge (2009). doi:10.1007/978-3-642-38466-0_28

Sina-Weibo Spammer Detection with GBDT

Yang Qiao[✉], Huaping Zhang, Min Yu, and Yu Zhang

School of Computer Science, Beijing Institute of Technology, 5 South Zhongguancun Street
Haidian District, Beijing, 100081, China
{qiaoyang2014,yumin,zhangyu}@nlpir.org, kevinzhang@bit.edu.com

Abstract. In China, Sina-Weibo, with its rising popularity as a microblogging website, has inevitably attracted the attention of spammers. Spammers use myriad of techniques to evade security mechanisms and post spam messages, which are either unwelcome advertisements for the victim or lure victims in to clicking malicious URLs embedded in spam tweets. With the extensive application of machine learning in social media mining and Sina-Weibo's development, we get many new ideas for the spammers detection. In this paper, we first make a comprehensive analysis specifically aiming at some new Sina-Weibo features rather than other social media, we further design a new feature set to detect spammers. We grab a large amount of Sina-Weibo data on the Internet and train the classifier with the algorithm GBDT. Through our experiments, we show that our new designed features are much more effective than some existing detector. And GBDT also has been significantly improved in both the accuracy and the FP-rate.

Keywords: Social media · Spammer · Detection · GBDT

1 Introduction

Weibo is an information sharing, dissemination and access platform based on user relationship, users can set up personal communities through WEB, WAP, and a variety of clients, with about 140 words of text updates, and to achieve instant sharing [1]. Statistics show that the average time spent on social network sites are far more than other sites [2]. Take Twitter as an example, every day there are at least 65 million tweets were sent [3]. Especially in China, the social media like micro blog, Weibo Microblog in Sina.com [4], is also developing much more rapidly.

With the development of micro-blog, there are more and more spammers. Spammers on micro-blog employ myriad of techniques to post unwanted tweets to users of an online social network such as micro-blog. Such tweets pose either as advertisements, scams and help perpetrate phishing attacks or the spread of malware through the embedded URLs. To gain a wider reach to potential victims, spammers are known to befriend (or to follow in micro-blog terminology) unrelated users, send unsolicited messages and masquerade malicious components (for instance, using URL shorterners to substitute malicious appearing URLs).

However, spammers are evolving to evade existing detectors. Such as spammers will switch IP frequently while reposting to evade the detecting of IP address [5]. And many of the Navy detection strategy is aimed at all kinds of social networking platform. So

© Springer Nature Singapore Pte Ltd. 2016
Y. Li et al. (Eds.): SMP 2016, CCIS 669, pp. 220–232, 2016.
DOI: 10.1007/978-981-10-2993-6_19

many strategies have ignored the characteristics of micro-blog itself [6]. In this paper, We plan to put forward some special features for micro-blog. To achieve our research goals, we use blacklist and honeypot [7] to build our dataset.

In summary, the contributions of this paper are as follows:

Set up a large weibo data set. Data contains some of the unique characteristics of Sina-Weibo.

We evaluate the detection rates of two state-of-the-art solutions on our collected dataset.

We design a new detecting feature set aiming at some new Sina-Weibo features. According to our evaluation, while keeping an even lower false positive rate, the detection rate by using our new feature set significantly increases to 80 % or higher.

We compare the result of different algorithms, we found that better detection results can be obtained by using GBDT.

2 Related Work

At present, detection of the navy is mainly divided into two kinds of methods: *Statistical Techniques for Spammer Detection* and *Supervised Learning Approaches.*

Statistical Techniques for Spammer Detection: Statistical Techniques is the main method for the detection of the spammers in the early stage of the study of spammer detection. Gao et al. [8] present a technique to detect and characterize spam campaigns on Facebook where connected component analysis of a graph of wall posts with common URLs or similar content is used to identify campaigns. Sarita et al. in [9] study structural properties of legitimate users and spammers and observe similarity between Web graph and Twitter's social graph. Song et al. [10] exploit the fact the spammers are usually not found in close proximity to legitimate users. The proximity is defined as the number of nodes between two accounts in the social graph. These graph based features are difficult to evade but are also time and resource intensive.

Supervised Learning Approaches: With the development of machine learning, it has been widely used. Benevenuto et al. in [11], discuss the rise of video spammers and promoters in video social networks like YouTube. Various features, including video-based, user-based, and social-network based features are used with supervised learning techniques for spammer detection. Monarch [12] analyzes the Twitter dataset for identifying spam URLs. The real-time detection approach uses L1-regularized Logistic Regression with features relying upon web browser based events, along with DNS, and network properties. We differ by proposing features which capture the behavior of spammers, in addition to the infra-structure oriented characteristics of malicious entities, as proposed above. The work in [13] highlights six features, also motivated by the spammer's behavior. The features include sender degree, rate of message sending, or the URLs sent. The features, however, differ in context where one of which (Unique URL number) contradicts our observation.

Algorithm and Feature Set

In this part, firstly we will introduce the algorithm we use to detect spammers, and then we will introduce the features we use.

2.1 Gradient Boosting

Gradient boosting is a machine learning technique for regression and classification problems, which produces a prediction model in the form of an ensemble of weak prediction models, typically decision trees. It builds the model in a stage-wise fashion like other boosting methods do, and it generalizes them by allowing optimization of an arbitrary differentiable loss function. In pseudocode, the generic gradient boosting method is:

Input: training set$\{(x_i, y_i)\}_{i=1}^n$, a differentiable loss function$L(y, F(x))$, number of iterations$M$.

Algorithm:

1. Initialize model with a constant value:

$$F_0(x) = \arg\min_\gamma \sum_{i=1}^n L(y_i, \gamma).$$

2. For $m = 1$ to M:

   1. Compute so-called *pseudo-residuals*:

   $$r_{im} = -\left[\frac{\partial L(y_i, F(x_i))}{\partial F(x_i)}\right]_{F(x)=F_{m-1}(x)} \quad \text{for } i = 1, \ldots, n.$$

   2. Fit a base learner$h_m(x)$ to pseudo-residuals, i.e. train it using the training set $\{(x_i, r_{im})\}_{i=1}^n$.
   3. Compute multiplierγ_m by solving the following one-dimensional optimization problem:

   $$\gamma_m = \arg\min_\gamma \sum_{i=1}^n L(y_i, F_{m-1}(x_i) + \gamma h_m(x_i)).$$

   4. Update the model:

   $$F_m(x) = F_{m-1}(x) + \gamma_m h_m(x).$$

3. Output $F_M(x)$.

According to our survey of existing detection methods used are the traditional classification model. So we choose to use the GBDT algorithm to try. The reason why we chose the GBDT algorithm has the following two aspects:

Comparing with SVM/Bayes/Regression, GBDT allows the combination of different features to have different discriminant not like SVM can only have a unique global discriminant. So it is particularly suited to different combinations of features that produce different results. This is more closed to the essence of spammers detection problem.

GBDT itself is a kind of boosting algorithm. Therefore, GBDT has inherited the characteristics of the boosting algorithm with low degree of overfitting.

2.2 Feature Set

In this part, we will detail the contents of the feature set and the reasons for the feature selection and verify the recognization ability of features. In previous studies, many of the features are presented in order to adapt to more social networking platforms. Of course, this can improve the universality of the spammers detection strategy. But the study of the unique characteristics of a social network can improve the accuracy of detection. So Most of the features are proposed based on the research of Sina-Weibo characteristics which have never been used.

We build an auxiliary data set which contains 1000 normal users and 1200 spammers to evaluate the discrimination ability of features.

Micro-blog level: Every Sina-Weibo user has a micro-blog level. It increases with the use of micro-blog. Users to use micro-blog more frequently, the higher the level of micro-blog. So this feature can be seen as a measure of user liveness. We have statistics on the data set of the Micro-blog level of account, the results are as follows (Table 1):

Table 1. Micro-blog level

Micro-blog Level	Spammers number	Routines number
0~5	1020	89
5~10	111	134
10~15	69	212
15~20	0	234
Over 20	0	331

We found that the spammer is usually low level users of Sina-Weibo. We think this is because the spammer account is idle in no task. So we use micro-blog level to measure the activity of the user and to deduce whether the user is the spammer.

Whether a Micro-blog member: Micro-blog member need to be acquired through the purchase of money. It allows the user to gain a series of micro-blog privileges such as: Dressing privilege, Mobile Phone privilege and some other value-added services. As a result of micro-blog membership is required to pay a certain fee, spammers is generally not the Micro-blog member, we can see in the following chart (Fig. 1):

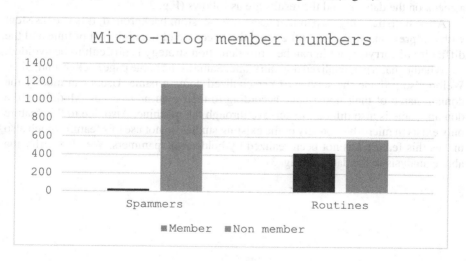

Fig. 1. Micro-blog member number

We can obviously see that most of the water is not a member of micro-blog. We think the reason for this situation is Micro-blog member's cost is too high for a large number of spammer accounts. Most of the spammer accounts are idle in no task, membership for no one to use the account no sense.

Integrity of personal data: Usually users registered micro-blog account will be asked to fill out personal information. Integrity of personal data is used to measure how much personal information is filled in by the user. The reason why we choose this feature is considering the way the spammer account registration. Usually the spammers are registered account through the machine automatically. Therefore, the spammers' Integrity of personal data users usually very close and relatively low. The specific performance as shown below (Table 2):

Table 2. Integrity of personal data

Integrity of personal data	Spammers number	Routines number
0 %~35 %	1116	345
35 %~70 %	84	423
70 %~	0	232

Obviously, spammers and routines have obvious differences in this feature. Although this feature does not apply to other social media, it is indeed an effective distinction between spammers and routines.

Whether has a home page background: This is a unique feature of the micro-blog social media. Sina-Weibo allows users to replace the background image for their personal home page. That is to say, this feature can be used to study whether a micro-blog account really is used rather than as a repost tool. But due to the huge number of spammer account usually can only use the default background. We have also carried out a check on the data set and the results are as follows (Fig. 2):

After statistics only 3 spammer users use a custom background, this is consistent with our previous analysis. At the same time because of the high cost of time and the difficulty of carrying out in batches, this detection strategy is difficult to be avoided.

Whether has a personalized domain name: Same as the home page background, Sina-Weibo also provide the service of personalized domain name. Users can modify the domain name of their home page according to their own preferences. Modifying the domain name is also difficult to achieve through the machine. Also due to this feature only exists in micro-blog, many of the existing studies do not use this feature which also makes this feature has not been realized by holders of spammers. We also verify the above analysis in the data set (Fig. 3):

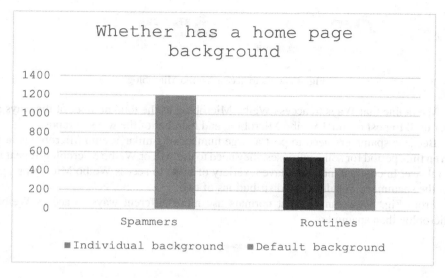

Fig. 2. Whether has a home page background

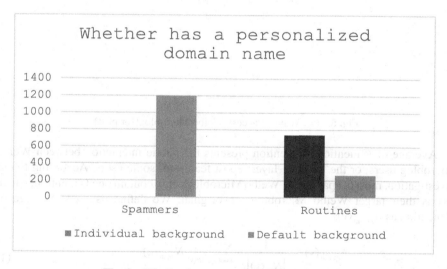

Fig. 3. Whether has a personalized domain name

We found that all spammers accounts do not use personalized domain. However routines more inclined to use a personalized domain name, over 700 users set personalized domain name. Therefore, we believe that users use personalized domain name are more likely to be real users.

Ways to access Weibo Microblog (Number of ways to post, repost): People have a lot of ways to access Weibo Microblog such as webpage or mobile client. In Fig. 4: we show some common ways.

Fig. 4. ways to access Weibo Microblog

We define that Ways to access Weibo Microblog as the total number of the ways a user used to post original Weibo Microblog and Number of the ways to repost.

Because spammers need to post a large number of similar Weibo Microblogs in a given time period for some purposes, they need to use API or Weibo Microblog-repeater to release. In contrast, normals have a variety of ways to access Weibo Microblog but not the spammers. We draw the distributions of two:

From Fig. 5 we can see that normals use more different ways to access Weibo Microblog than spammers.

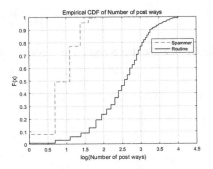

Fig. 5. (a). Ways to access Weibo Microblog(for post)

Average of @mention: @mention presents the public interaction between Weibo Microblog users, or the multiple layer repost feature of some users. According to our investigation, most of spammers' Weibo Microblogs only contain one @mention, which means their target Weibo Microblog are original. We define user v's Average of @mention as $A_{rp-at}(v)$:

$$A_{rp-at}(v) = \frac{1}{|N_{rp}(v)|} \cdot \sum_{u \in RP(v)} N_{r-at}(u) \tag{1}$$

Where $N_{rp}(v)$ is the total number of user v's reposts, $RP(v)$ is the set of user u's repost, N_{rp-at} is the number of @mentions per repost of user v. We also draw the curve of the Average number of @mention distribution as Fig. 6 We can see that there are obvious differences in the curve of distributions between normals and spammers (Fig. 7).

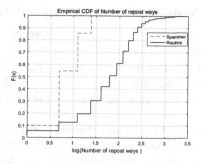

Fig. 6. (b). Ways to access Weibo Microblog(for repost)

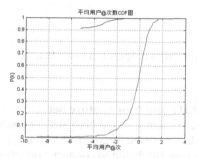

Fig. 7. Average of @ mentions

As for evasion tactics, spammers can randomly @someone while reposting to evade detection, but that may also cause accusation and lead to accounts suspended.

3 Experiment and Evaluation

In this part, we will verify the validity of our new feature set through the experimental method. Based on this, we will analyze the impact of the classification model and compare with existing research.

3.1 Experimental Data Preparation

We wrote a Sina-Weibo Microblog crawler crawling user information and Weibo Microblog message for our experiment. Details about the crawling information can be seen in Table 3.

Table 3. Weibo Microblog accounts crawling information

Category	Amount
Total of weibo accounts	721,563
Total of Weibo posts	121,555,716
Total of Fans' accounts	123,897,245
Total of Followings' accounts	144,659,845

Then, we need to identify Sina-Weibo spammers from our crawled dataset. We randomly selected 10 % of the accounts from each weibo arousal event and tag every account manually. What's more, we also bought spammers account on Internet authorities and collected their Sina-Weibo information. Finally, we collect 20,000 spammers (15,000 through purchasing) and 20,000 routines to build each of our cross-validation test data set.

3.2 Evaluation

In this part, we will apply the GBDT algorithm to the feature set which we have proposed and evaluate the results.

3.2.1 Evaluation of GBDT and New Feature Set
For the comparison the performance of the classifiers, we selected 3 popular machine learning classifiers, including Logistic Regression, SMO and Random Forest. For each classifier we use 10-fold cross-validation to conduct evaluation.

In order to simulate the real situation, considering spammers detection is a imbalanced classes problem, we randomly selected 1000,000 weibo posts from 2000 normal

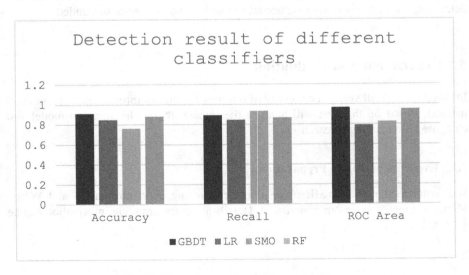

Fig. 8. Detection result of different classifiers

accounts and 600 spammer accounts to build experiment dataset. In Fig. 6, we show the detection result of different classifiers (Fig. 8):

From the result we can see that classifier based on GBDT has the highest detection accuracy of 91.07 % which means the best performance in distinguishing spammers from normals. The highest recall rate of 0.931 was obtained based on the SMO method, so we can use SMO to detect more spammers. However, the SMO algorithm leads to a much lower accuracy of 6.7 % than the other GBDT. We can think that the SMO algorithm is at the expense of accuracy and obtain a higher recall rate (Table 4).

Table 4. Detection result of different classifiers

Classifier	Accuracy	Recall	ROC area
GBDT	91.07 %	89.13 %	0.966
Logistic Regression	84.77 %	84.45 %	0.791
SMO	76.11 %	93.41 %	0.824
Random Forest	88.08 %	86.66 %	0.951

Further analysis we can get the following conclusions:

GBDT has the best detection results because it has the highest ROC. The conventional detection tasks we should use GBDT model. But when we do not consider the classification accuracy and consider only to find more spammers, wo should also choose SMO. Because it get the highest recall rate and we can get more spammers.

The method based on decision tree (GBDT and Random Forest) is superior to the other two methods in classification accuracy because they get much higher ROC. So we think decision tree is more suitable for our feature set under normal circumstances.

GBDT algorithm can achieve better results. This is in line with our previous expectations.

3.2.2 Comparison with Existing Strategies

In this part we implement two existing effective detection schemes [14, 15] and compare with our method. we also used the experiment dataset in Sect. 3.1.

3.2.2.1 Feature Set Comparison

Firstly, we compare the new feature set with the existing feature set.. In order to ensure the fairness of the comparison, we choose Logistic Regression method which was used both in [14, 15]. Assuming that our proposed method is A, [14] is B, [15] is C. The comparison results are shown in Fig. 9.

We can see that the result of our feature set is higher than two existing methods in Accuracy, Recall and ROC. We think what we have in our ascension is:

We use the feature set dimension is relatively high, it is conducive to enhance the classification effect. B and C use the feature dimension is too low, easy to lead to false classification and leakage classification.

According to our research, the spammer will take some anti detection strategies. Our feature set is new, can effectively avoid the existing spammer detection avoidance strategy.

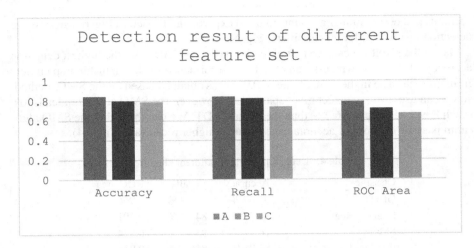

Fig. 9. Comparison of different detection methods

Our feature set is for micro-blog, which is more targeted. This also leads to the more difficult to avoid these strategies.

So, we add our features to the two strategies and retrain the model. We found that the classification accuracy of B and C were 5.5 % and 7.1 % respectively even more than just using our feature set. This also shows that our new features can be well combined with the existing research.

3.2.2.2 Algorithm Comparison

Secondly, we study whether the effect of the GBDT algorithm is only effective for our feature set. So we use the feature set B and C in Sect. 3.2.2.1 to evaluate. We still use the data we used before, the results are as follows (Fig. 10):

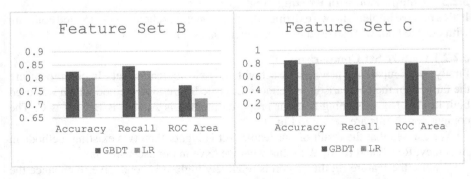

Fig. 10. Comparison of different detection methods with GBDT

It can be seen from the figure GBDT algorithm to detect the effect of the improvement is obvious. But the magnitude of the increase is not large. We think this is mainly because the dimension of the feature set is too low. Because the GBDT does not have a clear over fitting, we consider that the dimension of feature set can be increased appropriately in the case of low computational complexity.

4 Conclusion

In this paper, we propose a series of new classification features based on the based on an in-depth analysis of the new the characteristics of Sina-Weibo. We collected a large amount of spammer data on the Internet and do the examination of two state-of-the-art solutions. Then, we apply GBDT algorithm to spammers detection for the first time. According to our evaluation, while keeping an even lower false positive rate, the detection rate by using GBDT increases at least 3 % than other three different prevalent machine learning classifiers. At the same time, in the case of the same classification algorithm, we can make the recognition accuracy rate compared to the existing part of the study to improve at least 5 %. Finally, depending on the demand, we can choose different classification models or feature subsets in practical application.

References

1. http://baike.baidu.com/view/1567099.htm
2. http://www.businessinsider.com
3. Costolo: Twitter Now Has 190 Million Users Tweeting 65 Million Times A Day
4. https://en.wikipedia.org/wiki/Microblogging_in_China
5. http://tech.qq.com/a/20101126/000325.htm
6. Stringhini, G., Kruegel, C., Vigna, G.: Detecting spammers on social networks. In: Computer Security Applications Conference, pp. 1–9 (2010)
7. http://www.projecthoneypot.org/about_us.php
8. Gao, H., Hu, J., Wilson, C., et al.: Detecting and characterizing social spam campaigns. In: Proceedings of the 17th ACM Conference on Computer and Communications Security, pp. 681–683. ACM (2010)
9. Yardi, S., Romero, D.M., Schoenebeck, G., et al.: Detecting spam in a twitter network. First Monday **15**(1) (2010)
10. Song, J., Lee, S., Kim, J.: Spam filtering in twitter using sender-receiver relationship. In: Sommer, R., Balzarotti, D., Maier, G. (eds.) RAID 2011. LNCS, vol. 6961, pp. 301–317. Springer, Heidelberg (2011). doi:10.1007/978-3-642-23644-0_16
11. Benevenuto, F., Rodrigues, T., Almeida, J., et al.: Detecting spammers and content promoters in online video social networks. In: International ACM SIGIR Conference on Research and Development in Information Retrieval, SIGIR 2009, Boston, MA, USA, July 2009, pp. 337–338 (2009)
12. Thomas, K., Grier, C., Ma, J., et al.: Design and evaluation of a real-time URL spam filtering service **42**(12), 447–462 (2011)
13. Gao, H., Chen, Y., Lee, K., et al.: Poster: online spam filtering in social networks. In: ACM Conference on Computer and Communications Security, CCS 2011, Chicago, Illinois, USA, October 2011, pp. 86–93 (2011)

14. Wang, K., Xiao, Y., Xiao, Z.: Detection of internet water army in social network. In: Proceedings of the 2014 International Conference on Computer, Communications and Information Technology (CCIT 2014), pp. 189–192. Atlantis Press, Amsterdam (2014)
15. Lin, C., He, J., Zhou, Y., et al.: Analysis and identification of spamming behaviors in Sina Weibo Microblog microblog. In: Proceedings of the 7th Workshop on Social Network Mining and Analysis, p. 5. ACM (2013)

An Improved Top-N Recommendation
for Collaborative Filtering

Jiongxin Yang and Zhenyu Wang[⊠]

School of Software Engineering, South China University of Technology,
Guangzhou, People's Republic of China
seyangjx@mail.scut.edu.cn, wangzy@scut.edu.cn

Abstract. Information overload has become an increasingly important problem in the Internet era. The recommendation system has attracted great attention, since it can offer different users with personalized recommendations. Traditional collaborative filtering approaches, user-based collaborative filtering approaches and item-based collaborative filtering approaches tend to recommend some popular items. In order to solve this problem, we propose an algorithm to make penalty on the influence of the highly active users and highly popular items. Experimental results from the MovieLens and real-world dataset, show that our approaches improves precision and coverage, while decreasing the average popularity.

Keywords: Collaborative filtering · Recommendation system · Top-N · Active user · Popular item

1 Introduction

Information overload has been more and more important problem with the development of technology, meanwhile, recommendation system plays an increasingly important role in this era. Recommendation algorithm, as the core of recommendation system, can directly affect recommendation results.

In the field of recommendation system, there are two widely used predicting goal: rating prediction [1] and Top-N [2] prediction. Rating prediction requires recommendation system to predict the rating value that a user would give to an item, which concerns on accuracy, such as RMSE, MAE. Top-N prediction requires recommendation system to generate a list of items for a user, which can be measured by precision, recall, etc. [3] Most researches on collaborative filtering algorithm aim to increase recommendation accuracy. McNee et al. [4] thought that accuracy metrics were not perfect, because these metrics were designed to judge the accuracy of individual item prediction instead of the contents of entire recommendation lists. An effective recommendation system should be able to predict users' behaviors precisely, moreover, it should help users to explore those items which could be hardly found out but close to users' interest. Also, Greg Linden, a former Amazon scientist, pointed out that accuracy might not be what we want. In fact, the purpose of using recommendation system is not to make a prediction for any item, but find the best items for users in most situations [5]. It would be good to

© Springer Nature Singapore Pte Ltd. 2016
Y. Li et al. (Eds.): SMP 2016, CCIS 669, pp. 233–244, 2016.
DOI: 10.1007/978-981-10-2993-6_20

make higher accuracy if what we want is to understand how much users might like an item, however, what we actually want is to pick the best 10 items or so for someone.

In this paper, we would focus on Top-N recommendation issue. A method is proposed in this paper to improve traditional user-based collaborative filtering and item-based collaborative filtering by using user active index and item popular index to make adjustments in these two phases, finding neighbor-users (items) and predicting score, respectively. The experimental results on the public dataset and the real-world dataset indicate that the proposed methods can obtain better performance than traditional methods.

2   Related Work

Content-based filtering [6] and collaborative filtering [7–10] are most common approaches in the field of recommendation system since they are really effective in retail industry. Content-based recommendation system uses some features to represent items. There are many features. For example, an article can be represented by some keywords. Amazon uses a feature called "favorites" that represents the categories of items preferred by users. This approach has its own limitations, sometimes it is hard to obtain item features, and it could hardly recommend items from new category since item features may be different between different categories. Moreover, it would give poor recommendations if the content does not contain enough information to distinguish items the user likes from items the user does not like.

Collaborative filtering is different from content-based filtering, which does not need much extra information, so it can address the problems which content-based filtering cannot solve. The basic ideas of user-based collaborative filtering(User-CF) and item-based collaborative filtering(Item-CF) are similar. In real life, our hobbies are similar to our friends'. User-based collaborative filtering first finds a user's similar users by using similarity metrics, and then predicts this user's interest for an item-based on the weighted combination of ratings of those similar users. Item-based collaborative filtering takes similar steps to user-based collaborative filtering. Similarity metrics are used to measure how similar users or items are.

Recently, some researches revealed the influence of data sparsity on recommendation system, therefore, many approaches have been proposed to alleviate this problem. Xie et al. [11] proposed a method using similarity transitivity to alleviate data sparseness's influence on users' similarity computation. They thought that similarities were inaccurate due to the sparse user-item associations, thus, neighborhoods for each user or item could be inaccurate. By setting an intersection threshold, this method can filter out those inaccurate similarities and then replace them with transitivity similarity.

Some researches pointed out the relationship between recommendation accuracy and popularity of recommended items. It is well-known that recommendation accuracy tends to decrease towards the long tail [12], popular items can be recommended to more users [13]. Zhao et al. [14] proposed an opinion-based method to solve popularity bias problem. They introduced weighting function to measure users' similarities by considering users' opinions.

3 UAIB and IPIB Method

Collaborative filtering has been broadly applied in many industry system, what's more, it is beneficial to improve its algorithmic performance. Therefore, in order to improve recommendation quality, we introduce user active index and item popular index into collaborative filtering. User active index-based (UAIB) and item popular index-based (IPIB) algorithms are described in the proposed approaches. Generally, collaborative filtering approach needs user, item and user's feedback for item as its input. There are two forms of user's feedback, which are explicit feedback and implicit feedback [15]. Explicit feedback includes explicit input by users rating items, which is not always available. The other feedback is implicit feedback, such as purchasing history, searching history or even browsing history. As shown in Fig. 1, we use user-item rating matrix R to represent the association between users and items. For explicit feedback dataset, $R_{u,i}$ denotes the rating made by user u to item i. For implicit feedback dataset, $R_{u,i}$ represents whether user u has access to item i.

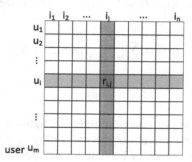

Fig. 1. User-item rating matrix

3.1 Collaborative Filtering

Collaborative filtering can be divided into two phases. The main task in the first phase is to generate neighbor users or items list. Then, in the second phase, the similarity and ratings of similar users on the same item or the user on the similar items are combined to generate a prediction on item for user.

After constructing a rating matrix for user-item association, for any user u, we use the following formula to calculate the similarity between u and v:

$$\text{sim}(u, v) = \frac{\sum_{i \in I_{u,v}} R_{u,i} * R_{v,i}}{\sqrt{\sum_{i \in I_u} R_{u,i}^2} * \sqrt{\sum_{i \in I_v} R_{v,i}^2}} \tag{1}$$

where $I_{u,v}$ means the items that both user u and user v have rated, I_u are items rated by user u. As for item-based CF, similarity between item i and j is calculated by:

$$sim(i, j) = \frac{\sum_{u \in U_{i,j}} R_{u,i} * R_{u,j}}{\sqrt{\sum_{u \in U_i} R_{u,i}^2} * \sqrt{\sum_{u \in U_j} R_{u,j}^2}} \tag{2}$$

where $U_{i,j}$ are users who have rated both item i and item j. After computing the nearest neighbors of users and items, we can generate Top-N recommendation list for a user by following method. We use $P_{u,i}$ to depict how much an item i should be recommended to user u, which can be calculated by combining user's neighbors' preferences on this item and how they are similar to user u. In User-CF, $P_{u,i}$ can be calculated by:

$$P_{User-CF}(u, i) = \sum_{v \in N_u \cap i \in I_v} sim(u, v) * R_{v,i} \tag{3}$$

User u's most similar users can be denoted as N_u, which is also called u's neighbors. In Item-CF, we compute the prediction on an item i for a user u by computing the sum of ratings given by the user on the items similar to i. Each rating is weighted by the corresponding similarity between i and j, $sim_{i,j}$. Formally, using the notion shown below, we can denote the prediction $P_{u,i}$ as:

$$P_{Item-CF}(u, i) = \sum_{j \in I_u \cap i \in N_j} sim(i, j) * R_{u,i} \tag{4}$$

3.2 User Active Index

In User-CF, $P_{u,i}$ is calculated by counting user u's neighbors' behaviors. Obviously, if user v has rated many items, moreover, the probability of v has rated items that u has rated is higher, it is easily to make v become u's neighbor since they both rated some items. Thus, there is higher probability for active user to make contribution to $P_{u,i}$. The penalty on user active index can be denoted as:

$$\alpha_u^{User-CF} = \frac{1}{\log_{10}(1 + |R_u|)} \tag{5}$$

where $|R_u|$ means the number of items that user u rated. Then, with penalty on user active index, $P_{u,i}$ can be calculated as:

$$P_{UAIB-User-CF}(u, i) = \sum_{v \in N_u \cap i \in I_v} sim(u, v) * R_{v,i} * \alpha_v^{User-CF} \tag{6}$$

In Item-CF, likewise, it is more possible that items rated by u have been rated by an active user v, then v's selected items would become u's selected items' neighbors with more chance. To reduce active users' contribution, we use following method:

$$\alpha_u^{Item-CF} = \frac{1}{|R_u|^\theta} \tag{7}$$

where θ is used to control the penalty intensity according to divergence of user active index or item popular index. For example, if divergence is large, θ should be assigned to a value larger than 1. Similarity between item i and item j with decreasing active users' influence is:

$$sim(i,j)' = \frac{\sum_{u \in U_{i,j}} R_{u,i} * R_{u,j} * \alpha_u^{Item-CF}}{\sqrt{\sum_{u \in U_i} R_{u,i}^2} * \sqrt{\sum_{u \in U_j} R_{u,j}^2}} \tag{8}$$

3.3 Item Popular Index

With the same idea as user active index, popular items can also influence recommendation results. Therefore, we use item popular index to reduce negative impact in a similar way to user active index. Popular item's contribution to the similarity between user u and user v can be reduced by:

$$\beta_i^{User-CF} = \frac{1}{|R_i|^\theta} \tag{9}$$

$$sim(u,v)' = \frac{\sum_{i \in I_{u,v}} R_{u,i} * R_{v,i} * \beta_i^{User-CF}}{\sqrt{\sum_{i \in I_u} R_{u,i}^2} * \sqrt{\sum_{i \in I_v} R_{v,i}^2}} \tag{10}$$

Item popular index can also be used in Item-CF. The penalty on popular item's weight can be depicted as Eq. (11) and $P_{u,i}$ is predicted by Eq. (12):

$$\beta_i^{Item-CF} = \frac{1}{\log_{10}(1 + |R_i|)} \tag{11}$$

$$P_{IPIB-Item-CF}(u,i) = \sum_{j \in I_u \cap i \in N_j} sim(i,j) * R_{u,i} * \beta_j^{Item-CF} \tag{12}$$

3.4 Integration of User Active Index and Item Popular Index

For both User-CF and Item-CF, we can integrate user active index based method and item popular index based method into one since they are adopted in different phases. We use following equations to represent $P_{u,i}$:

$$P_{IPIB-UAIB-User-CF}(u,i) = \sum_{v \in N_u \cap i \in I_v} sim(u,v)' * R_{v,i} * \alpha_v^{User-CF} \tag{13}$$

$$P_{UAIB-IPIB-Item-CF}(u,i) = \sum_{j \in I_u \cap i \in N_j} sim(i,j)' * R_{u,i} * \beta_j^{Item-CF} \tag{14}$$

4   Experimental Evaluation

4.1   The Experimental Data

For proving the effectiveness of proposed method, we use a popular publicly-available dataset MovieLens-100 K. The MovieLens-100 K dataset consists of 943 users, 1,682 movies, and 100,000 ratings. The ratings are represented as integer values ranging from 1 to 5. Each user has rated at least 20 movies.

Besides, we use a real-word dataset from GOMO to verify our proposed method further. This dataset is about Android themes. Each record indicates a user's behavior on a theme. There are multiple behaviors, including download, install, see details. In our view, these behaviors show users could be interested in the items. Since there are no explicit ratings available, we regard this dataset as an implicit dataset. This dataset includes 6,979 users, 693 themes and 130,585 records. These records are users' historical behaviors in 2 months in a country. Each user has access to at least 10 themes.

4.2   Evaluation Metrics

For a Top-N recommendation, recommendation system is going to generate a list containing N items for each user. As a result, we divide the dataset into the test set with N items for each user and training set with the remains of the data. There are two widely used metrics, precision and recall [3], while the coverage and popularity are used as the metrics to measure algorithmic diversity. For a specific test set, we set N according to how many items have been rated by each user. Consequently, the precision of recommendation always equals to recall in our metrics.

The coverage means the percentage of all items could be recommended:

$$\text{coverage} = \frac{\#Recommended\ items}{\#All\ items} \tag{15}$$

Since we are concerning the popularity bias problem, we need a measure index which can reflect the overall popularity of recommend recommended result. Apparently, the more users rated an item, the item is more popular. Lower popularity means recommended times reduction for extremely popular items, on the other hand, other items could be recommended with more opportunities. Popularity of item i can be easily represented by the number of users who rated item i. Average popularity is used to evaluate the overall popularity of recommended result. We use natural logarithm to smooth the average popularity on recommendation items:

$$\text{average popularity} = \frac{\sum_{i \in Recommended\ items} \ln(1 + popularity_i)}{\#Recommended\ items} \tag{16}$$

4.3 Experimental Results

MovieLens Dataset. In the first experiment, our concerns are the recall, coverage and average popularity by using different approaches and different K values. As shown in Fig. 2, the recall changes with different K values, meanwhile, penalty on item popular index and user active index can both increase the recall, in particular, combining two adjustment methods together can further increase the recall. The experimental results in Figs. 3 and 4 show coverage and the average popularity. According to Figs. 2, 3 and 4, IPIB-Item-CF has highest coverage and best performance on average popularity, moreover, improves recall slightly. UAIB-Item-CF makes great improvement on recall, however, coverage and average popularity are unsatisfactory. UAIB-IPIB-Item-CF can well balance the advantages of UAIB-Item-CF and IPIB-Item-CF, which has best recall while keeping satisfactory coverage and average popularity.

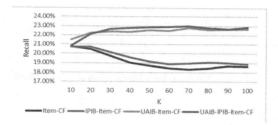

Fig. 2. The recall comparison for item-based approaches on MovieLens dataset

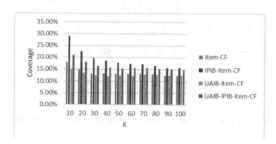

Fig. 3. The coverage comparison for item-based approaches on MovieLens dataset

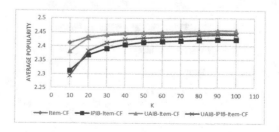

Fig. 4. The average popularity comparison for item-based approaches on MovieLens dataset

In the second experiment, we compare the proposed approaches to User-CF. Figure 5 illustrates the result could be inaccurate if number of neighbors is too small in User-CF, once neighbors' information is enough, all approaches can achieve higher accuracy. Both UAIB-User-CF and IPIB-User-CF can get better accuracy than the non-optimized approach. IPIB-UAIB-User-CF makes further improvement since it takes the advantages of each single approach. From Figs. 6 and 7, we can see the effectiveness of these three approaches. IPIB-UAIB-User-CF can improve the coverage to about 34 % and average popularity less than 2.29.

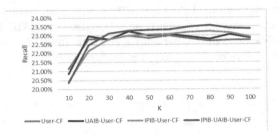

Fig. 5. The recall comparison for user-based approaches on MovieLens dataset

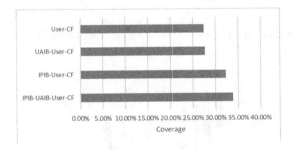

Fig. 6. The coverage comparison for user-based approaches on MovieLens dataset

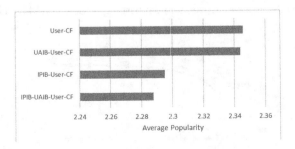

Fig. 7. The average popularity comparison for user-based approaches on MovieLens dataset

GOMO Android Themes Dataset. As mentioned above, the value of θ is related to divergence of user active index or item popular index. This dataset contains 6,979 users, so we set the K among 100 to 1000. More than 90 % users rated less than 20 items. Thus, we set θ as 0.5 for $\beta_i^{User-CF}$ and the results are better. The proposed UAIB-IPIB approach can always balance the tradeoff between accuracy and diversity. As can be seen from Figs. 8, 9 and 10, IPIB-Item-CF has the best performance on diversity while sacrificing some accuracy, and UAIB-Item-CF gets the most accurate result but lacks of diversity. UAIB-IPIB-Item-CF can take care of both. As shown in Figs. 11, 12 and 13, experimental results of improved approaches for User-CF can also verify the effectiveness of the proposed approach.

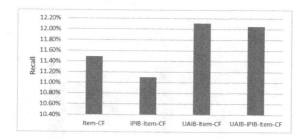

Fig. 8. The recall comparison for item-based approaches on GOMO dataset

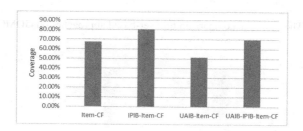

Fig. 9. The coverage comparison for item-based approaches on GOMO dataset

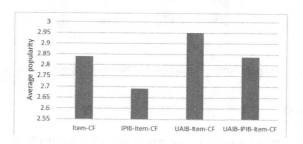

Fig. 10. The average popularity comparison for item-based approaches on GOMO dataset

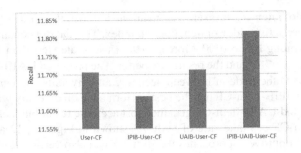

Fig. 11. The recall comparison for user-based approaches on GOMO dataset

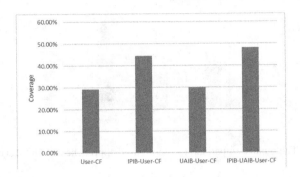

Fig. 12. The coverage comparison for user-based approaches on GOMO dataset

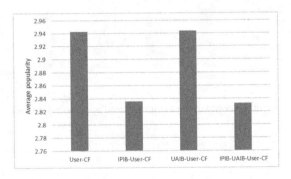

Fig. 13. The average popularity comparison for user-based approaches on GOMO dataset

5   Conclusion

This paper has proposed approaches to adjust the influence made by active user and popular item. With penalty on user active index and item popular index, we can improve both similarity quality and prediction quality. Proposed approaches are evaluated on the famous MovieLens-100 K dataset and real-world GOMO Android themes dataset. The experiments show that the proposed approaches have significant performance improvement, with better accuracy, coverage and average popularity.

Acknowledgements. This work is funded by the Science and Technology Program of Guangdong Province, China (No. 201604010017, No. 2015B010131003, No. 2013B090500062). The authors also thank the editors and reviewers for their constructive editing and reviewing, respectively.

References

1. Amatriain, X., Pujol, J.M., Tintarev, N., Oliver, N.: Rate it again: increasing recommendation accuracy by user re-rating. In: Proceedings of the Third ACM Conference on Recommender Systems, pp. 173–180. ACM, October 2009
2. Davidson, J., Liebald, B., Liu, J., Nandy, P., Van Vleet, T., Gargi, U., Sampath, D.: The youtube video recommendation system. In: Proceedings of the Fourth ACM Conference on Recommender Systems, pp. 293–296. ACM, September 2010
3. Cremonesi, P., Koren, Y., Turrin, R.: Performance of recommender algorithms on top-n recommendation tasks. In: Proceedings of the Fourth ACM Conference on Recommender Systems, pp. 39–46. ACM, September 2010
4. McNee, S.M., Riedl, J., Konstan, J.A.: Being accurate is not enough: how accuracy metrics have hurt recommender systems. In: CHI 2006 Extended Abstracts on Human Factors in Computing Systems, pp. 1097–1101. ACM, April 2006
5. Linden, G.: What Is a Good Recommendation Algorithm (2009). http://cacrrLacrn.org/blogs/blog-cacm/22925-what-is-a-good-recommendation-algorithm/fulltext. Accessed 24 Mar 2009
6. Pazzani, M.J., Billsus, D.: Content-based recommendation systems. In: Brusilovsky, P., Kobsa, A., Nejdl, W. (eds.) The Adaptive Web, vol. 4321, pp. 325–341. Springer, Heidelberg (2007)
7. Resnick, P., Iacovou, N., Suchak, M., Bergstrom, P., Riedl, J.: GroupLens: an open architecture for collaborative filtering of netnews. In: Proceedings of the 1994 ACM Conference on Computer Supported Cooperative Work, pp. 175–186. ACM, October 1994
8. Linden, G., Smith, B., York, J.: Amazon.com recommendations: item-to-item collaborative filtering. Internet Comput. IEEE 7(1), 76–80 (2003)
9. Sarwar, B., Karypis, G., Konstan, J., Riedl, J.: Item-based collaborative filtering recommendation algorithms. In: Proceedings of the 10th International Conference on World Wide Web, pp. 285–295. ACM, April 2001
10. Marlin, B.: Collaborative filtering: a machine learning perspective (doctoral dissertation, University of Toronto) (2004)
11. Xie, F., Chen, Z., Xu, H., Feng, X., Hou, Q.: TST: threshold based similarity transitivity method in collaborative filtering with cloud computing. Tsinghua Sci. Technol. 18(3), 318–327 (2013)
12. Steck, H.: Item popularity and recommendation accuracy. In: Proceedings of the Fifth ACM Conference on Recommender Systems, pp. 125–132. ACM, October 2011
13. Adomavicius, G., Kwon, Y.: Improving aggregate recommendation diversity using ranking-based techniques. IEEE Trans. Knowl. Data Eng. 24(5), 896–911 (2012)

14. Zhao, X., Niu, Z., Chen, W.: Opinion-based collaborative filtering to solve popularity bias in recommender systems. In: Decker, H., Lhotská, L., Link, S., Basl, J., Tjoa, A.M. (eds.) International Conference on Database and Expert Systems Applications, vol. 8056, pp. 426–433. Springer, Heidelberg (2013)
15. Hu, Y., Koren, Y., Volinsky, C.: Collaborative filtering for implicit feedback datasets. In: Eighth IEEE International Conference on Data Mining, ICDM 2008, pp. 263–272. IEEE, December 2008

Social Spammer Detection via Structural Properties in Ego Network

Baochao Zhang, Tieyun Qian[✉], Yiqi Chen, and Zhenni You

State Key Laboratory of Software Engineering, Wuhan University, Wuhan, China
{bczhang,qty,yiqi_chen,znyou}@whu.edu.cn

Abstract. Social media have become popular communication platforms in recent years. A huge number of users disseminate and share information on these websites. Due to their popularity, social media have attracted numerous malicious users (spammers) to send spams, spread malware and phish scams. It is highly desirable to automatically distinguish legitimate users from spammers. Existing approaches mainly use behavior, content, or profile information as features to characterize the social spammers. However, to avoid being caught by the websites, the spammers pretend to post normal messages sometimes and change their behaviors continuously. This makes the behavior and content based approaches less effective.

In this paper, we propose a novel method to detect social spammers via structural properties. Specifically, we adopt 12 types of topological features in users' ego network, including average degree, density, modularity, rich club connectivity, centrality, average shortest path, and cluster coefficient, to learn the classification model for spammer detection. Experimental results on a real world microblog data set demonstrate that the proposed method is very effective. It reaches an accuracy of 82.14 % with only structural features. Furthermore, its performance can be significantly improved to 94.00 % when combined with other features.

Keywords: Spammer detection · Structural properties · Ego network

1 Introduction

In recent years, social media have widely spread out all over the world. Twitter, Facebook, Wechat, and Sina Weibo have become popular communication platforms and aggregated a great deal of users who daily disseminate and share information on these websites. Social media greatly facilitate people's communication. However, they also attract numerous malicious users (spammers) to send spams, spread malware and phish scams. Spammers and spams are extremely harmful as (1) they may result in the uncontrolled dissemination of rumors and the leak of personal information in case of the phishing, (2) they may lead to the dissatisfaction and distrust of the users to service providers. Hence it is highly desirable to automatically distinguish legitimate users from spammers for both the service providers and end users.

© Springer Nature Singapore Pte Ltd. 2016
Y. Li et al. (Eds.): SMP 2016, CCIS 669, pp. 245–256, 2016.
DOI: 10.1007/978-981-10-2993-6_21

Previous approaches to spammer detection mainly used behavior, content, or profile information as features. For example, previous studies found that spammers tended to post duplicate messages [3,10,13]. Spammers were more likely to have out links than in links [9,20]. The time intervals for spammers were often short and there was a bursty shape for spammers' activities [12,17,22]. These features have been proved to be quite useful in building accurate classifiers and have been adopted in a number of commercial systems [17,20]. However, to avoid being caught by the websites, the spammers sometimes pretend to post normal messages and they continuously change their behaviors. This makes the behavior and content based approaches less effective.

A few researchers started to use network based topological features for spammer detection. For instance, Yang et al. extracted the density and average shortest path [19]. Bhat and Abulaish showed that the community-based node features could improve the performance of classification [2]. Yang et al. found that sybils in OSNs did not form tight-knit communities [20]. Existing structural features have the weakness in that it is easy to change the topology of a node. Spammers can follow many other users without the permission of the followee and thus have a large value of out-degree. More importantly, many legitimate users are likely to follow back the spammers considering the social etiquette, and this brings about the large in-degree of a spammer. In this paper, we propose a novel approach to detect the social spammers via structural properties in ego network. The key difference between our approach and existing methods is that we focus on the global topological features for the entire ego network rather than those for a single node.

Let's start from an example in Fig. 1, which shows the ego network for a legitimate user and a spammer. The red dot in Fig. 1(a) and (b) is the legitimate user and spammer him/her self. They have 153 and 161 followees (other black nodes in the figure), respectively. The edges are either between the user/spammer and his/her followees, or between two followees in the ego network.

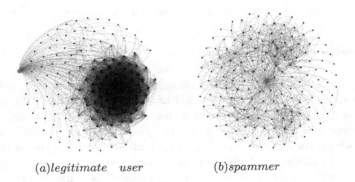

(a)legitimate user   (b)spammer

Fig. 1. Ego network for: (a) a legitimate user, and (b) a spammer (Color figure online)

It can be seen that although the number of followees of the spammer's is a bit large than that of the legitimate user's, the ego network for the spammer is significantly sparser than that for the legitimate user. We have two important observations for Fig. 1.

- The spammers can build as many social relations as the legitimate users. This contradicts the previous finding that it is extremely hard for spammers to get enough trust relations [6]. It is also informative in that the profile based features such as the number of followees, or the ratio of the followee number to the follower number may become less effective.
- While a single topological feature like the degree of a spammer is easy to forge and may be close to that of a legitimate user, their ego networks are indeed quite different. It is obvious the density in a legitimate user's network is much larger than that in a spammer's. Consequently, the averaged path length should be short for a legitimate user.

The above observations inspire our study. In particular, we are interested in the following questions. How about other structural properties for spammers' ego network? Are they different from those for legitimate users? If this is the case, what are the most distinguished features for building classification models? Hence we select 12 types of structural features, including weighted degree, average degree, density, modularity, rich club connectivity, four types of centrality, averaged shortest path, and cluster coefficient. These features are typical in network analysis to measure the key properties such as small world and robustness, and are normally used to identify whether a network is a social, biological, or internet network.

We evaluate the effects of structural features on a spammer detection task on a real world microblog data set. Experimental results demonstrate that the proposed method is very effective. It reaches an accuracy of 82.14 % with only structural features. Furthermore, its performance can be significantly improved to 94.00 % when combined with the content, profile and behavior features.

The rest of the paper is organized as follows. Section 2 reviews related work. Section 3 presents the novel structural features to characterize the social spammers. Section 4 introduces other commonly used content, behavior, and profile features for comparison. Section 5 provides experimental results. Section 6 concludes the paper finally.

2   Related Work

We first review the features used for spammer detection, and then survey the classification methods.

2.1   Features for Spammer Detection

Most of existing studies used the content features including duplicate reviews [3,10,11,13], the vocabulary size [5], the review length [10], if it is the first or second review [10,11], the rating score [11,13], the hash tags [1,12,15], the sentiment score [3,10], and the contact information such as URL or telephone [1,9,12,16,22]. Another type of feature is the activity or behavior feature such as the ratio of sharing or reposting [23], the ratio of being replied [3], the number of active days, the averaged time interval for posting [3], the date of register [1], the time distribution of the posting [12], the time stamps [22] and the time synchronization among users [7,17]. Several types of profile features, for instance, the number of followees or followers [1,9,16], the number of reviews or messages [10,12], the ratio of sent/acceptance invitation [20], are also used for spammer detection.

Recently, a few researchers evaluated the effects of topological features on spammer detection, for example, the relations among users [5] and messages [18], the density and the average shortest path [19], community based features like in/out degree and core node [2], and the clustering coefficient [20]. However, these features are either for single node or for the entire network containing all users and their connections. In contrast, our structural features are designed for the ego network for each user, which are much harder for spammers to change and have better effects on classification.

2.2   Classification Approaches

A number of supervised learning approaches have been explored to solve the problem of spammer detection, for instance, SVM [3,12,20], Naive Bayes, decision tree, and k-NN [3,12], logistic regression [8] and linear regression [11]. Among which, SVM is one of the most widely used approach and it has a relatively high performance.

Due to the lack of labeled data, attentions have also been paid to the semi-supervised methods like co-training [10] and PU learning [14]. In addition, several methods have been developed to incorporate the social relations. Typical ones are convex optimization [6], matrix factorization [5], and Expectation-Maximization (EM)-based label prediction [15].

Since we are interested in investigating the performance of structural features, the classification approaches are not the focus of this paper. We choose to use SVM as our classifier just as most of existing studies do.

3   Structural Properties in Ego Network

Ego networks consist of a focal node, and the nodes to whom ego is directly connected to plus the ties. In this paper, we treat the spammer or legitimate user as the ego or focal node, the social relations between the spammer and legitimate user and the people they follow (followee), and those between followees as the edges to build ego network for each spammer and legitimate user. Note that we do not include the followers of the ego into the network because in microblogging systems, a user can follow anyone else without the permission of the followee. This makes the followers of a user uncontrolled and diversified. Our preliminary study shows that the performance by using ego network of followers is poor. Due to the space limitation, we just present our results using followees.

We explore 12 types of topological features in ego network. We now give their formal definitions. G is a graph. V is the set of nodes and E is the set of edges in G. |V| and |E| are the number of V and E respectively. v, u, s and t mean a single node in G separately. D(v) is the degree of node v. A is an adjacency matrix of G and $A_{vu} = 1$ means an edge between nodes v and u. d(v, u) is the shortest distance between node v and node u.

(1) **Rich club coefficient.** This metric measures the extent to which well-connected nodes also connect to each other. It is defined as:

$$\phi(k) = \frac{2E_{>k}}{N_{>k}(N_{>k} - 1)} \tag{1}$$

where $N_{>k}$ is the number of nodes with degree larger than k and $E_{>k}$ is the number of edges among those nodes. In our experiments, we set k to the average degree of each network, i.e., all nodes.

(2) **Average clustering coefficient.** This metric gives an indication of the clustering in the whole network, and also can be called the transitivity. It is defined as:

$$ACC = \frac{3 \times N_t}{N_{ct}} \tag{2}$$

where N_t is the number of triangles and N_{ct} is the number of connected triplets of vertices in G.

(3) **Degree assortativity coefficient.** This metric measures the similarity of connections in the graph with respect to the node degree. It is defined as:

$$DAC = \frac{\sum_{jk} jk(p_{jk}, q_j q_k)}{\sigma_q^2} \tag{3}$$

where j and k are two degree values, p_{jk} is the probability that a randomly chosen edge with two nodes whose degrees are j and k respectively, q_k is the distribution of the remaining degree and σ_q is the standard deviation of q_k.

(4) **Modularity.** This metric is designed to measure the strength of division of a network into modules (also called groups, clusters or communities). It is defined as:

$$Q = \frac{1}{2|E|} \sum_{vu} (A_{vu} - \frac{D(v)D(u)}{2|E|})(\frac{m_v m_u + 1}{2}) \tag{4}$$

Consider G being partitioned into two communities using a membership variable m. If node v belongs to community 1, $m_v = 1$. If node u belongs to community 2, $m_u = -1$.

(5) **Average degree.** This metric gives basic information of a graph G. It is defined as:

$$AD = \frac{2|E|}{|V|} \tag{5}$$

(6) **Average weighted degree.** This metric is an extension of average degree for taking the weight of edges into consideration. It is defined as:

$$AWD = \frac{\sum_{e \in E} w_{in}(e) + w_{out}(e)}{2|V|} \tag{6}$$

(7) **Density.** This metric measures how many edges are in E compared to the maximum possible number of edges between vertices in V. It is defined as:

$$Den = \frac{|E|}{|V|(|V| - 1)} \tag{7}$$

(8) **Average path length.** This metric is a measure of the efficiency of information or mass transport on a network. It is defined as the average number of steps along the shortest paths for all possible pairs of network nodes. It is defined as:

$$APL = \frac{1}{|V|(|V| - 1)} \sum_{v \neq u} d(v, u) \tag{8}$$

(9) **Degree centrality.** This metric can be interpreted in terms of the immediate risk of a node for catching whatever is flowing through the network (such as a virus, or some information). It is defined as:

$$DC = \frac{\sum_{v \in V}(D(v^*) - D(v))}{\sum_{u \in U}(D(u^*) - D(u))} \tag{9}$$

Let graph X := (U, Z) be the |U| node connected graph that maximizes the denominator, v^* and u^* is the node with the highest degree centrality in G and X, respectively.

(10) **Eigenvector centrality.** This is a measure of the influence of a node in a network. It computes the centrality for a node based on the centrality of its neighbors. It is defined as:

$$x_v = \frac{1}{\lambda} \sum_{u \in G} a_{v,u} x_u \tag{10}$$

where λ is the eigenvalue of graph G, and x_v and x_u is the centrality score of node v and u.

(11) **Betweenness centrality.** This metric quantifies the number of times a node acts as a bridge along the shortest path between two other nodes. It is defined as:

$$BC(v) = \frac{\sum_{s,t \in V} nd(s, t|v)}{nd(s, t)} \tag{11}$$

where nd(s, t) is the number of shortest paths between node s and node t, and nd(s, t|v) is the number of those paths passing through some node v other than s, t.

(12) **Closeness centrality.** This metric is the reciprocal of the sum of the shortest path distances from node v to all other nodes. It is defined as:

$$CC(v) = \frac{|v| - 1}{\sum_{u \in V} d(u, v)} \tag{12}$$

4 Content, Behavior, and Profile Features

We then introduce a set of other content, behavior, and profile features for the purpose of comparison. These features have been widely used in the literature [1,3,9,10,12,12,15,17].

Content Features. We extract three types of content features from the microblogs, i.e., weiboFromRepostRate, topicRate, and textURLrate. The weiboFromRepostRate reflects the ratio of microblogs by reposting. The topicRate is defined as the ratio of microblogs which contain a hashtag #. The textURLrate is the ratio of microblogs which contain a URL links.

Behavior Features. The behavior features are used to measure how the users communicate with the others. We extracted atRate, commentRate and repostRate as the representatives for behavior features. The atRate is used to measure the ratio of microblogs being sent to a specific user. The commentRate and repostRate is the ratio of microblogs that have comments and are reposted by others.

Profile Features. We use nine profile features. Four of them are based on the number of followees and followers, including followeeNum, followerNum, followeeNumDivfollowerNum, and followeeNumDivAll. Two of them are about the length. One is the length (the number of characters) of the user name. The other is length of the description in the profile. If there is no description, the profileLen will be 0. The remaining ones are profileURL, hasProfile, and weiboAge. The hasProfile and hasProfileURL are boolean features, where 1 means the user has a profile or the profile contains a URL. The weiboAge is the number of years the account exists.

Table 1 summarizes three types of features.

Table 1. Content, profile, and behavior features

Type	Feature name	Description
Content	weiboFromRepostRate	The ratio of microblogs by reposting
	topicRate	The ratio of microblogs containing a hashtag #
	textURLrate	The ratio of microblogs containing a URL
Behavior	atRate	The ratio of microblogs being sent to a specific user
	commentRate	The ratio of microblogs that have comments
	repostRate	The ratio of microblogs are reposted by others
Profile	followeeNum	The number of followees
	followerNum	The number of followers
	followeeNumDivfollowerNum	The ratio of the number of followees to followers
	followeeNumDivAll	The ratio of the number of followees to all neighbors
	usernameLength	The number of characters in a username
	profileLength	The number of characters in the description
	hasProfileURL	Whether the profile containing a URL
	hasProfile	Whether the user having a profile
	weiboAge	The number of years the account existing

5   Experimental Evaluation and Discussion

In this section, we evaluate the proposed approach. We first introduce the experiment setup, and then present the results.

5.1   Experiment Setup

We conduct extensive experiments on a real world microblog data set. We collect and annotate a set of 700 users in Sina Weibo, the biggest social networking sites in China. We follow a supervised learning framework for spammer detection. There are two classes, i.e., spammer class and the legitimate user class. Each class has 350 samples. We further crawl the followees of these 700 examples to build their ego networks. The total number of followees is 253165 and there are 3592350 user-followee and followee-followee edges in total. The detailed statistics for the data set are shown in Table 2.

Table 2. The statistics for the data set

User type	User number	Followee number	Edge number
Spammer	350	175111	2513910
Legitimate user	350	78154	1078440
Total	700	253165	3592350

All our experiments use the LIBSVM classifier with default parameter settings [4]. The data are randomly split into five parts. The results are averaged over 5-fold cross validations. We report the accuracy as the evaluation metric.

5.2   Significance of Features

We first compute the average value of various features in spammers and legitimate users, as well as the χ^2 values to learn their significance. We show the top 15 distinguished features in Table 3. The features in bold are structural ones.

We see that among the top 10 features, 8 of them are structural features. This is a very informative finding. It strongly demonstrates that the structural features are more effective for spammer detection than other types of features. The degree and density metrics show that the spammers' ego network is much sparser than the legitimate users'. The high modularity for spammers shows that their networks have dense connections between the nodes within modules but sparse connections across different modules. Furthermore, we find that four centrality metrics all play important roles in classification.

We also see that textURLRate is the most distinguished feature. This is consistent with the previous studies [9,12,22], showing that spammers use URLs more frequently than the legitimate users. There are two profile features and

Table 3. The top 15 distinguished features

Rank	Feature name	Avg. in legitimate	Avg. in spammers	χ^2 significance
1	textURLRate	0.096346	0.431746	157.633144
2	**weighted degree**	0.040686	0.109298	110.309192
3	**average degree**	0.040686	0.109298	94.199311
4	**density**	0.169707	0.049015	61.23715
5	**modularity**	0.389015	0.608513	52.798309
6	followeeNum	0.124231	0.294027	50.473587
7	**closeness centrality**	0.072801	0.032455	49.259916
8	**rich club coefficient**	0.379513	0.227274	47.588268
9	**betweenness centrality**	0.044035	0.013423	44.342679
10	**degree centrality**	0.114153	0.054464	40.047002
11	**eigenvector centrality**	0.0313	0.126632	38.543364
12	**average path length**	0.121125	0.349441	38.543364
13	followeeNumDivfollowerNum	0.003715	0.014056	35.011692
14	topicRate	0.049453	0.050626	34.253097
15	userNameLength	0.18429	0.119765	22.289083

three content features rank high among all features. It is interesting that the χ^2 value for usernameLength feature is relatively high, indicating that legitimate users tend to have longer usernames than the spammers. The reason can be that spammers do not care about what their names look like and would like to save time by using short nick names [21].

To have a close look, we select six structural features and show their distributions in spammers and legitimate users in Fig. 2.

It can be seen that the spammers and legitimate users exhibit quite different statistic distributions. For example, in Fig. 2(d), we find the closeness centrality values for 70 % of spammers are less than 0.03. In contrast, only 22 % legitimate users are in this interval and half of them are located in the interval of (0.03, 0.1). Figure 2(e) shows that a great number of legitimate users (55.90 %) have a large rich club connectivity, indicating that there are many connections between nodes of high degree and these users may know each other in reality. On the contrary, the spammers have much smaller rich club connectivity in average, showing that those nodes of high degree may be followed by the spammers at random and thus they are not connected in the network.

5.3   Classification Performance

We now compare the performance of using different types of features. The results are shown in Table 4. For a fair comparison, we also conduct experiments on four structural features in profile, i.e., followeeNum, followerNum, followeeNumDivfollowerNum, and followeeNumDivAll and contain its result in Table 4.

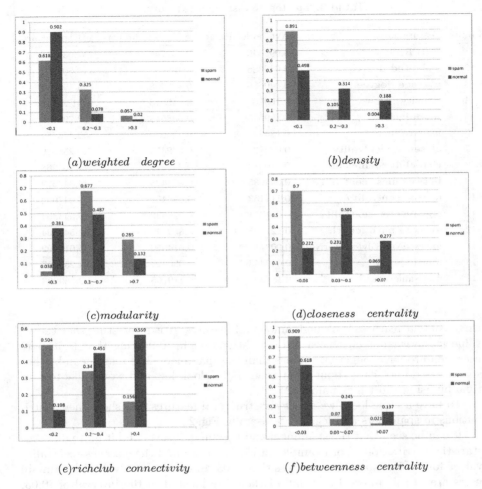

(a)weighted degree

(b)density

(c)modularity

(d)closeness centrality

(e)richclub connectivity

(f)betweenness centrality

Fig. 2. Distribution of spammers and legitimate users.

Table 4. Classification performance using various features

Feature type	Accuracy
Content features	89.71
Behavior features	49.42
Profile features	71.85
Structural features in profile	67.71
Structural features in ego network	82.14
All features	**94.00***

We can see that the content features perform the best among all single type of features. This reveals that the microblogs are the most informative for recognizing the spammers. The reason can be due to that the URLs, the hash tags #, and the reposts constitute the main contents in spammers' microblogs. They use URLs to promote products or redirect to phishing websites, and use hash tags to draw the readers' attentions. The reposts are used as disguise to make the spammers' microblogs more like the legitimate users'.

The structural features in ego network are the second best, reaching an accuracy of 82.14 %, significantly better than the behavior and profile features. More importantly, it is clear that the structural features in ego network outperform those in profile. The finding is very indicative, because those in profile are for the ego node him/her self while ours are for the entire ego network. This clearly demonstrates the hypothesis in the introduction that the topological features for a single node are relatively easy to forge and thus deteriorate the classification accuracy.

Finally, we combine all four types of features, i.e., content, behavior, profile, and structural features, by putting them together into a joint vector. The accuracy with all features reaches a surprisingly high value of 94.00 %. The * superscript denotes that its improvements over other methods are all significant under the 0.05 significance testing. That is to say, both the performances of content features and structural features can be further improved with the help of other features.

6   Conclusion

This paper presents a novel method to identify spammers with the structural properties. Our method employs 12 types of topological features in ego network. These features capture the difference between the network of spammers and that of legitimate users, and the key advantage is that they are hard to forge. We conduct extensive experiments on a real world data set. Experimental results demonstrate that structural features are very effective in detecting spammers. Moreover, we can incorporate the content, behavior and profile features to get extremely good performance.

While the experiments show that the structural properties are quite helpful in spammer detection. There are several weaknesses such as the high computational cost for computing centrality based metrics. In the future, we plan to select more efficient structural features and conduct experiments on other data sets.

Acknowledgements. The work described in this paper has been supported in part by the NSFC projects (61572376, 61272275), and the 111 project (B07037).

References

1. Benevenuto, F., Magno, G., Rodrigues, T., Almeida., V.: Detecting spammers on twitter. In: Proceedings of the 7th CEAS, pp. 6–12 (2010)

2. Bhat, S.Y., Abulaish, M.: Community-based features for identifying spammers in online social networks. In: Proceedings of the ASONAM, pp. 100–107 (2013)
3. Chen, C., Wu, K., Srinivasan, V., Zhang, X.: Battling the internet water army: detection of hidden paid posters. In: Proceedings of the ASONAM, pp. 116–120 (2013)
4. Fan, R.E., Chang, K.W., Hsieh, C.J., Wang, X.R., Lin, C.J.: Liblinear: a library for large linear classification. J. Mach. Learn. Res. **9**, 1871–1874 (2008)
5. Hu, X., Tang, J., Liu, H.: Leveraging knowledge across media for spammer detection in microblogging. In: Proceedings of the SIGIR, pp. 547–556 (2014)
6. Hu, X., Tang, J., Zhang, Y., Liu, H.: Social spammer detection in microblogging. In: Proceedings of the IJCAI, pp. 2633–2639 (2013)
7. Jiang, M., Cui, P., Beutel, A., Faloutsos, C., Yang, S.: CatchSync: catching synchronized behavior in large directed graphs. In: Proceedings of the KDD, pp. 941–950 (2014)
8. Jindal, N., Liu, B., Lim, E.P.: Finding unusual review patterns using unexpected rules. In: Proceedings of the CIKM, pp. 1549–1552 (2011)
9. Lee, K., Caverlee, J., Webb, S.: Uncovering social spammers: social honeypots+ machine learning. In: Proceedings of the SIGIR, pp. 435–442 (2010)
10. Li, F., Huang, M., Yang, Y., Zhu, X.: Learning to identify review spam. In: Proceedings of the IJCAI, pp. 2488–2493 (2011)
11. Lim, E.P., Nguyen, V.A., Jindal, N., Liu, B., Lauw, H.W.: Detecting product review spammers using rating behaviors. In: Proceedings of the CIKM, pp. 939–948 (2010)
12. McCord, M., Chuah, M.: Spam detection on Twitter using traditional classifiers. In: Calero, J.M.A., Yang, L.T., Mármol, F.G., García Villalba, L.J., Li, A.X., Wang, Y. (eds.) ATC 2011. LNCS, vol. 6906, pp. 175–186. Springer, Heidelberg (2011). doi:10.1007/978-3-642-23496-5_13
13. Mukherjee, A., Kumar, A., Liu, B., Wang, J., Hsu, M., Castellanos, M., Ghosh, R.: Spotting opinion spammers using behavioral footprints. In: Proceedings of the KDD, pp. 632–640 (2013)
14. Ren, Y., Ji, D., Zhang, H., Yin, L.: Positive and unlabeled learning for deceptive reviews detection. In: Proceedings of the EMNLP, pp. 488–498 (2014)
15. Sedhai, S., Sun, A.: Hspam14: a collection of 14 million tweets for hashtag-oriented spam research. In: Proceedings of the SIGIR, pp. 223–232 (2015)
16. Stringhini, G., Kruegel, C., Vigna, G.: Detecting spammers on social networks. In: Proceedings of the ACSAC, pp. 1–9 (2010)
17. Tian, T., Zhu, J., Xia, F., Zhuang, X., Zhang, T.: Crowd fraud detection in internet advertising. In: Proceedings of the 24th WWW, pp. 1100–1110 (2015)
18. Wu, F., Shu, J., Huang, Y., Yuan, Z.: Social spammer and spam message co-detection in microblogging with social context regularization. In: Proceedings of the CIKM, pp. 1601–1610 (2015)
19. Yang, C., Harkreader, R., Zhang, J., Shin, S., Gu, G.: Analyzing spammer social networks for fun and profit, a case study of cyber criminal ecosystem on Twitter. In: Proceedings of the WWW, pp. 71–80 (2012)
20. Yang, Z., Wilson, C., Wang, X., Gao, T., Zhao, B.Y., Dai, Y.: Uncovering social network sybils in the wild. ACM Trans. Knowl. Discov. Data **8**, Article No. 2 (2014)
21. Zafarani, R., Liu, H.: Connecting users across social media sites: a behavioral-modeling approach. In: Proceedings of the KDD, pp. 41–49 (2013)
22. Zhang, X., Li, Z., Zhu, S., Liang, W.: Detecting spam and promoting campaigns in Twitter. ACM Trans. Web **10**(1), 4:1–4:28 (2016)
23. Zhu, Y., Wang, X., Zhong, E., Liu, N.N., Li, H., Yang, Q.: Discovering spammers in social networks. In: Proceedings of the AAAI (2012)

News Events Elements Extraction Based on Undirected Graph

Xian Li[1], Zhengtao Yu[1,2(✉)], Shengxiang Gao[1], Xudong Hong[1], and Chunting Yan[1]

[1] School of Information Engineering and Automation,
Kunming University of Science and Technology, Kunming 650051, China
ztyu@hotmail.com
[2] School of Intelligent Information Processing,
Computer Technology Application Key Laboratory of Yunnan Province,
Kunming 650051, China

Abstract. News event elements extraction is a main task of information extraction. For news event correlation between sub-events, this paper proposes a kind of undirected graph model of news event element extraction merging associations of event elements. Firstly, splitting the news to multiple sub-event and extracting event elements. Then, the correlation between event elements and news events was analyzed, a undirected graph by extracting the correlation based on news event elements as node was established, and we transferred news event element extraction into a weighted undirected graph node calculation problem. At last, We conducted event elements extraction experiments. And comparing the experimental results show that the proposed method has good effect, correlation of sub-event can effectively improve the effect of extracting elements of news events.

Keywords: Information extraction · Event elements extraction · Undirected graph

1 Introduction

As the world becomes more informational, there is increasing number of textual information. Event extraction which is an essential part of information extraction is that automatically extract structured information from text. Events element extracted from text is helpful and supported for understanding the text and can characterize the main information of event. The current event extraction can be mainly divided into extraction method based on event template and event extraction method based on machine learning. The main idea of template event extraction method is that define event elements extraction template according to events feature, and extract event element by template matching. Among them, Xu [1] proposed using the trigger word argument semantics and transformation rules of template method to extract template, improving the effect of template

Y. Li et al. (Eds.): SMP 2016, CCIS 669, pp. 257–266, 2016.
DOI: 10.1007/978-981-10-2993-6_22

extract event element. Huang and Riloff [2] trained a multi-layer event extraction templates for every seed trigger word. The main ideal of extraction method based on classifier is that transfer event identification problem into a classification problem, and extract events characteristics to train event element classifier. Ji [3] extracted trigger word, entity type, event subcategory, entity, time expression, shortest path between trigger word and entity to train a classifier of the maximum entropy model to extract event. Liao and Grishman [4] proposed the theory of cross event that the events distribution of documents has a certain relationship, as a characteristic elements constructing classifier to recognition events. Xu et al. [5] proposed the reasoning method based on the correlation event and related event as characteristics to join in the training of the classifier in order to improve the effect of event element extraction. The above research work is mainly focused on the sentence level event element extraction which had made many achievements. Wang [6] put forward using the news special characteristics and indicative information of title to train classifier to get the topic sentence, and to get key events according to the topic sentence. Kastner [7] news used semantic, grammar and statistical characteristics in a single to design classifier which extract the most important sentence of news to automatically extract for CNN news.

The center of the news text which is the most important part for reading and understanding can be composed of several essential events of the element, this paper mainly study that extracting event elements from a single news which briefly portraying the news. Through the analysis of news texts, news and events contented cohesiveness, separability, relatedness and similarity [8], which make the news core may be repeatedly appeared in the title, introduction, plot description, and conclusion part, to portray news in different aspects. The co-occurrence relationship reflect that the event elements of the news is also repeatedly appeared in different part of the news, through this co-occurrence relationship of event elements can bridge a connection between child events which is benefit to extract event element. For example, the presence of the same time, place and figure in each child events is likely to be the essential element of news event. Based on this idea, we proposed that news core events element extraction method based on event element co-reference relation. With news event elements and event reference relation building into undirected graph model, we used the characteristics of graph to solve graph to realize the news elements extraction.

2 News Event Extraction

Research of sentence level event extraction has been conducted for many years. We realized the extraction method based on event trigger words proposed by Zhao [9] to extract events and event elements. According the defined trigger word set to identify candidate events, then select the event trigger word, up and down phraseology, the context entities as characteristics to training the

SVM classifier to identify the real news events. At last, we selected physical characteristics, syntactic structures and lexical characteristics to train to obtain the maximum entropy multiple classifiers. And we accorded the defined event elements template to extract candidate elements to implement sub-event element extraction.

3   Construction of Undirected Graph Based on News Sub-event Elements and Calculation of Edge Weight of Graph

Through the analysis of the news, we believe that a event elements which repeatedly appeared in different parts of the news text is more relevant to the news topics. Based on this idea, we use event elements as nodes, the co-occurrence relations of the extracted event element in news text and relation that event elements belong to a same sub-event as edge to construct an undirected graph model. With the aid of undirected graph model, we obtained the element's ability to influence other elements, which leading us to extract event element.

3.1   The Generation of Undirected Graph Nodes and Edges

According to the order of appearance of sub-event elements in the news we numbered event element nodes. If extracting n event elements from A news, thus an ordered set of these child elements can be expressed as:

$$V = \{V_1, V_2, V_3, \cdots, V_i, \cdots, V_n\} \tag{1}$$

where $V_i(i = 1, 2, \cdots, n)$ is sub-event element of the news text and n is number of sub-event. Sub-event element array V contains reduplicative events element, when creating undirected graph model we need to merge the reduplicative event elements into one to gather edges to a single node. Undirected graph edge consists of two parts, the first is that two events elements belonged to a same sub-event

Table 1. The information extracted from the news

Sub-event	Sub-event type	Trigger	Sub-event elements
Event 1	Earthquake	Earthquake	March 9; Songming County; 4.5 magnitude; Earthquake
Event 2	Earthquake	Earthquake	March 9, 2015 17:59; Songming County; 4.5 magnitude; Earthquake
Event 3	Call	Call	Reporter; Called; Zhe Yanyu
Event 4	Move	Move	Zhe Yanyu; Ran
Event 5	Move	Move	Office personnel; Went; Out
Event 6	Earthquake	Earthquake	September 6, 1833; Songming County; 8 magnitude; Earthquake

have a spontaneous correlation, so we build a edge between the elements. The second is that we merge reduplicative event element into the first same element, connecting with event elements that the reduplicative event element connected before merging. These relation formed E and V^* is the array that elements had merged. Concrete steps as Algorithm 1.

Table 2. News instance

Title	Content
The outskirts of Kunming occurred 4.5 earthquake felt strongly in umbra	March 9, 4.5 magnitude earthquake occurred in Songming County of Kunming City, Yunnan Province, the epicenter about 50 km from Kunming City, a main city of Kunming felt strongly. China seismic station officially measured, 17:59 on March 9 in Songming County of Yunnan Province, Kunming city (25.3°, 103.1° north latitude and longitude) occurred 4.5 magnitude earthquake, and the focal depth is 12 km. The epicenter is near in Xiaojie street town, Songming where about 7 km from the Songming County, and about 50 km from the urban area of Kunming. The glass door of 4 floor office area where reporter in shaken violently. Similarly, light 8 floor office where the people of Kunming Li Bin in, shaken badly for many seconds, and office personnel gradually went downstairs. Reporter called Zhe Yanyu who in the territory of the Dianchi College of Yunnan University Yang Lin campus located in the Songming county. When the earthquake came, he and his classmates were in the 2 floor of the dormitory. With suddenly shaking violently, the Zhe Yanyu immediately had ran out. At this time, many students have gathered on the playground. Songming county is located in central Yunnan, and is located in the northeast of the city of Kunming, and is under the jurisdiction of Kunming City suburb county, where away from the Kunming 43 km. Songming county had occurred 8 magnitude earthquake in September 6, 1833.

The following is an example, Table 1 and Fig. 1 showed a news and the event elements extracted by the above method. In the Table 1, the event elements, Songming and earthquake, belonged to event 1, 2 and 6, is co-occurrent in all three cases, which is the main content of the news. The elements of event 3, 4 and 5 is not co-occurrent in other events, which is not contained the core information of the news.

Algorithm 1. Algorithm merging undirected graph.

Input: V, n
Output: V^*, E
  for each V **do**
    if V_i and V_i belong to a same sub-event **then**
      put $e = \{V_i, V_j\}$;
    end if
  end for
  for each V **do**
    if V_i equals $V_j \in V^*$ **then**
      V_i replaces V_j in E where $V_j \in e$;
    else
      puts V_i into V^*;
    end if
  end for

3.2 Calculation of Edge Weights Based on Similarity

Undirected graph edge weights reflect the correlation between the degree of correlation between nodes and sub elements of the news event. In order to characterize the correlation between event element, we reference vector space model. With the news sub-event elements as space vector, we represented the sub event as a feature vector.

Construction Vector Space Characterized by Sub-event. Assuming event p is extracted from a news text, a sub-event set $K = \{W_1, W_1, \cdots, W_n\}$ is formed, and a sub event in K is used as one dimension of the vector space to construct a p dimensional vector space.

If an event element was associated with t event, it is said that the event element appeared at t event, which has a formula:

$$S_i = \underbrace{\cdots, W_k, \cdots}_{t} \tag{2}$$

K' is a array of the t sub events. Because there is $K' \subseteq K$, S_i can be expressed as:

$$S_i = \underbrace{\cdots, W_k, \cdots}_{t}, \underbrace{\cdots, W_e, \cdots}_{s}, \begin{cases} W_k \in K', & W_e = 0 \\ t \leq p, & t + s = p \end{cases} \tag{3}$$

Thus, any one of the news event elements can be expressed as a vector in the vector space.

Mapping News Sub Event Elements to a Vector Space. When the feature space is constructed, the sub events are characterized as a feature vector, and the feature value of each dimension is determined according to whether the sub-event element is a true value. The specific feature vector generation algorithm as Algorithm 2.

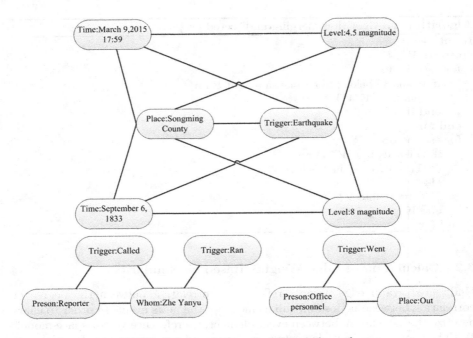

Fig. 1. Sub-event element undirected graph

After the Algorithm 2 processing, the feature vector of each news event element to the p dimension is characterized, and the matrix S is obtained:

$$S = \begin{bmatrix} V_{11} & V_{12} & \cdots & V_{1q} \\ V_{21} & V_{22} & \cdots & V_{2q} \\ \vdots & \vdots & \ddots & \vdots \\ V_{p1} & V_{p2} & \cdots & V_{pq} \end{bmatrix} \tag{4}$$

In the formula, q is the max number of V^*, V_{pq} represented the value of the element of q event in the p sub-event, $e_{pq} \in \{0,1\}$. S also can be expressed as:

$$S = \left[S_1, S_1, \cdots, S_1, \cdots \right]^T, i \in \{1,2,3,\cdots,p\} \tag{5}$$

Similarity Computing. With the news sub-event representation into a vector space, the feature vector of each news sub-event elements were got. Then calculating the similarity between the vector of the elements cosine angle on the element event.

$$Sim(S_i, S_j) = \cos q = \frac{\sum_{k=1}^{p} e_{ik} e_{jk}}{\sqrt{(\sum_{k=1}^{p} e_{ik}^2)(\sum_{k=1}^{2} e_{jk}^2)}} \tag{6}$$

Algorithm 2. Algorithm merging undirected graph.

Input: V^*, p, q, K
Output: S
  for $i = 0, 1, \cdots, p-1$ **do**
    for $j = 0, 1, \cdots, q-1$ **do**
      if $V_j \in W_i$ **then**
        $v_{ij} = 1$;
      else
        $v_{ij} = 0$;
      end if
    end for
  end for

θ is vector angle of S_i and S_j in the vector space. e_{ik} is the value of S_i in the K dimension, e_{jk} is the value of S_j in the K dimension. p is the number of dimension of the vector space constructed by the news event.

Calculating the similarity between news sub-event elements, the similarity matrix of the sub-event elements is obtained as shown below:

$$M = \begin{bmatrix} Sim_{11} & Sim_{12} & \cdots & Sim_{1i} & \cdots & Sim_{1q} \\ Sim_{21} & Sim_{22} & \cdots & Sim_{2i} & \cdots & Sim_{2q} \\ \vdots & \vdots & \ddots & \vdots & \ddots & \vdots \\ Sim_{i1} & Sim_{i2} & \cdots & Sim_{ii} & \cdots & Sim_{iq} \\ \vdots & \vdots & \ddots & \vdots & \ddots & \vdots \\ Sim_{q1} & Sim_{q2} & \cdots & Sim_{qi} & \cdots & Sim_{qq} \end{bmatrix} \tag{7}$$

In the formula, Sim_{ij} is the similarity between the i element and the j element, $i, j \in \{1, 2, \cdots, q\}$.

The similarity between event elements is used as the weight between the two nodes in the undirected graph. When the two sub event elements appear in the different sub events, the edges are overlapped in the undirected graph, and the weight of the edge is superimposed on calculating.

4   Weight Calculation and Event Element Extraction of Undirected Graph

In the constructed undirected graph, news event element extraction can be transformed into calculating the weights of the graph nodes, and then the event elements are extracted by weight. From the idea of PageRank algorithm, a calculation model of node weights was built. Using the correlation relationship between the nodes to calculate the importance of a node, the node is connected with other nodes, the more important the node is. Therefore, undirected graph node weights calculation can be expressed as:

$$SW(i) = (1 - d) + d \cdot \sum_{j=i, j \neq i}^{n} M_{ij} \cdot \frac{SW(j)}{\sum_{K=1, K \neq j}^{n} M_{jk}} \tag{8}$$

In the formula, $SW(i)$ is the weight of the node, and D is the damping coefficient, which generally set to 0.85 [10]. M_{ij} is the value of the similarity matrix M, which is the similarity between i and j sub-event element.

5   Experimental Results and Analysis

5.1   Experimental Data Preparation and Evaluating Indicator

In order to test the effect of news event elements extraction, we selected a set of news of earthquake, terrorist violence and corruption which is web crawling and labeled as corpus. If the model extracts the news events elements which is marked accounted for 80 %, it is considered that the news are correctly extracted. Precision (P), Recall (R) and F-Measure (F) was used to evaluate the system. A was defined as the total number of news, B is the number of extracted news event elements, C is the number of correct extracted news extraction news elements. The formula of Precision (P), Recall (R) and F-Measure (F) are respectively:

$$P = \frac{C}{B} \times 100\% \tag{9}$$

$$R = \frac{C}{A} \times 100\% \tag{10}$$

$$F = \frac{2PR}{R+P} \tag{11}$$

5.2   Experimental Results and Analysis

Extracting news events elements from 120 corpus, event element extraction methods based on trigger words [9] is selected as baseline to compare, the experimental results are shown in Table 3.

From Tables 3 and 4 experimental data, the average of F-measure of news event elements extraction reached 63.81 % compared with the method of event elements extraction based on trigger which increased by 3 % points, and compared with the traditional method that has a very good effect. We used the method of news event elements extraction based on new trigger words to eliminate counterexamples in news text which reasonably access graph nodes. But

Table 3. Event element extraction methods based on trigger words

Event type	Precision (P)	Recall (R)	F-measure (F)
Earthquake	58.12 %	66.81 %	62.16 %
Terrorist violence	51.64 %	62.15 %	56.41 %
Corruption	56.56 %	66.67 %	61.20 %
Average value	55.44 %	65.21 %	59.93 %

Table 4. Event element extraction method based on undirected graph

Event type	Precision (P)	Recall (R)	F-measure (F)
Earthquake	63.15%	67.27%	65.14%
Terrorist violence	60.37%	61.42%	60.89%
Corruption	64.48%	66.29%	62.08%
Average value	62.67%	64.99%	63.81%

the news element extraction is effected by performance of sub-event element extraction. The counterexamples introduced by sub-event element extraction and participle impacted on the accuracy of the selected elements.

6   Conclusion

This paper constructed the graph and computed weights of node and edge using the relationship between news events and event sub elements, and extracted news event elements according to the node weights. The experimental results confirm the validity of this method, the co-occurrence relationship can effectively improve the effect of extraction event element. Further research can be taken into account in extraction news event elements among multiple documents.

Acknowledgement. This paper is supported by the China National Nature Science Foundation (No. 61472168, 61672271, 61175068), and The Key Project of Yunnan Nature Science Foundation (No. 2013FA130). Corresponding author is Zhengtao Yu, his email is ztyu@hotmail.com.

References

1. Xu, X., Li, P.F., Zhu, Q.M.: Pattern filtering and conversion methods for semi-supervised Chinese event extraction. Comput. Sci. **42**, 253–255 (2015)
2. Huang, R., Riloff, E.: Bootstrapped training of event extraction classifiers. In: Proceedings of the 13th Conference of the European Chapter of the Association for Computational Linguistics, Association for Computational Linguistics, pp. 286–295 (2012)
3. Chen, Z., Ji, H.: Language specific issue and feature exploration in Chinese event extraction. In: Proceedings of the HLT-NAACL (2009)
4. Liao, S., Grishman, R.: Using document level cross-event inference to improve event extraction. In: Proceedings of the 48th Annual Meeting of the Association for Computational Linguistics, Association for Computational Linguistics, pp. 789–797 (2010)
5. Xu, X., Li, P.F., Zheng, X.: Event inference for semi-supervised Chinese event extraction. J. Shandong Univ. (Nat. Sci.) **49**, 12–17 (2014)
6. Wang, W., Zhao, D.Y., Zhao, W.: Identification of topic sentence about key event in Chinese news. ACTA Scientiarum Naturalium Universitatis Pekinensis **47**, 789–796 (2011)

7. Kastner, I., Monz, C.: Proceedings of the 12th Conference of the European Chapter of the Association for Computational Linguistics (EACL 2009), Athens, Greece, pp. 789–797 (2009)
8. Yang, E.H., Zen, Q.Q., Li, T.T.: Analysis of event information structure in text. J. Chin. Inf. Process. **26**, 92–97 (2012)
9. Zhao, Y.Y., Qin, B., Che, W.X.: Research on Chinese event extraction. J. Chin. Inf. Process. **22**, 3–8 (2008)
10. Sidorov, G., Gelbukh, A., Pinto, D.: Soft similarity and soft cosine measure: similarity of features in vector space model. Computación Y Sistemas **18**, 491–504 (2014)

An Unified One Class Collaborative Filtering Algorithm

Gai Li[1,2(✉)], Chao-bo He[4], Liyang Wang[1], Jin-cai Pan[1],
Qiang Chen[2,3], and Lei Li[2]

[1] Department of Electronic and Information Engineering,
Shunde Polytechnic, Foshan 528300, China
ligai999@126.com
[2] School of Data and Computer Science, Sun Yat-Sen University,
Guangzhou 510006, China
[3] Department of Computer Science, Guangdong University of Education,
Guangzhou 510303, China
[4] School of Information Science and Technology,
Zhongkai University of Agriculture and Engineering, Guangzhou 510225, China

Abstract. The problem of the previous researches on One Class Collaborative Filtering (OCCF) is that they focused on either rating prediction or ranking prediction, no concerted research effort has been devoted to developing recommendation approach that simultaneously optimize both ratings and rank of the recommended items. In order to solve this problem, a new unified OCCF approach (UOCCF) based on Probabilistic Matrix Factorization (PMF) approach and the newest Collaborative Less-is-More Filtering (CLiMF) approach was proposed. Experimental results on practical dataset showed that our proposed UOCCF approach outperformed existing OCCF approaches over different evaluation metrics.

Keywords: Recommended systems · Collaborative filtering · Collaborative ranking · Implicit feedback · Unified recommendation model

1 Introduction

One-Class Collaborative Filtering (OCCF) approaches can be divided into two categories: OCCF approaches based on rating prediction (OCCF_Rating) [1–6] and OCCF approaches based on ranking prediction (OCCF_Ranking) [7–10]. In OCCF approaches based on rating prediction, the system predicts the actual rating for an item that a customer has not rated yet, and then ranks the items according to the predicted ratings. On the other hand, for OCCF approaches based on ranking prediction, the system predicts a preference ordering over the yet unrated items without going through the inter-meditate step of rating prediction.

The problem of the previous researches on OCCF approach is that they focused on either rating prediction or ranking prediction rather than make full use of the advantages of both of the two OCCF approaches. However, previous studies show that the two OCCF approaches can produce very good recommended performance and could

© Springer Nature Singapore Pte Ltd. 2016
Y. Li et al. (Eds.): SMP 2016, CCIS 669, pp. 267–273, 2016.
DOI: 10.1007/978-981-10-2993-6_23

potentially complement each other. It is desirable to be able to unify these two kinds of approaches in order to generate more accurate recommendations. Research in this area is still very little. Shi et al. [11] proposed a novel unified recommendation model (URM) which combines a rating-oriented CF approach, i.e., probabilistic matrix factorization (PMF) [12], and a ranking-oriented CF approach, i.e., list-wise learning-to-rank with matrix factorization (ListRank) [13]. The URM benefits from the rating-oriented perspective and the ranking-oriented perspective by sharing common latent features of users and items in PMF and ListRank. The experiments show the proposed URM significantly outperforms other state-of-the-art recommendation approaches across different datasets and different conditions of user profiles. However, URM focuses on explicit feedback data. Until now, nobody has studied new OCCF approach by combining rating-oriented and ranking-oriented OCCF for personalized recommendation.

In order to overcome the defects of prior researches, this paper proposes a new unified OCCF approach (UOCCF) based on Probabilistic Matrix Factorization (PMF) approach and the newest Collaborative Less-is-More Filtering (CLiMF) approach was proposed. Experimental results on practical dataset showed that our proposed UOCCF approach outperformed existing OCCF approaches (both ranking-oriented and rating-oriented) over different evaluation metrics.

The rest of this paper is organized as follows: Sect. 2 demonstrates the problem formalization, PMF approach and CLiMF approach; a new unified OCCF approach (UOCCF) is proposed in Sect. 3; the experimental results and discussion are presented in Sect. 4, followed by the conclusion and future work in Sect. 5.

2 Problem Formalization and an Introduction of the PMF and CLiMF Approaches

2.1 Problem Formalization

In this paper, we use bold capital letters to denote a matrix (such as: Y). Given a matrix Y, Y_{ij} represents its element, Y_i indicates the *ith* row of Y, Y_j symbolizes the *jth* column of Y, and Y^T stands for the transpose of Y. If Y is a implicit feedback matrix, then Y_{ui} denotes the binary relevance score of item i to user u, i.e., $Y_{ui} = 1$ if item i is relevant to user u, 0 otherwise. As for RPIF, we need to approximate Y with a low rank matrix $\hat{Y} = (\hat{Y}_{ij})_{m \times n}$, where $\hat{Y} = U^T V$, $U \in C^{K \times M}$, $V \in C^{K \times N}$, U and V denotes the implicit feature matrix with ranks of K for users and items respectively, M is the number of users, and N is the number of items.

2.2 An Brief Introduction of the PMF Approach

The objective of PMF [12] is now to fit each rating Y_{ui} with the corresponding inner product $U_u^T V_i$, which can be formulated as follows:

$$L(U, V) = \frac{1}{2} \sum_{u}^{M} \sum_{i=1}^{N} I_{ui}(Y_{ui} - g(U_u^T V_i))^2 + \frac{\lambda_U}{2} \|U\|^2 + \frac{\lambda_V}{2} \|V\|^2. \tag{1}$$

In the above equation, $\lambda_U = \sigma^2/\sigma_U^2$, $\lambda_V = \sigma^2/\sigma_V^2$. Where $g(x)$ is a logistic function, i.e., $g(x) = 1/(1 + e^{-x})$. We can find a local minimum of the objective function in Eq. (1) by performing gradient descent on U_u and V_i for all users u and all items i. Detailed description of PMF can be found in Ref. [12].

2.3   An Brief Introduction of the CLiMF Approach

The objective function of CLiMF:

$$L(U, V) = \sum_{u}^{M} \sum_{i=1}^{N} Y_{ui}[\ln g(U_u^T V_i) + \sum_{j=1}^{N} \ln(1 - Y_{uj}g(U_u^T V_j - U_u^T V_i))]$$
$$- \frac{\lambda}{2}(\|U\|^2 + \|V\|^2). \tag{2}$$

We can see that maximizing Eq. (2) is equivalent to minimizing Eq. (3).

$$L(U, V) = -\sum_{u}^{M} \sum_{i=1}^{N} Y_{ui}[\ln g(U_u^T V_i) + \sum_{j=1}^{N} \ln(1 - Y_{uj}g(U_u^T V_j - U_u^T V_i))]$$
$$+ \frac{\lambda}{2}(\|U\|^2 + \|V\|^2), \tag{3}$$

in which λ denotes the regularization coefficient, and $\|U\|$ denotes the Frobenius norm of U. Note that the complexity of $L(U, V)$ is very low, and standard optimization methods, e.g., gradient ascend, can be used to learn the optimal model parameters U and V. Detailed description of PMF can be found in Ref. [8].

3   Unified One Class Collaborative Filtering

3.1   Combining PMF and CLiMF

As introduced in Ref. [8, 12], PMF and CLiMF learn the latent features of users and items by taking different views on the known data, i.e., PMF exploiting the individual ratings, and CLiMF exploiting the ranked lists. Our motivation of UOCCF is then straightforward so that the two different views can be exploited simultaneously, by which the knowledge encoded in individual ratings is expected to improve the latent features of users and items from CLiMF to achieve better ranking performance, as the example mentioned in Ref. [11]. Since both the PMF and the CLiMF are based on matrix factorization, we link the two by imposing common latent features for both models. Then, the UOCCF can be formulated by means of a new regularized loss function $L(U, V)$ as follows:

$$L(U, V)$$

$$= (1 - \alpha) \times - \sum_{u}^{M} \sum_{i=1}^{N} Y_{ui}[\ln g(U_u^T V_i) + \sum_{j=1}^{N} \ln(1 - Y_{uj}g(U_u^T V_j - U_u^T V_i))]$$

$$+ \alpha \times \frac{1}{2} \sum_{u}^{M} \sum_{i=1}^{N} (I_{ui}(Y_{ui} - g(U_u^T V_i))^2)$$

$$+ \frac{\lambda}{2}(\|U\|^2 + \|V\|^2).$$

(4)

The trade-off parameter α is used to control the relative contribution from PMF and CLiMF. Use the same strategy in ref. [11], we bias the loss function towards ranking. Consequently, the value of α should be relatively small.

3.2 Optimization

Since the objective function is smooth, a local minimum of the objective function given by Eq. (4) can be found by performing gradient descent in U and V. The gradients can be derived in a similar manner to PMF and CLiMF, as shown below:

$$\frac{\partial L}{\partial U_u} = (1 - \alpha) \times - \sum_{i=1}^{N} Y_{ui}[g(-f_{ui})V_i + \sum_{j=1}^{N} \frac{r_{uj}g'(f_{uj} - f_{ui})(V_i - V_j)}{1 - r_{uj}g(f_{uj} - f_{ui})}]$$

$$+ \alpha \times \sum_{i=1}^{N} I_{ui}(g(U_u^T V_i) - Y_{ui})g'(U_u^T V_i)V_i + \lambda U_u,$$

(5)

$$\frac{\partial L}{\partial V_i} = (1 - \alpha) \times - Y_{ui}[g(-f_{ui}) + \sum_{j=1}^{N} Y_{uj}g'(f_{ui} - f_{uj})(\frac{1}{1 - Y_{uj}g(f_{uj} - f_{ui})} - \frac{1}{1 - Y_{ui}g(f_{ui} - f_{uj})})]U_u$$

$$+ \alpha \times \sum_{u=1}^{M} I_{ui}(g(U_u^T V_i) - Y_{ui})g'(U_u^T V_i)U_u + \lambda V_i.$$

(6)

4   Experiment

4.1   Dataset

We conduct experiments using the Epinions dataset [8]. The Epinions dataset is publicly available, and it contains trust relationships between 49288 users. The Epinions dataset represents a directed social network, i.e., if user i is a trustee of user j, user j is not necessary a trustee of user i. Most microblogging social networks are also directed, such as Twitter. For the purpose of our experiments, we exclude from the dataset the users who have less than 25 trustees.

4.2 Evaluation Metrics

We use the Precision at top-k ($Pre@k$) [14] and Mean Reciprocal Rank (MRR) [8] as our metrics for the predictability of models.

4.3 Experiment Setup

We separate each dataset into a training set and a test set under various conditions of user profiles. For example, the condition of "Given 5" denotes that for each user we randomly selected 5 out of her trustees/friends to form the training set, and use the remaining trustees/friends to form the test set. The task is to use the training set to generate recommendation lists for individual users, and the performance is measured according to the holdout data in the test set. We investigated a variety of "Given" conditions for the training sets, i.e., 10, 15 and 20 for the Epinions dataset.

All the models were implemented in MATLAB R2009a. For UOCCF, the value of the regularization parameter λ was selected from range $\{10^{-5}, 10^{-4}, 10^{-3}, 10^{-2}, 10^{-1}, 1, 10\}$ and optimal parameter value was used. The trade-off parameter α is a real number, $\alpha = \{\alpha | 0 \leq \alpha \leq 1\}$, and the optimal parameter value of α was also used in our experimental comparison. In order to compare their performances fairly, for all matrix factorization models we set the number of features is 10. Detailed setting methods of the parameters for all the baselines can be found in the corresponding references. We repeated the experiment 5 times for each of the different conditions of each dataset, and the performances reported were averaged across 5 runs.

4.4 Experiment Results

In this section we present a series of experiments to evaluate UOCCF. We designed the experiments in order to address the following research questions:

1. Could UOCCF as a combination of a rating-oriented and a ranking-oriented OCCF approach outperform each of the individual approaches?
2. Does the proposed UOCCF outperform state-of-the-art personalized ranking approaches for top-N recommendation?

we compare the performance of UOCCF with that of three baseline algorithms. The approaches we compare with are listed below:

- PMF [12]. Probabilistic Matrix Factorization (PMF) is the most popular and widely used CF approach, experimental results show that PMF approach is also suit for OCCF settings.
- WMF [1, 3]. A state-of-the-art matrix factorization technique for implicit feedback data. The essential idea is to treat all missing user–item examples as negative and to assign proper weights to these entries.
- BPR [7]. Bayesian personalized ranking (BPR) represents the state-of-the-art optimization framework of CF for binary relevance data. BPR-MF represents the choice of using matrix factorization (MF) as the learning model with BPR optimization criterion.

Table 1. The performance comparison of UOCCF and baselines on Epinions dataset

	Given 10		Given 15		Given 20	
	Pre@5	*MRR*	*Pre@5*	*MRR*	*Pre@5*	*MRR*
PMF	0.050	0.138	0.057	0.148	0.056	0.148
WMF	0.059	0.143	0.063	0.155	0.059	0.153
BPR-MF	0.072	0.167	0.098	0.177	0.096	0.216
CLiMF	0.092	0.233	0.127	0.248	0.110	0.239
UOCCF	**0.110**	**0.248**	**0.147**	**0.265**	**0.128**	**0.255**

- CLiMF [8]. A state-of-the-art PR approach that optimizes the Mean Reciprocal Rank (*MRR*) measure for domains with implicit feedback data (e.g., click, follow).

The results of the experiments of UOCCF and the baseline approaches on the Epinions dataset are shown in Table 1. In order to attain further performance improvement, we tune the trade-off parameter more tightly for UOCCF approach across all the conditions on the dataset, and the optimal trade-off parameter value was used. Two main observations can be drawn from the results: First, the proposed UOCCF approach significantly outperforms the three baselines in terms of *Pre@k* and *MRR* across all the conditions. Especially, we can observe that UOCCF significantly improves upon CLiMF by ca. 3–8 % in the case of all the conditions on the Epinions dataset. The experimental result show that using PMF algorithm can explore the knowledge encoded in individual ratings, which is expected to improve the latent features of users and items from CLiMF to achieve better ranking performance. Second, the results show that the improvement of *MRR* aligns consistently with the improvement of *Pre@k*, indicating that optimizing *MRR* would not degrade the utility of recommendations that are captured by the *Pre@k* measure.

Hence, we give a positive answer to our two research questions.

5 Conclusion and Future Work

The problem of the previous researches on OCCF is that they focused on either rating prediction or ranking prediction, no concerted research effort has been devoted to developing recommendation approach that simultaneously optimize both ratings and rank of the recommended items. In order to overcome the defects of prior researches, a new unified OCCF approach (UOCCF) based on Probabilistic Matrix Factorization (PMF) approach and the newest Collaborative Less-is-More Filtering (CLiMF) approach was proposed. Experimental results on practical dataset showed that our proposed UOCCF approach outperformed existing OCCF approaches over different evaluation metrics.

For future work, we plan to extend our approach to richer ones, and we are also interested in the practical application of our UOCCF approach in the Internet domain.

Acknowledgments. This work is sponsored in part by the National Natural Science Foundation of China (No. 61370186), Natural Science Foundation of Guangdong Province (2016A0303 10018), Science and Technology Planning Project of Guangdong Province (No. 2014A01010

3040, No. 2014B010116001, No. 2015A020209178, No. 2016A030303058), Science and Technology Planning Project of Guangzhou (No. 201604010049, No. 201510010203), Appropriative Researching Fund for Professors and Doctors, Guangdong University of Education under Grant (No. 2015ARF25), Second batch open subject of mechanical and electrical professional group engineering technology development center in Foshan city (No. 2015-KJZX139), College Students' Science and Technology Innovation fund of Guangdong Province (No. G2016Z08).

References

1. Pan, R., Zhou, Y., Cao, B., et al.: One-class collaborative Filtering. In: Proceedings of the IEEE International Conference on Data Mining, pp. 502–511 (2008)
2. Hu, Y., Koren, Y., Volinsky, C.: Collaborative filtering for implicit feedback datasets. In: Proceedings of the IEEE International Conference on Data Mining. Pisa, Italy, pp. 263–272. IEEE (2008)
3. Pan, R., Scholz M.: Mind the gaps: weighting the unknown in large-scale one-class collaborative filtering. In: Proceedings of the 15th International Conference on Knowledge Discovery and Data Mining. Paris, France, pp. 667–676. ACM (2009)
4. Ning, X., Karypis, G.: SLIM: sparse linear methods for top-N recommender systems. In: Proceedings of the IEEE International Conference on Data Mining. Vancouver, BC, Canada, pp. 497–506. IEEE (2011)
5. Wang, C., Blei, D.: Collaborative topic modeling for recommending scientific articles. In: Proceedings of the 17th International Conference on Knowledge Discovery and Data Mining. San Diego, CA, pp. 448–456. ACM (2011)
6. Purushotham, S., Liu, Y., Kuo, C.: Collaborative topic regression with social matrix factorization for recommendation systems. In: Proceedings of the 29th ACM International Conference on Machine Learning. Edinburgh, Scotland, UK, pp. 1255–1265. ACM (2012)
7. Rendle, S., Freudenthaler, C., Gantner, Z., Schmidt-Thieme, L.: BPR: Bayesian personalized ranking from implicit feedback. In: Proceedings of the 22nd International Conference on Uncertainty in Artificial Intelligence. Montreal, Canada, pp. 452–461 (2009)
8. Shi, Y., Karatzoglou, A., Baltrunas, L., et al.: CLiMF: collaborative less-is-more filtering. In: Proceedings of the Twenty-Third International Conference on Artificial Intelligence. Beijing, China, pp. 3077–3081. ACM (2013)
9. Li, G., Ou, W.H.: Pairwise probabilistic matrix factorization for implicit feedback collaborative filtering. Neurocomputing **204**, 17–25 (2016)
10. Li, G., Wang, L.Y., Ou, W.H.: Robust personalized ranking from implicit feedback. Int. J. Pattern Recognit. Artif. Intell. **30**(1), 1–28 (2016). 1659001
11. Shi, Y., Larson, M., Hanjalic, A.: Unifying rating-oriented and ranking-oriented collaborative filtering for improved recommendation. Inf. Sci. **2013**(229), 29–39 (2013)
12. Salakhutdinov, R., Mnih, A.: Probabilistic matrix factorization. In: Proceedings of the 21st Annual Conference on Neural Information Processing Systems, Vancouver, B.C., Canada, pp. 252–260 (2007)
13. Shi, Y., Larson, M., Hanjalic, A.: List-wise learning to rank with matrix factorization for collaborative filtering. In: Proceedings of the Fourth ACM Conference on Recommender Systems, pp. 269–272. ACM, New York (2010)
14. Pan, W.K., Zhong, H., Xu, C.F., et al.: Adaptive Bayesian personalized ranking for heterogeneous implicit feedbacks. Knowl.-Based Syst. **73**, 173–180 (2015)

Knowledge Fragment Enrichment Using Domain Knowledge Base

Jing Zhang[1,3(✉)], Honglei Zhuang[2], Yanglei Song[2], Jiawei Han[2],
Yutao Zhang[3], Jie Tang[3], and Juanzi Li[3]

[1] Renmin University of China, Beijing, China
zhang-jing@ruc.edu.cn
[2] University of Illinois at Urbana-Champaign, Champaign, USA
{hzhuang3,ysong44,hanj}@illinois.edu
[3] Tsinghua University, Beijing, China
yt-zhang13@mails.tsinghua.edu.cn, {jietang,lijuanzi}@tsinghua.edu.cn
http://www.springer.com/lncs

Abstract. Knowledge fragment enrichment aims to complete user input concept fragment by augmenting each concept with rich domain information. This is a widely studied problem in cognitive science, but has not been intensively investigated in computer science. In this paper, we formally define the problem of knowledge fragment enrichment in domain knowledge base and develop a probabilistic graphical model to tackle the problem. The proposed model is able to model the dependencies among concepts in the input knowledge fragment and also capture the probabilistic relationship between concepts and domain entities. We empirically evaluate the proposed model on two different genres of datasets: PubMed and NSFC. On both datasets, the proposed model significantly improves the accuracy of label prediction task by up to 3–9 % (in terms of MAP) compared with several alternative enrichment methods.

Keywords: Heterogeneous information networks · Hierarchical topic modeling · Semi-supervised labeling

1 Introduction

Many human cognitive activities can be viewed as a process of enriching a given knowledge fragment. For example, in the quiz show Jeopardy![1], contestants are presented with knowledge clues (or knowledge fragment), and must answer related questions. Specifically, contestants need to first enrich the fragment with knowledge in their mind and then match the question with the enriched knowledge fragment. This problem has been intensively studied in cognitive science, such as the theory of knowledge representation—cognitive map proposed by [15] and cognitive model—spreading-activation model proposed by [7]. However, due

---

[1] http://en.wikipedia.org/wiki/Jeopardy!.

© Springer Nature Singapore Pte Ltd. 2016
Y. Li et al. (Eds.): SMP 2016, CCIS 669, pp. 274–286, 2016.
DOI: 10.1007/978-981-10-2993-6_24

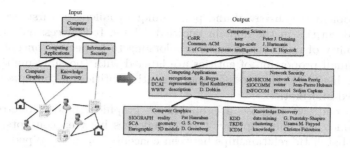

Fig. 1. Illustrative example of knowledge fragment enrichment. The left figure shows the input, where a knowledge fragment represented as a concept hierarchy of computer science and a bibliographic heterogeneous information network consisting of authors, papers, and venues are given. Some papers are labeled with concepts in the hierarchy (links in red). The right figure shows the output, an enriched hierarchy with each concept being represented by selected multi-typed entities. (Color figure online)

to the lack of large-scale data and also the lack of computing power, the study in cognitive science is limited in small group of people through interview. Recently, the problem has attracted increasing interests with the rapid development of big data analytics and artificial intelligence. IBM Watson is a system toward fulfilling this task by applying artificial intelligent techniques to process text such as Wikipedia. However, a fundamental problem is still open: how to formally define the problem of knowledge fragment enrichment and how to develop a general solution?

Consider a real scenario in Fig. 1, where one investigator in a funding agency only knows a high-level concept hierarchy of "Computer Science" (the left top part of Fig. 1), and he wants to identify potential funding reviewers, which is the most critical step in proposal processing. However, this is particularly challenging due to the lack of a complete domain knowledge. Suppose we are given a domain knowledge base (the left bottom part of Fig. 1), e.g., a heterogeneous information network consisting of papers, authors, and venues. Ideally, we can design a system to automatically generate an enriched concept hierarchy, in which each concept in the input concept hierarchy is associated with related entities (representative keywords, active authors, and reputed venues), as shown in the right part of Fig. 1. The investigator can further drill up and down into the concepts and related entities to acquire more detailed information. Immediately, the result helps the investigator to gain a quick glimpse of a research field. Moreover, the enriched results can also be applied in many other problems, e.g., conference paper-reviewer assignment and expert/citation recommendation.

To address this, we formalize a novel problem of *knowledge fragment enrichment* using domain knowledge base. More specifically, the input knowledge fragment is defined as a concept hierarchy (it may be further extended as a graph) and the domain knowledge base is represented as a heterogeneous information network (HIN). Our goal is to augment each concept in the input knowledge fragment with multiple types of entities extracted from HIN.

The problem is non-trivial and poses unique challenges. First, we consider multi-typed entities in the domain knowledge base. It is necessary to quantify the probability of multi-typed entities belonging to a specific concept. Second, usually a small proportion of entities are labeled with (possibly multiple) concepts in the hierarchy. How to infer representative entities for concepts with only little labeled information?

To this end, we propose a probabilistic graphical model, referred to as KEHIN, which not only captures the dependences between concepts, but also models probabilistic relationships between concepts and multi-typed entities in HIN. The model naturally supports supervised and semi-supervised learning. To train the model, we develop a variant algorithm of Collapsed Variational Bayes (CVB). We evaluate the proposed model on two different genres of datasets: PubMed (a bibliographic dataset in English) and NSFC (National Science Foundation of China). The experimental results indicate that KEHIN can significantly improve the accuracy of label prediction task by up to 3–9 % (in terms of MAP) compared with several alternative enrichment methods.

2   Related Work

The method used to solve knowledge fragment enrichment is related to hierarchical topic modeling and heterogeneous information network modeling. A few research studied the problem of extracting hierarchical topics from plain text. For example, [3,11] proposed two classical hierarchical topics models. A few papers constructed the hierarchical topics model by leveraging the human-defined hierarchy. For example, [2] restricted the concept sampling space for the documents with pre-labeled concepts in the hierarchy. [10] associated each node in the hierarchy with a K-dimension concept distribution. [5] sampled each word an arbitrary concept or a topic of the predefined hierarchy. However, all of them only consider the plain text and ignore the fact of heterogeneity of various objects, while we enrich the concept hierarchy via multi-typed entities in the heterogeneous network.

Extensive work has studied how to mine the common topics among the documents and their associated multi-typed entities. For example, [6,13] extended observed variables in the probabilistic models from the words to other entities. However, they usually treat topics independently of each other, while we leverage the hierarchical dependencies between topics. [16] also tried to generate a HIN-enriched hierarchy. However, it's not clear how to leverage the labeling information to enrich a pre-defined hierarchy. [9] leveraged the label information of heterogeneous entities to generate concepts, while ignored the hierarchical relationships between entities.

3   Problem Definition

Definition 1 *Knowledge fragment*. *A knowledge fragment is defined as a concept hierarchy $H = (Y, Par)$, where $y_k \in Y$ is the k-th concept, among which*

y_1 *is the root concept. Function* $Par : Y \setminus \{y_1\} \rightarrow Y$ *returns the parent of a non-root concept.*

A typical knowledge fragment is shown in the left top figure in Fig. 1, where each node corresponds to a sub-concept in computer science. We formalize the knowledge fragment as hierarchy structure because in early 1969, [8] propose the concepts are organized in hierarchy in cognitive science. In addition, hierarchy is prevalently adopted in various institutions, organizations, and professional societies (e.g., Medical Subject Headings by NIH[2], Computing Classification System by ACM[3], Principle Code by NSFC[4]), as it can greatly benefit browsing, searching entities and knowledge. We study the hierarchy structure in this paper and leave other structures, such as the graph, in the future.

Definition 2 *Heterogeneous star information network (HIN). A heterogeneous information network is a network with entities of multiple types, where the set of types is denoted by* $\mathcal{X} = \{x_t\}_{t=0}^{T}$. *Without loss of generality, it can be defined as a network* $G = (V, E; \phi, \mathcal{X})$ *with function* $\phi : V \rightarrow \mathcal{X}$ *mapping each vertex* $v \in V$ *to a particular type in* $\mathcal{X}$. *A HIN is said to have star schema, if* $\forall e = (v_i, v_j) \in E, \phi(v_i) = x_0 \wedge \phi(v_j) = x_t \in \mathcal{X} \setminus x_0$, *or vice versa. Type* x_0 *is called* **center type** *and type* $x_t \in \mathcal{X} \setminus x_0$ *are called* **attribute types**. *We denote the set of nodes with type* x_t *as* $V^{(t)}$.

We formalize domain knowledge base as HIN because the muti-typed entities and their relationships can capture rich information embedded in domain knowledge base. The star schema can well model a broad range of data sets, such as relational databases and document-centric domain knowledge. A typical example of star network is a bibliographic information network, with entity types as paper, venue, author, and term, where paper is the center type, and others are attribute types. The center-typed entity can capture the co-occurrence of different attribute-typed entities. The network reduces to a homogeneous network when $|T| = 1$.

Definition 3 *Entity distribution. We associate each concept* y_k *in H with T distributions* $\{\beta_k^{(t)} \in \mathbf{R}^{|V^{(t)}|}\}_{t=1}^{T}$, *where* $\sum_{w=1}^{|V^{(t)}|} \beta_{k,w}^{(t)} = 1$ *and* $\beta_k^{(t)}$ *is the multinomial distribution over* $V^{(t)}$ *of type* x_t.

Henceforth, we use node, concept, and label interchangeably. With above definitions, we formalize our problem as follows:

Problem 1. **Knowledge fragment enrichment using HIN (KEHIN).** Given a knowledge fragment H, and a heterogeneous star network HIN with V^L representing the entities with labels in H (L_i is the label set of v_i) and V^U representing the entities without labels in H, the objective is to learn the entity distributions $\{\beta_k^{(t)} \in \mathbf{R}^{|V^{(t)}|}\}_{t=1}^{T}$ for each concept y_k in H.

---

[2] http://www.nlm.nih.gov/bsd/disted/meshtutorial/.
[3] https://www.acm.org/about/class.
[4] http://www.nsfc.gov.cn/nsfc/cen/daima/.

The labels of center-typed entities, such as proposals in NSFC, are usually easier to be obtained, compared to the labels of attributed-typed entities, such as authors and keywords. Thus we only consider labels of center-typed entities.

4 Knowledge Fragment Enrichment

Basic Ideas. To solve the problem, a straightforward way is to enrich the concepts using the labeled center-typed entities. Specifically, for each concept in the knowledge fragment, we first extract all the center-typed entities with labels to it, and then use the most frequent attribute-typed entities linking to the center entities as the representative entities of the given concept. For example, several papers share the same authors or words. We select the authors or words shared in most papers labeled by one concept as representative entities. However, the method has several limitations. First, it ignores the hierarchical dependences between concepts in the knowledge fragment. Second, the entities' labels are usually lacking, due to the expensive cost of manual labeling. Thus, we consider leveraging the hierarchical dependences and unlabeled entities simultaneously. The basic idea is to construct a generative model to describe the generation of the heterogeneous network. More specifically, we regard each node in the hierarchy as a concept, associated with multiple generative processes, one for each attribute type. Each center-typed entity in the heterogeneous network is linked to a few concepts in the hierarchy. To establish an edge, it first chooses a concept in the hierarchy, and then samples an attribute-typed entity according to the generative process of that concept, and finally establishes an edge by connecting to the entity. The philosophy is similar to Latent Dirichlet Allocation (LDA) proposed by [4], while the difference is that first we consider multi-typed entities rather than single terms in LDA. In this way, the proposed model captures the co-occurrence of all the attribute-typed entities jointly via the connection of the same center-typed entity. We model the dependencies between concepts in the hierarchy, to allow the concepts in the higher-level shared by more center-typed entities, thus associated with more general attribute-typed entities than the lower-level concepts. In addition, we model the generation of both the labeled and unlabeled entities in a semi-supervised way.

Generative Model. We now explain the details of the generative model. Figure 2 shows the graphical structure of our proposed model.

Utilizing hierarchical structure. We select a concept for a center-typed entity $v_i^{(0)}$ in a top-down, recursive manner. We start from the root concept y_1, and decide to go down to which of its child concepts $C_{i,1}^{(0)}$ according to a multinomial distribution with parameter $\theta_{i,1}^{(0)}$. This process recurses at the chosen child concept. Note that there is a special child concept (i.e., exit concept), denoted by ε_k, associated with each node y_k. Once an exit concept ε_k is reached, the process terminates and the concept y_k is selected.

Generation of the heterogeneous network. To model the generation of edges in heterogeneous network G, we leverage the fact that links only exist between

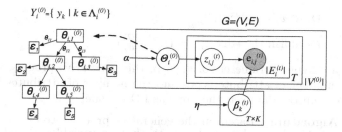

Fig. 2. The graphical representation of the KEHIN model. The dashed curve indicates that the variable $\Theta_i^{(0)}$ represents a collection of variables $\{\theta_{i,k}^{(0)} | k \in \Lambda_i^{(0)}\}$, where $\theta_{i,k}^{(0)}$ is the multinomial distribution over all children nodes of the node y_k in the tree structure.

center-typed and attribute-typed entities. For each center-typed entity $v_i^{(0)}$ in $V^{(0)}$, we generate the j-th edge $e_{i,j}^{(t)}$ of type x_t as follows: we first sample a concept $z_{i,j}^{(t)}$ in the hierarchy according to the aforementioned process, and then sample an entity $v_{i,j}^{(t)}$ from the corresponding multinomial distribution over entities, parameterized by $\beta_{z_{i,j}^{(t)}}^{(t)}$; finally, edge $e_{i,j}^{(t)}$ between $v_i^{(0)}$ and $v_{i,j}^{(t)}$ will be added into G. The co-occurrence pattern of attribute-typed entities can be captured via the connection of the same center-typed entity.

Leveraging labeling information. In many applications, a small proportion of entities are categorized into one or more concepts in the hierarchy. For those center-typed entities with labeling information, we restrict their potential concepts to be those on the paths from the root concept to their assigned concepts, denoted as $Y_i^{(0)} = \{y_k | k \in \Lambda_i^{(0)}\}$, where $\Lambda_i^{(0)}$ is the concept index set of $v_i^{(0)}$. For example, in Fig. 1, if a center-typed entity is linked to the concept "Computing Graphics", its potential concepts are restricted to concepts on the path from the root "Computer Science" to "Computing Graphics", i.e., {"Computer Science", "Computing Applications","Computing Graphics"}. The unlabeled entities have no such restrictions. Thus we sample their concepts from the whole hierarchical concepts, i.e., $\Lambda_i^{(0)}$ contains the indexes of all the concepts in Y. The labeled concepts can be viewed as prior information.

To summarize, the generative process is as follows:

- For each concept $y_k \in Y$, draw $\beta_k^{(t)} \sim Dir(\eta)$, where $t = 1, \ldots, T$;
- For each center-typed entity $v_i^{(0)} \in V^{(0)}$:
  - For each concept $k \in \Lambda_i^{(0)}$, draw $\theta_{i,k}^{(0)} \sim Dir(\alpha)$:
  - For each attribute type $t = 1, \cdots, T$:
    - For $j = 1, \cdots, |V_i^{(t)}|$:
      - Draw $z_{i,j}^{(t)} \in C_{i,1}^{(0)} \sim Mult(\theta_{i,1}^{(0)})$;
      - While $(z_{i,j}^{(t)} \neq \varepsilon_{Par(z_{i,j}^{(t)})})$ draw $z_{i,j}^{(t)} \in C_{i,z_{i,j}^{(t)}}^{(0)} \sim Mult(\theta_{i,z_{i,j}^{(t)}}^{(0)})$;

· Draw $v_{i,j}^{(t)} \sim Mult(\beta_{Par(z_{i,j}^{(t)})}^{(t)})$;

· Establish the edge $e_{i,j}^{(t)} = (v_i^{(0)}, v_{i,j}^{(t)})$

where α, η are hyper parameters of θ, β. In this generative process, we simply observe the number of attribute types and the number of attributes belonging to each type from the data set, the same as LDA model.

Inference Algorithm. Based on the generative process, we defines the joint distribution of the observed variables E, the hidden variables Z and the parameters $\Theta^{(0)}$ and B as :

$$p(E, Z, \Theta^{(0)}, B) = \prod_{t=1}^{T} \prod_{k=1}^{K} p(\beta_k^{(t)}|\eta) \prod_{i=1}^{|V^{(0)}|} \prod_{k \in \Lambda_i^{(0)}} p(\theta_{i,k}^{(0)}|\alpha) \prod_{i=1}^{|V^{(0)}|} \prod_{t=1}^{T} \prod_{j=1}^{|V_i^{(t)}|} p(z_{i,j}^{(t)}|\Theta_i^{(0)}) p(v_{i,j}^{(t)}|z_{i,j}^{(t)}, \beta_{z_{i,j}^{(t)}}^{(t)})$$

where $\Theta_i^{(0)} = \{\theta_{i,k}^{(0)}|k \in \Lambda_i^{(0)}\}$ is the collection of (center-typed) entity-specific multinomial distribution at each topic, and $\Theta^{(0)} = \{\Theta_i^{(0)}\}_{i=1}^{|V^{(0)}|}$. $\beta_k^{(t)}$ is the multinomial distribution over $V^{(t)}$ at topic y_k, and $B = \{\beta_k^{(t)}\}$; $p(v_{i,j}^{(t)}|z_{i,j}^{(t)}, \beta_{z_{i,j}^{(t)}}^{(t)})$ is the probability of generating entity $v_{i,j}^{(t)}$ (of type x_t) as the j-th neighbor of $v_i^{(0)}$ given topic $z_{i,j}^{(t)}$. We omit the dependence $\{\alpha, \eta\}$ for conciseness.

Our goal is to estimate the unknown hidden variables $\{Z, B, \Theta\}$ given observations E and small proportion of labels on center-typed entities. We adopt Collapsed Variational Bayes (CVB), which is widely used for inference in graphical models, such as the research conducted by [1,14].

The variational multinomial distribution parameters are derived as follows:

$$\gamma_{i,j,k}^{(t)} \propto \left[\prod_{\substack{y_m \in \\ \pi(y_1, y_k)}} \frac{\alpha + \mathbf{E}_q(n_{i,m,\cdot}^{(0),\neg i,j})}{\sum_{c \in C_{i,m'}^{(0)}} (\alpha + \mathbf{E}_q(n_{i,c,\cdot}^{(0),\neg i,j}))} \right] \frac{\alpha + \mathbf{E}_q(n_{i,\varepsilon_k,\cdot}^{(0),\neg i,j})}{\sum_{c \in C_{i,k}^{(0)}} (\alpha + \mathbf{E}_q(n_{i,c,\cdot}^{(0),\neg i,j}))} \frac{\eta + \mathbf{E}_q(n_{\cdot,k,v_{i,j}^{(t)}}^{(t),\neg i,j})}{|V_t|\eta + \mathbf{E}_q(n_{\cdot,k,\cdot}^{(t),\neg i,j})}$$

where the superscript $\neg i, j$ means the corresponding counts with $v_{i,j}^{(t)}$ and $z_{i,j}^{(t)}$ excluded, and $\mathbf{E}_q$, abbreviated for $\mathbf{E}_{q(Z^{(t)}, \neg ij)}$, denotes the expectation under the variational distribution $q(Z^{(t)}, \neg ij)$ with all variational variables fixed except $\gamma_{i,j}^{(t)}$; m' is the abbreviation of $Par(y_m)$, representing the parent topic of y_m. The above equation can be explained as the product of two terms: (1) the probability of generating an entity $v_{i,j}^{(t)}$ from topic y_k (the third product term); (2) the probability of selecting topic y_k in the hierarchy $Y_i^{(0)}$ by choosing the path from the root y_1 to y_k (the first term), and then choosing the exit topic ε_k (the second term). We update one variational variable $\gamma_{i,j,k}^{(t)}$ at a time with all others fixed. Finally, the parameter $\theta_{i,k}^{(0)}$ can be approximated by the product of the first fractions (in bracket) and the second fraction in the above equation, and $\beta_k^{(t)}$ can be approximated by the third fraction in the same equation.

5   Experiments

5.1   Experimental Setup

Datasets. The first dataset is collected from National Natural Science Foundation of China (NSFC), which includes a human defined hierarchy[5] and the adopted proposals from 2009 to 2013 in NSFC. NSFC receives more than 10K proposals every year and accepted 17 % of them. The domain-specific concept hierarchy is one of the most important factors for categorizing proposals or assigning reviewers. The hierarchy contains eight natural disciplines, named as Mathematical and Physical Sciences (Math. & Phy.), Chemical Sciences (Chem.), Life Sciences (Life), Earth Sciences (Earth), Engineering and Materials Sciences (Eng. & Mat.), Information Sciences (Info.), Management Sciences (Man.), Health Sciences (Health), of which each one contains at most three levels of hierarchical concepts. When submitting, the applicants are required to select one or more concepts from the hierarchy for the proposal. We construct the heterogeneous network by regarding every proposal as a center-typed entity, and its author (the principal investigator) and terms as attribute-typed entities linking to the proposal. The terms are segmented from the title and abstract of the proposal by a well-established Chinese word segmentation tool proposed by [17].

The second dataset is crawled from PubMed[6], which includes a human defined hierarchy MeSH[7] and the published papers. We select four disciplines from the hierarchy, including Disciplines and Occupations (Disc. & Occu.), Anthropology, Education and Sociology (Anth., Edu. & Sociol.), Technology, Industry and Agriculture (Tech., Ind. & Agr.), and Information Science (Info. Sci.), and crawl all the papers annotated by the four discipline concepts from 2009 to 2013. We regard every paper as a center-typed entity, and its authors, venues and terms as attribute-typed entities. The terms are extracted from the title and abstract using the method proposed by [18].

In both datasets, although all the center-typed entities are fully labeled, it would be too optimistic to extend this observation to other datasets in real world, as most organizations constructing concept hierarchy may not be affordable to further maintain hierarchical labels for massive entities. For the sake of generality of our experiments, we sample a subset of center-typed entities randomly, with probability r, while the labels of other center-typed entities are regarded as unknown.

We test our methods on proposals/papers of each discipline respectively. Table 1 summarizes the statistics of the two datasets.

---

[5] http://www.nsfc.gov.cn/nsfc/cen/daima/.
[6] http://www.ncbi.nlm.nih.gov/pubmed.
[7] http://www.nlm.nih.gov/mesh/trees.html.

Table 1. Statistics of datasets.

Dataset	#center entities	#attribute entities	#edges	#concepts	Hierarchy depth
PubMed	266,401	4,465,941	14,649,180	2,130	10
NSFC	207,665	610,112	16,593,458	2,768	4

Evaluation Methods. To evaluate the effect of the hierarchical modeling of the knowledge fragment, we compare our method *KEHIN* with a simple baseline method, named as *TopK*. To enrich one concept, TopK first selects center-typed entities labeled by the concept, and then selects the most frequent attribute-typed entities linking to those center-typed entities. We apply our method and TopK on both datasets, with only r = 0.1 of center-typed entities labeled, and partially show the enriched knowledge fragment as case studies. We also calculate topic coherence proposed by [12] to measure the quality of the learned concept:

$$C(k; V(k)) = \sum_{m=2}^{M} \sum_{l=1}^{m} \log \frac{D(v_m, v_l) + 1}{D(v_l)}$$

where $V(k) = (v_1, \cdots, v_M)$ is a list of the M most probable attribute-typed entities in concept y_k, $D(v)$ is the occurrence of v (the number of center entities v link to) and $D(v, v')$ is the co-occurrence of v and v' (the number of common center entities v and v' both link to). We set $M = 10$ in the experiments.

To further evaluate the effect of heterogeneous entities and the unlabeled entities on the enrichment results, we compare our method KEHIN with two modified baselines, named as *KEHO* and *KELA*. KEHO sets $T = 1$. In our setting, KEHO only considers the term entities in both datasets and ignores other entities such as authors and venues. KELA omits all the unlabeled center-typed entities as well as their edges in HIN while training. We use the performance of predicting the labels of center-typed entities as evaluation measure. Given r proportion of labeled center-typed entities to train the model, we aim to classify all the other center-typed entities into their corresponding labels. Specifically, after model learning, for each unlabeled entity $v_i^{(0)}$, we calculate the probability of selecting concept y_k as the product of the topic distributions from y_k to the root, i.e., $p(y_k|v_i^{(0)}) \propto \left[\prod_{y_m \in \pi(y_1, y_k)} \theta_{i, Par(y_m)}(y_m) \right] \theta_{i,k}(\varepsilon_k)$, where $\theta_{i, Par(y_m)}(y_m)$ indicates the probability of y_m being sampled from its parent concept $Par(y_m)$ and $\theta_{i,k}(\varepsilon_k)$ indicates the probability of the exit concept being selected from y_k. We rank top ten concepts based on $p(y_k|v_i^{(0)})$ and evaluate the ranked list by Mean Average Precision (MAP). The problem is new and no existing methods can be used directly to compare with our method fairly. Thus we compare with variational methods of our model.

Parameter Settings. We tried different settings of α and η for KEHIN and heuristically select 0.01 and 0.1 as optimal values respectively. We stop the iterative inference algorithm by checking the relative changes of perplexity and set the convergence threshold ϵ as 0.005. The perplexity is calculated based on the method in [4].

5.2 Experimental Results

Effect of Hierarchical Modeling . Figure 3 shows a selected branch of hierarchy for KEHIN and Topk in PubMed, where each concept (represented by a box) contains the top ranked terms/venues with the highest probability in the learned associated distribution β. Figure 3(a) shows the result of our model. We see that the top ranked terms/venues accurately reflect the corresponding concepts. More interestingly, terms/venues in high-level concepts tend to be more general and likely to be shared by more publications, such as the terms "development" and "application" illustrated at the root "Biological Science Disciplines", while terms/venues in lower-level concepts are more specific, such as "population" and "population genetics" illustrated in "Genetics, Population". However, TopK method presents poorer result in Fig. 3(b). For example, the general term "science" and the venue "Plos One" present in both top and bottom layers (mark in red color). We also present the topic coherence for term entities in both NSFC and PubMed in Table 2. From the table, we see that in all datasets, our method outperforms TopK in terms of topic coherence significantly.

Effect of Heterogeneous Entities. Table 3 shows the prediction performance for KEHIN and KEHO in terms of MAP ,while tackling the task of label prediction with r as 0.5. It can be observed that, in NSFC, our KEHIN method consistently outperforms the baseline in all datasets (+3.4–9.4 %), as KEHIN can take advantage of the information provided by multi-typed entities. These results verify the effect of enriching hierarchy by heterogeneous information network, implying that leveraging the links between multi-typed entities can benefit

Table 2. Topic coherence with r = 0.1.

| Method | NSFC | | | | | | | | PubMed | | | |
	Math. & Phy.	Chem.	Life	Earth	Eng. & Mat.	Info.	Man.	Health	Disc. &Occu.	Anth., Edu. & Sociol.	Tech., Ind. & Agr.	Info. Sci.
TopK	−135	−145	−148	−140	−146	−145	−118	−142	−177	−175	−192	−175
KEHIN	−109	−117	−121	−92	−116	−114	−103	−122	−73	−72	−89	−73

Table 3. MAP of prediction with r = 0.5 (%).

| Method | NSFC | | | | | | | | PubMed | | | |
	Math. & Phy.	Chem.	Life	Earth	Eng. & Mat.	Info.	Man.	Health	Disc. &Occu.	Anth., Edu. & Sociol.	Tech., Ind. & Agr.	Info. Sci.
KEHO	47.93	38.39	34.85	58.87	44.66	35.40	47.78	44.60	5.02	6.79	8.02	5.67
KEHIN	57.28	46.22	42.33	62.24	51.38	44.65	56.05	49.80	40.06	26.03	33.87	24.48

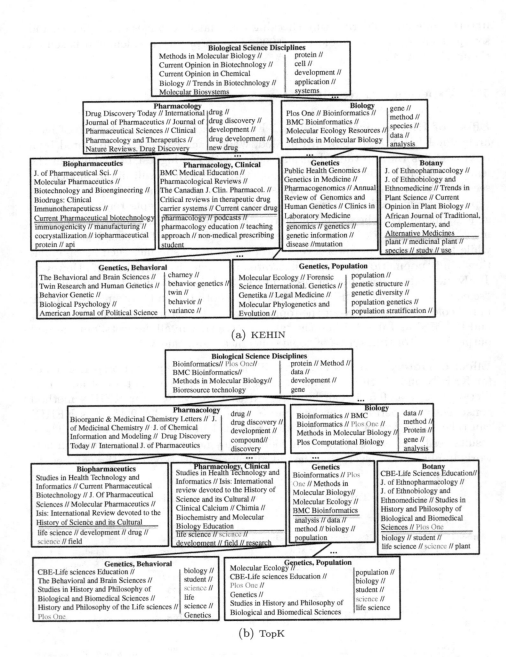

Fig. 3. Representative entities for partial PubMed hierarchy. The first line in each concept presents the name defined by humans. The following lines present the venue/term entities with highest probabilities given the concept.

a lot of applications, yielding significant improvement. Similar results are also observed in PubMed. We see that KEHO performs much worse in PubMed than that in NSFC. This can be explained that in PubMed, we only extract ten terms from the title and abstract of each paper, while all the phrases segmented from title and abstract are used in NSFC. Thus KEHO that leverages single terms performs much worse than KEHIN that not only considers terms but also author and venue entities, which further verifies the effect of heterogeneous information.

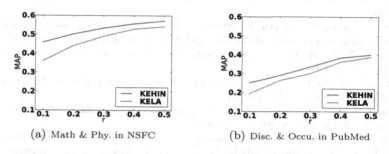

(a) Math & Phy. in NSFC   (b) Disc. & Occu. in PubMed

Fig. 4. MAP of prediction with different r.

Effect of Unlabeled Data. In order to test the effect of the unlabeled data, we adjust the ratio r of labeled data and compare our method KEHIN with baseline KELA in terms of label prediction performance. The results are shown in Fig. 4. It can be observed that as the proportion of the labeled data decreases, the performance of KELA drops significantly more than the performance of KEHIN does. When there is only 10 % of data labeled for training, MAP@10 of KEHIN is still above 45 %, while KELA has a performance around 35 % in NSFC dataset. The results verify the benefits of leveraging merely the network structure information without labels, while enriching a knowledge fragment.

6   Conclusion

In this paper, we solve the problem of enriching a knowledge fragment represented by a concept hierarchy via a heterogeneous information network. We propose a generative model to jointly model the dependencies between concepts in the hierarchy, the links among multi-typed entities, and the partial observed labels of the entities. The experiments present meaningful results on two datasets and also verify that our model outperforms several alternative baselines on the label prediction task.

References

1. Asuncion, A., Welling, M., Smyth, P., Teh, Y.W.: On smoothing and inference for topic models. In: UAI 2009, pp. 27–34. AUAI Press (2009)
2. Bakalov, A., McCallum, A., Wallach, H., Mimno, D.: Topic models for taxonomies. In: JCDL 2012, pp. 237–240 (2012)
3. Blei, D.M., Griffiths, T.L., Jordan, M.I., Tenenbaum, J.B.: Hierarchical topic models and the nested chinese restaurant process. In: NIPS 2003 (2003)
4. Blei, D.M., Ng, A.Y., Jordan, M.I.: Latent dirichlet allocation. JMLR **3**, 993–1022 (2003)
5. Chemudugunta, C., Smyth, P., Steyvers, M.: Text modeling using unsupervised topic models and concept hierarchies. arXiv preprint arXiv:0808.0973 (2008)
6. Chen, X., Zhou, M., Carin, L.: The contextual focused topic model. In: KDD 2012, pp. 96–104 (2012)
7. Collins, A.M., Loffus, E.F.: A spreading activation theory of semnatic processing. Psychol. Rev. **82**, 407–428 (1975)
8. Collins, A.M., Quiliam, M.K.: Retrieval time from semantic memory. J. Verbal Learn. Verbal Behav. **8**, 240–247 (1969)
9. Kang, D., Park, Y., Chari, S.N.: Hetero-labeled LDA: a partially supervised topic model with heterogeneous labels. In: Calders, T., Esposito, F., Hüllermeier, E., Meo, R. (eds.) ECML PKDD 2014, Part I. LNCS, vol. 8724, pp. 640–655. Springer, Heidelberg (2014)
10. Kim, D.K., Voelker, G., Saul, L.K.: A variational approximation for topic modeling of hierarchical corpora. In: ICML 2013, pp. 55–63 (2013)
11. Mimno, D., Li, W., McCallum, A.: Mixtures of hierarchical topics with pachinko allocation. In: ICML 2007, pp. 633–640 (2007)
12. Mimno, D., Wallach, H.M., Talley, E., Leenders, M., McCallum, A.: Optimizing semantic coherence in topic models. In: EMNLP 2011, pp. 262–272 (2011)
13. Sun, Y., Yu, Y., Han, J.: Ranking-based clustering of heterogeneous information networks with star network schema. In: KDD 2009, pp. 797–806 (2009)
14. Teh, Y.W., Newman, D., Welling, M.: A collapsed variational bayesian inference algorithm for latent dirichlet allocation. In: NIPS, vol. 6, pp. 1378–1385 (2006)
15. Tolman, E.C.: Cognitive maps in rats and men. Psychol. Rev. **55**(4), 189–208 (1984)
16. Wang, C., Danilevsky, M., Liu, J., Desai, N., Ji, H., Han, J.: Constructing topical hierarchies in heterogeneous information networks. In: ICDM 2013, pp. 767–776 (2013)
17. Zhang, H.P., Yu, H.K., Xiong, D.Y., Liu, Q.: HHMM-based Chinese lexical analyzer ICTCLAS. In: SIGHAN Workshop on Chinese Language Processing, pp. 184–187 (2003)
18. Zhang, K., Xu, H., Tang, J., Li, J.: Keyword extraction using support vector machine. In: Advances in Web-Age Information Management, pp. 85–96 (2006)

Author Index

Printed in the United States
by Bookmasters

Printed in the United States
By Bookmasters